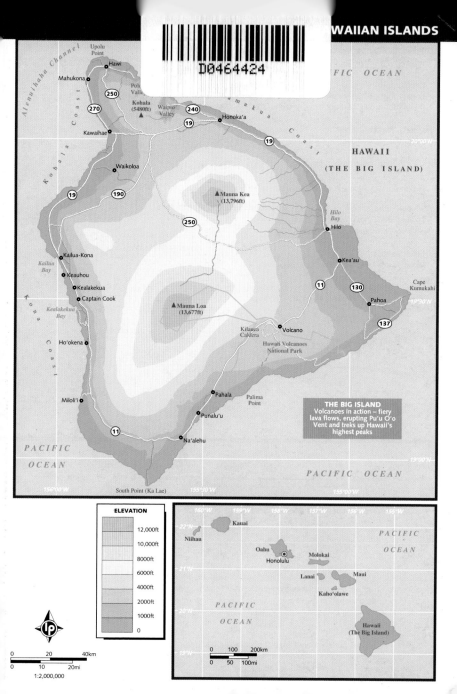

D0464424

Alenuihaha Channel
Upolu Point
Hawi
Mahukona
250
Kohala Coast
270
Kohala (5480ft)
Poli Valle
Waipio Valley
240
19
Honoka'a
19
Kawaihae
Kohala Coast
Hamakua Coast

HAWAII

(THE BIG ISLAND)

20°00'N

Waikoloa

19
190

▲Mauna Kea
(13,796ft)

250

Hilo Bay

Hilo

Kailua-Kona
Kailua Bay
Keauhou
Kealakekua
Captain Cook
Kealakekua Bay

Kea'au
11
130
Cape Kumukahi
Pahoa

19°30'N

Kona Coast

▲Mauna Loa
(13,677ft)

Kilauea Caldera
Volcano
Hawaii Volcanoes National Park

137

Ho'okena

Miloli'i

11

Pahala
Palima Point

Punalu'u

THE BIG ISLAND
Volcanoes in action – fiery
lava flows, erupting Pu'u O'o
Vent and treks up Hawaii's
highest peaks

Na'alehu

PACIFIC
OCEAN

19°00'N

PACIFIC OCEAN

156°00'W   155°30'W   155°00'W

South Point (Ka Lae)

ELEVATION

12,000ft
10,000ft
8000ft
6000ft
4000ft
2000ft
1000ft
0

160°W 159°W 158°W 157°W 156°W 155°W

22°N
Kauai
Niihau
PACIFIC
OCEAN
Oahu
Honolulu
Molokai
21°N
Lanai
Maui
Kaho'olawe

20°N
PACIFIC
OCEAN

19°N
Hawaii
(The Big Island)

LP

0   20   40km
0   10   20mi
1:2,000,000

0   100   200km
0   50   100mi

Hiking in Hawaii
1st edition – October 2003

Published by
Lonely Planet Publications Pty Ltd ABN 36 005 607 983
90 Maribyrnong St, Footscray, Victoria 3011, Australia

Lonely Planet Offices
Australia Locked Bag 1, Footscray, Victoria 3011
USA 150 Linden St, Oakland, CA 94607
UK 72-82 Rosebery Ave, London EC1R 4RW

Photographs
Many of the images in this guide are available for licensing from
Lonely Planet Images.
w www.lonelyplanetimages.com

Front cover photograph
View across Waimea Canyon, Kauai (John Borthwick)

Small front cover photograph
On the Halema'uma'u Trail (Scott Darsney)

ISBN 1 74059 426 6

text & maps © Lonely Planet Publications Pty Ltd 2003
photos © photographers as indicated 2003

Printed through Colorcraft Ltd, Hong Kong
Printed in China

Contents

TABLE OF MAPS   **3**

TABLE OF HIKES   **4**

THE AUTHORS   **6**

THIS BOOK   **8**

HIKE DESCRIPTIONS   **9**

MAPS   **10**

FOREWORD   **12**

INTRODUCTION   **13**

FACTS ABOUT HAWAII   **15**

History................................15	Ecology & Environment........26	Society & Conduct................29
Geography...........................16	Parks & Protected Areas........26	Language.............................29
Climate 18	Population & People..............28	
Watching Wildlife 19	Religion 28	

FACTS FOR THE HIKER   **32**

Suggested Itineraries 32	Food 37	Useful Organizations 40
When to Hike.......................33	Drinks...................................38	Digital Resources 41
What Kind of Hike? 33	Women Hikers 38	Books....................................41
Organized Hikes 33	Hiking with Children 39	TV 42
Permits & Fees.....................34	Dangers & Annoyances 39	Weather Information 42
Responsible Hiking...............34	Maps 39	Photography 42
Accommodations 35	Place Names 40	

CLOTHING & EQUIPMENT   **44**

Clothing...............................44	**Navigation Equipment..........46**	Equipment 48

HEALTH & SAFETY   **50**

Predeparture Planning 50	Medical Problems &	Safety on the Hike 59
Staying Healthy 51	Treatment.............................52	

HONOLULU   **62**

Information 62	Places to Stay.......................63	Getting There & Away 67
Supplies & Equipment...........62	Places to Eat........................66	Getting Around 67

OAHU   **69**

Manoa Falls to Jackass Ginger Pool 71	Maunawili Falls & Demonstration Trails 78	Kaunala Loop.......................86
Manoa Cliffs Circuit 73	Waimano Trail 81	Kaena Point 89
Wa'ahila Ridge.....................75	Manana Trail 83	Kealia Trail 91
Kuli'ou'ou Ridge 77	Hau'ula Loop 84	Kuaokala Trail 93
		Other Hikes........................95

2 Contents

THE BIG ISLAND 96

Muliwai Trail........................102
Mauna Kea...........................106
Captain Cook Monument
Trail 111
**Islands of Fire: Hawaii's
Volcanoes 115**

**Hawaii Volcanoes National
Park 120**
Halema'uma'u Loop............124
Kilauea Iki Loop 129
Crater Rim Trail 131
Napau Crater Trail 134

Mauna Iki Trail.....................136
Hilina Pali.............................138
Other Hikes 142

MAUI 144

Waihe'e Valley 149
Waihe'e Ridge 150
Hoapili Trail 151
Lahaina Pali Trail.................153

Haleakala Crater..................155
Polipoli Forest Loop 162
Hana.....................................164
Waianapanapa State Park....165

Waimoku Falls 167
Other Hikes 169

MOLOKAI 170

Kalaupapa National Historic
Park 175

Kamakou Preserve 179
Mo'omomi Dunes................181

Other Hikes 183

KAUAI 184

Kalalau Trail 188
East Kauai.............................194
Nounou Mountain East Trail..196
Moalepe & Kuilau Trails 197
Powerline Trail 199

Waimea Canyon State Park..201
Waimea Canyon Trail..........204
Kukui & Koaie Canyon
Trails.....................................206
Koke'e State Park.................209

Canyon Trail.........................211
Awa'awapuhi Lookout &
Nualolo Cliffs 212
Alakai Swamp 214
Other Hikes 217

TRAVEL FACTS 218

Tourist Offices 218
Visas & Documents 218
Embassies & Consulates 219
Customs................................219
Money..................................220
Post & Communications......221
Time 222

Business Hours....................222
Public Holidays....................222
Getting There & Away 223
Air 223
Sea 225
Getting Around 225
Air 225

Bus 226
Car & Motorcycle................226
Bicycle 226
Hitching 226
Boat......................................227
Taxi 227

GLOSSARY 228

INDEX 236

METRIC CONVERSION inside back cover

The Maps

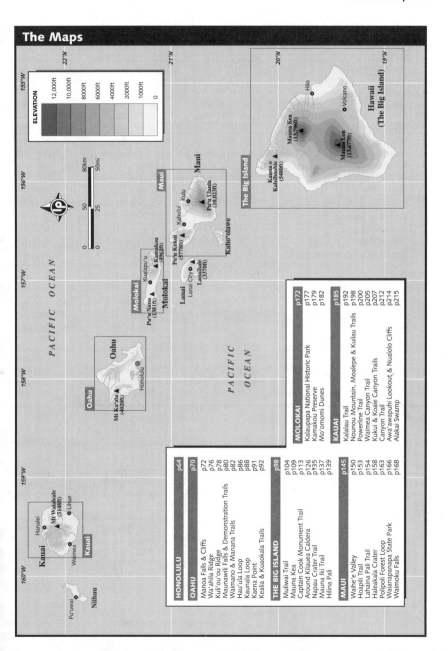

HONOLULU p64

OAHU p70

Manoa Falls & Cliffs	p72
Wa'ahila Ridge	p76
Kuli'ou'ou Ridge	p78
Maunawili Falls & Demonstration Trails	p80
Waimano & Manana Trails	p82
Hau'ula Loop	p86
Kaunala Loop	p88
Kaena Point	p91
Kealia & Kuaokala Trails	p92

THE BIG ISLAND p98

Muliwai Trail	p104
Mauna Kea	p109
Captain Cook Monument Trail	p113
Around Kilauea Caldera	p116
Napau Crater Trail	p135
Mauna Iki Trail	p137
Hilina Pali	p139

MAUI p145

Waihe'e Valley	p150
Hoapili Trail	p153
Lahaina Pali Trail	p154
Haleakala Crater	p158
Polipoli Forest Loop	p163
Waianapanapa State Park	p166
Waimoku Falls	p168

MOLOKAI p177

Kalaupapa National Historic Park	p179
Kamakou Preserve	p182
Mo'omomi Dunes	

KAUAI p185

Kalalau Trail	p192
Nounou Mountain, Moalepe & Kuilau Trails	p198
Powerline Trail	p200
Waimea Canyon Trail	p205
Kukui & Koaie Canyon Trails	p207
Canyon Trail	p212
Awa'awapuhi Lookout & Nualolo Cliffs	p214
Alakai Swamp	p215

The Hikes	Duration	Difficulty	Best Time
Oahu			
Manoa Falls to Jackass Ginger Pool	4½–6 hours	moderate	year-round
Manoa Cliffs Circuit	3½ hours	moderate	year-round
Wa'ahila Ridge	1½–2 hours	easy–moderate	year-round
Kuli'ou'ou Ridge	3 hours	moderate	year-round
Maunawili Falls & Demonstration Trails	4 hours	moderate	year-round
Waimano Trail	7–8 hours	demanding	year-round
Manana Trail	5–7 hours	demanding	year-round
Hau'ula Loop	1 hour	easy	year-round
Kaunala Loop	2 hours	easy	year-round
Kaena Point	3½–4 hours	easy–moderate	year-round
Kealia Trail	3 hours	moderate	year-round
Kuaokala Trail	2½ hours	moderate	year-round
The Big Island			
Muliwai Trail	2 days	demanding	Apr–Nov
Mauna Kea	7–9 hours	demanding	May–Oct
Captain Cook Monument Trail	2 hours	easy	Dec–Mar
Halema'uma'u Loop	3 hours	easy–moderate	year-round
Kilauea Iki Loop	1½ hours	easy–moderate	year-round
Crater Rim Trail	4½–5 hours	moderate	year-round
Napau Crater Trail	5½–7 hours	moderate–demanding	year-round
Mauna Iki Trail	2½ hours	easy	year-round
Hilina Pali	2 days	moderate–demanding	Dec–Mar
Maui			
Waihe'e Valley	2–2½ hours	moderate	year-round
Waihe'e Ridge	3 hours	moderate	year-round
Hoapili Trail	2–2½ hours	moderate	year-round
Lahaina Pali Trail	3–4 hours	demanding	Dec–Mar
Haleakala Crater	4 days	moderate–demanding	year-round
Polipoli Forest Loop	2½–3 hours	moderate	year-round
Waianapanapa State Park	2½–3 hours	moderate	year-round
Waimoku Falls	2 hours	moderate	year-round
Molokai			
Kalaupapa National Historic Park	2½–3 hours	moderate–demanding	year-round
Kamakou Preserve	2 hours	easy–moderate	year-round
Mo'omomi Dunes	4½ hours	moderate–demanding	year-round
Kauai			
Kalalau Trail	2 days	demanding	May–Oct
Nounou Mountain East Trail	1½–2 hours	easy	year-round
Moalepe & Kuilau Trails	3 hours	easy	year-round
Powerline Trail	3–3½ hours	moderate	year-round
Waimea Canyon Trail	5–6 hours	easy–moderate	Apr–Nov
Kukui & Koaie Canyon Trails	6½–8 hours	moderate–demanding	year-round
Canyon Trail	1½–2 hours	easy	year-round
Awa'awapuhi Lookout & Nualolo Cliffs	2½–3 hours	easy–moderate	year-round
Alakai Swamp	4–5 hours	moderate	year-round

Transport	Summary	Page
bus	See waterfalls and bamboo forests on a climb to a dramatic lookout	71
bus	Take a grand tour of the Makiki-Tantalus area	73
bus	Boulder-hop on a forest reserve ridge high above Honolulu	75
bus	Emerge from verdant Kuli'ou'ou Valley at the summit of the Ko'olau Range	77
bus	Amble beneath nearly vertical sea cliffs over to Oahu's Windward Coast	78
private	Cross streams and scale ridges below an elusive Ko'olau summit	81
bus	Try another Ko'olau summit trek on the way to Waimano Waterfall	83
bus	Stroll by ocean vistas and rare native flora species	84
private	Enjoy a peaceful valley and ridge walk above the wild North Shore	86
private	Traverse the island's northwestern tip and explore a natural area reserve	89
private	Brave breathtaking switchbacks over Kaena Point	91
private	Dare a narrow, windswept ridge above lush Makua Valley	93
private	Take the challenging ancient Hawaiian footpath into remote valleys	102
private	Hike to the summit of Hawaii's highest peak	106
bus	Walk down to historic Kealakekua Bay for first-rate snorkeling	111
bus	Cross lava flows to the still-smoking crater home of the volcano goddess	124
private	Venture across a lunar landscape that last erupted only 50 years ago	129
bus	Revel in rain forests and volcanic cinder deserts	131
private	Enter the heart of an active volcanic rift zone	134
private	Experience the golden silence and kaleidoscopic pit craters in the Kau Desert	136
private	Drop over sea cliffs to a castaway white-sand beach on the Puna Coast	138
private	Cross thrilling suspension bridges on a popular, easygoing jungle hike	149
private	Hike a lofty ridgeline with misty views of the West Maui Mountains	150
private	View spectacular coastal scenery on an ancient road over jagged lava	151
private	Climb through arid canyons on a historic bridle trail	153
private	Backpack through the unforgettable 3000ft-deep Haleakala crater	155
private	Relax with a quiet walk through a cool high-elevation forest	162
private	Follow an ancient lava trail over rugged sea cliffs to Hana	165
private	Discover pools and bamboo forests on the way to a 400ft waterfall	167
private	Trek down a plunging sea cliff to a historic leprosy colony	175
private	Ramble through native rain forest to a stunning cliff-top view	179
private	Take a long, lonesome walk to a fragile coastline preserve	181
private	Explore a classic backpack route on the Na Pali Coast	188
private	Reach a high point atop the fabled Sleeping Giant	196
private	Discover glorious valley and ocean lookouts on modest twin trails	197
private	Persevere up to head-spinning views of Mt Waialeale	199
private	Splash through cool river fords on a charming sugarcane haul road	204
private	Dive into Waimea Canyon by the banks of Kauai's longest river	206
private	Enjoy unbeatable views of the 'Grand Canyon of the Pacific'	211
private	Peer into hidden valleys of the Na Pali Coast	212
private	Spy rare bird life from boardwalks	214

The Authors

Sara 'Sam' Benson

Years ago Sara Benson graduated with a liberal arts degree from the University of Chicago. She soon found herself swept away to Maui. And she never forgot the sunrise over Haleakala, even as she ran through the wilds of Asia, traversing all kinds of roads on foot and racking up thousands of kilometers on rickety Laos buses, broken-down Chinese bicycles and Japanese *shinkansen*. After several jobs as an editor, high school teacher, journalist and corporate hack, both in the USA and abroad, she signed on with Lonely Planet many moons ago. A traveler by inclination and a writer by trade, this is her lucky 13th book with Lonely Planet. Much of it was penned while hanging out on the Big Island's Puna coast.

Jennifer Snarski

After spending most of her life in a small timber town on the southern Oregon coast, Jennifer beat it out to India, Sri Lanka and Thailand. She later put her liberal arts degree in religious studies to use, writing for a cultural guide to India. The writing assignments that followed sealed her fate as a travel writer. An avid hiker, Jennifer feels most at home exploring the wilderness areas of Oregon and Washington, and she happily grabbed this chance to escape the soggy northwest winter by hiking the warmer climes of Maui, Molokai and Lanai. She is also co-author of Lonely Planet's *Pacific Northwest*, *Hiking in the USA* and *USA* guides.

Jennifer lives in Portland, Oregon. When she's not puttering her Toyota up a dirt road you'll find her teaching Irish dance to nervous adults and dancing in bars.

From the Authors

Sara 'Sam' Benson *Mahalo* to Erva, Mike, Chris, and their menagerie of chickens, cats and dogs, for giving me that elusive home away from home. Thank you also to the Ala Moana YMCA, Makiki Forest Baseyard staff, the minivan family at Manoa Falls, Betsy at Kaena Point, Red Howard and Anne Davis in the Alakai Swamp, Bernie from Vancouver at Waimea Canyon, Mano on the Na Pali Coast, Thomas and Athene from Chicago, the surfers at Waipio Beach, the French scientists on Mauna Kea, Keola Awong and everybody at Hawaii Volcanoes National Park. Heartfelt gratitude to my family and to Josh for keeping those cell phone lifelines open.

Jennifer Snarski Life just doesn't get any better than when you're wandering around the guts of a 10,000ft volcano. For this I am grateful to Lindsay Brown and Andrew Bain at Lonely Planet. You've been great folks to work with.

Many generous folks on Maui, Molokai and Lanai extended a warm aloha and offered good advice. Staff and volunteers at the Nature Conservancy provided invaluable assistance on Molokai reserves. On Molokai, Kaipo Seales valiantly rescued my camp stove from airport security. Unexpected hospitality and an overwhelming aloha from John at the Adventure Lanai Ecocentre made a visit to Lanai an unforgettable experience. Jason good-naturedly drove me all over the island and helped me hunt for petroglyphs.

A huge thanks also to Krista Farmer, the best roommate ever! Anne Manning helped read over the entire manuscript and took good care of the car. Thanks to everyone who helped support Jupiter, who shall be very missed.

This Book

Coordinating author Sara Benson wrote the introductory, Honolulu, Oahu, Big Island, Kauai and Travel Facts chapters. Jennifer Snarski wrote the Maui and Molokai chapters. Some material from *Maui, Hawaii, Oahu* and *Hawaii: The Big Island* was used in this book.

From the Publisher

At Lonely Planet's Melbourne base the coordinating editors were Jennifer Garrett and Rebecca Chau. The coordinating cartographer was Helen Rowley. Assisting editors were Danielle North, Dan Caleo, Kate James, Nick Tapp and Melissa Faulkner. Assisting cartographers were Csanad Csutoros, Andrew Smith, Karen Fry and Adrian Persoglia. The color pages were put together by Katie Cason, and the layout designer was Vicki Beale. Sally Darmody and Cris Gibcus also lent a hand. The cover was designed by Wendy Wright. The project was managed through production by Glenn van der Knijff. Overseeing the entire process were series publishing manager Lindsay Brown and commissioning editors Andrew Bain and Marg Toohey. Technical assistance was provided by Chris LeeAck and Herman So.

Hike Descriptions

This book contains 41 hike descriptions ranging from day trips to four-day hikes, plus suggestions for side trips and alternative routes. Each hike description has a brief introduction outlining the natural and cultural features you may encounter, plus information to help you plan your hike – transport options, level of difficulty, time frame and any permits required.

Day hikes are often circular and are located in areas of uncommon beauty. Multiday hikes include information on campsites, huts, hostels or other accommodations and where you can obtain water and supplies.

Times & Distances

These are provided only as a guide. Times are based on actual hiking time and do not include stops for snacks, taking photographs, rests or side trips. Be sure to factor these in when planning your hike. Distances are provided but should be read in conjunction with altitudes. Significant elevation changes can make a greater difference to your hiking time than lateral distance.

In most cases, the daily stages are flexible and can be varied. It is important to recognise that short stages are sometimes recommended in order to acclimatize in mountain areas or because there are interesting features to explore en route.

Level of Difficulty

Grading systems are always arbitrary. However, having an indication of the grade may help you choose between hikes. Our authors use the following grading guidelines:

Easy – a hike on flat terrain or with minor elevation changes, usually over short distances on well-traveled routes with no navigational difficulties.
Moderate – a hike with challenging terrain, often involving longer distances and steep climbs.
Demanding – a hike with long daily distances and difficult terrain with significant elevation changes; may involve challenging route-finding and high-altitude or glacier travel.

True Left & True Right

The terms 'true left' and 'true right,' used to describe the bank of a stream or river, sometimes throw readers. The 'true left bank' simply means the left bank as you look downstream.

Maps

Our maps are based on the best available references, often combined with GPS data collected in the field. They are intended to show the general route of the hike and should be used in conjunction with maps suggested in the hike description.

Maps may contain contours or ridgelines, in addition to major watercourses, depending on the available information. These features build a three-dimensional picture of the terrain, allowing you to determine when the trail climbs and descends. Altitudes of major peaks, passes and localities complete the picture by providing the actual extent of the elevation changes.

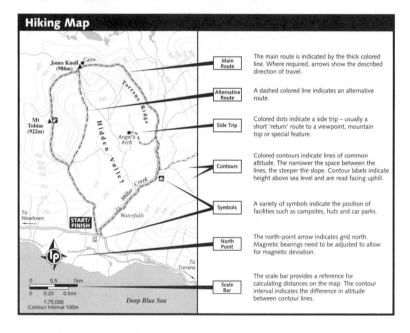

Hiking Map

Main Route — The main route is indicated by the thick colored line. Where required, arrows show the described direction of travel.

Alternative Route — A dashed colored line indicates an alternative route.

Side Trip — Colored dots indicate a side trip – usually a short 'return' route to a viewpoint, mountain top or special feature.

Contours — Colored contours indicate lines of common altitude. The narrower the space between the lines, the steeper the slope. Contour labels indicate height above sea level and are read facing uphill.

Symbols — A variety of symbols indicate the position of facilities such as campsites, huts and car parks.

North Point — The north-point arrow indicates grid north. Magnetic bearings need to be adjusted to allow for magnetic deviation.

Scale Bar — The scale bar provides a reference for calculating distances on the map. The contour interval indicates the difference in altitude between contour lines.

Route Finding

While accurate, our maps are not perfect. Inaccuracies in altitudes are commonly caused by air-temperature anomalies. Natural features such as river confluences and mountain peaks are in their true position, but the location of villages and trails is not always so. This may be because a village is spread over a hillside, or the size of the map does not allow for detail of the trail's twists and turns. However, by using several basic route-finding techniques, you will have few problems following our descriptions:

1. Always be aware of whether the trail should be climbing or descending.
2. Check the north-point arrow on the map and determine the general direction of the trail.
3. Time your progress over a known distance and calculate the speed at which you travel in the given terrain. From then on, you can determine with reasonable accuracy how far you have traveled.
4. Watch the path – look for boot prints and other signs of previous passage.

MAP LEGEND

BOUNDARIES

	International
	Regional
	Disputed

HYDROGRAPHY

	Coastline
	River, Stream
	Stream, Intermittent
	Canal or Flume
	Lake
	Spring, Waterfall
	Swamp

✪ **CAPITAL**	National Capital
◉ **CAPITAL**	Regional Capital
● Town	Town
● Village	Village

⬛	Campground
▣	Hut
●	Place to Stay
◰	Shelter

▣	Lookout
▼	Place to Eat
●	Point of Interest

ROUTES & TRANSPORT

(H-1)	Freeway
(50)	Primary Road
	Main Road
	Secondary Road
	One-Way Road
	Unsealed Road
	Fence
	Ferry Route

	Footbridge
	Powerline
	Tunnel
	Railway, Disused
	Described Walk
	Alternative Route
	Side Trip
	Hiking Track

AREA FEATURES

	Park (Regional Maps)
	Park (Hike Maps)
	Other Reserve
	Beach, Sand
	Reef
	Urban Area

MAP SYMBOLS

✈	Airport	▲	Mountain or Hill
✪	Bank	⛺	Park or Reserve
⊟	Bus	�	Parking
⌂	Cave	)(	Pass/Saddle
⛪	Church	☻	Picnic Area
	Cliff or Escarpment	✚	Police Station
100	Contour	✉	Post Office
✿	Garden	✖	Ruin
⋈	Gate	✪	Shopping Center
⛳	Golf Course	+100m	Spot Height
✚	Hospital	✦	Surf Beach
⚲	Lighthouse	△	Trigonometric Point
✖	Mine	ℹ	Visitor Center
⚱	Monument	▲	Volcano, Crater
🏛	Museum	⌨	Zoo

Note: not all symbols displayed above appear in this book

Foreword

ABOUT LONELY PLANET GUIDEBOOKS

The story begins with a classic travel adventure: Tony and Maureen Wheeler's 1972 journey across Europe and Asia to Australia. There was no useful information about the overland trail then, so Tony and Maureen published the first Lonely Planet guidebook to meet a growing need.

From a kitchen table, Lonely Planet has grown to become the largest independent travel publisher in the world, with offices in Melbourne (Australia), Oakland (USA), London (UK) and Paris (France).

Today Lonely Planet guidebooks cover the globe. There is an ever-growing list of books and information in a variety of media. Some things haven't changed. The main aim is still to make it possible for adventurous travelers to get out there – to explore and better understand the world.

At Lonely Planet we believe travelers can make a positive contribution to the countries they visit – if they respect their host communities and spend their money wisely. Since 1986 a percentage of the income from each book has been donated to aid projects and human rights campaigns, and, more recently, to wildlife conservation.

Although inclusion in a guidebook usually implies a recommendation we cannot list every good place. Exclusion does not necessarily imply criticism. In fact there are a number of reasons why we might exclude a place – sometimes it is simply inappropriate to encourage an influx of travelers.

UPDATES & READER FEEDBACK

Things change – prices go up, schedules change, good places go bad and bad places go bankrupt. Nothing stays the same. So, if you find things better or worse, recently opened or long-since closed, please tell us and help make the next edition even more accurate and useful.

Lonely Planet thoroughly updates each guidebook as often as possible – usually every two years, although for some destinations the gap can be longer. Between editions, up-to-date information is available in our free, monthly email bulletin *Comet* (**w** www.lonelyplanet.com/newsletters). You can also check out the *Thorn Tree* bulletin board and *Postcards* section of our website, which carry unverified, but fascinating, reports from travelers.

Tell us about it! We genuinely value your feedback. A well-traveled team at Lonely Planet reads and acknowledges every email and letter we receive and ensures that every morsel of information finds its way to the relevant authors, editors and cartographers.

Everyone who writes to us will find their name listed in the next edition of the appropriate guidebook. The very best contributions will be rewarded with a free guidebook.

We may edit, reproduce and incorporate your comments in Lonely Planet products such as guidebooks, websites and digital products, so let us know if you don't want your comments reproduced or your name acknowledged.

How to contact Lonely Planet:
Online: **e** talk2us@lonelyplanet.com.au, **w** www.lonelyplanet.com
Australia: Locked Bag 1, Footscray, Victoria 3011
UK: 72-82 Rosebery Ave, London EC1R 4RW
USA: 150 Linden St, Oakland, CA 94607

Introduction

Hawaii grants hikers a golden chance to do it all – from stealing across recent lava flows to cavorting beneath waterfalls or walking upon sacred footpaths once reserved for *ali'i* (royal chiefs) – and all in a relatively short time. Come for a week or a month, it makes no difference. After all, where else can you climb to a volcanic summit at over 13,000ft and then snorkel in warm tropical waters just hours later?

Even for novice hikers or expert trekkers, there are a dizzying number of island trails to choose from and most can be hiked year-round. Start with a half-day meander through cool bamboo forests and underneath cascading waterfalls? Spend a day wandering through history on the wild Kalaupapa Peninsula or strolling the boardwalks of the unique Alakai Swamp, a haven for rare bird life. Jonesing for an adrenaline rush? Try pushing your way up Oahu's knife-edged Ko'olau Range, venturing to the heart of the Big Island's active rift zone or planning a multi-day trek to remote valleys on the famous Na Pali Coast.

Hawaii has virtually all of the world's ecological zones represented and some of the only tropical rain forest in the USA. Cloud and rain forests, cinder deserts, majestic *pali* (sea cliffs) and coastal sand dunes all come bursting out of Hawaii's tropical trail mix. Kauai stakes a claim on the 'Grand Canyon of the Pacific' and the

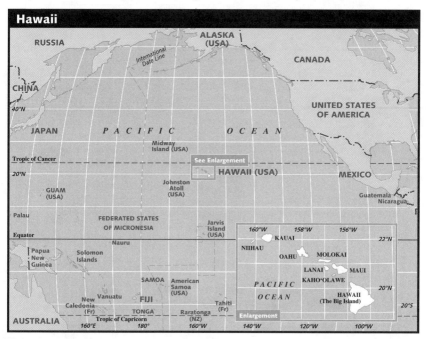

Big Island chalks up both the world's largest and most massive mountains, when measured from the ocean floor.

Hawaii's wealth of *aina* (land) is equaled only by its wildlife. Like on the Galapagos Islands, most of Hawaii's over 10,000 species of flora and fauna evolved from only a few ancestral types. Life thrives here. Adaptive radiation has produced a rainbow of honeycreepers, curious spiders with smiley faces on their backs, silversword plants that bloom only once in a lifetime and hibiscus that bloom for only one day. Even migrating North Pacific humpback whales prefer Hawaii's warm coastal waters above all others, often performing spectacular acrobatics during their winter sojourn in the islands.

Hiking is the perfect way to explore Hawaii. Island trails lead away from kitschy beach resorts and Vegas-style luau shows, letting you experience the aloha of Hawaii and its people as they are today. Skip ordering another mai tai from the poolside bar; instead pick *lilikoi* (passionfruit) straight from the vine or crack open fresh coconuts at beachfront campsites. Splash in a fern-covered waterfall grotto, instead of just glimpsing one on a helicopter tour or in a Hollywood film. Trade the keys to yet another bland hotel room for a cozy volcanic summit cabin, where all the stars of the Milky Way burn brightly outside the front door.

Real-life adventures await you here. *E komo mai*. Welcome to Hawaii, a paradise for hikers indeed.

Facts about Hawaii

HISTORY

c. 1000 BC – original settlers of Polynesia (literally 'many islands') migrate though Southeast Asia and across Melanesia, to settle Tonga and Samoa

c. AD 500–700 – first Polynesians arrive in Hawaii via double-hulled canoes sailed from the Marquesas Islands

c. 1000 – first wave of Tahitians reach Hawaii and force Marquesans to work as conscripted labor

c. 1200 – Pa'ao, a Tahitian *kahuna* (high priest), institutes *kapu* (system of taboos) to regulate social interaction and builds *luakini* (human sacrifice temples); later Pa'ao summons chief Pili, also from Kahiki (Tahiti), to start a new royal lineage

1778 – British explorer Captain James Cook chances upon Hawaii as he searches for a northwest passage to the Atlantic; Cook christens the archipelago the 'Sandwich Islands', in honor of the Earl of Sandwich

c. 1780 – Kahekili, the last of Maui's ruling *ali'i* (chiefs), brings Oahu, Molokai and Lanai under his unified rule

1782 – Captain George Vancouver lands on Maui at Kihei and befriends an ambitious young royal from the Big Island, later known as Kamehameha the Great

1790 – Kamehameha attacks Maui using Western cannons and the aid of two captured foreign seamen, Isaac Davis and John Young

1794 – Kahekili dies at Waikiki; Kamehameha invades Maui again and the next year conquers all of the Hawaiian islands, except for Kauai, which succumbs by treaty in 1810

1815 – Russian trading ship is wrecked off the coast of Kauai; Kaumuali'i, Kauai's last sovereign, confiscates the cargo, then later enters into (and reneges) on a treaty with the Russians, who built forts at Waimea and Hanalei

1819 – Kamehameha the Great dies, the crown passes to his reluctant son, Liholiho (Kamehameha II); Queen Ka'ahumanu brings down the *kapu* system, wiping out 600 years of taboos and restrictions, and a frenzy of temple-smashing and idol-burning quickly spreads across the islands

c. 1820s – whalers and the first missionaries arrive; Queen Ka'ahumanu converts to Christianity and becomes a great patron of the church in Hawaii

1831 – Lahainaluna Seminary, the first school west of the Rockies, is established above Lahaina Harbor

1840 – with the help of David Malo, the first native Hawaiian ordained at Lahainaluna Seminary, Kamehameha III pens a declaration of rights and Hawaii's first constitution, extending religious freedoms and universal male suffrage

1843 – Hawaii's only 'invasion' by a foreign power happens when George Paulet, an upstart British commander irate over a petty land deal, seizes Oahu for six months; Queen Victoria dispatches an admiral to restore Hawaiian independence

1848 – Kamehameha III signs the Great Mahele land act, under which land becomes a commodity, and foreigners buy up large tracts of land; many native Hawaiians are disenfranchised, drifting into urban ghettos or sugar plantations

c. 1850s – immigrant plantation laborers from around Asia start to bring a wealth of ethnic diversity to Hawaii

1861 – Walter Gibson, a charismatic Mormon elder, arrives in Lanai, where church members are trying to establish a 'City of Joseph' in Hawaii

1865 – as Hawaii's native population declines alarmingly, largely as the result of diseases introduced by foreigners, those afflicted with leprosy are forcibly exiled to Kalaupapa, Molokai

1870 – Samuel Alexander and Henry Baldwin, sons of prominent missionaries, plant a dozen acres of sugarcane in Haiku, Maui, and found what becomes Hawaii's biggest sugar company

1872 – General John Schofield sent by the USA to assess the strategic value of Pearl Harbor, the largest anchorage in the Pacific

1874 – King David Kalakaua, the 'Merrie Monarch,' elected as Hawaii's last king and supporters of rival Queen Emma riot in the streets; the king requests aid from US and British warships in Honolulu Harbor; Kalakaua goes on to reign as a cultural revivalist, bringing back the hula (traditional Hawaiian dance) and ensuring a measure of self-rule for Hawaiians

1887 – sugar barons, eager to eliminate tariffs, favor the annexation of Hawaii by the USA and form the Hawaiian League, which coerces Kalakaua to accept a new constitution and limits royal powers

1891 – Kalakaua dies in San Francisco; his sister, Liliuokalani, wife of Oahu governor John O Dominis, succeeds to the throne

1893 – while Queen Liliuokalani prepares to proclaim a new constitution restoring sovereign powers, a group of armed *haole* (Caucasian) businessmen declare the monarchy overthrown; Sanford Dole, son of a pioneer missionary, appeals to the USA for annexation, but President Grover Cleveland refuses

1894 – provisional government inaugurates itself as the 'Republic of Hawaii'; Liliuokalani forced to abdicate, then tried and placed under house arrest in Iolani Palace

1896 – Liliuokalani released and travels to Washington, DC to request help in restoring the Hawaiian monarchy

1898 – US Congress formally annexes Hawaii

1919 – Prince Jonah Kuhio Kalanianaole, Hawaii's first congressional delegate, introduces a statehood bill, but Hawaii's multiethnic community is deemed 'too exotic' to become American

1920 – US Congress passes Hawaiian Homes Commission Act, which sets aside 313 sq miles of land for 99-year-lease homesteading by Hawaiians who can prove at least 50% native ancestry

1922 – Jim Dole pays $1.1 million to purchase Lanai outright for his Hawaiian Pineapple Company

1936 – Pan American pilots the first passenger flight from the US mainland to Hawaii

December 7, 1941 – Japanese bombers attack Pearl Harbor; Hawaii placed under martial law and Oahu becomes the US military's WWII headquarters in the Pacific theater

1941–45 – Japanese-Americans are interrogated and sent to mainland internment camps; some Americans of Japanese Ancestry (AJAs) form the 442nd Regimental Combat Team, which later becomes the most decorated fighting unit in US history

1959 – after 61 years of territorial status, Hawaii becomes the 50th state of the USA; only the island of Ni'ihau votes against it; Daniel Inouye, among the veterans of the 442nd, is elected as Hawaii's first Congressional representative

1976 – successful voyage of the double-hulled canoe *Hokule'a* from Oahu to Tahiti and back, using only ancient navigation techniques, proves Polynesian theory of Hawaiian settlement

late 1970s – Hawaiian cultural renaissance of language and arts; native sovereignty movements emerge

1992 – Hurricane Iniki, the most powerful storm to strike Hawaii in a century, makes a direct hit on Kauai

1993 – President William J Clinton signs US Congress Public Law 103–150, an apology to native Hawaiians on behalf of the US for the overthrow of the Kingdom of Hawaii

2000 – US Supreme Court rules that native Hawaiians are a racial group, not a tribe that has a political relationship with the USA, resulting in far-reaching political as well as practical ramifications

2003 – Hawaiian representatives to US Congress continue to push for federal recognition for native Hawaiians as a sovereign people

History of Hiking

Most ancient Hawaiian footpaths connected villages to remote valleys and other settlements along the coast. The traditional land division system of *ahupua'a* (narrow strips of land that extended from the mountains to the sea) created inland trails used for trading and visiting. In the Polynesian tradition, ceremonial paths led from the ocean to important *heiau* (temples) and pilgrimage routes were established on sacred peaks, such as Mt Waialeale and Mauna Kea. Some *ali'i* built round-island highways of lava rocks and used them for tax collecting during the annual *makahiki* (harvest festival) processions.

After the arrival of Europeans, travel by horseback became common. Some existing footpaths were widened or rerouted, thanks in part to missionary activities. When more travelers were drawn to Hawaii in the late 19th century, visits to natural wonders like fiery Halemau'mau Crater or a sunrise atop Haleakala created new trails. The Hawaii Trail and Mountain Club (see Hiking Clubs, p41, under Useful Organizations) was established early the next century. Many of Hawaii's mountain and forest trails were built by the Civilian Conservation Corps, a 1930s-era federal work program. Nowadays trail preservation and development is coordinated by state-run Na Ala Hele (see Government Departments, p40, under Useful Organizations).

GEOGRAPHY

The Hawaiian Islands chain is 2500 miles from the nearest continental land mass, making it the most geographically isolated place in the world. The islands form the apex of the Polynesian triangle (with Easter Island and New Zealand as the other two

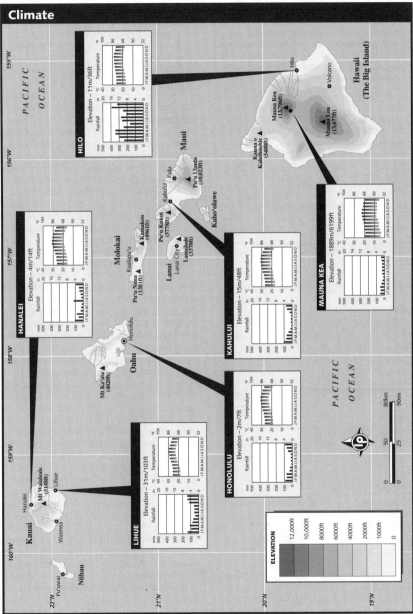

Super Superlative Islands

Hawaii's highest mountain is Mauna Kea, which is 13,796ft above sea level, on the Big Island. According to the *Guinness Book of Records,* Mauna Kea is technically the world's highest mountain (33,476ft) when measured from the ocean floor. Mauna Loa, also on the Big Island, is Hawaii's second highest mountain at 13,677ft. Again when measured from the ocean floor, it rates as the world's most massive mountain.

Guinness also considers Mt Waialeale, on Kauai, the world's wettest spot, averaging 486 inches of rainfall per year. Pu'u Kukui, which sits just 5 miles away from Maui's dry Wailuku plains, holds the US record for annual rainfall at an astoundingly soggy 739 inches.

vertices) and stretch from remote Kure Atoll in the northwest to the Big Island's South Point (Ka Lae), the southernmost point of the USA.

The equator lies 1470 miles south of the state capital Honolulu and all of the major Hawaiian Islands are south of the tropic of Cancer. Hawaii shares approximately the same latitude as Hong Kong, Bombay, Mexico City and Cuba. The total land mass (6423 sq miles) of all the Hawaiian Islands is slightly smaller than Fiji but larger than the state of Connecticut. The remote Northwestern Hawaiian Islands, which lie scattered across a thousand miles of ocean west of Kauai, contribute a total land mass of just under 5 sq miles.

CLIMATE

Most of the year, weather on the Hawaiian Islands is balmy, with northeasterly trade winds prevailing. Although it tends to be wetter in winter and hotter in summer, rainfall and temperature vary more with elevation and direction – whether *mauka* (toward the mountains) or *makai* (toward the sea), for example – than the season.

Most islands basically have two kinds of weather, at least along the coast. The western *kona* (leeward) side of the islands is dry and sunny year-round. On the *ko'olau* (windward) side, high mountains block trade winds, and moisture-laden clouds from the northeast bring abundant rainfall on exposed ridges, mountain slopes and into valleys.

The islands experience only two seasons, *kau* (summer) and *ho'oilo* (winter). Average temperatures differ only 8°F between summer and winter, and coastal waters are warm year-round. Keep in mind that the temperature drops an average of 3.5°F for every 1000ft of elevation above sea level. The lowest temperature ever recorded in Hawaii was 12°F atop Mauna Kea, although this did not count the wind-chill factor. Overnight lows regularly dip below freezing on all of Hawaii's highest volcanic peaks and snow occasionally falls.

Hawaii gets most of its rain somewhere between December and March. *Kona* weather sees the winds blow from the south, a shift from the typical northeast trades. The ocean swell pattern also changes at this time – snorkeling spots suddenly become surfing spots and vice versa. In summer, rain is more likely to fall as brief trade-wind showers.

Hurricane season is between June and early December. Strong winds and flash flooding do cause some injury and property damage. Tsunamis, or tidal waves, are not common in Hawaii, but when they do hit they can be severe. The largest to ever hit Hawaii was in 1946, the result of an earthquake in the Aleutian Islands. Waves reached a height of 55ft, entire villages were washed away and 159 people died.

Hawaii has since installed a tsunami warning system, which is aired through yellow speakers mounted on telephone poles around the islands. Any earthquake strong enough to cause you to grab onto something to keep from falling is a natural tsunami warning. If you're in a low-lying coastal area when one occurs, immediately head for higher ground.

See also Weather Information (p42).

[Continued on page 26]

WATCHING WILDLIFE

All living things that reached Hawaii's shores were carried across the ocean on wing, wind or wave – seeds clinging to a bird's feather, a floating *hala* plant or insect eggs in a piece of driftwood. The first Polynesian settlers brought chickens and pigs, along with medicinal plants and fruit. On the islands these species evolved in relative isolation. Today the majority of Hawaii's more than 10,000 endemic species of flora and fauna are found nowhere else on earth.

The legacy of Western contact has been the destruction of many of Hawaii's fragile ecosystems. Since the arrival of Europeans, invasive plants and animals have endangered, and even caused the extinction of, many Hawaiian species, which previously had few natural predators and only limited defenses. Introduced pigs, goats and cattle, which all grazed and foraged at will, spelled extinction for many Hawaiian plants by causing erosion and deforestation. Exotic songbirds and game birds spread avian diseases, to which native Hawaiian birds had no immunity. These islands didn't even have mosquitoes before water casks unloaded from whaling ships brought them – imagine: paradise without skeeters!

Hawaii accounts for 75% of extinct species in the USA and one-third of its endangered flora and fauna, even though the islands make up only 1% of the total US land mass. Although some species are slowly making a comeback, 20 new exotic species arrive on Hawaiian soil each year. Currently among the worst invaders is the *Miconia calvescens* or velvet tree, a tenacious South American plant that has already taken over 70% of Tahiti's rain forests.

Not Native?!

Many cultivated crops thought of as uniquely Hawaiian today are actually exotic imports, for example, macadamia nuts from Australia. Pineapples, which came from Brazil, belong to the bromeliad family of plants, some of which have showy decorative flowers. Sugarcane, called *ko,* was first planted by Polynesian settlers. Now cane stalks often grow wild alongside island highways, especially since many of Hawaii's commercial sugar operations have been shut down.

Plants

Climate zones vary from dry alpine desert to lush tropical rain forest in Hawaii, so hikers will find a wide variety of flora. Still, less than half of the islands' original forest cover remains today, due to widespread overgrazing, logging, erosion, invasive species and watershed pollution.

Flowers Found only on the volcanoes of Maui and the Big Island, the striking **silversword** *(ahinahina)* is a distant relative of the sunflower. Now endangered, the silversword was nearly wiped out in the early 20th century by grazing feral goats, pigs and cattle, as well as by people who cut them down for souvenirs. The silversword's shiny leaves have evolved fine silver hairs to reflect the sun's ultraviolet radiation. Each plant can grow for up to half a century, but blooms only once in a lifetime. In the summer of its final year, the silversword shoots up a flowering stalk with hundreds of maroon and yellow blossoms. When the flowers go to seed in late fall, the plant dies.

Common native plants include the **beach morning glory** *(pohuehue)*, with leathery green leaves and pale pink flowers, and the **beach naupaka**, which has delicate white flowers that look as if they've been torn in half and smooth green leaves. The yellow-orange flowers of the royal **ilima**, which has adapted to harsh coastal winds by growing as a ground cover, is used for making lei. Found in forests, the revered **maile** vine bears olive-looking fruit and has leathery green leaves that are woven into horseshoe-shaped lei. Also growing on vines are seed-filled **passionfruit** *(lilikoi)*.

More than 5000 varieties of **hibiscus** bush grow in Hawaii; on most, the colorful flowers bloom only for a day. There are a number of native hibiscus, including the **sea hibiscus** *(hau)*, known for its heart-shaped flowers that open as yellow and change to dark orange and red as day moves into the night. The **kokio keokeo**, a native white hibiscus tree that grows up to 40ft high, is the only Hawaiian hibiscus with a fragrance.

Hawaii is abloom with scores of other exotic tropical flowers, including blood-red **anthuriums** with heart-shaped leaves, brilliantly orange-and-blue or lily-white **bird-of-paradise**, **bougainvillea** heavily laden with bright red or purple flowers and various **heliconia**. Night-blooming **cereus**, actually a cactus plant, has scalloped green leaves and exquisitely fragrant white flowers along its trailing vines. Hundreds of varieties of both cultivated and native wild **orchids** and ornamental **ginger** varieties exist, including the white 'shampoo' ginger *(awapuhi)*, which has a fragrant soapy juice that is squeezed from its flowers.

Hawaii's **protea** are originally native to South Africa. The protea family, which is named after the Greek god Proteus who could change shape at will, comes in more than 1500 varieties, from macadamia nuts to spiky carnations to artichoke blossoms. There are also protea evergreens, shrubs and herbs. Hawaiian protea account for 90% of the world market, with 85 species alone situated solely on the slopes of Haleakala (Maui). Protea thrive on sandy, acidic soil and where cool nights follow warm days.

Ferns There are about 200 varieties of Hawaiian ferns and fern allies (such as mosses) found in rain forests and colonizing recent lava flows. **Hapu'u**, the most common of endemic tree fern varieties, has multiple fronds on each stalk that can grow over 20ft tall. **Amau** ferns have only a single leathery frond, which changes color from green to red over time, on each stalk. Growing in dense thickets, **false staghorn ferns** *(uluhe)* have repeatedly forked fronds. Fragrant, glossy **maile-**

scented fern (lauae) are favored by lei makers and resort gardeners. The **hare's foot fern** (lauae haole) has prominent sporangia, which are the spore capsules typically found on the undersides of fern fronds.

Shrubs & Trees

The most bewitching of native Hawaiian forest trees is **koa**, nowadays found only at higher elevations and even then rarely. It grows up to 100ft high. Young saplings have bizarre, fern-like compound leaves that are an evolutionary throwback to its African origins. This rich hardwood is traditionally used to make canoes, surfboards and even ukulele.

Hawaii was once rich in fragrant **sandalwood** (iliahi) forests, but these were sold off to foreign traders by the mid-19th century. Rare nowadays, these tall trees (of which there are many species, with varying types of green leaves, fruits and nuts) can be seen in Hawaii Volcanoes National Park. The dark green leaves of **false sandalwood** (naio) appear twisted, with tiny white or pinkish flowers, and are most common on Maui.

The versatile **ohia** is one of the first plants to colonize lava flows. It grows in barren areas as a shrub and on more fertile land as a tree. Found everywhere, its distinctive tufted flowers are petalless groups of red, orange, yellow and (rarely) white stamens.

Brought by early Polynesian settlers, the **candlenut tree** (kukui) has light silver-tinged foliage that stands out brightly in the forest, and it is Hawaii's state tree. Its oily nuts are used for making lei, dyes and candles. Another early Polynesian import was **bamboo**, now found in tall forest groves. It has a sweet edible root and its stalk sometimes grows six inches in a single day. Two coastal trees that also proved useful in ancient Hawaii were the **screw pine** (hala), a pandanus species, the spiny leaves of which were used for thatching and weaving, and the **coconut palm** (niu), which thrives in coral sands. Screw pines have prop roots around the trunk and produce an orangey pineapple-like fruit, which is inedible. Early Polynesian settlers used the coconut palm for food, material fibers and hale (dwelling) construction.

Stands of **ironwood**, a non-native conifer with drooping needles, act as natural windbreaks and prevent erosion from beaches. Majestic **banyan** trees have a canopy of hanging aerial roots with trunks large enough to swallow small children; they're also shady and a haven for bird life. Imported forest species from Australia include **rainbow eucalyptus**, which proves its name when its bark is peeled away; aromatic **blue gum** (with bluish bark); and **paperbark eucalyptus**, which has layered white bark.

Food & Medicine

The common Hawaiian taro plant has green heart-shaped leaves and purplish-white roots, which are pounded into the traditional dietary staple called poi. Waxy yellow-green leaves from Polynesian ti plants are used to wrap food, as well as to cure headaches when laid flat against the forehead. Polynesian breadfruit (ulu), a green, spiky football-sized fruit, can be a treatment for skin diseases, cuts and scratches. But unparalleled among traditional restoratives is Indian mulberry (noni), which is said to be effective against almost anything – and certainly tastes bad enough to prove it! A petite tree with knobby berries, noni often thrives on the mineral-rich soil of lava flows.

WATCHING WILDLIFE

Often mistakenly called Norfolk pines, stately **Cook pines** came to the islands from the South Pacific. More pesky are introduced species of **mangrove**, whose twisted root systems have completely choked natural ponds and sections of coastline. A member of the alien mesquite family, **kiawe** is a nuisance to beachgoers, as its sharp thorns easily pierce soft soles. Coastal *kiawe* often form shade cover with their long branches, compound leaves and dense flowers with white spikes.

Monkeypod are common shade trees and sport dark glossy green leaves, puffy pink flowers and longish seed pods. **Jacaranda** trees burst with blue and purple blooms in spring and summer, their tubular flowers carpeting upcountry roads. Both are native to South America.

Animals

Both of Hawaii's native mammals, the Hawaiian monk seal and a subspecies of hoary bat, are endangered. So are countless species of native birds, including a rainbow of honeycreepers. But hikers can still rejoice: Hawaii has *no* snakes.

Land Mammals The reclusive **Hawaiian hoary bat** *(opeapea)* has a heavy coat of brown-and-grayish fur and whitish ears, making it appear 'hoary'. Weighing only five to eight ounces, and with a wingspan of around a foot, not much is known about these nocturnal hunters. Having fallen victim to chemical pesticides and predatory species, today these tree-dwellers are thought to exist predominantly around forests on the leeward sides of the Big Island, Maui and Kauai.

Wild horses roam free and you'll see **cattle** grazing in the uplands of many islands, both species having been dropped off by Western explorers two centuries ago. The **axis deer** that run around Molokai, Lanai and Maui are descendants of eight deer sent from India in 1868 as a gift to King Kamehameha V. The deer, along with feral pigs, goats, sheep and game birds, are hunted for recreational purposes and to control the damage that all these non-native species wreak on the environment. Most insidious of all is the **mongoose**, a commonly seen ferret-like creature that was originally introduced to control sugarcane rats, but whose appetite for native birds and their eggs has led to a drastic decline in avian populations.

Marine Mammals The **Hawaiian monk seal**, so named apparently for its solitary habits and the cowl-like fold of neck skin, has remained nearly unchanged for 15 million years, but was almost wiped out last century. Extremely sensitive to human disturbance, the seals breed and give birth primarily in

Animal 911

Even short-term visitors can help Hawaiian conservation efforts in a variety of ways. Do not approach or otherwise disturb any endangered creatures, especially marine species such as whales, dolphins, seals and sea turtles; doing so is not only illegal, but subjects trespassers to a hefty fine. Please slow down while driving around the islands. Many nene (Hawaiian geese) have been backed over by careless drivers in parking lots or run over along park roads. Others have been tamed by too much human contact, so do not feed them. Finally, report any sightings of Hawaiian monk seals, or any wild animal in distress, to the State of Hawaii's **Division of Conservation & Resource Enforcement** *(DOCARE; ☎ 587-0077)*.

the remote Northwestern Hawaiian Islands. Of the world's two other monk seal species, the Caribbean monk seal is believed extinct and the Mediterranean monk seal numbers only in the hundreds.

Hawaii has several species of predatory **toothed whales** residing here year-round, plus a few migrating species of **baleen whales**, which have rows of horny elastic material (called whalebone or baleen) hanging from their upper jaw that acts as a filter to extract food, normally krill or small fish. Both are warm-blooded, air-breathing mammals.

It is the islands' most frequent visitor, the migrating **North Pacific humpback whale**, that everyone wants to see. These whales were hunted almost to extinction, and they were still being hunted as recently as the 1960s, when an international ban on their slaughter came into force. As the fifth largest of the great whales, the endangered humpback can reach lengths of 45ft and weigh up to 45 tons. These whales spend the summer feeding in the plankton-rich waters off Alaska, developing a layer of blubber that sustains them through the winter migration and breeding period. Some whales migrate to Mexico or the southern islands of Japan, but the largest numbers are found in the shallow waters between Maui, Lanai and Kaho'olawe, now declared a national marine sanctuary. Peak whale-watching season is January to March. Despite their size, humpbacks often put on quite an amazing acrobatic show, which includes arching dives, breaching and fin splashing.

Spinner dolphins are nocturnal feeders that often come into calm bays during the day to rest. These intelligent, wild dolphins are easily disturbed by noise, so it is illegal to swim out and join them. **Pacific bottle-nosed dolphins** and **spotted dolphins** are also common in Hawaiian waters.

Humpback whale

Amphibians All three Hawaiian sea turtle species are endangered, as human disturbance to nesting grounds and poaching have killed uncountable numbers. In ancient Hawaii, sea turtles served as *aumakua* (family gods and guardians) and their form often appears in petroglyphs. Among the **leatherback turtle, green sea turtle** (honu) and **Hawksbill sea turtle** (honuea) populations, the most threatened is the Hawksbill. These and green sea turtles weigh up to 200lbs when mature, while the soft-shelled leatherback can weigh 10 times that amount and grow up to 8ft long. Green sea turtles migrate hundreds of miles every few years to breed and nest in the remote Northwestern Hawaiian Islands, but are not uncommonly seen in waters off the main islands.

Leatherback turtle

Green sea turtle

Birds Native Hawaiian bird life is so varied, it deserves a book of its own.

Many of Hawaii's birds may have evolved from a single species in a spectacular display of adaptive radiation. The majority have evolved so thoroughly that it's not possible to trace them to any continental ancestors. Quite a few lost the ability to fly as well as many natural defenses, which were no longer needed in Hawaii, leaving them vulnerable to new predatory species and infectious avian diseases after Europeans arrived. Over half of Hawaii's native bird species are already extinct, and more than 30 of those remaining are still under threat.

One of the most critically endangered is the **Hawaiian crow** (alala), of which only a handful of birds remain in captive breeding programs on Maui and the Big Island. Hawaiians believe that the **Hawaiian short-eared owl** (pueo) has protective powers and represents a physical manifestation of ancestors' spirits. Seeing one is a good omen and the most likely place is atop volcanic peaks where it soars at high altitudes. From a distance some mistake it for the **Hawaiian hawk** (io), a symbol of royalty. Although both adult birds are predominantly dusty-brown colored, the Hawaiian hawk is restricted to the Big Island's volcanoes. Juvenile hawks have striking honey-colored bellies.

The endangered **nene** (Hawaiian goose), Hawaii's state bird, is a long-lost cousin of the Canada goose. Nene generally nest in high cliffs from 6000ft to 8000ft, surrounded by sparse vegetation and rugged lava flows, on the slopes of Haleakala, Mauna Kea and Mauna Loa. Their feet have gradually adapted by losing most of their webbing. Nene have black heads, light yellow cheeks, a white underbelly and dark

Creepy Crawlies

Hawaii's spiders are a diverse lot, but mostly non-poisonous. Long-legged brown cane spiders are common. So are Hawaiian happyface spiders, which live in rain forests, are less than ¼ inch long and active only at night. They have a variety of red and black markings on their waxy yellow bodies that uncannily resemble a 'happy face.' Happy hunting!

gray feathers. In 1946 only 50 nene remained alive anywhere in the world. In fact, there were no birds left inside Haleakala National Park at all until Boy Scouts carried junior birds back into the crater inside their backpacks! Thanks to a captive breeding and release program, the Hawaiian goose has slowly been brought back from the verge of extinction.

Finches, early ancestors of today's rainbow variety of Hawaiian honeycreepers, are theorized to be the first birds to colonize the islands. Most rain forest honeycreepers are sparrow-sized and have curved bills to suck nectar from Hawaiian flowers. Thriving common species include the yellow-green **amakihi**, the bright-red **apapane** with white feathers under its tail and wings that make a whirring sound, and the black-tailed **i'iwi**, recognized by its vermilion feathers and salmon-colored bill. The smallest species of honeycreeper, the **akepa**, has a beak with crossed tips that let it pry apart buds, seed pods and leaves to look for bugs; it's found above the 3000ft level in *ohia* forests. A non-native forest bird common to all the islands is the yellow-green **Japanese white-eye**, which has a white circle around its eye and a strident dawn song.

Native waterfowl include the **Hawaii coot** *(alae keokeo)*, which is all black except for its white bill and the front of its head, which can be white, yellow or blood-red. The coot is found in fresh or brackish-water ponds, where it builds floating nests, and it rarely flies. Although it can be seen on all the islands, it is most populous on Oahu. The endangered **Hawaiian stilt** *(aeo)* is a black-necked wading bird with a white underbelly that feeds along the marshy edges of ponds. It's a graceful bird in flight, with long orange legs that trail behind, and it has a yipping chirp. Even though the stilt population in all Hawaii is estimated at just 1500, the birds can still be spotted on Maui and Kauai.

Many long-distance migratory waterfowl use the Hawaiian islands as a stopping-off point. The **Pacific golden-plover** *(kolea)*, which nests in Alaska during the summer, returns to Hawaii with brown upper parts speckled with gold. As spring draws near, its coloring changes, showing black feathers with gray-brown upper parts. Most of the islets off Oahu's Windward Coast are sanctuaries for seabirds, including **terns**, **noddies**, **shearwaters**, **albatrosses**, **boobies** and **frigate birds**.

Frigate

[Continued from page 18]

ECOLOGY & ENVIRONMENT

Hawaii's native ecosystems have been decimated by the introduction of exotic flora and fauna since Europeans arrived. Erosion caused by free-ranging cattle, goats and pigs, and the monocrop cultures of sugarcane and pineapple have destroyed native ground covers, resulting in washouts that sweep prime topsoil into the sea and choke nearshore reefs.

Beach resorts and 'condoville' areas that sprang up from the mid-20th century were poorly planned, if they were even planned at all. This trend reached its epitome with the mainly Japanese-driven golf course megaresorts of the 1980s. When the Japanese economic bubble burst, many resorts went belly up, or suffered through environmental mismanagement, and some land sits unused or even worse, unusable. Today many special interest groups are in cut-throat competition for Hawaii's land and natural resources, including agriculture, ranching, forestry, tourism and resort development.

On a more positive note, the Hawaiian islands have no polluting heavy industry and not a single roadside billboard to blight natural vistas. The islands boast examples of virtually all of the world's ecological zones and some of the only tropical rain forest in the USA.

Conservation

On a day-to-day level, a wide coalition of environmentalists, scientists, activists and residents have made island conservation efforts a slow but steady success. They help fight invasive weeds, pulling up one plant at a time; monitor migrating whale and nesting turtle populations; advocate for the protection of coral reefs and tide pools; and protest against potentially harmful tourism, such as cruise ships visiting Molokai or shopping mall 'dolphinariums'.

One of the most tooth-and-nail battles waged on the islands today is over watershed resources. All the manicured greenery of resorts and golf courses comes with a price tag. It is mostly paid by Hawaiian farmers, whose water is drained through irrigation ditches to provide the millions of gallons required by resort guests daily. But as one activist slogan points out, 'No one can eat golf balls.' Plans for further resort development are fiercely opposed by a wide coalition of local and international environmental groups.

For endangered species conservation efforts, see Watching Wildlife (p19). Another conservation focus is on archaeological sites, such as *heiau*, petroglyph fields and Hawaii's traditional fishponds. Over recent decades, efforts have been made to rebuild and restock a few of the fishponds, mostly with *ama'ama* (mullet) and *awa* (milkfish). Some impressive ones lie along the shores of East Molokai, Maui and Kauai.

Currently there are more than 150 environmental groups in Hawaii, ranging from chapters of international organizations to neighborhood groups defending local beaches from encroaching development. Following are some of the more prominent groups:

Earthjustice Legal Defense Fund (☎ 599-2436, ⓦ www.earthjustice.org) 223 S King St #400, Honolulu, HI 96813. Earthjustice plays a leading role in protecting Hawaii's species diversity, natural environment and watershed resources through court action.

Malama Hawaii (ⓦ www.malamahawaii.org) This is a partnership network of community groups and other nonprofit organizations. Check the website for environmental news and volunteer opportunities, everything from public awareness campaigns to counting migrating whales.

The Nature Conservancy (TNC; ☎ 537-4508, ⓦ nature.org) 923 Nu'uanu Ave, Honolulu, HI 96817. TNC protects Hawaii's rarest ecosystems by buying up vast tracts of land or working out long-term stewardships with some of Hawaii's biggest landholders.

The Sierra Club (☎ 538-6616, ⓦ www.hi.sierra club.org) 1040 Richards St, Room 306, Honolulu, HI 96803. This club is one of the broadest-based groups engaging in local environmental activism.

PARKS & PROTECTED AREAS

Hawaii has two national parks, Haleakala National Park on Maui and Hawaii Volcanoes

National Park on the Big Island. You could have a splendid hiking vacation without leaving the parks. Each is uniquely fascinating, covering a variety of environments and natural phenomena. Both were nominated as international biosphere preserves in the 1980s and Hawaii Volcanoes has been declared a Unesco World Heritage site.

Prince Jonah Kalanianaole, the man who could've been king if the Hawaiian monarchy hadn't been overthrown, first proposed Haleakala as a national park. When

Kaho'olawe

For nearly a decade, this devastated island off Maui had the ironic distinction of being the only nationally registered historic place that was being used by its government for bombing practice. In many ways, the island's story mirrors the journey of the Hawaiian people, from early Polynesian settlement through US annexation, to the native sovereignty and environmental movements of today.

In ancient times Kaho'olawe was the place where *kahuna* (priests, healers or sorcerers) and navigators were trained, and it played an important role in early Pacific migrations to Tahiti. More than 500 archaeological sites have been identified on Kaho'olawe. Over time its native dryland forest was denuded by Hawaiian villagers, and by the time of Western contact it was largely uninhabited and barren.

Afterwards, Kaho'olawe was used and abused as a penal colony and smugglers' base, then sold as ranch land. By the early 1900s, feral goats, pigs and sheep had dug up, rooted out and chewed off so much of Kaho'olawe's vegetation that the island was largely a dust bowl. After the Pearl Harbor attack in 1941, the US military took control of Kaho'olawe and began bombing over the entire island.

By the 1970s, Hawaiian politicians were petitioning the federal government to cease its military activities and return Kaho'olawe to the state. In 1976, a small group of Hawaiian activists set out in boats for Kaho'olawe, trying to focus public attention on the bombing. There were a series of occupations and many activists were jailed. During one of the 1977 crossings, group members George Helm and Kimo Mitchell mysteriously disappeared in the waters off Kaho'olawe. Helm had been an inspirational Hawaiian-rights activist, and with his death the Protect Kaho'olawe Ohana (PKO) movement sprang up. Helm's vision of turning Kaho'olawe into a sanctuary of Hawaiian culture and identity quickly became widespread among islanders.

In 1980, in a court-sanctioned consent decree, the Navy reached an agreement that allowed the PKO regular access for religious, cultural, scientific and educational purposes. Although the bombing continued even after Kaho'olawe was listed on the National Register of Historic Places in 1981, the earlier decree restricted the Navy from using live munitions on part of the island and from bombing archaeological sites.

In October 1990, as Hawaii's two US senators, Daniel Inouye and Daniel Akaka, were preparing a congressional bill to stop the bombing, President Bush issued an order to halt military activities. On May 7, 1994, in a ceremony marked by Hawaiian rituals, chants and prayers, the US Navy signed over control of Kaho'olawe to the state and Hawaii's first native Hawaiian governor, John Waihe'e.

Proposals for the island's future range from establishing a marine sanctuary to making the island the center for a new Hawaiian nation. One enormous obstacle that remains is the cleaning up of live munitions from the island. The federal government has established a fund of up to $400 million for that purpose, but the cleanup now underway will take years to complete. Meanwhile two million tons of soil are still lost to erosion each year.

There's no general public access to the island. If you're interested in volunteering to work for the PKO, the members of which make regular trips to the island to plant vegetation, clean up cultural sites and rebuild ancient trails, take a look at W www.kahoolawe.org or write to Protect Kaho'olawe Ohana, PO Box 152, Honolulu, HI 96810.

the bill was signed into law in 1916, Hawai'i National Park officially comprised both Haleakala and its Big Island siblings, Mauna Loa and Kilauea. In the 1960s, Haleakala National Park and Hawaii Volcanoes National Park were separated and became independent entities. Currently there's a growing movement to turn the La Perouse Bay area of Maui's Keone'o'io coastline into Hawaii's third national park.

Across the islands there are dozens of registered national historic parks, sites and landmarks, including Pu'uhonua O Honaunau (Place of Refuge) on the Big Island and Kalaupapa Peninsula on Molokai. Some of Hawaii's national wildlife refuges (NWRs) are open to the public (see W www.refuge net.org for details). Birders will certainly delight in James Campbell NWR (Oahu), Kealia Pond NWR (Maui), and Kilauea Point and Hanalei NWRs (Kauai).

Each island in this book has its own system of state parks and recreation areas; county beach parks; forest reserves, petroglyph preserves and marine sanctuaries; and arboretums and botanical gardens, all of which protect at least equal diversity, if much smaller natural areas, than the national parks. Some are just stops on the headless chicken tour-bus circuit, while others are quite wild and natural. Keep an eye out for those run by private, nonprofit organizations or the state government.

POPULATION & PEOPLE

Around 1.25 million people live on the main Hawaiian islands, with nearly three-quarters of those residing on Oahu. Outside of urban sprawls, most islands have only scattered housing subdivisions or small towns. Population jumps in recent years due to the influx of mainland Caucasians have effectively 'haolefied' entire geographic areas. Most *malihini* (newcomers) are either older retirees or alternative types, like artists, surfers and organic farmers.

Some folks say that there is no real ethnic majority in Hawaii – everyone belongs to some minority. Half of islanders marry someone of a race different from their own, so the majority of children born in Hawaii

are *hapa* or mixed heritage. Over one-fifth of the population claim mixed ethnicity, with a majority of those having some Hawaiian blood. After that, Caucasians account for nearly 25% of the population, followed by Japanese (17%), Filipinos (14%), Chinese (5%), and small percentages of African-Americans, Koreans, Samoans and Pacific Islanders. There are about 9000 full-blooded Hawaiians, less than 1% of the total state population.

Ethnic tension, particularly between *haole* (Caucasians) and native Hawaiians does exist, but short-term visitors are usually given a free pass out of any such conflicts. One exception applies to surfers and windsurfers, who may encounter hostility if they hit the waves at some beaches without an introduction from a local resident.

RELIGION

Traditional Hawaiian religious ways are based on both older Polynesian gods and an animism that evolved unique to these islands. Many of the islands' outstanding natural features (mountains, cliffs and islets) have religious-mythological stories to explain their origins through the heroic or merely impulsive acts of deities.

Ku was the ancestor god for all generations of humankind, past, present and future. Like yin and yang, Ku and his wife Hina were responsible for heaven and earth. Ku had many manifestations, one as the benevolent god of fishing, the god of forests and the god of farming. One of the most fearful of Ku's manifestations was Kukailimoku (Ku, the snatcher of land), the war god whom Kamehameha the Great worshipped at the *luakini*, built for human sacrifice.

Lono was the god in charge of the elements, bringing rain and an abundant harvest. He was also the god of fertility and peace. The Hawaiians remembered Lono each year with a harvest festival, called the *makahiki*. It was from Kane (the word also means 'man' in Hawaiian) that all humans were said to have descended. Each family worshipped Kane under the image of its personal *aumakua* (family guardian spirit) with simple, everyday rituals.

Worship at *heiau* was abandoned in the late 19th century. After the *maka'ainana* (commoners) witnessed Queen Ka'ahumanu breaking *kapu* without suffering divine retribution, a frenzy of temple burning and smashing of *ki'i* (deity images) broke out. Most *heiau* are in ruins today, but a few of the old ways survive, commonly as folk superstitions about the wrath of Pele, goddess of volcanoes, or the good luck of seeing a *pueo* (Hawaiian short-eared owl).

Ever since the first missionaries and plantation workers arrived in the 19th century, Hawaii's population has been religiously diverse. Although half of all Hawaii residents today say they are unaffiliated with any religion, Christianity has the largest following. After that, Buddhism has the most adherents. You'll find many old-fashioned Christian mission churches scattered around the islands, some of which still hold Sunday services with hymns sung in the melodious Hawaiian language.

SOCIETY & CONDUCT
Traditional Culture

In many ways, Hawaii shares the same pop culture found on the US mainland. But mainland influences do not engulf the cultural traditions of the islands. Radio stations still play as much Hawaiian slack-key guitar and Jawaiian (Hawaiian-style reggae) as hiphop and rock, and local drive-in restaurants serving *kalua* pork, *laulau* (bundles of pork or beef with salted fish that are wrapped in leaves and steamed) and *poi* (a gooey paste made from taro root) are as widespread as McDonald's.

On a deeper level, Hawaiian aloha is much more than a simple greeting, but a way of life that unites islanders of whatever ethnic background in an everyday philosophy of tolerance, hospitality and generosity of spirit. Its various shades of meaning are like the rainbows that appear on Hawaii license plates, often, coincidentally, next to the ever-popular bumper sticker 'Live Aloha'.

'*Ua mau ke ea o ka aina i ka pono,*' meaning 'the life of the land is perpetuated in righteousness,' is Hawaii's state motto and one that people act upon. Unlike rampant consumerism on the US mainland, local values tend to focus on *ohana* (extended family) and *aina* (land). Entertainment revolves around spending time outdoors with family and friends, maybe camping out by the beach or practicing for outrigger canoe races.

Not only is traditional Hawaiian culture an integral part of the social fabric, but so are the customs of the ethnically diverse immigrants who have made Hawaii their home, merging together like the riot of tastes in a local mixed-plate lunch. In the words of the late musical phenomenon Bruddah Iz, 'Hawaiian to me is a way of getting somewhere without stepping on anybody's toes.'

Dos & Don'ts

Here as elsewhere in the USA, people generally stand in line, obey the rules and follow the instructions. Smoking is generally frowned upon in public places, including airports, restaurants and beaches, and on dry forest trails where there's a risk of fire danger. When driving in Hawaii, remember to slow down. Dress is casual, with a T-shirt, shorts and sandals acceptable almost anywhere. Donning a tropically inspired aloha print shirt and khaki pants, or a simple dress, and close-toed shoes usually suffices for 'dressing up', island-style. Most people take off their shoes before entering someone's private residence.

When passing someone on the trail, you should give advance notice by asking, 'Do you mind if I pass?', and be prepared to make a bit of small talk about the weather. Do not pass someone if the trail is crumbly and/or drops off steeply to one side. When you meet someone coming in the opposite direction, a simple, 'How's it going?' or 'Hey' is OK. People going uphill have the right of way, although usually the person with the most room to step aside usually does. See also Responsible Hiking (p34).

LANGUAGE

Hawaii is the only state in the union to have two official languages, Hawaiian and English. In everyday life, the unifying language is English, but it's liberally peppered with

The *Shaka* Sign

Islanders greet each other with the *shaka* sign, which is made by folding down the three middle fingers to the palm and extending the thumb and little finger. The hand is then held out, usually palm facing toward you, and shaken (hence the word 'shaka,' some say). Out on the highways, the *shaka* sign can mean 'I'm sorry, brah' if you cut someone off or *mahalo* (thanks) when someone else yields the right of way.

Where this humble and sweet little gesture came from, no one really knows. One apocryphal story claims that it originated in the early 1900s when a sugar plantation worker who had lost his middle three fingers in a mill accident (or gotten them bitten off by a shark) waved his hand to say hello or to warn hooligans against trespassing.

The *shaka* sign as seen by the person making it

Wherever it started, the *shaka* sign became the trademark of the King of Pidgin, Lippy Espinda, a used-car salesman from Honolulu. Lippy was a brilliant TV entertainer, appearing as the emcee of the program *Lanai Theater* as well as on *Hawaii Five-0* and *The Brady Bunch*. Lippy called himself the 'poor man's friend,' and his well-known salutation of 'Shaka, brah!' popularized the *shaka* sign as a symbol of island aloha forever.

Hawaiian phrases, pidgin slang as well as loan words from various immigrant mother tongues.

The Hawaiian language is most closely related to the other Polynesian languages of Tahitian, Maori and Indonesia-Malay. The Hawaiians had no written language until the 1820s, when Christian missionaries arrived and wrote down the spoken language in just 12 roman letters. Today, still spoken at home by about 9000 people, Hawaiian is phonetically simple, full of melodious vowels and repeated syllables.

Pronunciation

Pronunciation is easy, often just how the word looks on paper.

The consonant *w* is usually pronounced like a soft English 'v' when it follows the letters *i* and *e* (the town Haleiwa is pronounced ha-le-**i**-va) and like the English 'w' when it follows u or o. When w follows a, it can be pronounced either 'v' or 'w' – thus, you will hear Hawaii pronounced as both ha-**wai**-i and ha-**vai**-i.

Hawaiian uses both glottal stops and macrons, although in modern print they are often omitted. The glottal stop (') indicates a break between two vowels, which produces

an effect similar to saying 'oh-oh' in English. For example, when a hiker twists their ankle on *a'a* (rough, jagged lava) they may exclaim, Ah! Ah! (an easy way to remember how to pronounce glottal stops). A macron (a short straight line over a vowel) stresses the vowel. Glottal stops and macrons not only affect pronunciation, but can give a word a completely different meaning. For the purposes of this book, Hawaiian pronunciation marks have been streamlined and appear only when helpful in pronouncing common place names and words correctly.

Common Hawaiian Words

The following are some common Hawaiian words, including everyday pleasantries, signs and directions, that are useful to know.

aloha – welcome, goodbye
kane – man/men
kokua – help
mahalo – thank you
makai – toward the sea
mauka – toward the ocean
wahine – woman/women

Keep in mind that a noun can be singular or plural. Thus *keiki* can mean child or children. Technically it isn't correct to add an 's' to indicate the plural, but you'll often hear it done, for example when bars and restaurants call their appetizers *pupus*, not *pupu*. Some words are doubled to emphasize their meaning. For example: *wiki* means 'quick,' while *wikiwiki* means 'very quick.'

See also the Glossary (p228) for more Hawaiian terms used in this book.

Hawaiian Pidgin

Hawaii's early immigrants communicated with *luna* (plantation foremen) and each other in pidgin, a simplified, broken form of English mixed with Japanese, Hawaiian, Portuguese and anything else at hand. It was a creole language born of necessity, stripped bare of all but the most needed words.

Often speakers will drop just a word or two of pidgin into a standard English sentence, but lengthy conversations, poetry and literature can also take place in pidgin. Some characteristics of pidgin include a fast staccato rhythm, two-word sentences, dropping the soft 'h' sound from words that start with 'th' (the number three becomes 'tree'), loan words taken from various mother tongues and double meanings that trip up the uninitiated.

Visitors won't make any friends by trying to speak pidgin. It's more of an insider's code to be used only after you've lived in Hawaii long enough to understand the nuances. Following are a few basic Hawaiian pidgin terms you might hear used by locals.

aiyah – Oh wow!
'ass right – you're right; that's correct
brah – brother, friend; also used for 'hey you'
broke da mouf – delicious
buggah – guy, girl, friend; a pest
chance 'em – go for it
chicken skin – goose bumps
choke – lots, a vast amount
coconut wireless – word of mouth
cockaroach – to steal
da kine – whatchamacallit, thingamajig, etc; used whenever you can't think of the word you want but you know the listener knows what you mean
eat it – to fall down, wipe out or get totaled in an accident
geevum – go for it, beat them, try your hardest
grinds – food, eat; '*ono* grinds' is good food
hana hou – once more, do it again, encore
howzit? – hi, how's it going?
how you stay? – how are you?
humbug – a real hassle
junkalunka – a piece of junk
kau kau – food, meal; to eat
like beef? – wanna fight?
luna – boss
mo' bettah – much better, the best
okole – buttocks, butt
ono – number one, the best; delicious
rubbah slippah – flip-flops, thongs
shahkbait – very pale, untanned people
stick – surfboard
stink eye – dirty look, evil eye
talk story – to strike up a conversation, make small talk or gossip
tanks – thanks; more commonly, 'tanks brah' or 'tanks eh?'
you go, I go stay come – you go on ahead, I'll meet up with you soon

Facts for the Hiker

SUGGESTED ITINERARIES

You probably won't have time to visit all of the Hawaiian Islands. Think about what hikes most interest you and fit with your skill levels – be realistic and flexible, as anything from lava flows to booked-out campgrounds could disrupt the best-laid plans. Remember to factor in time for getting oriented, organizing permits and transport, buying supplies and – let's be honest – lazing along the beaches.

One Week

With limited time, fly directly to the Neighbor Island (one of the main Hawaiian Islands, apart from Oahu) of your choice. Those who must stop over in Honolulu could do a day hike in the Makiki-Tantalus area or southeast Oahu. Kauai claims the most rugged trails, including the classic Na Pali Coast hike. Nothing beats the Big Island's volcanoes, valleys and rain forests for multi-day backpacking trips and high-altitude adventures. Maui has an amazing variety of hikes, from waterfall gulches to the caldera summit of Haleakala National Park.

Two Weeks

Add another week and you can add another island to your itinerary: combine exploring Kauai's Grand Canyon with walking on the Big Island's lava flows; or detour to off-the-beaten-path Molokai, often said to be the most Hawaiian of the main islands. Alternatively, explore Oahu in more depth, spending time on the North Shore and Windward Coast.

WHEN TO HIKE

Peak tourist season is from December to mid-April, but that has more to do with snowbirds escaping cold winters back home than island weather. Essentially the tropical weather is agreeable for hiking all year round.

But winter gets about twice the rainfall of summer, and *kona* storms (when the wind shifts, blowing from the south) can hang around for days. This doesn't mean winter is a bad time to hike in Hawaii; it just means the weather is slightly more of a gamble. Keep in mind that daylight hours are shorter too. Between December and March be prepared for washed-out, muddy and slippery trails – but at the same time, to see migrating humpback whales, blooming foliage and waterfalls at their finest. Hikes involving difficult stream crossings, along Kauai's Na Pali Coast for example, may not be possible during the wettest months.

In contrast, the weather during summer is dependably dry, sunny and hot. When trekking over fields of lava becomes dehydrating, hikers and campers can still escape to cool upland forests. Trails at high altitudes on the Big Island's Mauna Kea and Mauna Loa (and to a lesser extent, Haleakala on Maui) are best attempted between May and October.

Visiting during the shoulder seasons affords you less extreme weather, the greatest range of hike environments and fewer crowds. An ideal time is from after the busy Easter holiday until summer school vacation starts in June. Early fall (September and October) can be exceedingly hot and dry, but November, when the temperature drops yet before heavy rains begin, can be another good time for hiking.

WHAT KIND OF HIKE?

Hawaii has countless invigorating day hikes and a few overnight backpacking trips. Many hikes can be combined with other outdoor activities, such as snorkeling, swimming or wildlife watching. Almost all trails are well signposted and manageable alone by reasonably experienced hikers. Hiking guides or organized hikes are the exception, not the rule. Some hikers stay in cabins or camp by the beach, while others prefer more creature comforts and rent beach condos and cottages, B&B rooms or hostel beds.

ORGANIZED HIKES

Rangers in Haleakala National Park and Hawaii Volcanoes National Park offer free hikes through volcano craters and rain forests. On Oahu, the University of Hawaii's

Campus Leisure Center (☎ 956-9777; non-student hike fee $10) organizes group hikes, which are open to the public, a few time per month. Nonprofit environmental groups lead organized hikes on public trails, private land and in nature reserves; volunteer guides are often scientists or trained naturalists, and advance reservations are usually required. On work service trips, hikers can volunteer to help with trail maintenance and the eradication of harmful exotic plants. See also Hiking Clubs (p41).

Following are some of the most active environmental groups.

Hawaii Audubon Society (☎ 528-1432, Ⓦ www .hawaiiaudubon.com) 850 Richards St, Suite 505, Honolulu, HI 96813. The society schedules bird-watching field trips, usually on weekends. Binoculars are recommended.

The Nature Conservancy (☎ 537-4508, fax 545-2019, Ⓦ nature.org) 923 Nu'uanu Ave, Honolulu, HI 96817. The conservancy offers guided hikes and work trips in its exclusive preserves around Oahu, Maui and Molokai.

The Sierra Club (☎ 538-6616, Ⓦ www.hi.sierra club.org) 1040 Richards St, Room 306, Honolulu, HI 96803. This club has a full monthly calendar of group outings, including historical walks, clean-up days at beaches and visits to wildlife refuges.

Private, commercial hiking guides usually stick to well-trodden trails that hikers could just as easily get to on their own. Joining a tour may be worthwhile to learn about native flora, fauna and geology, but make sure your guide is qualified before handing over a hefty chunk of change as a deposit.

PERMITS & FEES

Some wilderness areas managed by the state, national park agencies, conservation groups or private landowners grant access only by permit. Getting any of these permits is usually free and straightforward, although it requires some advance planning. Hikers may be required to sign a liability waiver for through-access after reading over some basic safety guidelines.

Hawaii's national parks charge an entry fee of $10 per car, or $5 per person arriving on foot, bicycle or motorcycle. Fees are collected at park entry gates and a multiple-entry ticket is good for seven days. An annual pass to both Hawaiian national parks costs $20. If you're a US resident, considering buying an annual national parks pass ($50), good for unlimited entry to all US national parks for one year from the month of issue. Seniors aged 62 and over who are US citizens or permanent residents qualify for the life-time Golden Passport ($10), which grants unlimited free entry to all national parks and 50% off camping fees.

RESPONSIBLE HIKING

Over the past couple of centuries, Hawaii's unique ecosystem has been devastated first by the introduction of non-native plants and animals, then by heavy industrial and military development, and finally by mass tourism. The islands' natural reserves, parks and wild backcountry are all fragile environ-ments that cannot support ecologically care-less or insensitive activity.

Following are a few basic guidelines for responsible hiking on the Hawaiian Islands:

Access
- Respect all 'Kapu – No Trespassing' signs. Often these are posted as much for hikers' own safety as to protect private landowners from unwel-come intrusions into their backyard. Remember that the goodwill of landowners depends upon the continuing cooperation of all visitors.
- A few of the walks in this book pass through pri-vate property (although it may not be obvious at the time) along recognized routes where ac-cess is freely permitted. If there seems to be some doubt about this, ask someone nearby if it's OK to walk through.

Trail Use
- On multi-use trails, horseback and mule riders always have the right-of-way and mountain bikers must yield to hikers. Those heading downhill should yield to anyone coming up the trail if feasible.
- Stay on trails at all times – no trailblazing into the wilderness. Shortcutting over a trail switch-back could erode it entirely over time. Wandering off-trail could mean trampling an endangered plant seedling or even finding yourself falling through cracks in unstable lava.

- When visiting *heiau* (temples) do not walk atop them, because not only is it disrespectful but you may loosen already unstable stones and injure yourself in the process. Similarly, refrain from walking across petroglyphs, which dam-ages them; instead view them from a distance (bring binoculars) and walk only along board-walks or roped-off areas provided.
- Volcanic rock is crumbly and porous, so rock climbing on this type of terrain is extremely dangerous.

Conservation
- To avoid importing new hazardous species of plants and insects to Hawaii, thoroughly wash all of your hiking and camping gear before ar-rival. Do not bring any fresh fruit, produce or plant cuttings either.
- Before *and* after entering each hiking area, clean your hiking boots by scraping them with a sharp stick or vigorously brushing off small seeds and mud. This helps prevent the spread of pest species to other natural areas. Some invasive plants have nearly microscopic seedlings that cling to clothes too.
- Drive cautiously and tread softly where endan-gered species are known to take refuge. Hawai-ian monk seals and nesting sea turtles, for example, are easily disturbed by any sign of human activity. Keep the nene and other species wild by not feeding them.
- Taking cuttings of plants, breaking off pieces of coral and pocketing lava rocks as souvenirs is not only illegal, but also very bad luck accord-ing to island legends.

Rubbish
- If you've carried it in, you can carry it back out – everything, including empty packaging, citrus peel and cigarette butts, can be stowed in a dedicated rubbish bag. Make an effort to pick up rubbish left by others.
- Sanitary napkins, tampons and condoms don't burn or decompose readily, so carry them out, whatever the inconvenience.
- Burying rubbish disturbs soil and ground cover, and it also encourages erosion and weed growth. Buried rubbish really does take years to decompose, and it will probably be dug up by wild animals who may then be injured or poi-soned by it.
- Before you go on your hike remove all surplus food packaging and put small-portion packages in a single container to minimize waste.

Human Waste Disposal
- If a toilet is provided at a campsite, please use it.
- Where there isn't one, bury your waste. Dig a small hole 6 inches deep and at least 35yd from any stream, 55yd from paths and 220yd from any buildings. Take a lightweight trowel or a large tent peg for the purpose. Cover the waste with a good layer of soil.
- Toilet paper should *not* be burned due to dangerously flammable backcountry conditions, so carry it out – burying is a last resort. Ideally, use biodegradable paper.
- Contamination of water sources by human feces can lead to the transmission of giardia, a human bacterial parasite.

Camping
- In remote areas, use a recognized site rather than create a new one. Keep at least 35yd from watercourses and paths. Move on after a night or two.
- Pitch your tent away from hollows where water is likely to accumulate so that you won't need to dig damaging trenches if it rains heavily. At beaches, choose a site far back from the high-tide mark, as ocean surf and swells can be unpredictable.
- Have respect for your neighbors. Avoid intrusive noise, and keep your gear tidy.
- Leave your site as you found it.
- Fires are prohibited at backcountry campsites. Some developed campgrounds have picnic pavilions with fire pits or barbecue grills, and cabins may have wood-burning stoves. In certain places it is illegal to gather kindling, so bring fire-starters instead.

Washing
- Don't use detergents or toothpaste in or near streams or lakes; even if they are biodegradable they can harm fish and wildlife.
- To wash yourself, use biodegradable soap and a water container at least 55yd from the watercourse. Disperse the waste water widely so it filters through the soil before returning to the stream.
- Wash cooking utensils at least 55yd from watercourses using a scourer or gritty sand rather than detergent.

ACCOMMODATIONS
The accommodations rates given throughout this book don't include the 11.41% room tax.

High season commonly applies to the winter period of December 15 to March 31. During this time, many of the places offering the best deals, particularly the smaller hotels, B&Bs and condos, are booked up well in advance. You'll need reservations at almost any time of year to lock in the best deals.

Consider basing yourself in just one or possibly two different areas on each island. This way you can save money on weekly rental rates and avoid the hassle of constantly moving around. Even on the Big Island, almost all hikes are within reasonable driving distance of each other.

Camping & Cabins
Hawaii has numerous public campgrounds but no full-service private campgrounds of the Kampgrounds of America (KOA) type found on the US mainland. Developed public campgrounds generally have picnic tables, barbecue grills, drinking water, toilets and showers, although the maintenance of the facilities varies greatly. Costs are low, around $5 per person per night, with a typical maximum stay of five days or a week. Camping permits are available in advance, but reservations are not always necessary, depending on the location.

As a general rule of thumb, national park campgrounds are the safest, cleanest and most well equipped. Camping in the national parks is better than in the state parks, and the state parks are better choices than the county parks. State parks often have caretakers and better security than county parks. Due to trash, late-night partying and drinking, or exposure to busy highways, some county beach parks can be unappealing. Evaluate a campground on its vibe; if you don't like it, move on.

Backcountry camping is generally safe on all the islands; your biggest safety concern might be an encounter with a wild boar or cross-eyed hunter. Women should avoid camping alone in isolated spots, however, particularly on Kauai. Camping on private land is not normally allowed. Many Hawaiian families informally camp out at different beaches, but this is illegal unless it's a designated campground.

Private campgrounds can be good value, although their standards vary. Some are church-sponsored, while others are run by private organizations or individuals. Sites may cost $10 or more per person. A few hostels found in urban and rural areas also allow camping.

Cabins at national parks are extremely popular and require advance reservations, sometimes even a lottery drawing months beforehand. The state parks system also offers simple (or deluxe) housekeeping cabins with varying amenities like kitchens or hot showers. Overnight fees start at $45, depending on the location and group size.

For state park cabin reservations and camping permits, contact any Division of State Parks office (see Useful Organizations, p40), either in person, by mail or by phone.

Hostels

Offering generally the cheapest accommodations available, hostels are useful for meeting other hikers and finding out about the region. Prices average around $20 per night for a shared dorm, at least double that for a private room. Hostels typically offer a range of perks, friendly staff and a comfortable, unhurried atmosphere. Some have a kitchen and coin-operated laundry facilities, information boards, TV room and lounge area, and will arrange excursions and offer limited local transportation for a fee. That said, Hawaiian hostels don't compare favorably with those on the US mainland. Many are shockingly lax about cleanliness, security and civility. In our experience, Waikiki Beach hostels are the worst offenders, with sky-high guest turnover rates, suddenly 'lost' reservations and deceptive advertising. Beware of 'semiprivate' rooms, which may be nothing more than a curtained-off section of a dormitory, although the term usually means a separate, lockable room inside a large dormitory with shared bathroom facilities.

B&Bs

If there are two of you who don't mind sharing a room, B&Bs may work out to be almost as cheap as hostels. Amenities vary, but a room with cable TV/VCR, kitchenette and private bathroom is standard. Simple rooms with shared bath rent for as little as $40. Expect to pay up to $125 per night for something special, like a historic inn or luxury beachfront property.

B&Bs are typically scattered in only a few pockets on each island. Some of the B&Bs also handle vacation home rentals. In addition to the following booking services, Internet sites such as w www.alternative -hawaii.com and w www.purpleroofs.com list smaller B&Bs, often single-family operations offering great privacy and rates, or those catering to specific clientele.

Affordable Paradise (Oahu ☎ 261-1693, fax 261-7315, w www.affordable-paradise.com) This agency rents a wide range of properties on Oahu and Neighbor Islands.

Bed & Breakfast Hawaii (☎ 800-733-1632, Kauai ☎ 822-7771, fax 822-2723, w www.bandb -hawaii.com) This long-running service offers special car rental and interisland flight rates.

Hawaii's Best B&Bs (☎ 800-262-9912, the Big Island ☎ 885-4550, fax 885-0559, w www .bestbnb.com) These ladies get rave reviews for high standards for hand-picked properties on all islands.

Condos

The Hawaiian Islands tend to have many more condominium units than hotel rooms, especially near beach resorts. Some condo complexes are booked only through rental agents or private owners who advertise on the Internet. Others operate more like a hotel with a front desk, although even in those places some units are usually handled by rental agents.

Some condos can work out as cheaply as staying in hostels if two or more hikers share, while others may cost as much as a luxury hotel room. Most condos require deposits within one to two weeks of booking, with full payment due 30 days prior to arrival. The minimum stay is usually three to seven days, depending on the place and season. In some cases you might have to pay security deposits and cleaning fees, especially for shorter stays. Cancellation policies vary, but expect a hefty charge (or no refund at all) for canceling within the last month.

FOOD
Local Food
Local food refers to anything eaten in Hawaii and almost nowhere else in the world. If it's full of starches, fats and gravies, you're probably eating local. Basically, it's Hawaiian soul food.

Loco moco is a morning wake-up call for the strong-stomached, with a bed of rice topped by a fried egg, hamburger patty and rivulets of brown gravy. Local mixed-plate lunches are sold everywhere, from drive-ins to *kaukau* wagons, which are basically kitchens on wheels. Typically, a plate lunch averages 1400 calories and consists of 'two scoop rice,' a helping of macaroni salad and a serving of meat or fish. *Saimin* is the local version of ramen noodle soup.

A favorite *pupu* (appetizer) is *poke,* which is cubed, raw fish marinated in salt, soy sauce, chili peppers and *limu* (seaweed). *Haupia,* the standard dessert, is a stiff pudding made of coconut cream thickened traditionally with arrowroot. Crack seed is a Chinese snack food that can be sweet, sour, salty or some combination of the three. It's often made from dried fruits, such as mangoes and apricots; more exotic flavors include *li hing mui* plums.

Traditional Hawaiian Dishes Wetland taro is one of the world's few purple foods and is used to make *poi,* a paste pounded from cooked taro corms. It is sometimes fermented for a few days to give it more zing. It's highly nutritious, but an acquired taste. Foods often eaten with *poi* include *laulau* (ti-leaf bundles of steamed fish, pork and taro) and *lomi* salmon, made by massaging and marinating thin slices of raw fish. Baked *ulu* (breadfruit), *opihi* (tiny limpet shells picked off the reef at low tide) and *pipikaula* (beef jerky) are traditional island fare, too.

On the Hike
Remember that food is fuel for hikers and backpackers, and you'll burn more calories on the trail. Since you won't have any opportunities to buy food along the way, always carry enough to sustain you for the duration, even if it's only a day hike, and then some extra snacks for emergencies or weather delays. On multiday backpacking trips, pre-measure your rations and employ the strictest willpower. Try to balance bulk and weight against nutritional value.

Eat constantly while hiking – your body needs more fuel than while sitting at home, and many small meals are easier to digest on the go and at altitude. This does not mean eat to excess. As a rule of thumb, eat enough to keep your energy up but not until you're full. A general guideline is to eat 50% carbohydrates, 27% proteins and 23% fats while you're on the trail.

Cooking For information on camp stoves and fuel availability, see p49. Know how much your backpacking mug holds and use it as a measuring cup. When heating water, insulate the stove by surrounding it with rocks or an aluminum shield, and keep the lid on the pot until you know it's boiling (when the pot starts vibrating). It's advisable to avoid strong-smelling foods, which may attract feral animals to your campsite.

Buying Food Wherever you purchase food, it's likely to be expensive compared to the US mainland. Some supermarkets are open 24 hours and sometimes even have a bakery and deli as well as a pharmacy all under one roof. Natural foods stores are found even in small towns. Some have hot-and-cold buffets with food sold by the pound, as well as fresh sandwiches and deli items; they also stock trail mix, dried fruit and muesli. For even fresher, cheaper produce, visit a farmers market. Outdoor stores sell freeze-dried meals, which rapidly rehydrate when hot water is added. They're convenient, but rarely feed more than one hungry hiker, making them expensive at $5 to $8 each.

DRINKS
Alcoholic Drinks
All of Hawaii has become synonymous with those rum-defiling tropical cocktails

dolled up with paper umbrellas, cherries and the odd plastic monkey. The classic favorite is a mai tai, mixing rum, grenadine, and lemon and pineapple juices. For natural flavor, however, nothing beats a coconut fresh from the palm, whacked open, and the milk spiked with rum.

The drinking age in the USA is a retrograde 21 years, and you may be asked to produce photo ID when purchasing alcohol. It's illegal to have open containers of alcohol in motor vehicles and, although it's commonplace, drinking at public parks or beaches is against the law. Alcohol (and substance) misuse is often a factor in driving accidents and other mishaps in the backcountry. Alcohol can impair judgment and mislead a person into feeling warm in conditions likely to cause hypothermia (p54).

Nonalcoholic Drinks

Most tap water is OK to drink, except if the tap water supply comes from private rain catchment systems, which are more common on the *ko'olau* (windward) sides of the islands. Bottled water is readily available everywhere. Purified water dispensers outside supermarkets will fill a gallon jug for about 50¢.

Hawaii is one of the main kava-growing regions in the USA. This root has a long history in Polynesia, and when steeped with water and extracted through a fine cloth, makes a pleasing, mildly narcotic drink. Cures-what-ails-you smoothies made with *lilikoi* (passionfruit), banana, coconut, pineapple, guava or papaya are other tropical elixir delights. If it's caffeine you crave, try 100% Kona coffee grown on the Big Island. Hawaiian herbal teas are popular, especially those containing medicinal *noni* (Indian mulberry).

On the Hike

Hydration is crucial. It's recommended that hikers drink at least 3L per day. People who sweat a lot will benefit from sports drinks containing salts to restore the body's natural electrolyte balance. It's best to avoid caffeinated beverages (tea, coffee etc) early in the day as they have a diuretic effect that will contribute to dehydration. Hands-free 'hydration bags' (such as those made by Camelbak or Platypus) have drinking tubes and are easier to carry comfortably, especially in day packs.

Unfortunately, paradise is not always what it seems. Even pristine waterfalls, springs and mountain streams may contain harmful pathogens (especially those causing leptospirosis). Any freshwater available along the trail must be treated before drinking (see Water Purification, p51).

WOMEN HIKERS

This book was researched by solo women hikers. That said, hiking with a trustworthy companion is preferable. Apart from the natural hazards of hiking, the greatest danger to women is of being attacked on lonely stretches of trail or at remote campgrounds. Be especially careful on Kauai. If you like plenty of people around, stick to well-trodden trails; it's best to choose campgrounds with a caretaker.

Otherwise, the normal safety precautions apply. Avoid hitchhiking if you can. Don't drink by yourself at local bars. Avoid deserted areas after dark – walking along a tropical beach at night under the stars may sound romantic, but it actually puts you at high risk for mugging or other violent crimes.

Women are usually treated with respect and should trouble occur, help is usually quickly forthcoming. Hawaiian *ho'okipa* (hospitality) means that women may find themselves invited to hike with families, join beach picnics or campground barbecues, almost becoming part of someone's *ohana* (extended family) in no time. Naturally, be wary of anyone who seems just too eager to show you around the islands.

For local resources for women, check in the Yellow Pages phone directory. These local, state and federal governmental and private agencies are usually aimed at women residents in need, but can make referrals on a wide range of subjects.

HIKING WITH CHILDREN

Hawaii is a family-friendly vacation destination and nearly all of the islands offer day-hiking opportunities for families with children. It's important to choose hikes that have scope for variety – visiting a national park or unusual archaeological sites, swimming in waterfalls or watching wildlife. The distance and duration of the hike should be firmly based on the children's actual capabilities and experience. For easy nature walks, see the 'Other Hikes' sections at the end of each hiking chapter.

Since children can be slow to adapt to changes of diet, temperature and altitude, make sure you carry plenty of spare food and drink. Tired, hungry and thirsty is no fun, for adult hikers or youngsters. It's also important to bring along a generous range of warm clothing. Always be prepared for any weather eventuality. If you are traveling with children, be aware that some B&Bs and historic inns prohibit children from staying, so it's important to inquire about their policies before making reservations. All of the paraphernalia necessary for traveling with kids is readily available at supermarkets, pharmacies and convenience stores.

DANGERS & ANNOYANCES

Hiking in Hawaii is generally a safe and hassle-free activity, if you are prepared for natural hazards and variable climatic conditions. Some trails follow razorback ridges and sheer cliffs, with fearful footing over loose lava scree. Know your own abilities and don't attempt tricky bits when you're exhausted and heavily laden with a pack. It's better to turn back than risk serious injury. See also Safety on the Hike (p59).

Crime rates are lower than in much of the US mainland. Drunk driving is an all-too-frequent cause of traffic accidents, whether on highways or remote backcountry roads. County beach parks are often a nexus for petty theft, public drunkenness, violence or worse. Generally the less you look like a tourist, the less likely you are to be targeted. Car break-ins predictably occur at beach parking lots and trailheads, even during daylight hours. Do not leave any valuables in your car and keep any possessions you must leave behind in the trunk. Renting an older compact car and hanging cheap plastic

shell or flower lei around the rearview mirror may help you look local. Some people advise purposely leaving car doors unlocked so that thieves don't break any windows or locks trying to get inside.

Divide your money, credit cards etc, and stash them in several places. Leave copies of all your important documents in your car or at your accommodations, but keep the originals with you. While on the trail, you may want to keep them in an inside pocket of your pack, but in public areas (like campgrounds), it's best to keep them on your person. A waterproof Ziploc bag placed inside a standard (waist) money belt protects your documents, money and other valuables from becoming sweat-soaked.

MAPS

Specific topographical map recommendations appear under individual hikes, although you'll find that large-scale maps are not strictly necessary for the majority of hikes in this book. For general map and compass information, see Navigation Equipment (p46). For a description of maps in this book, see Maps (p10).

Small-Scale Maps

Free island maps distributed by state tourism offices, activity operators and hotels are usually woefully inadequate for navigating anything but major highways and resorts. The National Park Service (NPS) gives out excellent orientation maps at national park entrances, but these can't be relied upon 100% for hiking.

A lightweight fold-out map series with good street detail and topographic shading is published by Nelles Maps ($5.95 each). University of Hawaii Press island maps ($3.95 each) are less helpful, even though they are readily available and cost less. DeLorme's *Hawaii Atlas & Gazetteer* ($19.95) covers all the main Hawaiian Islands with scaled contour maps.

The Ready Mapbook series is an invaluable resource for exploring the Neighbor Islands, especially with 4WDs. Admittedly, these stapled map books are bulky, but comprehensive in their coverage of island road networks. Choose from *West Hawaii* or *East Hawaii* (the Big Island), *Maui County* (including Molokai) or *Kauai* ($10 each).

Large-Scale Maps

The United States Geological Survey (USGS) publishes detailed topographical maps of Hawaii. Due to their large scale, topographic maps reproduce detail quite accurately, but having to use numerous maps is inconvenient and expensive. Many maps have not been revised for decades, so trails and infrastructure may not be shown correctly. The 7.5-minute topographic series is the USGS standard. Most 7.5-minute maps, known as quadrangles or quads, are scaled at 1:24,000 (1 inch = 2000ft). Entire island and detailed sectional maps are both available.

Buying Maps

Maps sold at tourist and convenience shops are usually not high-quality and are of little use. Good maps can be bought at bookstores, national park visitor centers and surprising places like museums. For a comprehensive selection of all-islands topographic maps, stop by Oahu's **Pacific Map Center** (☎ 545-3600; *Gentry Pacific Design Center, Suite 206A, 560 N Nimitz Hwy, Honolulu; open 9am-noon & 1pm-5pm Mon-Fri)* or the Big Island's **Basically Books** (☎ 961-0144, 800-903-6277; *w www.basicallybooks.com; 160 Kamehameha Ave, Hilo).*

USGS maps can also be ordered about three weeks in advance from the **US Geological Survey** (☎ 888-275-8747, fax 303-202-4693; *w www.usgs.gov; USGS Information Services, PO Box 25286, Denver, CO 80225).* Maps cost $7 per sheet, plus a $5 mailing fee per order. It's usually faster and costs about the same to source the maps from a private online or local retailer.

PLACE NAMES

Most main roads are called 'highways' whether they're busy four-lane thoroughfares or just quiet country roads. What's more, islanders refer to highways by name, rarely by number. On Oahu, if you ask someone how to find Highway 72, chances are they aren't going to know; ask for the Kalanianaole Highway instead. Keep in mind that any road may have several common usage names, often disagreeing with what's printed on maps.

USEFUL ORGANIZATIONS

For other groups active in promoting hiking and preserving Hawaii's unique ecological systems, see Conservation (p34).

Government Departments

To find regional offices for government agencies listed here, check the blue section of the local White Pages directory. Many branch offices handle all the services of the main Honolulu office, including issuing permits, making reservations and answering questions about recreational activities – even for other islands!

Department of Land & Natural Resources (DLNR, ☎ 587-0320, W www.state.hi.us/dlnr/) Kalanimoku Bldg, 1151 Punchbowl St, cnr S Beretania St, Honolulu. DLNR issues camping and hunting permits at its 1-Stop Permit Shop on the ground level of the state office building. Many of its useful publications, including brochures on safe hiking, conservation and aquatic safety, are available online.

The DLNR oversees all of the following divisions and programs, which have their own offices in the same building.

Division of Forestry & Wildlife (DOFAW, W www .dofaw.net) This division supervises public land management of Hawaii's forests and natural area reserves (NARs). Public outreach efforts focus on outdoor recreation, conservation and watershed protection.

Division of State Parks (☎ 587-0300, W www .hawaii.gov/dlnr/dsp/) This division administers over 50 state parks on five islands, and also handles permits for camping, housekeeping cabins and A-frame shelters on various islands. The website lists a variety of outdoor safety tips.

Na Ala Hele Trail & Access Program (☎ 587-0051, W www.hawaiitrails.org) Na Ala Hele (Trails to Go On) coordinates public access to hiking trails, as well as historical trail preservation and maintenance. The excellent website contains useful island overview maps, guidelines for safe hiking and announcements of recently developed or reopened trails.

Hiking Clubs

Hawaiian Trail and Mountain Club (HTMC, W www.geocities.com/yosemite/trails/3660/) PO Box 2238, Honolulu, HI 96804. This hiking club has been based on Oahu since 1910. Group hikes usually take place on Saturday or Sunday mornings (suggested donation $2). HTMC also participates in trail maintenance and occasionally organizes excursions to Neighbor Islands.

Like Hike (☎ 455-8193 before 9pm Hawaii Standard Time, W www.gayhawaii.com/likehike) This is a gay Oahu hiking group that leads twice-monthly Sunday morning hikes. First-time hikers must call or email before joining the group.

DIGITAL RESOURCES

The Web is crowded with sites about Hawaii; those relating to particular regions are mentioned in the respective hike chapters. See also Accommodations (p35), Travel Facts (p218), Conservation (p34) and Useful Organizations (p40). Following are some other useful sites.

Conservation Hawaii (W www.conservation hawaii.org) A visually appealing resource for learning about Hawaii's watersheds, native forest birds, other endangered species and invasive threats to the environment.

Great Outdoors Recreation Pages (W gorp.com) Helpful articles, including advice for beginning hikers on purchasing gear, packing smart and trail skills, plus links.

The Lightweight Backpacker (W www.backpack ing.net) A fantastic place to find information on high-tech, lightweight backpacking equipment, plus off-the-wall tips that really work.

Lonely Planet (W www.lonelyplanet.com) Information on most places on earth, linked to the Thorn Tree bulletin boards and Postcards, where you can catch up with postings from other travelers; the Travel Ticker, for news and hot travel updates; and the subwwway section that zips you to some of the most useful travel resources elsewhere on the Internet.

Wildernet (W www.wildernet.com) Skeleton background information for enjoying outdoors recreation all over Hawaii; it sells customized, waterproof topographical maps.

BOOKS

The following are just some of the gems you can dig out from libraries and bookstores.

Lonely Planet

Hawaii is a comprehensive guide to all of the Hawaiian Islands, with complete coverage of beaches, culture and much more. *Oahu*, *Maui* and *Hawaii: The Big Island* are vibrant, in-depth island guides. *Travel with Children*, by Cathy Lanigan, has lots of practical advice on the subject, along with first-hand stories from Lonely Planet authors and readers.

Travel & Exploration

Six Months in the Sandwich Islands, by Isabella Bird, is a quirky Victorian-era travelogue that is both offensive and insightfully opinionated, with lyrical glimpses of old Hawaii. *Stories of Hawaii*, by Jack London, who sailed to the islands in the early 1900s, tells first-hand tales of surfing at Waikiki and watching the sunrise atop Haleakala volcano. *A Hawaiian Reader*, edited by A Grove Day & Carl Stroven, is an excellent anthology with selections by the preceding writers, plus Captain Cook, Mark Twain, David Malo and others.

Natural History

There are dozens of specialized field guides to Hawaii, for example entire volumes just on ginger varietals, ferns or Kauai's birds.

Hawaii's Birds (Hawaii Audubon Society) is indeed the best pocket-sized guide to the birds of Hawaii. *Hawaii's Floral Splendor*, by Angela Kay Kepler, introduces nearly 400 of the common native and non-native species found alongside Hawaii's trails. *Legacy of the Landscape*, by Patrick Vinton Kirch, visits 50 of Hawaii's most important archaeological sites, including *heiau*, fishponds and petroglyphs. *Plants in Hawaiian Medicine*, by ethnobotanist Beatrice H Krauss, talks about the traditional uses of common plants, including herbal remedies and their history. *A Pocket Guide to Hawaii's Trees and Shrubs*, by H Douglas Pratt, is an introduction to common species, arranged by environment (dry lowland forest, native rain forest etc), with thumbnail color photographs. *Roadside Geology of Hawaii*, by Richard Hazlett & Donald Hyndman, is a layperson's science textbook for the volcanic and other awesome natural forces that shaped the islands.

Buying Books

These days every tourist shop stocks enough Hawaiiana books to keep anyone reading for weeks. Independent bookstores carry a selection to rival chains such as Borders and Waldenbooks. Nonprofit organizations like museums, botanical gardens and national parks also sell books.

Publishers that specialize in Hawaiian titles include the following.

Bamboo Ridge Press (W www.bambooridge.com)
 PO Box 61781, Honolulu, HI 96839

Bess Press (☎ 734-7159, W www.besspress.com)
Bishop Museum Press (☎ 848-4159, W www .bishopmuseum.com/press)
University of Hawaii Press (☎ 956-8255, 888-847-7377, W www.uhpress.hawaii.edu)

TV

Hawaii's local hiking TV show, *Let's Go Hiking!*, airs on Oahu's Oceanic Cable channel 52 every Tuesday night at 6pm. New half-hour documentary episodes are taped almost monthly.

WEATHER INFORMATION

Many Hawaiian radio stations broadcast weather, surf and traffic reports throughout the day. The *Honolulu Star-Bulletin* newspaper has excellent Hawaiian weather forecasts. Local island weather reports are sometimes posted on national and state park

---

Taking Photos Outdoors

For walkers, photography can be a vexed issue – all that magnificent scenery but such weight and space restrictions on what photographic equipment you can carry. With a little care and planning it is possible to maximize your chance of taking great photos on the trail.

Light & Filters In fine weather, the best light is early and late in the day. In strong sunlight and in mountain and coastal areas where the light is intense, a polarizing filter will improve color saturation and reduce haze. On overcast days the soft light can be great for shooting wildflowers and running water and an 81A warming filter can be useful. If you use slide film, a graduated filter will help balance unevenly lit landscapes.

Equipment If you need to travel light carry a zoom in the 28–70mm range, and if your sole purpose is landscapes consider carrying just a single wide-angle lens (24mm). A tripod is essential for really good images and there are some excellent lightweight models available. Otherwise a trekking pole, pack or even a pile of rocks can be used to improvise.

Camera Care Keep your gear dry – a few Ziploc freezer bags can be used to double-wrap camera gear and silica-gel sachets (a drying agent) can be used to suck moisture out of equipment. Sturdy cameras will normally work fine in freezing conditions. Take care when bringing a camera from one temperature extreme to another; if moisture condenses on the camera parts make sure it dries thoroughly before going back into the cold, or mechanisms can freeze up. Standard camera batteries fail very quickly in the cold. Remove them from the camera when it's not in use and keep them under your clothing.

For a thorough grounding on photography on the road, read Lonely Planet's *Travel Photography*, by Richard I'Anson, a full-color guide for happy-snappers and professional photographers alike. Also highly recommended is the outdoor photography classic *Mountain Light*, by Galen Rowell.

Gareth McCormack

bulletin boards. The Weather Channel (available on cable TV) broadcasts national, international and regional weather reports 24 hours a day.

The National Oceanic and Atmospheric Administration (NOAA) frequently updates its weather reports and forecasts for the Hawaiian Islands online at ⓦ www.prh.noaa.gov/pr/hnl/ or via recorded telephone services.

Kauai	☎ 245-6001
Maui, Molokai & Lanai	☎ 877-5111
Oahu	☎ 973-5286
The Big Island	☎ 961-5582

PHOTOGRAPHY
Film
Print film and disposable underwater cameras (around $10) are available at supermarkets, drugstores and tourist convenience shops. B&W or slide (transparency) film is rarely sold anywhere except specialty photography stores.

Processing your film in Hawaii will not only avoid rapid deterioration of exposed film due to heat and humidity, but make sure you don't take any chances passing undeveloped film through airport X-ray machines. Another advantage is that local photo labs are experienced in developing tropical scenes, ensuring the bright Hawaiian colors are not washed out.

One-hour photo processing shops are quick, but drugstores like Longs Drugs tend to be half as expensive – about $6 for a roll of 24 color prints.

Airport Security
All airline passengers have to pass their luggage through X-ray machines; those used for checked baggage can damage (ie, fog) *any* unexposed film that passes through, while those for carry-on luggage do not damage lower-speed film. If you have high-speed film (1600 ASA) and above, carry your film spools loose in a clear-plastic container and ask the X-ray inspector to visually examine the film. Always finish off the roll in your camera, rewind it and take it out before packing your camera in either checked or carry-on baggage.

Clothing & Equipment

You don't need to spend a fortune on gear to enjoy hiking, but you do need to think carefully about what you pack to make sure you're comfortable and prepared for an emergency. Taking the right clothing and equipment on a hike can make the difference between an enjoyable day out or a cold and miserable one; in extreme situations, it can even mean the difference between life and death.

The gear you need will depend on the type of hiking you plan to do. For day hikes, clothing, footwear and a backpack are the major items; you might get away with runners, a hat, shorts, T-shirt and rain poncho. For longer hikes, or those at higher elevations, especially if you're camping, the list becomes longer.

We recommend spending as much as you can afford on good hiking boots, a tent, a waterproof jacket and a synthetic pile jacket. These are likely to be your most expensive items but are a sound investment, as they should last for years.

The following section is not exhaustive; for more advice, visit outdoor stores, talk to fellow hikers and read product reviews in outdoor magazines.

CLOTHING

It's better to wear several thin layers of clothing than one or two thicker items. Layering allows you to add or remove layers as you get colder or hotter depending on your exertion or the weather. In cooler weather, begin with lightweight thermal underwear (made of a 'wicking' fabric such as Capilene or polypropylene, that moves the sweat away from your body). Your lightweight shorts/trousers and shirt make up the middle layer. Outer layers can consist of sweaters (jumpers) or fleece jackets. Finally, there is the 'shell' layer, or windproof and waterproof jacket and pants.

Look for clothes that offer insulation from the elements, but still breathe and wick moisture away from your skin. Avoid

wearing heavy cotton or denim, as these fabrics dry slowly and are very cold when wet. When you are choosing clothes, prepare for the worst weather that a particular region might throw at you. The body loses most of its heat through its extremities, particularly the head; wearing a fleece hat and gloves can prevent this warmth being lost. When deciding between long sleeves and trouser legs, weigh up the advantages of sun and insect protection against discomfort in the heat.

Waterproof Jacket

The ideal specifications are a breathable, waterproof fabric, a hood which is roomy enough to cover headwear but still allows peripheral vision, capacious map pocket, and a good-quality, heavy-gauge zip protected by a storm flap. Make sure the sleeves are long enough to cover warm clothes underneath.

Overpants

Although restrictive, these are essential if you're hiking in wet and chilly conditions. As the name suggests, they are worn over your pants (trousers). Choose a model with slits for pocket access and long leg zips so that you can pull them on and off over your boots.

Footwear

Your footwear will be your friend or your enemy, so choose carefully. The first decision you will make is between boots and shoes. Runners or walking shoes are fine over easy terrain but, for more difficult trails and across lava rocks and scree, most hikers agree that the ankle support offered by boots is invaluable. Leather boots are heavier and less water resistant than fabric boots lined with a breathable membrane such as Gore-Tex, but pierce a hole in a Gore-Tex–lined boot – a more likely occurrence than with a leather boot – and the water resistance will go from hero to zero in an instant. Some

Check List

This list is a general guide to the things you might take on a hike. Your list will vary depending on the kind of hiking you want to do, whether you're camping or planning on staying in hostels or B&Bs, and on the terrain, weather conditions and time of year.

Clothing
- ☐ **boots** and spare **laces**
- ☐ **hat** (warm) and **gloves**
- ☐ **jacket** (waterproof)
- ☐ **overpants** (waterproof)
- ☐ **runners** (training shoes), **sandals** or **thongs** (flip-flops, *rubbah slippah*)
- ☐ **shorts** and **trousers**
- ☐ **socks** and **underwear**
- ☐ **sunhat**
- ☐ **sweater** or **fleece jacket**
- ☐ **thermal underwear**
- ☐ **T-shirt** and **shirt** (long-sleeved with collar)

Equipment
- ☐ **backpack** with **liner** (waterproof)
- ☐ **first-aid kit***
- ☐ **flashlight** (torch) or **headlamp**, spare **batteries** and **bulb** (globe)
- ☐ **food** or **snacks** (high energy), and one day's **emergency supplies**
- ☐ **insect repellent**
- ☐ **map**, **compass** and **guidebook**
- ☐ **map case** or **clip-seal plastic bags**
- ☐ **pocket knife**
- ☐ **sunglasses**
- ☐ **sunscreen** and **lip balm**
- ☐ **survival bag** or **blanket**
- ☐ **toilet paper** and **trowel**
- ☐ **watch**
- ☐ **water container**
- ☐ **whistle** (for emergencies)

Overnight Hikes
- ☐ **cooking**, **eating** and **drinking utensils**
- ☐ **dishwashing items**
- ☐ **groundsheet** (lightweight)
- ☐ **insulating mat**
- ☐ **matches** (waterproof) and **lighter**
- ☐ **stove** and **fuel**
- ☐ **sewing/repair kit**
- ☐ **sleeping bag** and **bag liner/inner sheet**
- ☐ **spare cord**
- ☐ **tent, pegs, poles** and **guy ropes**
- ☐ **toiletries**
- ☐ **towel** (small)
- ☐ **water purification tablets**, **iodine** or **filter**

Optional Items
- ☐ **backpack cover** (waterproof, slip-on)
- ☐ **binoculars**
- ☐ **camera**, **film** and **batteries**
- ☐ **candle**
- ☐ **emergency distress beacon** or **flares**
- ☐ **gaiters**
- ☐ **GPS receiver**
- ☐ **hiking poles**
- ☐ **cell phone**
- ☐ **notebook** and **pen/pencil**
- ☐ **swimwear**

* see First-Aid Check List, p51

boots can be made more water-resistant by applying a waterproofing agent, preferably a fluoropolymer spray or a water-based sealant; the latter can be used on the trail even when your boots are already wet.

Buy boots in warm conditions or go for a hike before trying them on, so that your feet can expand slightly, as they would on a hike.

Most hikers carry a pair of 'camp shoes,' thongs (also called flip-flops or, in Hawaiian pidgin, *rubbah slippah*) or sport sandals. These will certainly relieve your tired feet from the heavy boots at night as well as during rest stops, and sport sandals are useful when you are fording waterways.

[Continued on page 48]

NAVIGATION EQUIPMENT

Maps & Compass

You should always carry a good map of the area you are hiking in (see Maps, p39), and know how to read it. Before setting off on your hike, ensure that you understand the contours and the map symbols, plus the main ridge and stream systems in the area. Also familiarize yourself with the true north–south directions and the general direction in which you are heading. On the trail, try to identify major landforms such as mountains and gulches, and locate them on your map. This will give you a better understanding of the region's geography.

Buy a compass and learn how to use it. The attraction of magnetic north varies in different parts of the world, so compasses need to be balanced accordingly. Compass manufacturers have divided the world into five zones. Make sure your compass is balanced for your destination zone. There are also 'universal' compasses on the market that can be used anywhere in the world.

How to Use a Compass

This is a very basic introduction to using a compass and will only be of assistance if you are proficient in map reading. For simplicity, it doesn't take magnetic variation into account. Before using a compass we recommend you obtain further instruction.

1. Reading a Compass

Hold the compass flat in the palm of your hand. Rotate the **bezel** so the **red end** of the **needle** points to the **N** on the bezel. The bearing is read from the **dash** under the bezel.

1	Base plate
2	Direction of travel arrow
3	Dash
4	Bezel
5	Meridian lines
6	Needle
7	Red end
8	N (north point)

2. Orientating the Map

To orientate the map so that it aligns with the ground, place the compass flat on the map. Rotate the map until the **needle** is parallel with the map's north–south grid lines and the **red end** is pointing to north on the map. You can now identify features around you by aligning them with labeled features on the map.

3. Taking a Bearing from the Map

Draw a line on the map between your starting point and your destination. Place the edge of the compass on this line with the **direction of travel arrow** pointing towards your destination. Rotate the **bezel** until the **meridian lines** are parallel with the north-south grid lines on the map and the **N** points to north on the map. Read the bearing from the **dash**.

4. Following a Bearing

Rotate the **bezel** so that the intended bearing is in line with the **dash**. Place the compass flat in the palm of your hand and rotate the **base plate** until the **red end** points to **N** on the bezel. The **direction of travel arrow** will now point in the direction you need to hike.

5. Determining Your Bearing
Rotate the **bezel** so the **red end** points to the **N**. Place the compass flat in the palm of your hand and rotate the **base plate** until the **direction of travel arrow** points in the direction in which you have been hiking. Read your bearing from the **dash**.

GPS

Originally developed by the US Department of Defense, the Global Positioning System (GPS) is a network of more than 20 earth-orbiting satellites that continually beam encoded signals back to earth. Small, computer-driven devices (GPS receivers) can decode these signals to give users an extremely accurate reading of their location – to within 30m, anywhere on the planet, at any time of day, in almost any weather. The cheapest hand-held GPS receivers now cost less than $100 (although these may not have a built-in averaging system that minimizes signal errors). Other important factors to consider when buying a GPS receiver are its weight and battery life.

Remember that a GPS receiver is of little use to hikers unless used with an accurate topographical map. The receiver simply gives your position, which you must then locate on the local map. GPS receivers will only work properly in the open. The signals from a crucial satellite may be blocked (or bounce off rock or water) directly below high cliffs, near large bodies of water or in dense tree cover and give inaccurate readings. GPS receivers are more vulnerable to breakdowns (including dead batteries) than the humble magnetic compass – a low-tech device that has served navigators faithfully for centuries – so don't rely on them entirely.

Altimeter

Altimeters determine altitude by measuring air pressure. Because pressure is affected by temperature, altimeters are calibrated to take lower temperatures at higher altitudes into account. However, discrepancies can still occur, especially in unsettled weather, so it's wise to take a few precautions when using your altimeter.

1. Reset your altimeter regularly at known elevations such as spot heights and passes. Do not take spot heights from villages where there may be a large difference in elevation from one end of the settlement to another.

2. Use your altimeter in conjunction with other navigation techniques to fix your position. For instance, taking a back bearing to a known peak or river confluence, determining the general direction of the track and obtaining your elevation will usually give you a pretty good fix on your position.

Altimeters are also barometers and are useful for indicating changing weather conditions. If the altimeter shows increasing elevation while you are not climbing, it means the air pressure is dropping and a low-pressure weather system may be approaching.

[Continued from page 45]

Gaiters If you will be hiking through deep mud or scratchy vegetation, consider using gaiters to protect your legs and help keep your socks dry. The best are made of strong fabric, with a robust zip protected by a flap, and with an easy-to-undo method of securing around the foot.

Socks The best hikers' socks are made of a hard-wearing mix of wool (70% to 80%) and synthetic (30% to 20%), and are free of ridged seams in the wrong places (toes and heels). Socks with a high proportion of wool are more comfortable when worn for several successive days without washing. Spare socks are valuable, especially in wet hiking conditions.

EQUIPMENT
Backpack
For day hikes, a day-pack will usually suffice, but for multi-day hikes you will need a backpack between 45L and 90L in capacity. It can be tough deciding whether to go for a smaller or bigger pack. This can depend on the destination and whether you plan to camp, stay in cabins hostels, etc. Your pack should be large enough that you don't need to strap bits and pieces to the outside where they can become damaged or lost or, like foam mats, leave unsightly souvenirs in trackside bushes. However, if you buy a bigger pack than you really need there's the temptation to fill it simply because the space is there. Its weight will increase and your enjoyment decrease. Assemble the gear you intend to take and try loading it into a pack to see if it's big enough.

A good backpack should:

• be made of strong fabric such as canvas, Cordura or similar heavy-duty woven synthetic, with high-quality stitching, straps and buckles, a lightweight internal or external frame and resilient and smoothly working zips
• have an adjustable, well-padded harness that evenly distributes weight
• be water-resistant, with a minimum of external nooks and crannies for water to pool or seep into; stitched seams can be treated with a sealant such as beeswax
• be equipped with a small number of internal and external pockets to provide easy access to frequently used items such as snacks and maps

Even if the manufacturer claims your pack is waterproof, use heavy-duty liners (garden refuse bags are ideal; custom-made sacks are available) or an easily adjustable waterproof backpack cover.

Tent
A three-season tent will fulfill the requirements of most hikers. The floor and the outer shell, or fly, should have taped or sealed seams and covered zips to stop water leaking inside. Weight will be a major issue if you're carrying your own tent so a roomy tent may not be an option; most hikers find tents of around 5lb to 8lb (that will sleep two or three people) a comfortable carrying weight. Popular shapes include dome and tunnel, which are better able to handle windy conditions than flat-sided tents.

Check you know how to pitch your tent before taking it away, and always check your poles and pegs are packed.

Sleeping Bag & Mat
Choose between down and synthetic fillings, and mummy and rectangular shapes according to your needs. Down is warmer than synthetic for the same weight and bulk but, unlike synthetic fillings, do not retain warmth when wet. Keep in mind that at higher elevations in Hawaii, camping areas are often cold and damp. Mummy bags are best for weight and warmth, but can be claustrophobic. Sleeping bags are rated by temperature. The given figure (23°F/-5°C, for instance) is the coldest temperature at which a person should feel comfortable in the bag. However, the ratings are notoriously unreliable. Work out the coldest temperature at which you anticipate sleeping, assess whether you're a warm or a cold sleeper, then choose a bag accordingly.

An inner sheet will help to keep your sleeping bag clean, as well as adding an insulating layer. You'll find that silk 'inners' are the lightest, but they also come in cotton or polypropylene.

Self-inflating sleeping mats are popular and work like a thin air cushion between you and the ground; they also insulate from the cold. Foam mats are a low-cost, but less comfortable, alternative. A mat is probably unnecessary if you are staying in cabins.

Stove

As a general guideline, the fuel stove you choose needs to be stable when sitting on the ground and to have a good wind shield.

Fuel stoves fall roughly into three categories: pressurized (Coleman fuel/white gas), unpressurized (denatured alcohol) and propane/butane gas. Pressurized stoves are small, efficient and, because they can burn a variety of fuels, ideal for places where a reliable fuel supply is difficult to find. However, they tend to be sooty and require frequent maintenance. Stoves running on denatured alcohol are slower and less efficient, but are safe, clean and easy to use. Propane/butane gas stoves are clean and reliable, but can be slow, and the gas canisters can be awkward to carry and a potential litter problem.

Fuel Carry your fuel in a clearly labeled and sturdy plastic or aluminum bottle. Note that fuel cannot be carried on airplanes and US airport security may confiscate reusable fuel canisters (even if they are empty).

Propane gas and Coleman fuel are widely available in Hawaii. Coleman fuel is actually a refined brand-name version of white gas called naphtha; it is compatible with most stoves designed to burn white gas. Butane/propane gas canisters that puncture on top are very difficult to find. Expect to pay higher prices than on the US mainland.

Army surplus outlets, sporting goods retailers, and some grocery and hardware stores sell camp stove fuel. Large chains like The Sports Authority, Wal-Mart, Kmart and Sears carry different kinds of fuel too. As different locations are often sold out, call ahead.

Hiking Poles

Think about packing a pair of lightweight, telescopic poles. They help you keep your balance on eroded scree trails and ease the jarring on your knees during steep descents. Using a fallen tree branch as a walking stick may be convenient, but is not always as durable.

Buying & Hiring Locally

Bring as much of your hiking and camping gear from home as you can. Only Oahu has outdoor stores carrying top-notch brands like North Face, Patagonia and REI. Retail chains like Wal-Mart, Kmart, The Sports Authority and Sears carry camping and hiking supplies, but their selection is limited and typically of poor quality. Prices are also higher than on the US mainland.

Health & Safety

Keeping healthy on your hikes and travels depends on your predeparture preparations, your daily health care while traveling and how you handle any medical problems that develop. While the potential problems can seem quite frightening, in reality few travelers experience anything more than an upset stomach. The sections that follow aren't intended to alarm, but they are worth reading before you go.

PREDEPARTURE PLANNING
Health Insurance

Travel health insurance is essential – health care in the US is exceedingly expensive and some hospitals may refuse treatment unless you have some form of insurance. See Travel Insurance (p218).

Physical Preparation

Some of the hikes in this book are physically demanding and most require a reasonable level of fitness. Even if you're tackling the easy or easy–moderate hikes, it pays to be relatively fit, rather than launch straight into them after months of fairly sedentary living. If you're aiming for the demanding hikes, fitness is essential.

Unless you're a regular hiker, start your get-fit campaign at least a month before your visit. Take a vigorous walk of about an hour, two or three times per week and gradually extend the duration of your outings as the departure date nears. If you plan to carry a full backpack on any walk, carry a loaded pack on some of your training jaunts. Older hikers with little previous experience should have a medical checkup beforehand.

Immunizations

No immunizations are required for Hawaii (or even to enter the US, although evidence of cholera and yellow fever vaccinations may be required if you're arriving from an infected area). It is worth noting that rabies vaccinations are not needed since Hawaii (unlike other parts of the US) is rabies-free.

Still, before any trip it's a good idea to make sure you are up to date with routine vaccinations such as diphtheria, polio and tetanus. It's particularly important that your tetanus is up to date – the initial course of three injections, usually given in childhood, is followed by boosters every 10 years.

First Aid

It's a good idea at any time to know the appropriate responses to make in the event of a major accident or illness, and it's especially important if you are intending to backpack in a remote area. Consider learning basic first aid on a recognized course before you go, or including a first-aid manual with your first-aid kit. Although detailed first-aid instruction is outside the scope of this guidebook, some basic points are listed under Traumatic Injuries (p56). Prevention of accidents and illness is as important – read Safety on the Hike (p58) for more advice. You should also know how to summon help should a major accident or illness befall you or someone with you – see Rescue & Evacuation (p58).

Other Preparations

If you have any known medical problems or are concerned about your health in any way, it's a good idea to have a full checkup before you go. It's far better to have any problems recognized and treated at home than to find out about them halfway up a mountain. It's also sensible to have a dental checkup since toothache on the trail can be a miserable experience, and dental fillings are more likely to come loose at high altitude. If you wear glasses, take a spare pair and your prescription.

If you need a particular medicine, take enough with you to last the trip. Take part of the packaging showing the generic name, rather than the brand, as this will make getting replacements easier. It's also a good idea to have a legible prescription label or letter from your doctor to prove that you

First-Aid Check List

Following is a list of items you should consider including in your first-aid kit – consult your pharmacist for brands available in your country.

Essentials

- [ ] adhesive tape
- [ ] bandages and safety pins
- [ ] elasticized support bandage – for knees, ankles etc
- [ ] gauze swabs
- [ ] nonadhesive dressings
- [ ] paper stitches
- [ ] scissors (small)
- [ ] sterile alcohol wipes
- [ ] sticking plasters (Band-Aids, blister plasters)
- [ ] sutures
- [ ] thermometer (note that mercury thermometers are prohibited by airlines)
- [ ] tweezers

Medications

- [ ] antidiarrhea and antinausea drugs
- [ ] antifungal cream or powder – for fungal skin infections and thrush
- [ ] antihistamines – for allergies, eg, hay fever; to ease the itch from insect bites or stings; and to prevent motion sickness
- [ ] antiseptic (such as povidone-iodine or Neosporin) – for cuts and grazes
- [ ] cold and flu tablets, throat lozenges and nasal decongestant
- [ ] painkillers (eg, aspirin or acetaminophen) – for pain and fever

Miscellaneous

- [ ] calamine lotion, sting relief spray or aloe vera – to ease irritation from sunburn and insect bites or stings
- [ ] eye drops – for washing out dust
- [ ] multivitamins – consider for backpacking trips, when dietary vitamin intake may be inadequate
- [ ] rehydration mixture – to prevent dehydration, eg, due to severe diarrhea; particularly important when traveling with children

legally use the medication to avoid any problems at customs.

Digital Resources

You can find a number of excellent travel health sites on the Internet. The health page of the Lonely Planet website (ⓦ www.lonely planet.com/health) offers extensive travel health information, with links to many useful sites. Visit the Hawaii Department of Health website (ⓦ www.state.hi.us/health) for local updates and information.

STAYING HEALTHY
Hygiene

To reduce the chances of contracting an illness, you should wash your hands frequently, particularly before handling or eating food.

Water

Many diseases are carried in water in the form of bacteria, protozoa, viruses, worms and insect eggs, etc. The number one rule is if you don't know for certain that the water is safe, assume the worst.

Water Purification The simplest way of purifying water is to boil it thoroughly. Vigorous boiling should be satisfactory; however, at high altitude water boils at a lower temperature, so germs are less likely to be killed. Be sure to boil it for longer in these environments.

If you cannot boil water you can use a chemical agent to purify water. Chlorine and iodine are usually used, in powder, tablet or liquid form, available from outdoor-equipment suppliers and pharmacies. Follow the recommended dosages and allow the water to stand for the correct length of time. Chlorine tablets will kill many pathogens, but not some parasites like giardia and amoebic cysts. Iodine is more effective in purifying water. Follow the directions carefully and remember that too much iodine can be harmful.

You could also consider purchasing a water filter. There are two main kinds of filter. Total filters take out all parasites, bacteria and viruses and make water safe to drink. They are often expensive, but they can be more cost effective than buying bottled water. Simple filters (which can be a nylon mesh bag) take out dirt and larger foreign bodies from the water so that chemical solutions work much more effectively; if water is dirty, chemical solutions may not work at all. It's very important when buying a filter to read the specifications, so that you know exactly what it removes from the water and what it doesn't.

Food

Food hygiene standards in Hawaii are typical of any first-world country. However, when on a hike or buying food from roadside stands, unpeeled fruit and uncooked vegetables should be washed with purified water or peeled where possible.

When foraging for food, always have a reliable Hawaiian field guide at hand. Sweet, bright-red berries from the *ohelo* plant, which thrives in arid volcanic environments, look deceptively similar to the berries of the *akia* plant, which can be poisonous to touch, let alone consume.

Note that steaming does not make contaminated shellfish safe for eating. Neither does cooking reduce your risk of contracting ciguatera poisoning (p54) from certain Hawaiian fish. Contact the **Hawaii Department of Health, Epidemiology Branch** (on Oahu ☎ 586-4586) to find out which fishing areas are known to be affected by ciguatoxins. Always clean fish immediately after they've been caught and do not eat the head, guts or eggs (roe) of any fish, particularly sharks and eels.

Common Ailments

Blisters This problem can be avoided. Make sure your walking boots or shoes are well worn in before your visit. At the very least, wear them on a few short walks before tackling longer outings. Your boots should fit comfortably with enough room to move your toes; boots that are too big or too small will cause blisters. Similarly for socks – be sure they fit properly and are specifically made for walkers; even then, check to make sure that there are no seams across the widest part of your foot. Wet and muddy socks can also cause blisters, so even on a day walk, pack a spare pair of socks. Keep your toenails clipped but not too short.

If you do feel a blister coming on, treat it sooner rather then later. Apply moleskin, or preferably one of the special blister plasters that act as a second skin, and follow the maker's instructions for replacement.

Fatigue A simple statistic: more injuries of whatever nature happen towards the end of the day than earlier, when you're fresher. Although tiredness can simply be a nuisance on an easy walk, it can be life-threatening on narrow exposed ridges or in bad weather. You should never set out on a walk that is beyond your capabilities on the day. If you feel below par, have a day off. To reduce the risk, don't push yourself too hard – take rests every hour or two and build in a good half-hour's lunch break. Towards the end of the day, take down the pace and increase your concentration. You should also eat properly throughout the day, to replace the energy used up.

Knee Strain Many walkers feel the judder on long steep descents. When dropping steeply, to reduce the strain on the knee joint (you can't eliminate it) try taking shorter steps, which leave your legs slightly bent, and ensure that your heel hits the ground before the rest of your foot. Some walkers find that tubular bandages help, while others use hi-tech supports with straps. Hiking poles are very effective in taking some of the weight off the knees.

MEDICAL PROBLEMS & TREATMENT
Environmental Hazards

Hikers are at more risk than most groups from environmental hazards. However, the risk can be significantly reduced by applying common sense – and reading the following section.

Altitude Lack of oxygen at high altitudes (over 8000ft) affects most people to some extent. The effect may be mild or severe, and occurs because the air pressure is reduced,

Warning

Self-diagnosis and treatment can be risky, so you should always seek medical help. A five-star hotel, your accommodations hosts or a local tourist information office can usually recommend a local doctor or clinic, or check the Yellow Pages.

Although we do give drug advice in this section, they are for emergency use only. Correct diagnosis is vital. Note that we have used generic rather than brand names for drugs throughout this section – check with a pharmacist for locally available brands.

and the heart and lungs must work harder to oxygenate the body. Acute Mountain Sickness (AMS) is a possibility while on Hawaii's highest peaks, including the Big Island's Mauna Kea and Mauna Loa, and also Haleakala on Maui. However, most hikers on Mauna Kea and Mauna Loa ascend slowly enough to acclimatize en route. Lower summit elevations on Haleakala usually present fewer problems. Anyone who has been scuba diving within the past 24 to 48 hours should wait at least a full day before hiking at high altitude to avoid getting the bends. Children, pregnant women and those with cardiac, pulmonary or high blood-pressure problems are more susceptible to AMS.

Mild symptoms of AMS include headache, lethargy, dizziness, difficulty breathing and loss of appetite. AMS may become more severe without warning and can be fatal. Severe symptoms include breathlessness, a dry, irritating cough (which may progress to the production of pink, frothy sputum), severe headache, lack of coordination and balance, confusion, irrational behavior, vomiting, drowsiness and unconsciousness. If you experience any of the early warning signs of AMS, *descend immediately*.

To help prevent AMS:

- Ascend slowly – have frequent rest stops; don't overdo it.
- Drink extra fluids. The mountain air is dry and cold and moisture is lost as you breathe. Evaporation of sweat may occur unnoticed and result in dehydration.

- Eat light, high-carbohydrate meals for more energy.
- Avoid alcohol as it may increase the risk of dehydration.
- Avoid sedatives.

Sun Protection against the sun should always be taken seriously. Particularly in the rarified air and deceptive coolness of the mountains, or over lava fields that reflect and intensify the sun's rays, sunburn occurs rapidly. Slap on the sunscreen and a barrier cream for your nose and lips, wear a broad-brimmed hat and protect your eyes with good quality sunglasses with UV lenses, particularly when walking near water, sand or snow. If, despite these precautions, you get yourself burnt, calamine lotion, aloe vera or other commercial sunburn relief preparations will soothe.

Heat Take time to acclimatize to high temperatures and humidity, drink sufficient liquids and do not do anything too physically demanding until you have fully acclimatized to the tropics.

Prickly Heat This is an itchy rash caused by excessive perspiration trapped under the skin. It usually strikes people who have just arrived in a hot climate. Keeping cool, bathing often, drying the skin and using a mild talcum or prickly heat powder may help. Fungal infections of the skin also occur more commonly in hot, humid conditions – for more details, see Infectious Diseases (below).

Dehydration & Heat Exhaustion Dehydration is a potentially dangerous and generally preventable condition caused by excessive fluid loss. Sweating combined with inadequate fluid intake are one of the most common causes in hikers, but other important causes are diarrhea, vomiting, and high fever – see Diarrhea (below) for more details about appropriate treatment in these circumstances.

The first symptoms are weakness, thirst and passing small amounts of very concentrated urine. This may progress to drowsiness,

Everyday Health

Normal body temperature is up to 98.6°F (37°C); more than 4°F (2°C) higher indicates a high fever. The normal adult pulse rate is 60 to 100 per minute (children 80 to 100, babies 100 to 140). As a general rule the pulse increases about 20 beats per minute for each 2°F (1°C) rise in fever.

Respiration (breathing) rate is also an indicator of illness. Count the number of breaths per minute: between 12 and 20 is normal for adults and older children (up to 30 for younger children, 40 for babies). People with a high fever or serious respiratory illness breathe more quickly than normal. More than 40 shallow breaths a minute may indicate pneumonia.

dizziness or fainting on standing up, and finally, coma. It's easy to forget how much fluid you are losing via perspiration while you are hiking, particularly when hiking over lava or if a strong breeze is drying your skin quickly. You should always maintain a good fluid intake – a minimum of 3L a day is recommended.

Dehydration and salt deficiency can cause heat exhaustion. Salt deficiency is characterized by fatigue, lethargy, headaches, giddiness and muscle cramps; salt tablets are overkill, just adding extra salt to your food is probably sufficient.

Heatstroke This is a serious, occasionally fatal, condition that occurs if the body's heat-regulating mechanism breaks down and the body temperature rises to dangerous levels. Long, continuous periods of exposure to high temperatures and insufficient fluids can leave you vulnerable to heatstroke.

The symptoms are feeling unwell, not sweating very much (or at all) and a high body temperature (102° to 106°F or 39° to 41°C). Where sweating has ceased, the skin becomes flushed and red. Severe, throbbing headaches and lack of coordination will also occur, and the sufferer may be confused or aggressive. Eventually the victim will become delirious or convulse. Hospitalization

is essential, but in the interim get victims out of the sun, remove their clothing, cover them with a wet sheet or towel and then fan continually. Give fluids if they are conscious.

Cold Too much cold can be just as dangerous as too much heat.

Hypothermia This occurs when the body loses heat faster than it can produce it and the core temperature of the body falls.

It is frighteningly easy to progress from very cold to dangerously cold due to a combination of wind, wet clothing, fatigue and hunger, even if the air temperature is above freezing. If the weather deteriorates, put on extra layers of warm clothing: a wind and/or waterproof jacket, plus fleece hat and gloves are all essential. Have something energy-giving to eat and ensure that everyone in your group is fit, feeling well and alert.

Symptoms of hypothermia are exhaustion, numb skin (particularly toes and fingers), shivering, slurred speech, irrational or violent behavior, lethargy, stumbling, dizzy spells, muscle cramps and violent bursts of energy. Irrationality may take the form of sufferers claiming they are warm and trying to take off their clothes.

To treat mild hypothermia, first get the person out of the wind and/or rain, remove their clothing if it's wet and replace it with dry, warm clothing. Give them hot liquids – not alcohol – and some high-kilojoule, easily digestible food. Do not rub victims: instead, allow them to slowly warm themselves. This should be enough to treat the early stages of hypothermia.

Infectious Diseases
Diarrhea Simple things like a change of water, food or climate can all cause a mild bout of diarrhea, but a few rushed toilet trips with no other symptoms is not indicative of a major problem. More serious diarrhea is caused by infectious agents transmitted by fecal contamination of food or water, by using contaminated utensils or directly from one person's hand to another. Paying particular attention to personal hygiene, drinking purified water and taking care of what

you eat are important measures to take to avoid getting diarrhea.

Dehydration is the main danger with any diarrhea, particularly in children or the elderly as dehydration can occur quite quickly. *Fluid replacement* (at least equal to the volume being lost) is the most important thing to remember. Weak black tea with a little sugar, soda water, or soft drinks allowed to go flat and diluted 50% with clean water are all good. With severe diarrhea a rehydrating solution is preferable to replace minerals and salts lost. Commercially available oral rehydration salts are very useful; add them to boiled or bottled water. In an emergency you can make up a solution of six teaspoons of sugar and half a teaspoon of salt to a liter of boiled or bottled water. You need to drink at least the same volume of fluid that you are losing in bowel movements and vomiting. Urine is the best guide to the adequacy of replacement – if you have small amounts of concentrated urine, you need to drink more. Keep drinking small amounts often. Stick to a bland diet as you recover.

Gut-paralyzing drugs such as diphenoxylate or loperamide can be used to bring relief from the symptoms, although they don't cure the problem. Only use these drugs if you do not have access to toilets, eg, if you *must* travel. These drugs are not recommended for children under 12 years, or if you have a high fever or are severely dehydrated. Seek medical advice if you pass blood or mucus, are feverish, or suffer persistent or severe diarrhea.

Leptospirosis This is caused by bacteria found in freshwater (streams, waterfalls, pools etc) that passes through habitats contaminated by animal urine. Hawaii's feral animals, such as pigs and rats, are leptospirosis carriers. While swimming or wading in affected freshwater, bacteria can enter the human body through the mouth, nose, eyes or cuts in the skin. Sensible precautions include wearing waterproof *tabi* (reef walkers) and avoiding unnecessary stream crossings, especially if you have open cuts. Do not drink *any* freshwater without filtering or chemically treating it first (see Water Purification, p51).

Symptoms usually occur within 20 days after exposure, and may include fever, chills, sweating, headaches, red eye (conjunctivitis); muscle pain, vomiting and diarrhea, or occasionally jaundice and a rash. Because symptoms of leptospirosis resemble the flu or hepatitis, only a few dozen cases of leptospirosis are confirmed each year. Symptoms may persist for several weeks. Deaths attributed to the disease are relatively rare, but organ and tissue damage may occur if left untreated by antibiotics prescribed by a doctor.

Giardiasis This is caused by a common parasite, *Giardia lamblia*, found in freshwater contaminated by human feces. Symptoms include stomach cramps, nausea, a bloated stomach, watery and foul-smelling diarrhea and frequent gas. Giardiasis can appear several weeks after you have been exposed to the parasite. The symptoms may disappear for a few days and then return; this can go on for several weeks. Seek medical advice if you think you have giardiasis.

Ciguatera Poisoning This is a serious illness caused by eating reef fish (raw or cooked, it doesn't matter) that have ingested ciguatoxic algae. Symptoms of ciguatera poisoning usually occur within a few hours, and may include: numbness and tingling around the mouth; vomiting, nausea and diarrhea; headache and dizziness; joint and muscle pain with weakness and cramps; and a reversal of temperature sensation (hot objects feel cold, and vice versa). Extreme cases can result in unconsciousness or even death. See Food (p52) for preventative measures. If you get sick, make sure you seek medical help immediately.

Insect-Borne Diseases

Dengue Fever This viral disease is transmitted by mosquitoes and is fast becoming one of the top public health problems in the tropical world. Unlike the malaria mosquito, the *Aedes aegypti* mosquito, which transmits the dengue virus, is most active during the day and is found mainly in and around human dwellings.

How to Prevent Mosquito Bites

- Wear light-colored clothing
- Wear long trousers and long-sleeved shirts
- Use mosquito repellents containing the compound DEET on exposed areas (prolonged overuse of DEET may be harmful, especially to children, but its use is considered preferable to being bitten by disease-transmitting mosquitoes)
- Avoid perfumes, scented soaps or aftershave
- Impregnating clothes with mosquito repellant (permethrin) effectively deters mosquitoes and other insects

Signs and symptoms of dengue fever include a sudden onset of high fever, headache, joint and muscle pains and nausea and vomiting. A rash of small red spots sometimes appears three to four days after the onset of fever. In the early phase of illness, dengue may be mistaken for other infectious diseases, including malaria and influenza. Minor bleeding such as nose bleeds may occur in the course of the illness, but this does not necessarily mean that you have progressed to the potentially fatal dengue hemorrhagic fever (DHF). This is a severe illness, characterized by heavy bleeding, which is thought to be a result of second infection due to a different strain (there are four major strains, of which only the comparatively benign Type 1 has been found so far in Hawaii). Recovery even from simple dengue fever may be prolonged, with tiredness lasting for several weeks.

You should seek medical attention as soon as possible if you think you may be infected. A blood test can exclude malaria and indicate the possibility of dengue fever. There is no specific treatment for dengue. Aspirin should be avoided, as it increases the risk of hemorrhaging. There is no vaccine against dengue fever. The best prevention is to avoid mosquito bites at all times – see the boxed text 'How to Prevent Mosquito Bites.'

Traumatic Injuries

Sprains Ankle and knee sprains are common injuries among hikers, particularly when crossing rugged terrain. To help prevent ankle sprains, wear an all-leather boot that has adequate ankle support. If you do suffer a sprain, immobilize the joint with a firm bandage, and, if feasible, immerse the foot in cold water. Distribute the contents of your pack among your companions. Once you reach shelter, relieve pain and swelling by keeping the joint elevated for the first 24 hours and, where possible, by putting ice on the swollen joint. Take simple painkillers to ease the discomfort. If the sprain is mild, you may be able to continue your walk after a couple of days. For more severe sprains, seek medical attention as an X-ray may be needed to find out whether a bone has been broken.

Major Accidents Falling or having something fall on you, resulting in head injuries or fractures, is always possible when walking, especially if you are crossing steep slopes or unstable terrain. Following is some basic advice on what to do if a major accident does occur; detailed first-aid instruction is outside the scope of this book. If a person suffers a major fall:

1. Make sure you and other people with you are not in danger
2. Assess the injured person's condition
3. Stabilize any injuries, such as bleeding wounds or broken bones
4. Seek medical attention – see Rescue & Evacuation (p60) for details

If the person is unconscious, immediately check whether they are breathing – clear their airway if it is blocked – and check whether they have a pulse – feel the side of the neck rather than the wrist. If they are not breathing but have a pulse, you should start mouth-to-mouth resuscitation immediately.

In these circumstances it is best to move the person as little as possible in case their neck or back is broken.

Check for wounds and broken bones – ask the person where they have pain if they are conscious, otherwise gently inspect them all over (including their back and the back of the head), moving them as little as possible. Control any bleeding by applying firm pressure to the wound. Bleeding from the nose or ear may indicate a fractured skull. Don't give the person anything by mouth, especially if they are unconscious.

You'll have to manage the person for shock. Raise their legs above heart level (unless their legs are fractured); dress any wounds and immobilize any fractures; loosen tight clothing; keep the person warm by covering them with a blanket or other dry clothing; insulate them from the ground if possible, but don't heat them.

Some general points to bear in mind are:

- Simple fractures take several weeks to heal, so they don't need fixing straight away, but they should be immobilized to protect them from further injury. Compound fractures need urgent treatment.
- If you do have to splint a broken bone, remember to check regularly that the splint is not cutting off the circulation to the hand and foot.
- Most cases of brief unconsciousness are not associated with any serious internal injury to the brain, but as a general rule of thumb in these circumstances, any person who has been knocked unconscious should be watched for deterioration. If they do deteriorate, seek medical attention straight away.

Fractures Indications of a fracture (broken bone) are pain (tenderness of the affected area), swelling and discoloration, loss of function or deformity of a limb. Unless you know what you are doing, you shouldn't try to straighten an obviously displaced broken bone. To protect from further injury, immobilize a nondisplaced fracture by splinting it, usually in the position found, which will probably be the most comfortable position.

Fractures of the thigh bone require urgent treatment as they involve massive blood loss and pain. Seek help and treat the patient for shock. Fractures associated with open wounds (compound fractures) also require more urgent treatment than simple fractures as there is a risk of infection. Dislocations, where the bone has come out of the joint, are very painful, and should be set as soon as possible.

Broken ribs are painful but usually heal by themselves and do not need splinting. If breathing difficulties occur, or the person coughs up blood, medical attention should be sought urgently, as it may indicate a punctured lung.

Internal Injuries These are more difficult to detect, and cannot usually be treated in the field. Watch for shock, which is a specific medical condition associated with a failure to maintain circulating blood volume. Signs include a rapid pulse and cold, clammy extremities. A person in shock requires urgent medical attention.

Cuts & Scratches

Coral cuts can be particularly severe. Because living matter gets left behind in the wound, coral cuts can take a painfully long time to heal. Wash the cut thoroughly with soap and water, then with a half-water solution of hydrogen peroxide. Apply an antibacterial topical gel and cover the wound with a dry, non-adhesive dressing. Repeat cleaning and dressing twice daily until fully healed.

Even small cuts and grazes should be washed well and treated with an antiseptic such as povidone-iodine or Neosporin. Dry wounds heal more quickly, so where possible avoid bandages and Band-Aids, which can keep wounds wet.

Infection in a wound is indicated by the skin margins becoming red, painful and swollen. More serious infection can cause swelling of the whole limb and of the lymph glands. The patient may develop a fever, and will need medical attention.

Burns

Immerse the burnt area in cold water as soon as possible, then cover it with a clean, dry, sterile dressing. Keep this in place with plasters for a day or so in the case of a small mild burn, longer for more extensive injuries. Seek medical help for severe and extensive burns.

Bites & Stings

Bedbugs These critters live in various places, but particularly in dirty mattresses and bedding, evidenced by spots of blood on bedclothes or on the wall. Bedbugs leave itchy bites in neat rows. Calamine lotion or a sting relief spray may help.

Bees & Wasps These are usually painful rather than dangerous. However, in people who are allergic to them severe breathing difficulties may occur and urgent medical care is required. Calamine lotion or a commercial sting relief spray will ease any discomfort and ice packs will reduce the pain and swelling.

Leeches Often present in damp rain forest conditions, leeches attach themselves to your skin to suck your blood. Hikers may get them on their legs or in their boots. Salt or a lighted cigarette end will make them fall off. Do not pull them off, as the bite is then more likely to become infected. Clean and apply pressure if the point of attachment is bleeding. An insect repellent may keep them away.

Scorpions, Centipedes & Spiders These pesky critters are notoriously painful. Centipedes and scorpions often shelter in shoes or clothing, so always check the inside of your hiking boots before putting them on. Centipedes especially lurk under leaf litter found on trails and around campsites, and will crawl inside your tent during rainstorms There are some spiders with dangerous bites, but antivenins are usually available.

Ticks If a tick is found attached to the skin, press down around the tick's head with tweezers, grab the head and gently pull upwards. Avoid pulling the rear of the body as this may squeeze the tick's gut contents through its mouth into your skin, increasing the risk of infection and disease. Smearing chemicals on the tick will not make it let go and is not recommended.

Women's Health
Being aware of, and more importantly prepared for, any potential health problems will help you ease any particular discomforts encountered along the trail.

Menstruation A change in diet, routine and environment, as well as intensive exercise can all lead to irregularities in the menstrual cycle. This, in itself, is not a huge issue and your cycle should return to normal when you return to a more regular lifestyle. It is also important to note that failure to menstruate could indicate pregnancy. If concerned about irregularities seek medical advice.

Pregnancy If you are pregnant, see your doctor before you travel. Even normal pregnancies can make a woman feel nauseated and tired. Although little is known about the possible adverse effects of altitude on a developing fetus, almost all authorities recommend not traveling above 11,500ft while pregnant. Pregnant women should also avoid hiking through the Big Island's active rift zones, where volcanic steam vents emit a toxic cocktail of sulfuric and hydrochloric acids.

Thrush (Vaginal Candidiasis) Anitbiotic use, synthetic underwear, tight trousers, sweating, contraceptive pills and unprotected sex can each lead to fungal vaginal infections, especially when traveling in hot, humid or tropical climates. The most common is thrush (vaginal candidiasis). Symptoms include itching and discomfort in the genital area, often in association with a thick white discharge. The best prevention is to keep the vaginal area cool and dry, and to wear cotton rather than synthetic underwear and loose clothes. Thrush can be treated by clotrimazole pessaries or vaginal cream.

Urinary Tract Infection Dehydration and 'hanging on' can result in urinary tract infection and the symptoms of cystitis, which can be particularly distressing and an inconvenient problem when out on the trail. Symptoms include burning when urinating, and having to urinate frequently and urgently. Blood can sometimes be passed in the urine. Drink plenty of fluids and empty your bladder at regular intervals. If symptoms persist, seek medical attention because a simple infection can spread to the kidneys, causing a more severe illness.

SAFETY ON THE HIKE

You can significantly reduce the chance of getting into difficulties by taking a few simple precautions. These are listed in the boxed text 'Hike Safety – Basic Rules'; a list of the clothes and equipment you should take appears in the Clothing & Equipment chapter (p44).

Crossing Rivers & Streams

Sudden downpours are common in mountains and valleys, and can speedily turn a gentle stream into a raging torrent. If you're in any doubt about the safety of a crossing, look for a safer passage upstream or wait. If the rain was short-lived, water levels should subside relatively quickly. As a general rule, any stream or river that reaches above your knees is too high to cross.

If you decide it's essential to cross (late in the day, for example), look for a wide, relatively shallow stretch of the stream rather than a bend. Take off your trousers and socks, but keep your boots on to prevent injury. Put dry, warm clothes and a towel in a plastic bag near the top of your pack. Before stepping out from the bank, unclip your chest strap and belt buckle. This makes it easier to slip out of your backpack and swim to safety if you lose your balance and are swept downstream. Use a hiking pole, grasped in both hands, on the upstream side as a third leg, or go arm in arm with a companion, clasping at the wrist, and cross side-on to the flow, taking short steps.

Flash Floods

Many hikers in Hawaii have been killed by flash flooding. Floods are more common during the winter rainy season, especially

Hike Safety – Basic Rules

- Allow plenty of time to accomplish a walk before dark, particularly when daylight hours are shorter.
- Study the route carefully before setting out, noting the possible escape routes and the point of no return (where it's quicker to continue than to turn back).
- Monitor your progress during the day against the time estimated for the walk, and keep an eye on the weather.
- It's wise not to walk alone. Always leave details of your intended route, number of people in your group, and expected return time with someone responsible before you set off; let that person know when you return.
- Before setting off, make sure you have a relevant map, compass, whistle, emergency beacon or flare, and that you know the weather forecast for the area for the next 24 hours. On some trails (especially on Oahu), bringing along a cell phone could be a life-saver.

during *kona* storms (when the wind shifts, blowing from the south). Check for flash flood warnings issued by the National Weather Service (see Weather Information, p42) and take any warning signs posted at trailheads seriously. If rain starts falling on a trail known to be subject to flash flooding, *immediately* get to higher ground – don't wait to see raging waters headed your way – and then exit the area by the safest and quickest route.

Dogs

During walks in settled and hunting areas, you're likely to encounter barking dogs – tethered or running free. Do not take away lost dogs encountered on trails around hunting areas, as their owners will be back to claim them. Regard any dog as a potential attacker and be prepared to take evasive action: even just crossing the road can take you out of its territory and into safety. A hiking pole may be useful, though use it as a last resort, especially if the owner is in sight. Knowing your tetanus immunization is up to date is reassuring.

Wild Animal Attacks

Hawaii has an abundance of feral animals, including wild goats, pigs and horses. Most of these animals will flee at the sounds of people approaching; however, some may attack if they feel threatened (eg, a wild boar protecting her piglets). Always cede the right-of-way and wait for wild animals to clear the trail area before proceeding. Keeping a clean campsite will prevent unpleasant late-night encounters with foraging animals as well. Common sense dictates that any bite, scratch or even lick from a feral animal should be cleaned immediately to prevent infection.

Hunting Accidents

Each hunting area on public lands has its own regulations, meaning the hunting season on a particular trail could be seasonal or year-round, daily or on weekends only, etc. Hunters and hikers often use the same trails; regulations are usually clearly posted at trailheads.

Most hunting actually takes place off-trail, but sometimes only a few feet away. Keep your wits about you, especially at the sounds of gunfire, as accidents can occur. Safety-conscious hunters wear fluorescent orange vests and/or caps to alert others of their presence. Hikers are advised to wear bright or fluorescent colors in hunting areas. Any hunting violations should be reported to the Department of Land & Natural Resources **Division of Conservation & Resource Enforcement** (DOCARE; on Oahu ☎ 587-0200).

Rockfall

Even a small falling rock (or coconut!) could shatter your hand or crack your skull, so always be alert to the danger of rockfall. Rockfall often happens under waterfalls, beneath cliff faces and on unstable trail sections. If you accidentally let loose a rock along a trail, loudly warn other hikers below. Wild horses and feral goats, sheep and pigs occasionally let loose rocks, too. If caught in a rockfall, try to protect your head with your pack.

Rescue & Evacuation

If someone in your group is injured or falls ill and can't move, leave somebody with them while another one or more goes for help. They should take clear written details of the location and condition of the victim, and of helicopter landing conditions. If there are only two of you, leave the injured person with as much warm clothing, food and water as it's sensible to spare, plus the whistle and torch. Mark the position with something conspicuous – an orange bivvy bag, or perhaps a large stone cross on the ground. Remember, the rescue effort might be slow, perhaps taking days to remove the injured person.

Emergency Communications The national emergency number is ☎ 911. Only call out a rescue team in a genuine emergency – not for relatively minor discomfort, such as a barely sprained ankle. Be ready to give information on where an accident occurred, how many people are injured and the injuries sustained. If a helicopter needs to come in, what are the terrain and weather conditions like at the place of the accident?

Telephone Emergency call boxes or pay-phones can be found near some trailheads and campgrounds. All US cell phones (mobile phones) sold after October 2001 are equipped with GPS-based location-tracking technology that can help rescuers locate overdue or missing hikers. But cell phones should not be relied on too heavily. They will often not function in remote backcountry areas and batteries run down quickly – keep the cell phone turned off to save power for emergencies.

Distress Signals If you need to call for help, use these internationally recognized emergency signals. Give six short signals, such as a whistle, a yell or the flash of a light, at 10-second intervals, followed by a minute of rest. Repeat the sequence until you get a response. If the responder knows the signals, this will be three signals at 20-second intervals, followed by a minute's pause and a repetition of the sequence.

Search & Rescue Organizations Back-country search and rescue is normally handled by the local law enforcement using civilian volunteers, but state police, Department of Land & Natural Resources (DLNR) personnel, local firefighters, hiking club volunteers or even the military may be called on. Especially where irresponsibility, negligence or unlawful activity is a factor, rescued persons may be billed for major expenses. Note that rescue workers will normally not start searching for hikers unless they are reported still missing 24 hours after their expected time of return. Call ☎ 911 to report a missing hiker.

Helicopter Rescue & Evacuation If a helicopter arrives on the scene, there are a couple of conventions you should be familiar with. Standing face on to the chopper:

- Arms up in the shape of a letter 'V' means 'I/We need help'
- Arms in a straight diagonal line (like one line of a letter X) means 'All OK'

For the helicopter to land, there must be a cleared space of 30yd x 30yd (25m x 25m), with a flat landing pad area of 7yd x 7yd (6m x 6m). The helicopter will fly into the wind when landing. In cases of extreme emergency, where no landing area is available, a person or harness might be lowered. Take extreme care to avoid the rotors when approaching a landed helicopter.

Honolulu

In 1809, Kamehameha I moved his royal court to Honolulu from nearby Waikiki Beach. Almost 200 years later, Honolulu is Hawaii's only major city, and the state's center of business, culture and politics. Its ethnic diversity can be seen on almost every corner – the sushi shop next door to the Vietnamese bakery, the Catholic church around the block from the Chinese Buddhist temple, and the rainbow of school children waiting for the bus. The downtown area is an architectural miscellany of past and present, with both stately 19th-century buildings and sleek high-rises. Chinatown is at the northeastern edge of downtown, roughly bounded by Honolulu Harbor, Bethel St, Vineyard Blvd and River St. Hotel St, a line of bars and strip joints a few blocks from the harbor, has been the city's red-light district since the whaling days.

INFORMATION

Click to Ⓦ www.chinatownhi.com for an independent low-down on the arts, entertainment and cuisine scene around Chinatown.

You can pick up brochures and general tourist literature at the Hawaii Visitors and Convention Bureau's **visitor information office** (☎ 924-0266; *Waikiki Shopping Plaza, Suite 502, 2250 Kalakaua Ave; open 8am-4:30pm Mon-Fri, 8am-noon Sat-Sun*).

The Department of Land and Natural Resources (DLNR) has a **1-Stop Permit Office** (☎ 587-0166; *Kalanimoku Bldg, ground level, 1151 Punchbowl St, cnr S Beretania St; open 8am-3:30pm Mon-Fri*), in downtown Honolulu, for camping, hunting and hiking permits. There are racks of free outdoor-safety brochures and photocopied handouts of topographic trail maps.

Camping permits are issued at the **Department of Parks & Recreation** (☎ 523-4525; *Honolulu Municipal Bldg, ground floor, 650 S King St, cnr Alapai St; open 7:45am-4pm Mon-Fri*) in downtown Honolulu and from satellite city halls, including one at the **Ala Moana Center** (☎ 973-2600; *1450 Ala Moana Blvd, No 1286; open 9am-5pm Mon-Fri, 8am-4pm Sat*).

Foster Botanical Garden (☎ 522-7066; *180 N Vineyard Blvd; adult/child $5/1; open 9am-4pm daily*), at the north side of Chinatown, is Oahu's main botanical garden, with an impressive 14-acre collection of tropical flora. A free self-guided tour booklet is available upon entrance. Volunteer guides lead hour-long walking tours at 1pm weekdays.

SUPPLIES & EQUIPMENT

You'll never be far from one of the ubiquitous **ABC Discount Marts**, which stand on nearly every other street corner in Waikiki. They're often the cheapest place to pick up everyday necessities and sundry items. Beyond Waikiki, the easiest supermarket to get to without a car is the **Foodland** (*Ala Moana Center, 1450 Ala Moana Blvd; open 6am-10pm Mon-Fri, 7am-10pm Sat, 7am-8pm Sun*).

Down to Earth Natural Foods (☎ 947-7678; *2525 S King St; open 7:30am-10pm daily*), near the University of Hawaii, is Honolulu's largest natural food supermarket and carries local organic produce. It has a vegetarian deli and salad bar with hot dishes such as tahini-tofu balls or vegetable curry for $6 a pound. There's a conventional grocery store, **Star Market**, across the street.

Hawaii's biggest shopping center, the **Ala Moana Center** (☎ 955-9517; *1450 Ala Moana Blvd*), has 200 stores, from chain department stores to specialty shops. The two other large shopping centers between downtown Honolulu and Waikiki are the **Ward Center** (☎ 591-8411; *1200 Ala Moana Blvd*) and the adjacent **Ward Warehouse** (☎ 593-2376; *1050 Ala Moana Blvd*).

The Powder Edge (☎ 593-2267; Ⓦ *www.powderedge.com; Ward Village Shops, 1142 Auahi St; open 9am-9pm Mon-Sat, 9am-7pm Sun*), across from Ward Center, has Hawaii's best selection of top-quality outdoor gear. Quantities may be limited, but they do stock just about everything – hiking boots, lightweight camp stoves, reusable fuel canisters, dehydrated food and even waterproof backpack covers. Unfortunately, the Powder Edge's Ala Moana Center **store** (☎ 947-3100; street level, 1450 Ala Moana Blvd; open 9:30am-9pm Mon-Sat, 10am-7pm Sun) is not as well stocked.

The Bike Shop (☎ 596-0588; W www.bike shophawaii.com; 1149 S King St; open 9am-7pm Mon-Fri, 9am-5pm Sat, 10am-5pm Sun), west of downtown Honolulu, rents excellently maintained bicycles and sells outdoor accessories, such as Camelbaks, water bottles and maps.

West of downtown Honolulu, **Pacific Map Center** (☎ 545-3600; Gentry Pacific Design Center, Suite 206A, 560 N Nimitz Hwy; open 9am-noon & 1pm-5pm Mon-Fri) sells specialist maps and USGS topographic quadrangles for all Hawaiian Islands.

Borders Books Music & Cafe (☎ 591-8995; Ward Center, 1200 Ala Moana Blvd; open 9am-11pm Mon-Thur, 9am-midnight Fri & Sat, 9am-10pm Sun) carries road maps. So does **Bestsellers** (☎ 528-2378; Bishop Square, 1001 Bishop St; cnr S King St; open 7:30am-5:30pm Mon-Fri, 9am-4pm Sat), a well-stocked downtown bookstore.

Native Books (☎ 599-5511; 222 Merchant St, cnr Richards St; open 8am-5pm Mon-Fri, 10am-3pm Sat) and **Native Books & Beautiful Things** (☎ 596-8885; Ward Warehouse, 1050 Ala Moana Blvd; open 10am-9pm Mon-Sat, 10am-5pm Sun) are excellent Hawaiian-owned stores in downtown and near Ala Moana respectively.

PLACES TO STAY

Most accommodations are found at Waikiki Beach. Booking at least a few weeks in advance is essential for securing a room.

Budget

Despite a mishmash of erratically run private hostels, Honolulu has a few internationally affiliated hostels and budget-priced hotels that won't disappoint.

Central Branch YMCA (☎ 941-3344, fax 941-8821; 401 Atkinson Dr; W www.central ymcahonolulu.org; rooms $30-53) is conveniently located on the east side of the Ala Moana Center. Guests receive YMCA

privileges, including free use of the sauna, pool and gym. It's popular, so call for reservations (accepted no less than two weeks before arrival).

Hostelling International (HI) Honolulu (☎ 946-0591, fax 946-5904; W www.hostel saloha.com; 2323A Seaview Ave; dorm beds $14-17, family rooms $38-44; office open 8am-noon, 4pm-midnight) is a well-run hostel in a quiet residential neighborhood near the University of Hawaii.

Hostelling International Waikiki (☎ 926-8313, fax 922-3798; e ayhaloha@lava.net; 2417 Prince Edward St; dorm beds $17, doubles $42-48; office open 7am-3am) is a few short blocks from the beach. Like other Waikiki hostels, it's in an older low-rise apartment complex, with the units converted for hostel use mainly by adding extra beds.

Private hostels around Waikiki all cater to backpackers and draw a fairly international crowd. To avoid taking on local boarders, the hostels may require you to show a passport or an onward ticket. The private hostels seem to go in cycles, with the standards varying whenever there are changes in management or staffing – and that can be frequent. You can sometimes get a discount on stays of a week or more, but these typically require advance payment and allow no refunds.

Seaside Hawaiian Hostel (☎ 924-3303, fax 923-2111; W www.seasidehawaiianhostel .com; 419 Seaside Ave; beds in 6-bed/2-bed dorm $17/20, semiprivate doubles $44) tends to be quieter and has an open-air courtyard.

Hokondo Waikiki Beachside (☎ 923-9566, fax 923-7525; W www.hokondo.com; 2556 Lemon Rd; beds in 8-bed/4-bed dorm $18/22.50, semiprivate doubles $50, doubles with bath $90) has air-con dorm rooms, each with cable TV and a kitchen.

Pacific Ohana Hostel (☎/fax 921-8111; 2552 Lemon Rd; beds in 6-bed/2-bed dorms $19/30-40, doubles with bath $60) has private rooms that are essentially one-bedroom apartments with their own kitchen, air-con and bath.

Polynesian Hostel Beach Club (☎ 922-1340, fax 262-2817; W www.hawaiihostels .com; 2584 Lemon Rd; dorm beds $15-19.50,

HONOLULU

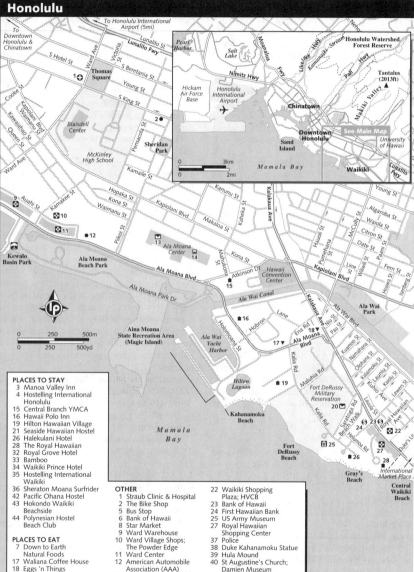

Honolulu

PLACES TO STAY
3 Manoa Valley Inn
4 Hostelling International
   Honolulu
15 Central Branch YMCA
16 Hawaii Polo Inn
19 Hilton Hawaiian Village
21 Seaside Hawaiian Hostel
26 Halekulani Hotel
28 The Royal Hawaiian
32 Royal Grove Hotel
33 Bamboo
34 Waikiki Prince Hotel
35 Hostelling International
   Waikiki
36 Sheraton Moana Surfrider
42 Pacific Ohana Hostel
43 Hokondo Waikiki
   Beachside
44 Polynesian Hostel
   Beach Club

PLACES TO EAT
7 Down to Earth
   Natural Foods
17 Waliana Coffee House
18 Eggs 'n Things
29 Perry's Smorgy
30 Ono Hawaiian Food
31 Irifune's

OTHER
1 Straub Clinic & Hospital
2 The Bike Shop
5 Bus Stop
6 Bank of Hawaii
8 Star Market
9 Ward Warehouse
10 Ward Village Shops;
   The Powder Edge
11 Ward Center
12 American Automobile
   Association (AAA)
13 Post Office
14 Bus Terminal
20 Waikiki Post Office

22 Waikiki Shopping
   Plaza; HVCB
23 Bank of Hawaii
24 First Hawaiian Bank
25 US Army Museum
27 Royal Hawaiian
   Shopping Center
37 Police
38 Duke Kahanamoku Statue
39 Hula Mound
40 St Augustine's Church;
   Damien Museum
41 Waikiki-Kapahulu
   Public Library
45 Kapiolani Bandstand

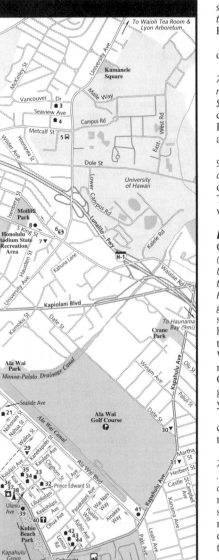

semiprivate singles/doubles $34/39, double/ triple studios $56/64) is typical of Lemon Rd's run-of-the-mill hostels.

Budget hotel rooms are a much better deal than what's offered by Waikiki hostels.

Royal Grove Hotel (☎ 923-7691, fax 922-7508; W www.royalgrovehotel.com; 151 Uluniu Ave; doubles with bath & kitchenette $43-60, triple 1-bedroom suites $75) is a charming no-frills hotel with a small pool. Rooms in the oldest wing are small, have no air-con and are exposed to traffic noise.

Waikiki Prince Hotel (☎ 922-1544, fax 924-3712; 2431 Prince Edward St; singles/ doubles $45/55, with kitchen $50/60) is next door to Hostelling International Waikiki. The rooms are simple, but they're equipped with air-con, TV and bath.

Mid-Range & Top End

Over the years, the **Outrigger & Ohana** (☎ 303-369-7777, fax 303-369-9403, from the USA & Canada ☎ 800-688-7444, from Australia, New Zealand, Germany & the United Kingdom ☎ 800-688-74443; W www.outrigger.com, www.ohanahotels.com) chain has snapped up and renovated many of Waikiki's hotels. With one phone call, you can check on the availability of 25% of the hotel rooms in Waikiki! Ask about promotional deals when making reservations. Both Outrigger and Ohana commonly offer a 'Free Ride' program, which provides a free rental car when you book at the regular room rate.

There is also a smorgasbord of other chain and independent hotels catering to all tastes and expectations.

Hawaii Polo Inn (☎ 949-0061, 800-669-7719, fax 949-4906; W www.hawaiipolo .com; 1696 Ala Moana Blvd; doubles $89-109, double suites $129-169) has motel-style rooms and a small pool. When things are slow, they'll commonly offer discounted rates as low as $55, which is certainly a good deal. Request a room in back to minimize the traffic noise.

Bamboo (☎ 922-7777, fax 922-9473; W www.aquabamboo.com; 2425 Kuhio Ave; doubles $145, double studios $165-185, quad 1-bedroom suites $215) is a Eurasian-style small hotel in the heart of Waikiki. Poolside continental breakfast is complimentary. Internet specials and weekly discounts can slash rates by as much as half.

Manoa Valley Inn (☎ 947-6019, 800-634-5115, fax 946-6168; e manoavalleyinn@ aloha.net; 2001 Vancouver Dr; doubles without bath $99-120, doubles with bath $140-190), on a quiet side street near the university, is a restored Victorian inn that's on the National Register of Historic Places. The inn is away from the beach and the peaceful rooms are furnished with antiques. Rates include continental breakfast.

W Honolulu Diamond Head (☎ 922-1700, 888-625-5144, fax 923-2249; w www.whotels.com; 2885 Kalakaua Ave; doubles with Diamond Head/ocean view from $265/330) is an upscale boutique hotel that is right on Sans Souci Beach, on the quieter Diamond Head side of Waikiki. It has stylish rooms with high-end amenities such as 27-inch Web TVs, high-speed Internet access, Aveda bath products and down-feather bedding.

Sheraton Moana Surfrider (☎ 922-3111, 800-325-3535, fax 923-0308; w www.sheraton-hawaii.com; 2365 Kalakaua Ave; doubles from $275), built in 1901, was Hawaii's first beachfront hotel. Despite the fact that modern wings have been attached, the Moana has survived with much of its gracious plantation-era character intact.

Halekulani Hotel (☎ 923-2311, 800-367-2343, fax 926-8004; w www.halekulani.com; 2199 Kalia Rd; doubles with garden/ocean view from $325/440) is widely regarded as Waikiki's premier hotel. Staff are pampering. Rooms are tastefully subdued rather than posh, have large balconies, deep soaking tubs, and little touches like bathrobes and fresh flowers.

The Royal Hawaiian (☎ 923-7311, 866-500-8313, fax 924-7098; w www.sheraton-hawaii.com; 2259 Kalakaua Ave; doubles in historic wing/oceanfront rooms from $380/605), which is a fantasy of Moorish architecture, is a throwback to the era when Rudolph Valentino was *the* romantic idol, and travel to Hawaii was by luxury liner. The 'Pink Palace of the Pacific' is now Sheraton-owned.

PLACES TO EAT

For self-catering options see Supplies & Equipment (p62).

Chinatown

Although it's predominantly Chinese, this downtown neighborhood has Vietnamese, Thai and Filipino influences as well. Good, cheap restaurants abound. There are also half a dozen noodle factories in Chinatown. One easy-to-find shop, **Yat Tung Chow Noodle Factory** (150 N King St), makes nine sizes of noodles, from skinny golden threads to fat *udon*.

The heart of Chinatown is **Oahu Market** (cnr Kekaulike & N King Sts; open daily), a lively, open-air smorgasbord of stalls since 1904. These days it gets a lot of competition from the nearby **Maunakea Marketplace** (N Hotel St; meals around $5; open 6am-6pm Mon-Sat, 6am-3pm Sun), which has about 20 stalls with mom-and-pop vendors dishing out home-style Chinese, Thai, Vietnamese, Korean and Japanese food.

Pho To Chau (☎ 533-4549; 1007 River St; soup $4-6; open 8am-2:30pm daily) is a Vietnamese restaurant serving fantastic *pho*, a rice noodle soup. It's so popular that even at 10am patrons may have to line up outside the door for one of the 16 tables. Indeed, it's worth the wait.

Indigo (☎ 521-2900; 1121 Nu'uanu Ave; dinner mains $16-26; open 11:30am-2pm Tues-Fri, 6pm-9:30pm Tues-Sat) has a relaxed, open-air courtyard and good contemporary Eurasian-Pacific cuisine. For cocktails, swing by the Indigo's **Green Room** (open until midnight Tues, 1.30am Wed-Sat), a hybrid Tiki-lounge-meets-opium-den affair.

Ala Moana & Ward Centers

The Ala Moana shopping center's food court, **Makai Market** (open 8am-9pm Mon-Sat, 9am-6pm Sun), is a circus with neon signs, hundreds of tiny tables crowded together and some 50 fast-food stalls. There's something for everyone, from salads to Japanese, Korean, Hawaiian, Thai and Mexican specialties.

Ward Center has a couple of top-rated dining spots.

Kaka'ako Kitchen (☎ 596-7488; meals $6-10; open 7am-9pm Mon-Sat, 7am-5pm Sun) is a spin-off of the upscale restaurant 3660 On the Rise. Kaka'ako uses fresh ingredients and creative flair to create gourmet 'mixed plate' meals with brown rice and a salad of locally grown greens.

Brew Moon (☎ 593-0088; appetizers & sandwiches $6-9, lunch/dinner mains $12/18; open 11am-2am daily), a stylish, high-energy place, brews its own ales, ranging from a low-calorie 'moonlight' brew to the copper-colored 'Hawaii 5' malt. It serves a wide variety of creative food.

Waikiki

This area is full of fast food and overpriced pre-fab eateries, but there are some A1 spots if you know exactly where to look.

Eggs 'n Things (☎ 949-0820; 1911-B Kalakaua Ave; dishes $3-8; call for opening hours) is a bustling, all-night diner specializing in breakfast fare, with a variety of waffles, pancakes, crepes and omelettes.

Waliana Coffee House (☎ 955-1764; 1860 Ala Moana Blvd; meals $6-12; open 24hr), opposite Hilton Hawaiian Village, is a vintage coffee shop serving heaping portions with plenty of aloha around the clock.

Perry's Smorgy (☎ 926-0184; 2380 Kuhio Ave; breakfast/lunch/dinner $5.50/6.50/9.50; open 7am-11am, 11:30am-2:30pm & 5pm-9pm daily) features all-you-can-eat buffets in a garden-like setting. It's a tourist crowd and the food is cafeteria quality, but the price is right.

Irifune's (☎ 737-1141; 563 Kapahulu Ave; lunch specials $7, dinner combo plates $10-15; open 11:30am-1:30pm & 5:30pm-9:30pm Tues-Sat) serves hearty Japanese country food. A top choice is the *tataki ahi*, tuna that's seared lightly on the outside, sashimi-like inside. Alcohol is not served, but you can bring your own.

Ono Hawaiian Food (☎ 737-2275; 726 Kapahulu Ave; meals $8-10; open 11am-7:45pm Mon-Sat) is *the* place in the greater Waikiki area to get traditional Hawaiian food served Hawaiian-style. It's a simple little diner, crowded with aging tables and sports memorabilia.

Elsewhere in Honolulu

Not surprisingly, students at the University of Hawaii at Manoa support a number of reasonably priced ethnic restaurants, coffee shops and health food stores. Most are within a 10-minute walk of the three-way intersection of King St, Beretania St and University Ave.

In Manoa Valley, **Waioli Tea Room** (☎ 988-5800; 2950 Manoa Rd; breakfast & lunch $8-12, high tea $18.75; open 8am-4pm daily, high tea 2:30pm Tues-Sun, dinner served weekends), between the University of Hawaii and the Lyon Arboretum, is delightfully like stepping back 100 years to a simpler, more refined time. In one of the gardens is the restored grass hut that author Robert Louis Stevenson stayed in during his retreat at Waikiki Beach. For high tea, reservations are required at least a day in advance.

Between Chinatown and the airport, **Sam Choy's Breakfast, Lunch & Crab** (☎ 545-7979; 580 N Nimitz Hwy; Sun brunch buffet $12.50, lunch mains $9-$16, dinner $12-$35; open 6:30am-3pm Mon-Fri, dinner 5pm-9:30pm daily) offers huge portions of local Hawaiian-style food for breakfast; fresh crab, crab cakes or other sandwiches for lunch; and more crab for dinner. The food is great, a high-quality change from overpriced hotel fare, and there's an on-site Big Aloha Brewery.

GETTING THERE & AWAY

Honolulu is the main hub for both domestic and international airlines (see Air, p223) as well as interisland carriers (see Air, p225). Oahu really is a very easy island to get around, whether by public bus or rental car; just see individual hikes in the Oahu chapter for details on getting both to and from trailheads.

GETTING AROUND

You'll probably find that driving around Waikiki is always a headache, so it's best to take the bus. Traffic in and out of Honolulu can get quite jammed during rush hours, from 6:30am to 9am and 3pm to 6pm on weekdays.

To/From the Airport.

Public buses stop at the roadside median on the terminal's 2nd level. Luggage is limited to what passengers can hold on their laps or store under their seat, the latter comparable to the space under an airline seat. City bus No 19 or 20 runs via downtown Honolulu ($1.50, 25 minutes) to Waikiki ($1.50, one hour) about once every 30 minutes from 5am until 11:15pm on weekdays, and to 11:45pm on weekends.

A taxi to Waikiki from the airport will cost about $25. A few private companies offer shuttle services between the airport and Waikiki hotels. Fares are around $8 one-way, or $13 round-trip. The ride averages 45 minutes, but can be more or less depending on how many passengers are dropped off before reaching your hotel. Board at the roadside median on the ground level, in front of the baggage claim areas.

The main car rental agencies have booths or courtesy phones in the airport baggage claim area. **Tradewinds U-Drive Inc** (☎ 834-1465, 888-388-7368, fax 839-6255; W www .drive-me.com; 2875A Koapaka St) offers free airport pick-ups.

Bus

Oahu's public bus system, called **TheBus** (☎ 848-5555; W www.thebus.org), is fairly extensive and easy to use. TheBus has about 80 routes, which collectively cover most of Oahu. All buses are equipped with front-loading bicycle racks. Buses usually operate from about 5:30am to 8pm, although some main routes, such as some of those that serve Waikiki, continue until around 10pm or even midnight. Printed timetables are available free at any satellite city hall, including the one at Ala Moana Center.

Buses generally keep the same number when inbound and outbound. For instance, bus No 8 can take you either into the heart of Waikiki or away from it toward Ala Moana – so take note of both the number and the written destination before you jump on. When possible, take one of the express buses, which cost the same but make limited stops. The one-way fare for adults is $1.50 (exact change or $1 bills only). Transfers, which have a two-hour time limit stamped on them, are free. Visitor passes ($15), valid for unlimited rides over four consecutive days, can be purchased at any ABC Store. Monthly bus passes ($27) are sold at satellite city halls, 7-Eleven convenience stores, and Foodland and Star supermarkets.

Common Routes Buses Nos 8, 19 and 20 run between Waikiki and the Ala Moana Center, Honolulu's central transfer point. It's hardly worth checking timetables, as one of these buses comes by every few minutes throughout the day. From Ala Moana you can connect with a broad network of buses to points around the island. Buses Nos 2, 19 and 20 also run between Waikiki and downtown Honolulu every 10 minutes or so. Bus No 4 shuttles between Waikiki and the University of Hawaii every 15 minutes. Bus No 6 connects the University of Hawaii and downtown Honolulu every 20 minutes via Ala Moana.

Oahu

Oahu, covering 597 sq miles, is the third-largest Hawaiian Island. It is by far the most developed of the islands and, quite appropriately, has long been nicknamed 'The Gathering Place.' It's an urban scene, with highways, high-rises and crowds. Oahu is probably also the cheapest Hawaiian Island to visit, but if you're looking for a getaway vacation, you'd best continue on to one of the Neighbor Islands (the main islands apart from Oahu).

When people think of Hawaii it's often places on Oahu that spring to mind – such famous sightseeing attractions as Waikiki Beach, Pearl Harbor, Diamond Head and Sunset Beach. Despite its tourism and military development, the island still maintains its scenic beauty, with steeply fluted *pali,* deep aquamarine bays, thickly forested peaks and valleys carpeted with pineapple fields. Two separate volcanoes form Oahu's two mountain ranges, Waianae and Ko'olau; Oahu's highest point, Mt Ka'ala (4025ft), is in the Waianae Range.

HISTORY
In 1795 Kamehameha swept through Maui and Molokai, conquering those islands before crossing the channel to Oahu. On the quiet beaches of Waikiki he landed his fleet of canoes and marched up toward Nu'uanu Valley. Kamehameha's taking of Oahu marked the last battle ever fought between Hawaiian troops.

The Oahuans, prepared for the usual spear-and-stone warfare, panicked when they realized Kamehameha had brought in a handful of Western sharpshooters. The foreigners picked off the Oahuan generals and blasted into their ridge-top defenses. What should have been the advantage of high ground turned into a death trap for the Oahuans when they found themselves wedged up into Nu'uanu Valley, unable to redeploy.

Fleeing up the cliff sides in retreat, the Oahuans were forced to make their last

Highlights

ANN CECIL

Along the North Shore

- Perching at Nu'uanu Valley lookout en route to Jackass Ginger Pool (p71)

- Stepping in the shadows of ancient *pali* (cliffs) above Maunawili Falls (p78)

- Triumphing over the high-peaked Ko'olau Range via the rugged Waimano or Manana Trails (p83)

- Scrambling over large boulders above Kaena Point Satellite Tracking Station for vistas of Mt Ka'ala on the Kealia Trail (p91)

stand at the narrow, precipitous ledge along the current-day Nu'uanu Pali Lookout. Hundreds were driven over the top of the *pali* to their deaths. Some Oahuan warriors, including Kalanikupule, the *ali'i nui* (high chief), escaped into upland forests. When Kalanikupule surfaced a few months later, he was sacrificed by Kamehameha to the war god Ku.

OAHU

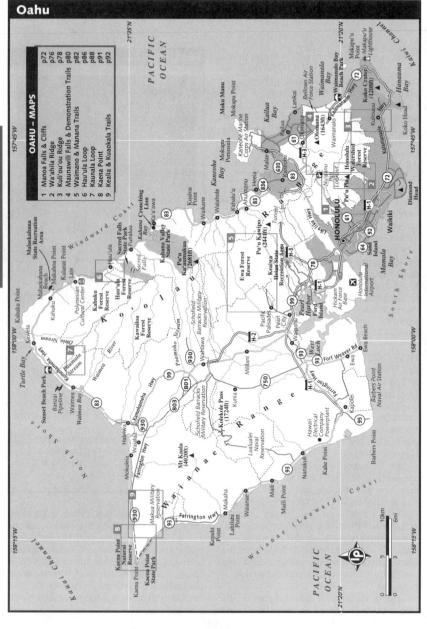

Oahu

OAHU – MAPS

1 Manoa Falls & Cliffs	p72
2 Wa'ahila Ridge	p76
3 Kuli'ou'ou Ridge	p78
4 Maunawili Falls & Demonstration Trails	p80
5 Waimano & Manana Trails	p82
6 Hau'ula Loop	p86
7 Kaunala Loop	p88
8 Kaena Point	p91
9 Kealia & Kuaokala Trails	p92

INFORMATION

When to Hike

Oahu is a year-round hiking destination. Heavy winter rains may make trails slick but not impassable. Stopping over on Oahu to get acclimated and do some warm-up hikes before visiting Neighbor Islands is a good idea.

Books

Excellent photography and documentary books on Oahu's ancient Hawaiian sites include the UH Press books *Pana Oahu: Sacred Stones, Sacred Land*, compiled by Jan Becket and Joseph Singer, *Sites of Oahu* by Elspeth Sterling and Catherine Summers, and *Ancient Sites of Oahu* by Van James. UH Press' *Na Wahi Pana O Ko'olau Poko*, by Anne Kapulani Landgraf, treats the Windward Coast.

Information Sources

Oahu Hiking Enthusiasts *(OHE;* W *www2 .hawaii.edu/~turner/ohe/ohe.html)* is an online forum for backcountry trail notes, valuable hiking pointers and community discussions.

Place Names

Basically Oahu has four sides, with distinct windward and leeward coasts and north and south shores. Southeast Oahu is the region around Diamond Head, Koko Head and Makapu'u Point. The Windward Coast stretches northwest from Kailua Bay and Kaneohe up past Laie to the North Shore, famous as a surfer's paradise. There you'll find Sunset Beach, Waimea Bay and Haleiwa town. The North Shore is separated from the leeward Waianae Coast by Kaena Point.

Permits & Fees

Camping is free at several county beach parks, but permits are required. County camping is allowed from 8am Friday to 8am Wednesday, except at Bellows Field Beach Park, which is open only on weekends. The Department of Land and Natural Resources (DLNR) has a **1-Stop Permit Office** *(☎ 587-0166; Kalanimoku Bldg, ground level, 1151 Punchbowl St, cnr S Beretania St; open 8am-3:30pm Mon-Fri)* in downtown

Honolulu. Permits are also issued at the **Department of Parks & Recreation** *(☎ 523-4525; Honolulu Municipal Building, ground floor, 650 S King St, cnr Alapai St; open 7:45am-4pm Mon-Fri)* in downtown Honolulu and from satellite city halls, including one at the **Ala Moana Center** *(☎ 973-2600; 1450 Ala Moana Blvd, No 1286; open 9am-5pm Mon-Fri, 8am-4pm Sat)*.

GATEWAY

See Honolulu (p62).

Manoa Falls to Jackass Ginger Pool

Duration	4½–6 hours
Distance	9 miles (14.5km)
Difficulty	moderate
Start/Finish	end Manoa Rd
Nearest Town	Honolulu (p62)
Transport	bus

Summary Stride past a 100ft-high waterfall and musically rustling bamboo groves up to the breathtaking Nu'uanu Valley lookout, then drop to a natural pool surrounded by wild ginger plants.

The upper Manoa Valley, inland from the University of Hawaii campus, ends at forest reserve land in the hills above Honolulu. The road into the valley runs through a well-to-do residential neighborhood before reaching Lyon Arboretum and the trailhead to Manoa Falls.

Lyon Arboretum *(☎ 988-0456;* W *www .hawaii.edu/lyonarboretum/; 3860 Manoa Rd; suggested donation $2.50; open 9am-3pm Mon-Sat)* is a good place to learn how to identify native Hawaiian trees and plants. Call for schedules of tours, guided hikes, bird-watching and horticultural classes. The arboretum has restrooms, drinking fountains and a nonprofit shop selling excellent field guides and Hawaiiana books. The arboretum, at the end of a short paved drive, is just west of the Manoa Falls trailhead.

This is a beautiful hike, especially for one so close to the city. It traverses both popular and more peaceful sections of the Honolulu Mauka Trail System, enjoying a variety of native forest environments, bird song and scenic vistas almost the entire way.

PLANNING

When the sun shines on Waikiki, it may be raining up here in the mountains. Hiking poles or a walking stick will help with steep, slippery slopes. Pack a swimsuit, towel and flip-flops. Bring water, since any available freshwater must be filtered or treated before drinking. Keep to established trails at all times to avoid quickly becoming lost.

Maps

The USGS 1:24,000 map *Honolulu* covers the Makiki-Tantalus area and the Manoa Valley, but doesn't depict all of the trails. Instead pick up the free, photocopied *Honolulu Mauka Trail System* handout, which has an up-to-date topographic map and brief trail notes. It's available from the DLNR permit office in downtown Honolulu.

GETTING TO/FROM THE HIKE

From the Ala Moana Center take the No 5 Manoa Valley bus to the end of the line, at the junction of Manoa Rd and Kumuone St

Manoa Falls & Cliffs

($1.50, 25 minutes, once or twice hourly). It's a 10-minute walk up through Paradise Park subdivision to the end of Manoa Rd. The trail begins from a small parking lot beyond the arboretum turn-off.

THE HIKE (see map p72)

Follow the signposted Manoa Falls Trail across a concrete bridge. Surrounded by lush, damp vegetation and moss-covered stones and tree trunks, the trail runs ¾ mile above a rocky streambed before ending at the falls. Be careful of exposed tree roots. There are *hau* (hibiscus) thickets, flowering orange African tulip trees, tall, swamp mahogany groves with spongy reddish bark and other lofty arboreal varieties that creak like wooden doors in old houses. Many of them were planted by the Lyon Arboretum, which at one time held a lease on the property.

Up ahead the vertical falls drop 100ft into a small, shallow pool. Wild purple orchids and red ginger grow nearby. The pool isn't deep enough for swimming, and falling rocks make it dangerous. Do not venture beyond the safe viewing area established after the last landslide. About 50ft back from Manoa Falls, the inconspicuous Aihualama Trail starts to the west of a chain-link fence and scrambles over some boulders. Passing some healthy ti plants, the trail enters a tall bamboo forest with some massive old banyan trees and then contours around the ridge, offering broad views of Manoa Valley. Another mile of gradual switchbacks (ignore any shortcuts or misleading trails-of-use) brings hikers to an intersection with the Pauoa Flats Trail, which ascends to the right for ½ mile over muddy tree roots to spectacular **Nu'uanu Valley lookout**. Here atop the Ko'olau Range, where Oahu's steep *pali* are visible all around, it's possible to peer through a gap out to the Windward Coast.

When ready, backtrack to the intersection with the Aihualama Trail, but continue downhill on the Pauoa Flats Trail. At the next intersection, turn right onto the Nu'uanu Trail. This 1½-mile footpath starts off innocently enough, walking breezily along a narrow ridge, which offers panoramic views of Honolulu and the harbor.

Abruptly the trail plunges down through koa, ohia and *uluhe* (false staghorn ferns). After a stumbling and skidding descent of about 15 minutes, the trail eases into shady, but still steep switchbacks. Watch out for ankle-twisting tree roots, large boulders and a few muddy rockslides. Eventually the trail becomes carpeted with ironwood and pine needles as it reaches the valley floor.

A Na Ala Hele sign marks the intersection with the Judd Trail, which is actually a ¾-mile loop. Walk left and soon a tumbling stream and a series of pools come into view. Look for a metal stake marking a steep trail-of-use down to the biggest pool, **Jackass Ginger Pool**, surrounded by yellow-flowering ginger (a local donkey once grazed here, hence the name). After taking a dip, climb back to follow the Judd Trail as it moves up and away from the stream. As it curves back over tree roots to the Nu'uanu Trail intersection, look for small trail signs and arrows pointing the way.

From the bottom of the Nu'uanu Trail, it's at least a two-hour hike back to the Manoa Falls trailhead. Be sure to leave enough daylight for the return trip. Darkness falls quickly in the upper reaches of the forest and obscures trail junctions; the last legs of the trip through bamboo forest and over rocks on the way back from the falls are especially hazardous after dark.

Manoa Cliffs Circuit

Duration	3½ hours
Distance	6.2 miles (10km)
Difficulty	moderate
Start/Finish	Makiki Forest Baseyard
Nearest Town	Honolulu (p62)
Transport	bus

Summary A grand tour of the Makiki-Tantalus area, racing up tree-root staircases and along cliff faces to the awesome Nu'uanu Valley lookout, and visiting an endangered species habitat.

Presided over by Tantalus (2013ft), the fertile Makiki Valley was the site of an ancient Hawaiian agricultural settlement.

OAHU

The archaeological remains of stone walls and evidence of a 19th-century coffee plantation can still be seen. Today the area is part of the Honolulu Watershed Forest Reserve, which incorporates Hawaii's first state nursery and arboretum, and is crisscrossed by the Honolulu Mauka Trail System. This hike loops through some of the best scenery that the Makiki-Tantalus area has to offer, with almost no backtracking.

For a shorter (2½-mile) hike along this route, try the Makiki Valley Loop. Link the first and final sections of the Manoa Cliffs Circuit by staying on the Makiki Valley Trail, which passes through small gulches and across gentle streams with patches of ginger. There are some fine views of the city below.

Another short (4 mile) option is to tackle the middle of the circuit, incorporating Tantalus and the Nu'uanu Valley lookout (see Pu'u Ohia Trail, p95).

Naturalists from the **Hawaii Nature Center** (☎ 955-0100; W www.hawaiinaturecenter .org) lead low-cost guided hikes and family-oriented nature workshops in the forest reserve; reservations are required. The center's trailer offices are located alongside the main baseyard road, below the forestry service gate.

PLANNING

Even when it's sunny in downtown Honolulu, it may be raining up here in the mountains. Hiking poles or a walking stick will help with steep, occasionally slippery slopes. Carry water on the trail; drinking water is available from a spigot outside the public rest rooms behind the Hawaii Nature Center and a drinking fountain hidden by a soda vending machine outside the Division of Forestry & Wildlife (DOFAW) office.

Maps

The USGS 1:24,000 map *Honolulu* covers the Makiki-Tantalus area, but doesn't accurately depict all trails. Instead pick up the free photocopied 'Honolulu Mauka Trail System' handout, which has an up-to-date topographic map and brief hiking notes. It's available from the **DOFAW office** (open

Jewels of the Forest

Oahu has an endemic genus of tree snail, the *Achatinella*. In former days the forests were loaded with these colorful snails, which clung like gems to the leaves of trees. They were too attractive for their own good, however, and hikers collected them for souvenirs by the handfuls around the turn of the 20th century. Even more devastating has been the deforestation of habitat and the introduction of a cannibal snail and predatory rodents. Of 41 known *Achatinella* species, only 19 remain and all are endangered.

❀ ❀ ❀ ❀ ❀ ❀ ❀ ❀ ❀ ❀ ❀ ❀ ❀ ❀

weekdays) in Makiki Forest Baseyard, just uphill from the Hawaii Nature Center. Note that the 2.3-mile Manoa Cliff Trail is no longer 3.4 miles long, as erroneously stated on a number of trail maps and outdated signboards.

GETTING TO/FROM THE HIKE

From downtown Honolulu (a convenient bus stop is on Alapai St at the corner of S Hotel St) take the No 15 Makiki-Pacific Heights bus up past Roosevelt High School and get off just before the Contemporary Museum at the intersection of Mott-Smith Dr and Makiki Heights Dr ($1.50, 25 minutes, at least hourly). Turn right and walk ½ mile downhill on Makiki Heights Dr; where the road makes a sharp bend, proceed left through a green gate into the Makiki Forest Recreation Area and continue up the paved road to the baseyard.

THE HIKE (see map p72)

Past the Hawaii Nature Center, turn right and walk by the rest rooms toward the signposted Maunalaha trailhead. After crossing over a small stream and a few tame switchbacks, the trail makes a no-holds-barred ascent of the Makiki Valley's east ridge over a giant staircase of tree roots, passing Norfolk pine, banyans, leafy ti plants and a hidden taro patch along the way. Behind are views of Honolulu's skyscrapers and harbor. After climbing for half an hour, the trail comes to a four-way intersection. Follow the Makiki Valley Trail straight ahead (*not* left) and proceed uphill on a forest path carpeted with leaves. At the next junction, turn left onto the ¾-mile-long Moleka Trail, where artificial steps give way to a narrow footpath made slippery by wet leaves and *kukui* (candlenut tree) nuts rolling underfoot. As the trail slides along, there are prime valley views framed by wild orchids and only slightly spoiled by subdivision housing.

Another steep set of steps leads into the shade where a few palm trees wave and rustling bamboo groves are filled with bird song. Power lines and traffic noise from Round Top Dr draw near as the trail ends. Stop and use the boot brush to wipe off invasive plant seeds before crossing the road to the next trailhead. Step onto the Manoa Cliff Trail, which rises through palm ferns, Christmas berries, big ol' ficus and a host of native trees, past some striking valley viewpoints. Traffic noise finally disappears as the trail curves left into bamboo forest and meets a **bench** framed by berry plants, offering some excellent views of the Ko'olau Range to the northeast and *pali* beyond.

It's another muddy mile of lush ferns, mossy boulders and guava trees as the trail switchbacks down to a large trail map signboard near the intersection with the Pu'u Ohia Trail. Keep going and, at the next three-way intersection with the Kalawahine Trail, turn right onto the Pauoa Flats Trail for a quick side trip to the **Nu'uanu Valley lookout** at a Ko'olau summit, boasting views that sweep over to the Windward Coast. When ready, backtrack to the junction and turn right, then take a left onto the Kalawahine Trail. A muddy path descends under large banyans and *kokio keokeo* (white-flowered hibiscus) trees, eventually gaining ocean and harbor views.

After passing over rocks, boulders and a few narrow stream gulches, the trail enters the specially protected habitat of the Oahu tree snail (see the boxed text 'Jewels of the Forest', p74). Please obey all posted rules while passing through this fragile area. Soon afterwards it emerges into sunlight and descends to meet Tantalus Dr. Turn

right on this paved road and walk downhill as it narrows to one lane and parallels a retention wall. Watch for a Na Ala Hele trailhead sign on the east side of the road at the end of the guardrail.

The Nahuina Trail takes off from Tantalus Dr. The next ½-mile trail segment is short, but steep and often overgrown, not to mention annoyingly within earshot of traffic. In some spots, the soil is soft and crumbly. At the junction with the Makiki Valley Trail, turn left and scramble over some boulders, then take a sharp right at the next intersection with the Kanealole Trail, which descends for ¾ mile through dense forest alongside a streambed. The trail leads down through a field of Job's tears; the beadlike bracts of the female flowers of this tall grass are often picked to be strung in lei. The trail ends in the forest baseyard just above the DOFAW office.

Wa'ahila Ridge

Duration	1½–2 hours
Distance	4.8 miles (7.7km)
Difficulty	easy–moderate
Start/Finish	Wa'ahila Ridge State Recreation Area
Nearest Town	Honolulu (p62)
Transport	bus
Summary	Skedaddle over boulders and tree roots along a wonderfully bumpy trail up Wa'ahila Ridge, with views of Manoa Valley, Honolulu and the Ko'olau Range as a reward.

Popular even with novice hikers, the boulder-strewn Wa'ahila Ridge Trail covers a variety of terrain in a short time, making for an enjoyable afternoon walk. Native plants are common all along the trail, and birders should watch for *amakihi* and *apapane*.

Experienced hikers can combine this trail with an excursion to the top of Pu'u Pia for more jaw-dropping 360-degree views (see Side Trip: Pu'u Pia, p77). There is also a shorter (one-hour) option to the top of Pu'u Pia, which can be used as an alternative finish for the Wa'ahila Ridge Trail. The signposted

OAHU

Na Ala Hele trail begins from a paved drive-way running between private houses at Nos 3670 and 3689 on Woodlawn Dr, at the intersection of Alani Dr. In rain forest the trail passes a picnic shelter, which is the junction with the Kolowalu Trail. The No 6 University/Woodlawn bus from downtown Honolulu stops nearby the trailhead ($1.50, every 30 minutes).

PLANNING

Some steep and narrow sections can become dangerously slippery after heavy rains. Hiking poles or a walking stick are helpful for Kolowalu Trail on the Pu'u Pia side trip. Bring water, as none is available at the trailhead or anywhere along the trail. The state recreation area has rest rooms and covered picnic pavilions.

Maps

The USGS 1:24,000 map *Honolulu* covers Wa'ahila Ridge, but not the side trip to Pu'u Pia. The free, photocopied *Honolulu Mauka Trail System* handout has an up-to-date topographic map and brief trail notes. It's available from the DLNR's permit office in downtown Honolulu.

GETTING TO/FROM THE HIKE

Near Honolulu Zoo at the east end of Waikiki, from the intersection of Kapahulu and Paki Aves, take the No 14 St Louis Heights bus up through the St Louis Heights subdivision and get off at the top of Peter Place ($1.50, 20 minutes, approximately hourly). The trailhead is about a 15-minute walk from the bus stop. Head west on Ruth Place through the gates of Wa'ahila Ridge State Recreation Area and curve right to the upper end of the parking lot.

THE HIKE

Pause by the picnic tables on the west side of the parking lot for a broad overview of Manoa Valley before heading uphill past the barbecue pits to the Na Ala Hele trailhead sign. Please clean all stray seeds and soil off hiking boots using the brush provided, both before *and* after hiking, to prevent the spread of invasive species.

Framed by ironwood trees and wild straw-berry guava, the trail ascends on a rutted dirt road past a water tank. Watch for a small arrow pointing off to the left where the trail leaves the road and enters the forest reserve. Scattered with soft ironwood needles, the trail contours for a bit before sliding steeply downhill over tree roots. The terrain becomes dry and rocky at the bottom, with a few grasses and Christmas berries growing around the trail.

Only partly shaded now, the trail labors up and down a series of small saddles and knobs, while granting views over Manoa Valley and downtown Honolulu. At one point, the trail drops sharply over a series of boulders that require some minor scrambling, but then continues rhythmically on its roller-coaster pattern for another mile.

There is a big koa tree with spreading roots across the trail just before you make a more arduous, partly exposed climb to a wide grassy **clearing**. Bird's-eye views over

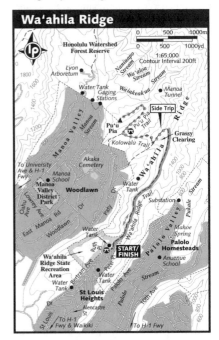

the Manoa Valley and greater Honolulu make it worth stopping here. Beyond this clearing, the trail keeps going for only another five minutes, becoming more muddy and overgrown. From the end it may be tempting to continue on a trail-of-use uphill into the restricted watershed area, doing so is strictly prohibited. The trail is not maintained and hazards may exist.

Side Trip: Pu'u Pia
2 hours, 3.5mi (5.6km)
Beyond the end of the Wa'ahila Ridge Trail, the Kolowalu Trail starts a muddy, often overgrown and precipitous 1-mile descent to visit Pu'u Pia, a lookout that offers even grander views. At various points, it's pure scree and hikers will have to hang onto tree trunks or slide downhill on their *okole* (tush)! When the eroded path becomes anchored by tree roots once again, the worst is over. Keep descending to a covered picnic table, then turn right at the junction with the Pu'u Pia Trail. Cross a few streambeds and ascend steeply on a muddy footpath that ends at a **summit bench**; the views of Honolulu city and harbor, surrounding valleys and the Ko'olau Range are impressive.

On the return trip from Pu'u Pia, turn left at the same picnic table to backtrack up into Wa'ahila Ridge State Recreation Area.

Kuli'ou'ou Ridge

Duration	3 hours
Distance	5.4 miles (8.7km)
Difficulty	moderate
Start/Finish	end Kuli'ou'ou Rd
Nearest Town	Honolulu (p62)
Transport	bus

Summary Amble along forest switchbacks rising out of Kuli'ou'ou Valley before making a stiff, but highly satisfying climb to the windy summit of the Ko'olau Range for ocean vistas.

Of all Oahu's classic trails to the top of the Ko'olau mountain range, the comparatively easy Kuli'ou'ou Ridge Trail is the most well traveled. Why? Simply put, it manages to get there without any unduly hazardous segments. That's not to say this hike is easy, since the final ascent is steep enough to make anyone's breath labored. But the varied terrain and 360-degree view of Koko Head, Makapu'u Point, the Windward Coast and Honolulu are rewarding enough to make hikers forget any minor hardships.

PLANNING
Bring water as none is available at the trailhead or along the trail. Hiking poles or a walking stick will help on the final scramble to the Ko'olau summit. Basic supplies, drinking water, groceries and take-out meals are sold at the **Aina Haina shopping center** *(Kalanianaole Hwy, cnr W Hind Dr)*, about 2 miles west of Kuli'ou'ou Rd on Hwy 72.

Maps
The USGS 1:24,000 map entitled *Koko Head* shows the trail. The free, photocopied *East Honolulu-Kuliouou Area* handout has an up-to-date topographic map and brief trail notes. It's available from the DLNR's permit office in downtown Honolulu.

GETTING TO/FROM THE HIKE
From stops along S King St in downtown Honolulu, catch the No 1 Hawaii Kai or Lunalilo bus eastbound along the Kalanianaole Hwy (Hwy 72) to Kuli'ou'ou Rd ($1.50, 50 minutes, twice hourly). It's just over a mile's walk inland up Kuli'ou'ou Rd through Kuli'ou'ou Homesteads subdivision to the trailhead, curving left at Haleloa Place, then turning sharply right and eventually reaching a cul-de-sac at the end of the road.

THE HIKE (see map p78)
Walk north across the cul-de-sac past a Na Ala Hele trailhead sign and a cable gate. Do not detour to the right up a private road. At the hunter/hiker check-in station, sign the log sheet inside the mailbox before continuing ahead on a wide forested path lined with *koa haole* and *kiawe* trees, which ascends slightly to a trail junction. Straight ahead the Kuli'ou'ou Valley Trail meanders almost ½ mile along a streambed, but it's a

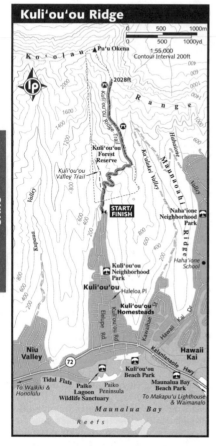

Kuli'ou'ou Ridge

with soft needles. After half an hour of hiking, switchbacks give way to a sinuous path up the ridge accompanied by ti plants and Norfolk pines. Bear up over a particularly eroded stretch of trail and reach a covered picnic shelter. Stop here to catch a few breaths, then veer left and walk generally uphill. The trail picks a very steep path over tree roots and under dense forest cover before emerging at a break in the foliage where a **bench** has views back over Southeast Oahu and Honolulu, but nothing compared to what lies ahead.

Press on through scratchy *uluhe* ferns and shrubby ohia, occasionally using artificial steps built into the trail or a rope tied around a tree for support. Just when it seems that this near-vertical ascent will go on forever, the trail abruptly ends on a small flat **summit** (2028ft) of the Ko'olau mountain range. Be prepared for strong winds here. Amazing views take in Honolulu, Diamond Head, Koko Head, Makapu'u Point and all the way around to Kailua Bay on the Windward Coast.

Maunawili Falls & Demonstration Trails

Duration	4 hours
Distance	9 miles (14.5km)
Difficulty	moderate
Start	Waikupanaha Rd
Finish	Maunawili Rd
Nearest Towns	Waimanalo (p79), Honolulu (p62)
Transport	bus

Summary Walk underneath graceful, near-vertical *pali* toward Oahu's Windward Coast, enjoying the island's best-cut trail as it winds through waterfall gulches above the fertile Maunawili Valley.

dull hike since the water levels are typically too low to produce any waterfalls.

Instead turn right onto the Kuli'ou'ou Ridge Trail, using the boot brush to clean off any seeds before entering the forest reserve. The trail makes nearly a dozen switchback turns, running back and forth between the *mauka* (inland) valley and the *makai* (ocean) side of the ridge, all the while rising through koa forest. When confronted with forks, stay on the lower path. Avoid shortcuts to prevent trail erosion.

The trail gradually becomes steeper, entering ironwood groves that carpet the path

Venturing outside Honolulu is worthwhile solely for the joys of this hike. Planned and built in the early 1990s through the Na Ala Hele program, the exemplary Maunawili Demonstration Trail was made possible by combined volunteer efforts from the Sierra

Club and other hiking groups. The trail gently contours around Oahu's impressive *pali* for a series of unique viewpoints over lush valleys and the Windward Coast. A connector trail leads down from the cliffs to lovely Maunawili Falls, a popular day-trip from Maunawili Rd.

Although there are a few variations to the described route, none is feasible on public transport. Only hikers able to shuttle two vehicles, or someone who's willing to hitch along a busy highway, can hike the entire 10-mile Maunawili Demonstration Trail to its end out on the Pali Hwy (Hwy 61). But why bother, when the best views are on the first seven miles of trail before the turn-off to the falls anyway?

PLANNING

Unlike many trails on Oahu, hiking in the rain isn't much of a problem here; waterfalls are likely to be at their best. Carry water as any available freshwater must be filtered or chemically treated before drinking. Pack swimwear and a towel if you plan to take a dip at the falls.

Maps

The USGS 1:24,000 maps *Honolulu* and *Koko Head* cover the entire area, but don't show the trails. The free, photocopied *Koolaupoko Trail Complex* handout has a more recent, but not entirely accurate topographic map and brief trail notes. It's available from the DLNR's permit office in downtown Honolulu.

NEAREST TOWNS & FACILITIES

See Honolulu (p62).

Waimanalo

Waimanalo Bay boasts the longest contiguous beach on Oahu, with over 5 miles of white sand stretching from Makapu'u Point. Although the area isn't highly regarded for safety, Waimanalo has a few county beach parks with camping facilities, rest rooms, showers and drinking water. Set a third of a mile inland from the Kalanianaole Hwy, **Waimanalo Bay Beach Park** has campsites shaded by ironwood trees. The long beach

fronting **Bellows Air Force Base** has fine sand and a natural setting backed by ironwood trees; the marked entrance is a ¼ mile north of Waimanalo Bay Beach Park, and from there it's about 1½ miles to the beach. For camping permits, see Permits & Fees (p34).

Waimanalo Town Center Shopping Plaza *(41-1537 Kalanianaole Hwy)*, at the main crossroads, has some convenience marts, fast-food eateries and casual Hawaiian restaurants. **Keneke's BBQ** *(☎ 259-5266; 41-857 Kalanianaole Hwy; snacks and meals $3-7; open daily)*, a local soul-food eatery with $5 plate lunches, is just north of Waimanalo Beach Park, near the post office.

Getting There & Away From the Ala Moana Center, take eastbound bus No 57 (Kailua Waimanalo/Sea Life Park), which stops at Waimanalo Town Center and all of the beach park entrances ($1.50, around one hour, at least hourly).

GETTING TO/FROM THE HIKE

The Maunawili Demonstration Trail starts just outside town. From Waimanalo Town Center, walk north for ½ mile along the Kalanianaole Hwy (Hwy 72). Turn inland onto Kumuhau St and walk 1 mile to the end of the road, then turn right onto Waikupanaha Rd. About ¼ mile along this road, keep an eye out for a break in the fence at a gravel pull-out and the familiar Na Ala Hele trailhead sign.

From the Maunawili Falls trailhead at the end of this hike, turn right and follow Maunawili Rd as it curves around for about 1½ miles to the Pali Hwy (Hwy 61). Walk east to the Kailua Rd intersection near Castle Medical Center. Stand on the north side of the highway to catch bus No 57 for Honolulu Ala Moana ($1.50, 40 minutes). Otherwise, stand on the south side of the highway for bus No 57 (Kailua Waimanalo/Sea Life Park) back to Waimanalo ($1.50, 25 minutes).

THE HIKE (see map p80)

From the Na Ala Hele trailhead sign on Waikupanaha Rd, walk up over the pipes and onto an old 4WD road. Keep going past the Maunawili Ditch Trail turn-off, staying

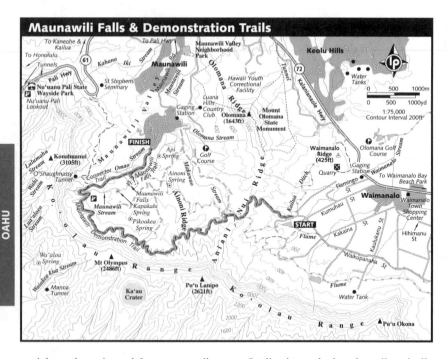

Maunawili Falls & Demonstration Trails

straight on the main road. Ignore any trails-of-use to the left. After about ½ mile, the road narrows to a footpath, pushing through koa and ohia trees, stands of bamboo, ti plants, ferns and guava. Although muddy, the path remains comfortably wide as it switchbacks up and gains ever-better views over Waimanalo Valley and ahead, the *pali*. At a signed junction around the 1-mile mark, the Demonstration Trail continues uphill to the left.

The footpath grows even more narrow as it sidles around the ridge. Power lines that come into view don't detract much from the gloriously wide vistas or the melodious chatter of native birds. Continue straight across the next four-way intersection (don't take the muddy 'steps' on the left.) The trail soon crosses its first stream gulch, ambling by ti plants and *niu* (coconut) palms before passing a striking number of waterfall cascades dropping into fern-covered pools over mossy rocks.

Settling into a rhythm, the trail gradually ascends by working in and out of gulches set beneath the misty *pali*, each time heading back out to the edge of the cliffs for unique vantage points over the Maunawili Valley and coast. Ironwood trees, banana plants and *kukui* nuts can be seen, and perhaps a stray mongoose. Look for an upright brown post marked 'Mile 4.5' on the *makai* side of the trail. Scuffle marks from pig activity and grooves worn by mountain bikers are all telltale signs of deteriorating trail conditions after this point. Expect lots of mud.

Trail markers appear almost every ½ mile, counting backwards to the trail's opposite end on the Pali Hwy. Around where the 2½-mile marker should be, an exceptional view opens up across the valley and its experimental agricultural complex out to sea. Then the trail switchbacks left, rising moderately with mountain apples underfoot and eucalyptus trees all around. Although slippery, the trail benefits from a boardwalk or two later. Ethereal waterfalls stream down the *pali* now towering overhead. Ferns start to creep in from all sides near the junction with the Maunawili Falls connector trail.

For the best views of the *pali,* walk another 10 minutes down the Demonstration Trail before turning around. Back at the junction, turn downhill and towards the ocean onto the steep connector trail, which has some artificial steps for support. After descending quickly through ferns and mossy trees, it enters ironwood forest and dries out. Just beyond the end of the connector, turn right to get to Maunawili Falls via a steep stairway down to the streambed. Skip over rocks up the true-left bank of the stream (don't ford it) and pick up the trail further on as it goes over a few small boulders to reach the falls. The falls are pretty enough to merit a detour, even without swimming in the pool below.

Walk back alongside the stream and up the staircase to the trail junction. Turn right onto the official Maunawili Falls Trail, a gentle but extremely muddy, insect-laden route that descends and makes three minor stream crossings on its way out of the forest. Follow the 1-mile trail all the way back to Maunawili Rd, looking for coffee trees along the way.

Waimano Trail

Duration	7–8 hours
Distance	14.5 miles (23.3km)
Difficulty	demanding
Start/Finish	end Waimano Home Rd
Nearest Town	Honolulu (p62)
Transport	private

Summary Go boulder hopping, bushwhacking, stream crossing and ridge scaling, all in pursuit of an elusive Ko'olau summit for astounding ocean views over knife-edged *pali.*

Most of the trails atop the Ko'olau Range were constructed by the Civilian Conservation Corps in the 1930s. Many have fallen into disrepair or are no longer open to the public, but a blessed exception is the challenging Waimano Trail (another is the Manana Trail, p83). Depending on when the Waimano was last maintained, it may or may not be possible to reach the end of the trail at a Ko'olau summit. But it's worth making the attempt, both for the solitude and the spectacular views, plus a chance to see relatively untouched native Hawaiian forest along the way.

PLANNING

Be forewarned that this trail is only irregularly maintained. Some narrow, overgrown sections of the hike can hide hazardous drop-offs and unstable soil. If the trail becomes too risky, turn around. It may be worth contacting the **Hawaiian Trail and Mountain Club** *(HTMC;* Ⓦ *www.geocities.com/ yosemite/trails/3660/; PO Box 2238, Honolulu, HI 96804)* to check when the final part of the route was last cleared or join a guided hike. Wear lightweight pants to guard against scratchy *uluhe* ferns and thorny plants along the way. Hiking poles or a walking stick may help with balancing on precariously narrow stretches of trail. Bring lots of water, as any available freshwater must be filtered or chemically treated before drinking. Keep an eye out for hunting activity. At times the trail may be deserted, so it's best not to hike alone.

Maps

The USGS 1:24,000 maps *Waipahu* and *Kaneohe* cover the trail. The free, photocopied *Manana-Waimano Area* handout has an up-to-date topographic map and brief trail notes. It's available from the DLNR's permit office in downtown Honolulu.

GETTING TO/FROM THE HIKE

From Ala Moana Center the No 53 Pacific Palisades bus travels up Waimano Home Rd only as far as the Koko Mai Drive intersection ($1.50, 45 minutes, at least hourly). From there it's a 2-mile walk uphill on Waimano Home Rd to the trailhead.

Considering the demanding length of the hike itself, driving is the only realistic option. Drivers coming from Honolulu should take westbound H1 to exit 10, staying right

OAHU

on Moanalua Rd. At the stoplight, turn right onto Waimano Home Rd and follow it up past Waimano Training School to the end of the public access road. Park in a dirt pull-out opposite the security gatehouse.

THE HIKE

Near the Na Ala Hele trailhead sign is a hunter/hiker check station with a mailbox containing handwritten log sheets. After signing in, start walking on an extremely narrow footpath that follows alongside a chain-link fence. At the first junction keep right on the Upper Waimano Trail, which later runs away from the fence and joins the forest. Step over the run-off canal as the trail wanders through swamp mahogany, ferns and strawberry guava.

Walk straight over an eroded hump with excellent valley views, ignoring a trail-of-use to the right. From this point the trail gets wetter before arriving at an abandoned irrigation ditch, once used to feed sugar cane fields in the valley below. The ditch soon flows through a tunnel, which hikers pass around via a rock face on the left side and continue to the next junction with the Lower Waimano Trail, which heads off to the left.

Stay straight along the ditch and detour around another two tunnels, each bypass getting a bit dicier. Some ropes are tied around tree trunks to help hikers navigate over jumbled boulders, but test them before trusting them with your full weight.

Hiking alongside the increasingly overgrown ditch, shaded by *kukui* and *hau* trees, look for lush valleys spreading out in most directions. Watch also for a small trail sign that points left and across a streambed. On the opposite side, turn sharply right to pick up the trail again, moving away from the stream and up moderately steep switchbacks to a picnic table shelter. Keep going straight out to the edge of Waimano Valley, then turn right onto the trail downhill.

By now the trail has narrowed to a muddy single-track and is probably somewhat overgrown as it descends to a confluence of boulder-strewn streams, which may be dry. Cross the first streambed, heading slightly up and to the right, then veer left across the second streambed and look for a yellow-arrowed trail sign pointing up through *hau* thickets. Rejoin the trail and begin a moderate ascent, being careful of steep dropoffs obscured by vegetation.

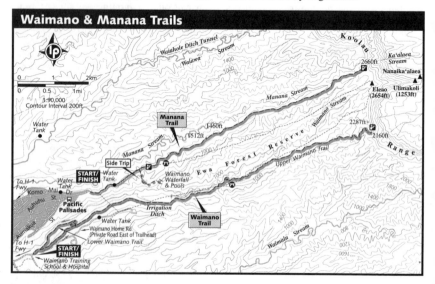

Soon the trail ascends on boggy, fern-covered and narrow switchbacks, then exits the shade and rises past a few lonely palm trees as it contours alongside the ridge. Behind remain views of the streams and Waimano Valley. Look for a sunken white pipe labeled '5' on the right side of the trail, at about two hours from the trail start. This is the 5-mile marker. The trail keeps ascending, eventually passing under ohia trees, scratchy *uluhe* ferns and some buzzing bees.

Another white pole marked '6' signals there's just over a mile left. After making a little switchback turn, the trail passes over to the exposed side of the ridge. Views improve, but don't let them distract from carefully watching every footfall, as eroded sections and camouflaged drop-offs are serious hazards. At one point, the trail jumps a deep, narrow ravine. Mountain *naupaka* (flowering, beach plant), scented ohia lehua and white-flowering *kopiko* trees, which are members of the coffee family, escort hikers on the final push up to a windy **summit** (2160ft) on the Ko'olau Range, with breathtaking views over valleys and cliffs to the Windward Coast. The trail officially ends here, and hiking beyond the viewpoint is foolhardy. On the way back to Waimano Home Rd, you could detour near the end of the route along the Lower Waimano Trail loop for a little variety.

Manana Trail

Duration	5–7 hours
Distance	12 miles (19.3km)
Difficulty	demanding
Start/Finish	end Koko Mai Dr
Nearest Town	Honolulu (p62)
Transport	bus

Summary Yet another way to reach a summit of the Ko'olau Range, blessed by sunshine and broad valley- and ocean-vistas en route, plus a chance to scramble down 'Heart Attack Hill' to Waimano Waterfall.

Both the rugged Manana and Waimano (p81) Trails climb to spectacular viewpoints atop the Ko'olau Range, but there the similarities end. The more challenging Manana Trail traces the ridge line that goes between Manana and Waimano Valleys, taking an adventurous journey over numerous exposed saddles and knobs, as opposed to the comparatively steady and shaded ascent of the Waimano Trail. If summiting is your goal, take the Waimano Trail. But even if it's not possible to go beyond the first couple of miles of the Manana Trail, for natural beauty this trip can't be beat and a dip into waterfall pools only sweetens the prospect.

PLANNING
See Planning (p81) for the Waimano Trail.

Maps
The USGS 1:24,000 maps *Waipahu* and *Kaneohe* cover the trail. The free, photocopied *Manana-Waimano Area* handout has an up-to-date topographic map and brief trail notes. It's available from the DLNR's permit office in downtown Honolulu.

GETTING TO/FROM THE HIKE
From the Ala Moana Center, the No 53 Pacific Palisades bus travels up Koko Mai Dr to the Auhuhu St intersection ($1.50, one hour, at least hourly). It's a ½-mile walk to the trailhead at the end of Koko Mai Dr.

Drivers coming from Honolulu should take the H1 westbound to exit 10, veering right onto Moanalua Rd. At the stoplight, turn right onto Waimano Home Rd. Drive uphill and hang a left onto Koko Mai Dr.

THE HIKE (see map p82)
From the Na Ala Hele trailhead sign, start walking uphill on a wide forest path lined with eucalyptus and guava. After about ½ mile, the trail passes a water tank and two sets of power lines cross overhead before it reaches a power installation. Ignore any trails-of-use made by hunters and keep to the main path, which curves left and starts descending over tree roots. A signed junction with the trail to Waimano Waterfall (see Side Trip: Waimano Waterfall, p84) appears after approximately 1 mile.

Veer left on the trail to the Ko'olau summit, which, despite what the sign says, is

OAHU

actually about 5 miles away. Listen for native bird song as the trail rises and falls through forest to where artificial steps lead down over an extremely bare and exposed area still in the stages of recovering from a massive fire that swept through here decades ago. The colors of the soil are fascinating. Stop in the middle of this devastated stretch for great views of the Ko'olau Range and lush *makai* valleys.

Contouring around the ridge, the trail breezes through a hilltop meadow and passes a 1½-mile marker shortly before the **picnic table shelter**, which has even better views than before. Be sure to rest here before pushing onward since the trail gets more challenging quickly. Past the 2-mile marker, scratchy native vegetation already threatens to choke the trail.

After another ½ mile, the trail's repeating pattern becomes clear. From this point onward it crosses a long series of dry saddles and wet, muddy knobs, alternating through eroded sections of loose scree (sometimes with ropes tied to trees) and thickly overgrown switchbacks that are completely mined with tree roots and loose soil, all of which could result in an unlucky tumble over the side of the ridge, so be careful.

During the struggle toward the Ko'olau summit, occasionally look behind for views of Pearl Harbor. Keep an eye out for *elepaio* (a native flycatcher) and *apapane* birds darting about. Walk carefully, as the trail drops off steeply in the summit area. The trail ends on top of the Ko'olau Range at a **lookout** (2660ft) with grand views of Honolulu, over southeast Oahu down to Makapu'u Point and around Kaneohe Bay on the Windward Coast. Be prepared for strong winds here.

Side Trip: Waimano Waterfall
1 hour, 1½mi (2.4km)
Some locals take the Manana Trail just to go swimming at this waterfall. As a side trip after hiking the main route, it makes an excellent diversion, especially for those who couldn't reach the Ko'olau summit. Since this is not an officially maintained trail, it won't appear on maps and hikers should exercise caution, especially during hunting season. Flash floods are possible, but in summer the pools may be dry.

The waterfall trail starts from the signed junction about 1 mile inland from the Manana Trail start. It's soon obvious why folks have nicknamed this hike 'Heart Attack Hill' as it zooms down over tree roots, the grade becoming steeper with every step. There are some strawberry-guava tree trunks to hold onto, and there may be ropes to assist hikers over the worst bits. Although the path is vague, just keep heading left and stay atop the ridge until reaching some ohia trees at a clear fork in the trail. Veer right down to the streambed to meet the lower pool. Turn left and walk further upstream to reach the main pool and waterfall.

Hau'ula Loop

Duration	1 hour
Distance	2.5 miles (4km)
Difficulty	easy
Start/Finish	Hau'ula Homesteads Rd
Nearest Towns	Hau'ula (p85), Laie (p85)
Transport	bus

Summary A quick stroll with ocean vistas, gently rolling over streambeds and valley ridges, with a chance to see a variety of rare native forest species.

The Division of Forestry & Wildlife maintains two trails in the forest reserve above Hau'ula. Both trails share the same access point and head into beautiful hills in the lower Ko'olau Range. The Hau'ula Loop, which clambers through Waipilopilo Gulch and onto a ridge over Kaipapa'u Valley, is not only better maintained but more rewarding, both for its views and the rainbow of native flora along the way. It's a popular path with locals and families.

PLANNING
Maps
The USGS 1:24,000 map *Hau'ula* covers the area. The free, photocopied *Hauula Trail System* handout has an up-to-date topographic map and brief trail notes. It's

available from the DLNR's permit office in downtown Honolulu.

NEAREST TOWNS & FACILITIES

Hau'ula

This is a small coastal town set against a scenic backdrop of hills and majestic Norfolk pines. Although unappealing for swimming, the **county beach park** allows camping. For camping permits and information, see Permits & Fees (p34). **Zoe's** (☎ 232-0095; *Hau'ula Kai Shopping Center, 54-316 Kamehameha Hwy; sandwiches & burgers $3-8; open 11am-9pm Tues-Sun*), about ½ mile north of the beach park, makes remarkably fresh falafel pita wraps and smoothies. Hau'ula also has a **convenience store**.

Getting There & Away From the Ala Moana Center take the No 55 Kaneohe Circle Isle bus to Hau'ula ($1.50, 1½ hours, once or twice hourly). Take the No 55 Honolulu Ala Moana bus in the opposite direction on the return trip.

Laie

Outside the Polynesian Cultural Center, **Laie Inn** (☎ 293-9282, 800-526-4562; W *www.laieinn.com; 55-109 Laniloa St; doubles $84-99*) is a two-story motel with a courtyard swimming pool. Each room has a *lanai* (veranda), cable TV, air-con and refrigerator. Rates include continental breakfast. About ½ mile further north, **Laie Shopping Center** (*55-510 Kamehameha Hwy*) has a Foodland grocery store and an Ace Hardware for camping supplies.

Getting There & Away From the Ala Moana Center the No 55 Kaneohe Circle Isle bus via Hau'ula stops in Laie at the Polynesian Cultural Center ($1.50, 1 hour 35 minutes, once or twice hourly).

Malaekahana State Recreation Area

This recreation area has the best campgrounds at this end of the Windward Coast. **Kalanai Point**, the main section of the state park, is less than 1 mile north of Laie and has picnic tables, barbecue grills, rest rooms

A Place of Refuge

Laie is thought to have been the site of an ancient *pu'uhonua* – a place where *kapu* (taboo) breakers could escape being put to death. Today, Laie is the center of the Mormon community in Hawaii.

The first Mormon missionaries to Hawaii arrived in 1850. After an attempt to establish a Hawaiian 'City of Joseph' on the island of Lanai failed amidst a land scandal, the Mormons moved to Laie. In 1865 they purchased thousands of acres in the area and slowly expanded their influence.

In 1919 the Mormons constructed a smaller version of their Salt Lake City (Utah) temple here at the foot of the Ko'olau Range. This stately temple, reached at the end of a wide promenade, appears like nothing else on the Windward Coast.

❀ ❀ ❀ ❀ ❀ ❀ ❀ ❀ ❀ ❀ ❀ ❀ ❀

and showers. Camping is allowed between 8am Friday and 8am Monday. Sites cost $5 per night and permits are issued at the DLNR office in downtown Honolulu. You can also rent a rustic cabin or enjoy camping with outdoor hot showers at **Makahoa Point**, which has a separate entrance off Kamehameha Hwy, ¾ mile further north. Gates are locked to private vehicles after 6:45pm. You can just contact **Friends of Malaekahana** (☎ 293-1736, fax 293-2066; *tent sites per person $5, four-person cabins Mon-Thur/Fri-Sun $55/66, eight-person cabins $66/80; office hours 10am-4pm Mon-Fri*) for reservations.

Getting There & Away From the Ala Moana Center, the No 55 Kaneohe Circle Isle bus stops outside both park entrances ($1.50, 1 hour 40 minutes, once or twice hourly).

GETTING TO/FROM THE HIKE

The signposted trailhead is at a bend in Hau'ula Homestead Rd, about ¼ mile up from Hau'ula County Beach Park and the Kamehameha Hwy (Hwy 83), where the bus stops.

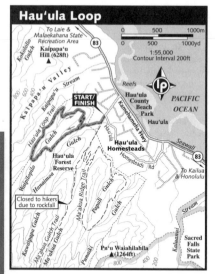

Hau'ula Loop

To Laie &
Malaekahana State
Recreation Area
Kokololio Gulch
Kaipapa'u Hill (628ft)
Kaipapa'u Valley
Kaipapa'u Stream
Hau'ula Loop Trail
Gulch
START/FINISH
Reefs
Hau'ula County Beach Park
Hau'ula
Kamehameha Hwy
PACIFIC OCEAN
Seawall
Hau'ula Homesteads
Homesteads Rd
To Kailua & Honolulu
Hau'ula Forest Reserve
Closed to hikers due to rockfall
Ma'akua Ridge Trail
Waipilopilo Gulch
Hanaimoa
Papali Gulch
Gulch
Kawaipapa Gulch
Ma'akua Gulch Trail
Ma'akua Gulch
Panaili
Pu'u Waiahilahila (1264ft)
Kaluanui Stream
Sacred Falls State Park

0   500   1000m
0   500   1000yd
1:55,000
Contour Interval 200ft

THE HIKE

Follow the paved access road inland, past a hunter/hiker check-in station. The Hau'ula Loop trail forks off to the right immediately after the road enters the forest reserve, rising quickly through native ohia, *hala* (screw pine) and palms, as well as sweet-smelling guava and bizarre octopus trees, with their spreading tentacle-like branches of pink to reddish flowers. Birds fly about and ocean vistas open up as the trail climbs through ironwood trees, then splits into a loop around the ½-mile point.

By going left, the trail remains easier to follow and more clearly laid out. Under ironwoods and towering Norfolk pines, the trail switchbacks up and over a ridge into Waipilopilo Gulch, passing rare endemic flora such as *a'ali'i* plants with red seed pods, *akia* shrubs and *lama* (Hawaiian persimmon). Ocean breezes and forest shade are a relief from the humidity. The trail crosses a streambed and muddily climbs out of the gulch to empty out atop of another ridge with fine overlooks of Kaipapa'u Valley.

Instead of heading uphill left on a hunting trail-of-use, turn right. As the footpath rolls up and down along the ridge, there are even more spectacular views into the valley. Eventually the trail descends back into ironwood trees, Norfolk pines and Hawaiian ferns, all displaying an infinite number of shades of green. The trail crosses a streambed, then ascends again and levels out into a wide forest path with views of Hau'ula town, ocean beaches and off-shore islets. Even the roar of the surf reaches up here. Contouring around the ridge, which drops off steeply, tree roots emerge underfoot as the trail starts descending. Keep a sharp eye out for any obscure turnings in the switchbacks. Turn left at the loop trail junction to reach the trailhead and the paved road.

Kaunala Loop

Duration	2 hours
Distance	4.5 miles (7.2km)
Difficulty	easy
Start/Finish	end Pupukea Rd
Nearest Towns	Haleiwa (p87), Waimea (p87)
Transport	private

Summary Mix an easy, peaceful valley walk with a moderate ridge climb for sweeping views of the North Shore out to Kaena Point and the Waianae Range.

This little-known trail sits quietly above Waimea Valley. In ancient Hawaii, the lowlands were terraced in taro, the valley walls dotted with house sites and the ridges topped with *heiau*. Just about every crop thrived in the valley, including a rare pink taro favored by Hawaiian royalty. When Captain Cook's ships sailed into Waimea Bay to collect water in 1779, an entry in the ship's log noted that the valley was uncommonly picturesque. However, Western contact wasn't kind to the area. Deforestation above the valley, from logging and the introduction of plantations, contributed to a devastating flood in 1894. After the flood, most residents abandoned the valley. Waimea has a beautiful, deeply inset bay with turquoise waters and a wide white-sand beach. Ancient Hawaiians believed its waters were

OAHU

sacred, and after seeing the bay from viewpoints high atop this trail, it'd be hard not to agree.

PLANNING

This trail is officially open to the public only on weekends and state holidays. Hunting is allowed, so hikers should wear bright colors and not go wandering off-trail. Bring water, as none is available at the trailhead or anywhere along the trail.

Maps

The free, photocopied *Pupukea Area* handout has an up-to-date topographic map and brief trail notes. It's available from the DLNR's permit office in downtown Honolulu.

NEAREST TOWNS
Haleiwa

This is the southern gateway to the North Shore and the main town. The townspeople are a mix of families who have lived here for generations and more recently arrived surfers, artists and New-Age folk.

Supplies & Equipment Haleiwa caters to the multitude of day-trippers who make the circle-island ride.

In the Haleiwa Shopping Plaza, **Haleiwa IGA Super Market** (66-197 Kamehameha Ave; open 8am-8pm Mon-Sat, 8:30am-5:30pm Sun) is the place for general grocery items, while **Celestial Natural Foods** (66-443 Kamehameha Ave; open 9am-6:30pm Mon-Sat,

Surf & Cultural Museum

You can get a sense of how integral surfing is to the town's character by visiting the **North Shore Surf & Cultural Museum** (☎ 637-8888; W www.surfmuseum.net; 66-250 Kamehameha Ave, Haleiwa; admission by donation; open most afternoons), in the North Shore Marketplace, which has a collection of vintage surfboards, period photos and surf videos. It's run by volunteers, so the hours are flexible. When the surf's up, expect the place to be padlocked!

10am-6pm Sun) carries a good variety of health foods and also has a vegetarian deli. **Fujioka's Market** (66-190 Kamehameha Hwy; open 10am-8pm daily) has fresh seafood and beer, while a few trucks outside in the parking lot next door to **Waiola Bakery** sell hot *malasadas* (Portuguese fried dough served warm, similar to a doughnut), smoked fish and wild boar. Pick up camping supplies at **Ace Hardware** (66-134 Kamehameha Hwy; open 9:30am-5:30pm daily).

Places to Stay & Eat About 1 mile west of town, county-run **Kaiaka Bay Beach Park** has shady ironwood trees, rest rooms, picnic tables and showers as well as campsites. For camping permits and information, see Permits & Fees (p34).

Surfhouse Hawaii (☎ 637-7146; W www .surfhouse.com; 62-203 Lokoea Place; tent sites for 1 person/2 people $9/15, dorm beds $15, single/double bungalows $40/45), north of Rainbow Bridge, is within walking distance of the town center. The owner speaks French.

Kua Aina (66-214 Kamehameha Ave; sandwiches $4-7; open 11am-8pm daily) grills up the North Shore's reputedly best burgers and fish sandwiches. **Cholo's Homestyle Mexican** (☎ 637-3059; 66-250 Kamehameha Ave; meals $7-11; open 8am-9pm daily), in the North Shore Marketplace, serves particularly hearty portions of super-fresh Mexican food. Don't miss lining up for extraordinary shave ice at **Matsumoto's** (66-087 Kamehameha Ave; 8:30am-6pm daily) tin-roofed general store.

Getting There & Away From Ala Moana Center, take the No 52 Wahiawa Circle Isle bus to Haleiwa ($1.50, 1½ hours, every 30 minutes).

Waimea

There's no town here per se, just beach accommodations and a few scattered places to pick up basic supplies. **Foodland** (☎ 638-8081; 59-720 Kamehameha Hwy; open 6am-10pm daily), opposite Pupukea Beach Park, has the best grocery selection on the North Shore.

OAHU

OAHU

Places to Stay Pretty much a surfers hangout, **Backpackers** (☎ 638-7838, fax 638-7515; W *www.backpackers-hawaii.com; 59-788 Kamehameha Hwy; dorm beds $17-20, semiprivate doubles $45-65, doubles with shared bath $80-115, 4- to 8-person cabins $110-200)* offers free scheduled pickups from the Honolulu airport and Waikiki. A durable place that's been in business for years, it has a few different setups, mostly beach-house casual.

Ke Iki Beach Bungalows (☎ 638-8229, 866-638-8229; W *www.keikibeach.com; 59-579 Ke Iki Rd; double garden-view/triple beachside apartments from $65/130)* fronts a beautiful white-sand beach just north of Pupukea Beach Park. Each apartment has a kitchen, TV and phone, and guests have access to a barbecue and hammocks strung between coconut trees. The location is a real gem.

Ulu Wehi B&B (☎/fax 638-8161; W *www.uluwehi.com; 59-416 Alapio Rd; double studios $85)* is 1½ miles up the hill from Pupukea Beach Park. Breakfast includes tropical fruit from the gardens and homemade baked goods. The house has a lovely 75ft lap pool in the backyard and a poolside barbecue. The toilet and open-air shower are in a rustic bathhouse in the rear garden. French is spoken.

Getting There & Away From Ala Moana Center take the No 52 Wahiawa Circle Isle bus to Waimea ($1.50, 1¾ hours, every 30 minutes). A 5-mile bicycle lane connects Haleiwa and Waimea.

GETTING TO/FROM THE HIKE
To get to the trailhead, turn up Pupukea Rd at the Foodland supermarket. Continue past Pu'u O Mahuka Heiau state monument to the end of the road, about 2½ miles from the Kamehameha Hwy (Hwy 83).

THE HIKE
Walk past Pupukea Boy Scout Camp down a dirt road and hop over a gate by the Na Ala Hele trailhead sign. Framed by eucalyptus, koa, *kukui* and then ironwood trees, the main road passes under power lines; ignore any private access roads on the right-hand side. Descending gradually, look for where a footpath leaves the main road on the left, at a Na Ala Hele sign. Take this footpath, veering left at the first fork onto a forest path layered with leaves. The trail becomes a grassy single

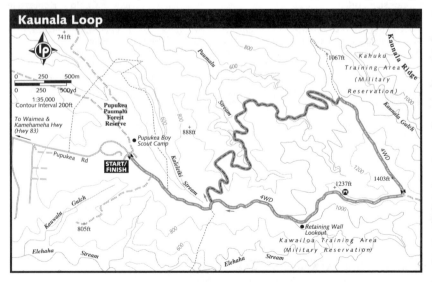

track lined by Philippine orchids, contouring over tree roots.

It's windy and soon the ocean comes into view far off to the left. Around the 1-mile point, look carefully for a smaller trail that takes off to the left. Follow this trail downhill as it slips over some mud and descends into a gully. It then switchbacks further down through ferns, ti plants and exotic Java plum trees, the fruit of which resembles a boysenberry-raspberry hybrid, with butterflies keeping company. Keep going in roughly the same direction past the next junction, the trail continuing to switchback moderately down over tree roots and allowing glimpses of different valleys. Again, do not veer off onto trails-of-use.

Eventually the trail crosses a few streambed gullies that may be dry before ascending back up the ridge. A meadow of native ferns spreads out below, but the ocean is not quite visible yet. Amongst ti plants, the trail works its way up and down, going in and out of more gullies. After about an hour of hiking, the footpath shows soft, crumbly switchbacks so narrow it feels like walking on a balance beam. After a quick nip back into forest, the trail makes one more sharp switchback to the left and then empties onto the dirt 4WD road.

Start climbing on the exposed, eroded jeep road by turning right. All along this road are beautiful ocean views. The road, pocked with huge craters and rocks, repeatedly ascends steeply and then levels out. Norfolk pine stand alongside the road like sentries. At its highest point (1403ft), hikers are rewarded with amazing views of the Waianae Range, and the North Shore surf and blowholes.

Veering right now, the road tumbles steeply downhill through a yellow gate. At a T-intersection with another 4WD road, turn right 90° and begin a gentle descent through koa and ohia, passing a picnic table shelter with wind blowing softly through the ironwood trees. As the road runs up, down and around, it passes lookouts over the coast. Be sure to stop at a wooden retaining wall on the *makai* side to see remote Kaena Point out to the west, then continue straight down the road, all the way back to the trailhead.

Kaena Point

Duration	3½–4 hours
Distance	9.5 miles (15.3km)
Difficulty	easy–moderate
Start/Finish	end Farrington Hwy (Hwy 930)
Nearest Towns	Haleiwa (p87), Waimea (p87)
Transport	private

Summary Ease onto a level shoreline hike around Oahu's northwestern tip, visiting a seabird sanctuary, coastal sand dunes, lighthouse and lava blowholes, all set beneath dramatic *pali*.

OAHU

Kaena Point State Park is an undeveloped 778-acre coastal strip that runs mainly along the south side of Kaena Point, the westernmost point of Oahu. Until the mid-1940s the Oahu Railroad ran up here from Honolulu and continued around the point on Haleiwa on the North Shore. On the south side of the point, Yokohama Bay, with its attractive 1-mile-long sandy beach, was named for the large number of Japanese fishers who came here during the railroad days.

In addition to being part of a state park, Kaena Point has been designated a natural area reserve because of its unique ecosystem. The extensive dry, windswept coastal dunes that rise above the point are the habitat of many rare native plants. The endangered *Kaena akoko* (pale-green leafed plant), which grows on the talus slopes, is found nowhere else. Seabirds seen at Kaena Point include shearwaters, boobies and the common noddy – a dark-brown bird with a grayish crown. The coastal sand dunes are once again a nesting site for the rare Laysan albatross, which can be seen in winter and spring. Spinner dolphins can often be seen off-shore, and in winter humpback whale sightings are not unusual.

PLANNING

Do not hike the southern part of this hike during high surf. Since the hike is unshaded (Kaena means 'the heat'), bring plenty of water, sunscreen as well as wrap-around

The End of the World

Early Hawaiians believed that when people went into a deep sleep or lost consciousness, their souls would wander. Souls that wandered too far were drawn west to Kaena Point. If they were lucky, they were met here by their *aumakua* (ancestral spirit helper), who led their souls back to their bodies. If unattended, their souls would be forced to leap from Kaena Point into the endless night, never to return.

❀ ❀ ❀ ❀ ❀ ❀ ❀ ❀ ❀ ❀ ❀ ❀ ❀

sunglasses. Binoculars are handy for birdwatching and spotting whales in winter. This hike could just as easily be done in the reverse direction, but nearby visitor facilities on the Waianae Coast aren't as good as on the North Shore. Be aware that mountain bikers share the trail with hikers, as do some ATVs and motorbikes. Weekdays tend to be quieter.

Maps

The USGS 1:24,000 map *Kaena* covers the trails and all 4WD roads around Kaena Point, but isn't really necessary for hiking the main trail.

NEAREST TOWNS & FACILITIES

See Haleiwa (p87) and Waimea (p87).

Mokuleia Beach Park Campground

Mokuleia Beach Park, opposite Dillingham Airfield, has a large, open, grassy area with picnic tables, rest rooms and showers. Camping is allowed with a county camping permit (see Permits & Fees, p34).

Getting There & Away There is no bus service, but bicycles and scooters can be rented in Haleiwa. Whether cycling or driving, head south to Waialua and take the Farrington Hwy (Hwy 930) west for about 7 miles to the beach park.

GETTING TO/FROM THE HIKE

There is no bus service out to Kaena Point, but bicycles and scooters can be rented in Haleiwa. Heading west from Waialua, take the Farrington Hwy (Hwy 930) past Mokuleia Beach Park and Dillingham Airfield to the end of the paved road. Park in any of the gravel pull-outs next to the ocean.

THE HIKE

From where the paved Farrington Hwy ends, start walking along the coast on a dirt 4WD road below fern-covered *pali*. On some days strong winds can knock off hats and whip the sand up into small storms; just making headway can be problematic. Otherwise, the level, graded road is an easy walk. A couple of gates block vehicular traffic, but hikers pass through them on the left side. Ignore any spur roads or trails that head *mauka* toward the cliffs. Although it's possible to detour closer to the shore on trails-of-use in the dunes instead of staying on the main road, be cautious of high surf and roads.

Telephone poles start off on the left side of the road, which is lined by boulders and eventually passes over a mossy gulch. Soon the Kaena Point Satellite Tracking Station comes into view atop the cliffs, and this is where the telephone poles leave off. Keep walking straight ahead on the main road. Common plants are the beach *naupaka,* with white flowers that look like they've been torn in half; *pau-o-Hi'iaka,* a vine with blue flowers; beach morning glory, sometimes found wrapped in the parasite plant *kaunaoa,* which looks like orange plastic fishing line; and spiky sisal plants growing wild.

Another locked vehicle gate comes in at about the 2-mile point as the road draws ever nearer to the coast and sand dunes. Where the trail splits, stay on the lower right-hand path and head for the **lighthouse beacon** set on concrete pilings. On clear days, Kauai can be seen from the point. According to legend, it was at Kaena Point that the demigod Maui attempted to cast a huge hook into Kauai and pull it next to Oahu to join the two islands. But the line broke and Kauai slipped away, with just a small piece of it remaining near Oahu. Today, this splintered rock, off the end of Kaena Point, is known as Pohaku o Kauai.

From the lighthouse, head back through the dunes toward the cliffs, veering right to

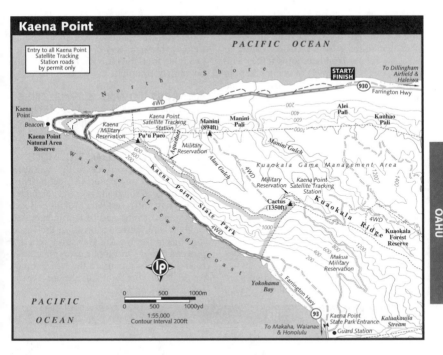

walk southeast along the Waianae Coast. Lava blowholes spout in the crashing surf and ocean spray blows over the trail, which continues over some old railroad ties and beside tide pools, sea arches and jet-black fingers of *a'a* (rough, jagged lava) that stretch out into foamy waters. Keep an eye on the ocean for rogue waves.

Shortly the trail, which follows a former road, reaches a washed-out section that requires some careful picking down and over rocks with a rope to aid hikers. After a large sea arch appears, the trail may see some passing jeep traffic and up ahead are the white installations of the tracking station. In another mile or so, the trail ends at Kaena Point State Park Beach. There are rest rooms (no potable water) near the state park's southern entrance.

When ready, hike back toward Kaena Point. At about the same time the lighthouse beacon comes into view, veer right at the fork in the road. Hiking inland closer to the

cliffs shaves some distance from the return leg of this route along the North Shore.

Kealia Trail

Duration	3 hours
Distance	5 miles (8km)
Difficulty	moderate
Start/Finish	Dillingham Airfield
Nearest Towns	Haleiwa (p87), Waimea (p87)
Transport	private

Summary Ride breathtaking switchbacks up the sea cliffs over the North Shore and, after a stiff ascent on a 4WD road, emerge at a spectacular overlook on the nearby Kuaokala Trail.

Originally built by the Civilian Conservation Corps in the 1930s, the Kealia Trail ascends from Dillingham Airfield on over a mile of cliff-face switchbacks above Kaena Point. Although the segment of dirt 4WD road that follows isn't very interesting to hike, the Kealai Trail later joins forces with the Kuaokala Trail (p93) to bring hikers to a justly celebrated viewpoint over Makua Valley and the high Waianae Range.

PLANNING

This trail is best for those wishing to avoid the hassle of securing a permit and driving around the Waianae Coast just to hike the Kuaokala Trail. After heavy rains, the dirt 4WD road sections can become slippery. Hiking poles or a walking stick will help ease steep grades. Carry a lot of water, as none is available along this hot, dusty route. Note the gates to Dillingham Airfield are only open from 7am to 6pm daily.

Maps

The USGS 1:24,000 map *Kaena* covers the trail and some 4WD roads, but not always accurately. The free, photocopied *Kuaokala-Mokuleia Area* handout has an up-to-date topographic map and brief trail notes. It's available from the DLNR's permit office in downtown Honolulu.

NEAREST TOWNS & FACILITIES

See Haleiwa (p87) and Waimea (p87). Mokuleia Beach Park Campground (p90) is closest to the trailhead.

GETTING TO/FROM THE HIKE

There is no bus service to the trailhead. Whether you are driving or cycling from Haleiwa, head south and take the Farrington Hwy (Hwy 930) west past Mokuleia Beach Park almost to the end of Dillingham Airfield. Where there is a break in the fence, turn left at the Na Ala Hele trail sign and proceed through the public gates on a paved road. Follow it around to the left and park (or lock up your bike) in the air control tower's parking lot.

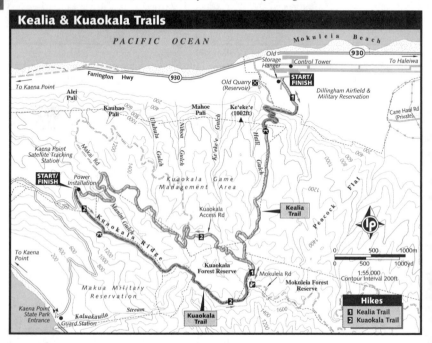

THE HIKE

Just before the air control tower parking lot, there's a turn-off *mauka* on a short gravel access road marked with a Na Ala Hele trailhead sign. Follow it around to the left of an old storage hangar and, after about five minutes, turn right and pass through a green fence marked by another sign. Head toward the *pali* on a soft forest path littered with leaves from *kukui*.

Numerous birds and insects can be heard, although they may be drowned out by the noise from quirky small aircraft flying overhead. Watch out for rockfall ahead as the trail, strewn with rubble and boulders, starts switchbacking up, slowly at first, but then more steeply. Rare *a'ali'i* plants comprise part of the vegetation and butterflies flutter about in great quantity. Far below is an old rock quarry reservoir, and from the cliff face are views of the white sands of lovely 6-mile-long Mokuleia Beach.

After about 1 mile, the switchbacks curve inland and up through ironwoods to a picnic-table shelter. Go straight across the picnic area to meet a dirt road, turn right and start climbing uphill past an old water tank. Ignore any hunting trails or smaller 4WD roads that stray off to either side. The main road is sunny and exposed, although some silk oaks provide shade relief. Keep struggling uphill to the signposted major junction with Mokuleia Rd. Ascend by turning left and look for another Na Ala Hele sign, for the Kuaokala Trail, staked into the ground ahead. Keep rising (except more gently now) through eucalyptus trees to come out abruptly atop a ridge. Swivel right and scramble down over tree roots and red dirt, rock hopping up the other side of the saddle to reach the Kuaokala Trail's premier **overlook** of the verdant Makua Valley and weather permitting, Mt Ka'ala (4025ft), Oahu's highest peak.

On the way back down from the Kuaokala Trail, be sure to head straight across the first dirt 4WD road intersection, then turn right at the next junction to return to the picnic-table shelter. At the bottom of the switchbacks, bear left at the trail fork right after the green gate to meet the paved road back to the air-control tower.

Kuaokala Trail

Duration	2½ hours
Distance	5.5 miles (8.9km)
Difficulty	moderate
Start/Finish	Kuaokala Trailhead
Nearest Towns	Makaha (p94), Honolulu (p62)
Transport	private

Summary A roller-coaster ride over a narrow, windswept ridge leads to a lookout, with dramatic panoramas of Makua Valley and the Waianae Mountains.

The satellite-tracking station above Kaena Point has odd-looking antennas and domes sitting atop the mountains, a couple of them looking like giant white golf balls perched on the ridge. The DLNR maintains a few hiking trails above the tracking station, including the Kuaokala Trail, a 2½-mile ridge route that enters Mokuleia Forest Reserve. The final lookout can also be accessed via the Kealia Trail (p91) from the North Shore.

PLANNING

After heavy rainstorms, some narrow and exposed sections of this trail can become slippery. High winds can also make the trail too risky. Carry all water, as none is available anywhere along the trail, and watch out for hunting activity.

Maps

The free, photocopied *Kuaokala-Mokuleia Area* handout has an up-to-date topographic map and brief trail notes. It's available from the DLNR's permit office in downtown Honolulu.

Permits & Regulations

You'll need to obtain a hiking permit in advance from the **Division of Forestry & Wildlife** (*DOFAW;* ☎ *587-0166*) at the DLNR's permit office in downtown Honolulu. Despite what staff may tell you, a 4WD vehicle isn't necessary to get to the Kuaokala trailhead, however, a permit is absolutely required to get past the military guard station.

OAHU

OAHU

NEAREST TOWNS & FACILITIES

Make this hike a day trip from Honolulu (p62), as visitor accommodations are sparse along the Waianae Coast.

Makaha

Makaha is best known for its world-class surfing. There are some places to grab a bite along the Farrington Hwy (Hwy 93). **Makaha Drive-In** (☎ 696-4811; 84-1150 Farrington Hwy, cnr Makaha Valley Rd; snacks $1-3.50, meals $6; open 6am-8pm Mon-Sat) serves plate lunches, burgers as well as sandwiches.

Getting There & Away From the Ala Moana Center, buses on County Express Route C travel on the Farrington Hwy (Hwy 93) up the leeward coast to Makaha Beach Park ($1.50, 1¾ hours, twice hourly).

Kea'au Beach Park Campground

Although a rough reef, sharp drop and high seasonal surf make swimming uninviting, the **county beach park** has well-manicured campsites with showers, drinking water, picnic tables and rest rooms. See Permits & Fees (p34) for permit information.

Getting There & Away There is no bus service past Makaha. Drive about 2 miles north of Makaha Beach Park on the Farrington Hwy (Hwy 93).

GETTING TO/FROM THE HIKE

There is no bus service, so driving is the only option. The Farrington Hwy (Hwy 93) continues about 5 miles past Makaha and, immediately before the gate to Kaena Point State Park, a road on the right leads up to Kaena Point Satellite Tracking Station, which is operated by the US Air Force. After showing your permit and ID to the guard, continue uphill to a T-junction. Turn right and drive past the administration buildings as the road curves left and park in a gravel pull-out near the DLNR trailer, close to the signposted trailhead. The paved access road, which leads downhill to the left of the trailhead, is the return route for this hike.

THE HIKE (see map p92)

Start by heading to the right, past the Na Ala Hele trailhead sign, and following the trail as it contours through forest. At about the ½-mile point, turn left at the junction with a dirt road that climbs atop the ridge through ironwood and pine trees. Soon a picnic table appears and the road drops into a gully infested with strawberry guava. Keep heading straight uphill to the very edge of the ridge, where the trail abruptly turns left and climbs over an eroded stretch with partial views into Makua Valley.

Veer back up into ironwood forest, and brace yourself against the strong wind blowing up from the coast by sidling along the upslope side of the trail. The trail narrows as it continues over a series of saddles and knobs. There are spectacular views on this open and exposed section of the route, where rainbow-colored rocky patches alternate with grassy areas and tree roots. It can be challenging, especially in high winds, but it's nothing technical.

At the trail's highest point (1960ft) is an **overlook**, with tremendous views. On a clear day hikers can see Mt Ka'ala, the highest peak on Oahu, and part of the Waianae Range. From here the trail drops over rocks and less steeply than it may at first look. Then it heads across a bare saddle and scrambles up over loose dirt and more tree roots to a secondary viewpoint.

Here hikers need to make a choice. Those who'd like to return the same way along the scenic Kuaokala Trail should turn around here. Otherwise there's a scenic 4WD road that makes a complete loop back to the trailhead on a different, longer route. Along the way are broad views over the North Shore and a variety of native forest growth.

To get to the road, follow the trail inland and descend gently through ironwoods. At a junction with the 4WD keep heading straight and walk downhill past a small water catchment. The road that you are now hiking on, called the Kuaokala Access Rd, has been cut anew and regraded. Overgrown sections of the old road can be seen leading off to either side of the main road at various points, but unless you're keen on exploring damp gullies, it's best to keep on the main road, which is signed for hikers at confusing junctions.

Eventually the white golf-ball–shaped domes of the tracking station come back into view. At the road's westernmost point are some excellent lookouts over Kaena Point and the entire coast. At the junction with Makai Rd, which takes off right toward the ocean, go straight down the main road into Mahini Gulch, where the road levels out briefly before passing out of the game management area. Curve uphill on the paved road near the power installation and in about five minutes emerge back at the trailhead sign.

Other Hikes

HONOLULU & AROUND
Pu'u Ohia Trail
This trail, in conjunction with the Pauoa Flats Trail, leads up to the Nu'uanu Valley lookout. It's nearly 2 miles one way. Start at the Pu'u Ohia trailhead at the very top of Tantalus Dr, 3.6 miles up on the left from its intersection with Makiki Height Dr. After about a ½-mile walk uphill, the Pu'u Ohia trail reaches a service road. A small detour to the left takes in a trail-of-use to the top of Tantalus. Otherwise continue right by walking north on the service road, at the end of which there's a telephone company building. Pick up the trail again behind the left side of this building and head downhill to join the Manoa Cliff Trail. From here, follow the description for the Manoa Cliffs Circuit (p73) out to the lookout and back.

Aiea Loop
Keaiwa Heiau State Recreation Area (☎ 483-2511; Aiea Heights Dr; admission free; open 7am-sunset daily) in Aiea, north of Pearl Harbor, contains an ancient temple used by *kahuna lapa'au* (herbalist healers) and a scenic 4½-mile, easy–moderate hiking trail, which starts from the top of the paved loop road and comes back out at the campground, about a third of a mile below the trailhead. There are sweeping vistas of Pearl

Harbor, Diamond Head and the Ko'olau Range en route. About two-thirds of the way in, the wreckage of a C-47 cargo plane that crashed in 1943 can be spotted through the foliage on the east ridge. To get here from Honolulu, drive west on Hwy 78 and take the exit 13A Aiea turn-off onto Moanalua Rd. Turn right onto Aiea Heights Dr at the second traffic light. The road winds up through a residential area 2½ miles to the park.

SOUTHEAST OAHU
Diamond Head
Diamond Head (☎ 587-0300; admission $1; open 6am-6pm daily) is a tuff cone and crater that was formed by a violent, steam explosion long after most of Oahu's volcanic activity had stopped. As the backdrop to Waikiki, it's one of the best-known landmarks in the Pacific. The trail to the summit was built in 1908 to service the military observation stations along the crater rim. It's a moderately steep hike, with a gain in elevation of 560ft, but only ¾-mile long and fully paved. Tote along a flashlight for the tunnels. From the top there's a fantastic 360-degree view taking in the southeast coast to Koko Head and Koko Crater and the leeward coast to the Waianae Range. From downtown Honolulu, Ala Moana Center or Waikiki, take bus No 58 ($1.50, every 30 minutes). It's a 20-minute walk along the signed access road from the bus stop to the trailhead. Maps and interpretive brochures are given out at the admission gate when you pay the entrance fee.

Makapu'u Point
Makapu'u Point and its coastal lighthouse mark the easternmost point of Oahu. The service road to the lighthouse is locked to keep out private vehicles, but visitors can park off the highway just beyond the gate and walk in 1 mile from there. Although not difficult, it's an uphill path, and conditions can be both hot and windy. Along the way there are fine coastal views of Koko Head, Haunama Bay and, in winter, migrating whales. Note that actually climbing down the rocks to the lighthouse is illegal trespassing on federal property. From Honolulu take bus No 22, No 57 (Kailua/Sea Life Park) or No 58 (Hawaii Kai/Sea Life Park) and ask the driver which stop is closest to Makapu'u Lighthouse Rd (about one hour from Honolulu).

The Big Island

The island of Hawaii, aka the Big Island, is nearly twice the size of all the other Hawaiian Islands combined. With climates ranging from tropical to subarctic, the island's geographical variety resembles a minicontinent. Landscapes include one of almost everything: desolate lava flows, lush coastal valleys, high sea cliffs, rolling pastures, rain-forest oases and desert.

The island is divided up into five districts: Kona, Kohala, Hilo, Puna and Kau. Hilo and Kona are the island's two population centers. Kona catches the biggest waves of tourists, but it is the charming Hilo area that has the lion's share of hiking opportunities. This windward east coast has a predominantly rugged coastline with pounding surf, tropical rain forests, deep ravines and majestic waterfalls. The island's most impressive scenery is at Hawaii Volcanoes National Park, which offers miles of backcountry adventures in locales from tropical beaches to the icy 13,677ft summit of Mauna Loa.

HISTORY

By and large, the history of the Big Island is the history of Hawaii. It was here that the first Polynesian settlers arrived between AD 500 and 700. Both *luakini* (temples of human sacrifice) and the *kapu* system of strict taboos, which regulated all aspects of daily life in ancient Hawaii, were introduced here by the 12th-century Tahitian high priest, Pa'ao. It was also on the Big Island, seven centuries later, that the old Hawaiian gods were overthrown and replaced by those of the Christian missionaries. English explorer Captain Cook died on the island in 1779, and this is where Kamehameha the Great, the great unifier of the Hawaiian Islands, was born and rose to power.

NATURAL HISTORY

Geologically, it is the youngest Hawaiian island – and the only one still growing, as new lava spews into the sea. The Big Island was formed by five large shield volcanoes:

Highlights

Mauna Kea looming above the palm trees of the Kohala coast

- Sleeping under a full moon beside crashing surf in Waimanu Valley (p105)
- Reaching the true summit of Mauna Kea (p106), Hawaii's highest peak
- Navigating the lunaresque lava landscapes of Halema'uma'u and Kilauea Iki Craters (p129)
- Gazing into the heart of an active volcanic eruption on the Napau Crater Trail (p134)

Kohala, Hualalai, Mauna Kea, Mauna Loa and Kilauea. The last two are still active, with Kilauea having the distinction of being the most active volcano on earth. Mauna Loa (Long Mountain) makes up more than half the landmass of the Big Island.

CLIMATE

The Big Island has Hawaii's highest mountains, which rise almost 14,000ft above sea

Maunawili Demonstration Trail, Oahu

Windward beach, Waimanalo, Oahu

Honolulu, gateway to the Hawaiian Islands, and Ko'olau Range, Oahu

Kaluahine Falls in the Waipio Valley, on the Muliwai Trail, Hamakua Coast, the Big Island

Near the Hamakua Coast, the Big Island

Halemaʻumaʻu Trail, the Big Island

level. The mountains create a giant barrier that blocks the moist northeasterly trade winds and makes the sunny leeward side of the Big Island the driest region in Hawaii, a perfect proving ground for iron-man triathletes every year. The Kona and Kohala coasts have the island's finest beaches.

On the windward side of Mauna Kea, which is near the 2500ft elevation, around 300 inches of rain fall annually. So much rain is squeezed out of the clouds as they rise up Mauna Kea and Mauna Loa that only about 15 inches of precipitation reaches the summits, much of it as snow. Heavy subtropical winter rainstorms in Hilo occasionally bring blizzards to the mountains as low as the 9000ft level.

INFORMATION
When to Hike
No season is ideal for doing all of the Big Island hikes. A summit attempt on Mauna Kea or Mauna Loa is best done only in summer. Winter is the coolest time for coastal lava trekking, but at that time the Muliwai Trail out of Waipio Valley may be washed out by flooded streams. All of the hikes within the main section of Hawaii Volcanoes National Park are accessible year-round.

Information Sources
The Big Island's branch of the Sierra Club in Hilo schedules a monthly calendar of island-wide group outings, including guided hikes, clean-up days at beaches and visits to wildlife refuges.

Permits
Camping permits are required at all state, county and national parks.

State park camping reservations can be made at state park offices on any island. The maximum length of stay at any state park is five nights a month. Campsites cost $5 per night. The Division of State Parks in Hilo issues permits.

County camping is allowed for up to two weeks in each park, except between June and August when it's limited to one week only. County camping costs $5 per adult per

Vog

'Vog' is a word coined on the Big Island to define the volcanic haze that has been hanging over the island since Kilauea's latest eruptive phase began in 1983. It usually blows toward Kona, and conditions can resemble city smog when the trade winds falter. Vog consists of water vapor, carbon dioxide and significant amounts of sulfur dioxide. The sulfur dioxide level exceeds standards set by the US Environmental Protection Agency an average of 22 days a year. While vog shouldn't present health problems for short-term visitors, scientists are currently studying the link between vog and respiratory problems for residents. It's best to avoid long periods of intense exposure, however, especially in the areas around Hawaii Volcanoes National Park.

night. Permits are issued at the Department of Parks & Recreation in Hilo. You can also make reservations by phone through the Hilo office and then pick up the camping permit at branch offices in Kailua-Kona or Captain Cook. The on-line reservation system at ⓦ www.ehawaiigov.org using credit cards is convenient.

Place Names
The Hawaii Belt Rd circles the island, taking in the main towns and many of the sights. Different segments of the road have different highway numbers and names, but it's easy to follow. When a road or town takes several names, go with local usage. 'East Hawaii' refers to the windward Hilo side, and 'West Hawaii' to the dry Kona and Kohala coasts.

GATEWAY
Hilo
Hilo happens to be the oldest city in Hawaii, and shows its age with character. It has a diverse multiethnic population, plus an alternative community that's taken root since the 1970s. Most folks call it 'old Hilo town,' befitting its pace; original wood facades with corrugated eaves make up the waterfront

THE BIG ISLAND

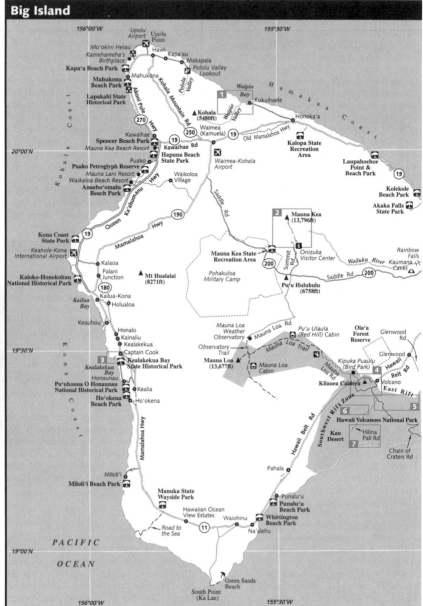

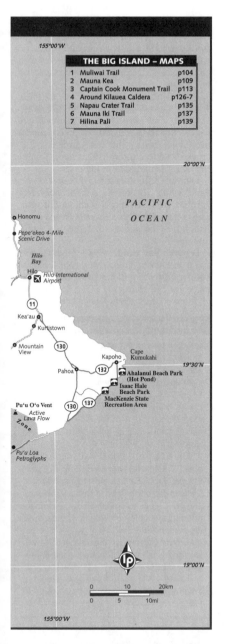

THE BIG ISLAND – MAPS

1	Muliwai Trail	p104
2	Mauna Kea	p109
3	Captain Cook Monument Trail	p113
4	Around Kilauea Caldera	p126-7
5	Napau Crater Trail	p135
6	Mauna Iki Trail	p137
7	Hilina Pali	p139

THE BIG ISLAND

business district. The city's graceful beauty seeps into the subconscious as you catch sight of Mauna Kea standing guard over Hilo Bay.

According to official statistics, measurable rain falls in Hilo 278 days of the average year, adding up to just over 129 inches annually. Indeed, this has led to the saying that 'in Hilo, people don't tan, they rust.'

Information You can pick up brochures and general tourist literature at the **Big Island Visitors Bureau** (☎ 961-5797, 800-464-2924; Ⓦ www.gohawaii.com; 250 Keawe St). The bureau can send you a glossy vacation planner (☎ 800-648-2441) in advance.

The **Sierra Club** (☎ 965-9695; Ⓦ www.hi.sierraclub.org/Hawaii/mokuloa.html; PO Box 1137, Hilo, HI 96721) runs island-wide group outings.

The **Division of State Parks** (☎ 974-6200; 75 Aupuni St, Room 204; open 8am-3:30pm Mon-Fri) issues permits for camping in state parks. Permits for county camping are issued at the **Department of Parks & Recreation** (☎ 961-8311; Ⓦ www.ehawaiigov.org; 25 Aupuni St, Room 210; open 7:45am-4pm Mon-Fri).

The **Division of Forestry & Wildlife** (DOFAW; ☎ 974-4221, fax 974-4226; 19 E Kawili St; open 7:45am-4:30pm Mon-Fri) handles hiking permits and camping reservations for places such as the Waimanu Valley.

Supplies & Equipment Hilo has lots of places where you can pick up the raw materials for a great meal. The **farmers market** (cnr Mamo St & Kamehameha Ave; open 7am-noon Wed & Sat) has vendors selling island fruits, vegies and flowers direct from the growers at bargain prices. Don't miss the delicious selection of *poke* (marinated, bite-sized raw fish) at the **Suisan Fish Market** (☎ 935-9349; 85 Lihiwai St; open 8am-5pm Mon-Sat).

Abundant Life Natural Foods (☎ 935-7411; 292 Kamehameha Ave; open 8:30am-7pm Mon-Tues & Thur-Fri, 7am-7pm Wed & Sat, 10am-5pm Sun) has all the quality cheeses, juices and bulk foods you'd expect of a health food store, plus a simple deli and smoothie bar. **O'Keefe & Sons Bread Bakers** (☎ 934-9334; 374 Kino'ole St; items $2.75-7; open 6am-5pm Mon-Fri, 6am-4pm Sat) sells gorgeous artisan breads, pastries and stuffed sandwiches.

KTA Supermarket (321 Keawe St; open 7am-9pm Mon-Sat, 7am-6pm Sun) is a convenient downtown grocery store. The **Puainako Town Center** (Hwy 11) has both a **KTA Superstore** selling 30 types of poke and a **Sack N Save** that sells coffee and doughnuts from 5am.

Maps are usually sold at bookstores. **Basically Books** (☎ 961-0144, 800-903-6277; W www.basicallybooks.com; 160 Kamehameha Ave), specializing in out-of-print books and Hawaiiana titles, carries general travel maps and USGS topographic maps for all Hawaiian islands.

Borders Books & Music Café (☎ 933-1410; Waiakea Center, 301 Makaala St, off Hwy 11; open 9am-9pm Sun-Thur, 9am-10pm Fri & Sat) sells road maps.

Conveniently located downtown, **Hilo Surplus Store** (☎ 935-6398; 148 Mamo St; open 8am-5pm Mon-Sat) sells hiking and camping supplies, such as rain gear, backpacks, tents, sleeping bags, camp stoves and fuel.

Pacific Rent-All (☎ 935-2974; 1080 Kilauea Ave; open 7am-5pm Mon-Sat, 9am-11am Sun) rents three-person tents ($23/46 per day/week), sleeping bags ($8/24), Coleman stoves, lanterns, water jugs and other supplies. The selection is limited and is generally geared more for drive-up camping than backcountry use.

Places to Stay & Eat The majority of hikes in this chapter are all within an hour's drive of Hilo, so consider making this your base. Always ask about weekly discounts when making reservations.

Arnott's Lodge & Hiking Adventures (☎ 969-7097; W www.arnottslodge.com; 98 Apapane Rd; tent sites $9, dorm beds $17, semiprivate singles/doubles $37/47, doubles with bath $57-65, five-person 2-bedroom suites $120) really is the place to connect with other travelers, if you don't mind being on the outskirts of town. Doug Arnott's

well-run hostel has sex-segregated dormitories, claustrophobic urban camping in the front yard and a slew of private rooms, all with access to kitchen facilities; rates include taxes. Adventure island tours cost $48 per guest.

Wild Ginger Inn (☎ 935-5556, 800-882-1887; W www.wildgingerinn.com; 100 Pu'ueo St; dorm beds $19, doubles without/with bath from $50/70), a colorful 1920s plantation house amid exuberant gardens with a creek meandering through, is decent value. Breakfast is included in the rates.

Lannan's Lihi Kai (☎ 935-7865; 30 Kahoa Rd; doubles $60-65) is a laid-back B&B perched on a cliff directly above Hilo Bay. The two guest rooms share a bath and a half. Amenities include a small heated swimming pool.

Dolphin Bay Hotel (☎ 935-1466, fax 935-1523; W www.dolphinbayhilo.com; 333 Iliahi St; single/double studios $66/69, superior single/double studios $76/79, double 1-/2-bedroom units $89/99) is a very popular

---

Soul Food, Hawaiian-style

Good ol' Hilo town boasts some of the most famous local-style Hawaiian food joints in the islands.

Ka'upena (1710 Kamehameha Ave; items $1.50-7; open 9am-6pm Mon-Sat) is the town's favorite for ono (delicious) Hawaiian food. It's the 'home of the foot-long laulau', which comes full of tender fish and pork wrapped in a ti leaf.

Cafe 100 (969 Kilauea Ave; meals $4-6; open 6:45am-8:30pm Mon-Fri, 6:45am-9:30pm Sat & Sun) is the original home of the loco moco (rice topped with a hamburger and fried egg accompanied by a cardiac-arresting amount of brown gravy), now in 17 different varieties.

Surprisingly, some of the best local Hawaiian food is found at strip malls. **Island Infusion** (Waiakea Center, 315 Maka'ala St; meals $5-7.50; open 10am-9pm Mon-Sat, 10am-8pm Sun) is next to Wal-Mart, off Hwy 11.

family-run hotel full of aloha. All of the apartment-like units have full kitchens, TVs and bathrooms. Fresh-picked fruit from the backyard is available, along with free morning coffee.

Shipman House Bed & Breakfast (☎/fax 934-8002, 800-627-8447; w www.hilo-hawaii.com; 131 Kaiulani St; doubles $155-185), on a knoll above town, is a beautiful Victorian mansion that has been in the Shipman family since 1901. Past visitors at this national historic site have included Queen Liliuokalani and Jack London.

The bulk of Hilo's restaurants are downtown by the waterfront. **Ocean Sushi Deli** (☎ 961-6625; 239 Keawe St; dishes $1.50-20; open 10am-2:30pm & 4:30pm-9pm Mon-Sat) slices up traditional sushi, accompanied by scores of contemporary rolls, such as a tuna-avocado-*kukui* (candlenut) combo, and lots of vegetarian options.

Ken's House of Pancakes (☎ 935-8711; 1730 Kamehameha Ave, cnr Hwy 11; meals $6-12; open 24 hrs daily) diner never closes, making it the perfect spot after Mauna Kea stargazing. Ken's has hundreds of menu combos, including huge Spam omelettes, macadamia nut pancakes and milkshakes like ambrosia.

Seaside Restaurant (☎ 935-8825; 1790 Kalanianaole Ave; meals $18-24; open 5pm-8:30pm Tues-Thur, 5pm-9pm Fri & Sat) has the island's freshest fish. Outdoor tables sit prettily above the family's aquafarm. Everything is delicious; try the mullet steamed in ti leaves with lemon and onions. Meals include rice, salad, apple pie and coffee. Call for reservations.

Getting There & Around Kona gets the bulk of mainland and international flights, so flying directly to Hilo can certainly be prohibitively expensive. You'll probably find that it is cheaper to fly to Honolulu first, then board an interisland flight to Hilo. These flights sell out fast, so book seats well in advance. If you don't have any luck, then consider flying into Kona on the leeward coast and traveling overland, especially easy if you're already planning on renting a car.

See the Travel Facts chapter (p218) for details on international, domestic and inter-island flights, commuter airlines and discount flight coupons. Behind the Minit Stop gas station, **Cut Rate Tickets** (☎ 969-1944; Hwy 11 & Leilani St; open 8am-7pm Mon-Fri, 9am-5pm Sat, 9am-2pm Sun) sells interisland flight coupons at reasonable prices. Bring cash to avoid credit card surcharges.

At the Hilo airport, taxis can be picked up curbside, and car rental booths line the road just outside the arrival areas. Expect to pay about $15 for the taxi ride into downtown Hilo. Some accommodations will do airport pick-ups for free, such as Arnott's Lodge.

The **Hele-On Bus** (☎ 961-8744; Mo'oheau Bus Terminal, Kamehameha Ave; open 7:45am-4:30pm Mon-Fri), in downtown Hilo near Mamo St, offers limited island-wide services. There are a few intracity routes, all costing 75¢. The bad news is buses only operate Monday to Friday, and there is an extra $1 charge for luggage or backpacks. Following are details for the most important routes and stops:

No 4 Kaumana – this bus goes five times a day (the first leaves at 7:35am, the last at 2:20pm) from Mo'oheau Bus Terminal–Hilo Library–Hilo Medical Center.

No 6 Waiakea-Uka – this bus goes five times a day (the first leaves at 7:05am, the last at 3:05pm) from Mo'oheau Bus Terminal–Hilo Shopping Center–University of Hawaii–Prince Kuhio Plaza–Wal-Mart.

Getting around town by bike is totally feasible. Following are some reliable rental shops:

Da Kine Bike Shop (☎ 934-9861) 12 Furneaux Lane. This is a friendly place, renting bikes from $5-a-day rusty cruisers to $50-a-day pro models. It also offers island cycling tours.

Hilo Bike Hub (☎ 961-4452) 318 E Kawili St. The Bike Hub rents cruisers, rock hoppers and full-suspension mountain bikes for $20 to $45 per day. Ask about weekly discounts.

Mid-Pacific Wheels (☎ 935-6211) 1133-C Manono St. Mid-Pacific rents 21-speed bikes for $15 per day.

THE BIG ISLAND

Muliwai Trail

Duration	2 days
Distance	19 miles (30.6km)
Difficulty	demanding
Start/Finish	Waipio Valley Overlook
Nearest Towns	Honoka'a (p103), Kukuihaele (p104)
Transport	private

Summary Starting from the Big Island's most beautiful valley overlook, take the challenging switchbacks of an ancient Hawaiian footpath past waterfall gulches and over cliffs to pristine Waimanu Valley.

Waipio Valley is the largest of seven spectacular amphitheater valleys on the windward side of the Kohala Mountains. Everything down in Waipio (Curving Water) is a fertile tangle of jungle, flowering plants, taro patches and waterfalls, all fronted by a black-sand beach cleaved by a stream. Some of the near-vertical *pali* (cliffs) wrapping around the valley reach heights of 2000ft. The whole place pulsates with *mana* (spiritual power), beckoning hikers to venture down.

Doing part of the Muliwai Trail makes a good day hike from Waipio, but hoofing it all the way to Waimanu Valley and back in a day is unrealistic. Be forewarned that the last mile or so of the trail is precipitous and only irregularly maintained, making this one of the most technically challenging hikes in this book. The final switchbacks are especially tough because hikers will probably be carrying a heavy backpack with gear for camping out in Waimanu Valley. Still, the rewards are many on this overnight adventure into the Hawaii of days gone by.

HISTORY

Waipio is often referred to as the 'Valley of the Kings.' In ancient times it was the political and religious center of Hawaii and home to the highest *ali'i* (chiefs). Waipio's sacred status is evidenced by a number of important ruins, including *hale* (house) sites and *heiau* (temple) terraces.

According to oral histories, at least 10,000 people lived in this fertile valley before the arrival of Westerners. Umi, the Big Island's ruling chief in the early 16th century, is credited with laying out Waipio's taro fields, many of which are still in production today. Waipio is also the site where Kamehameha the Great received the statue of his fearsome war god, Kukailimoku.

In 1823, William Ellis, the first missionary to visit Waipio Valley, guessed the population to be about 1300. Later in the 19th century, immigrants, mainly Chinese, began to settle in Waipio. At one time, the valley had schools, restaurants and churches, as well as a hotel, post office and jail.

In 1946, Hawaii's most devastating tsunami slammed great waves far back into the valley. Coincidentally or not, no one in this sacred place perished (every resident was also spared during the great 1979 flood). But afterwards, most people resettled 'topside' and Waipio has been sparsely populated ever since.

PLANNING

Most people hike all the way into Waimanu Valley on the first day, camp for two nights and then walk back out on the third day. Those who want to get a head start can camp at Waipio Beach the night before.

There are a few creeks that cross the trail, as well as streams into both Waipio and Waimanu Valley, which can become torrents after rainstorms. Especially in the rainiest winter months, the streams can quickly swell to impassable, usually for just a few hours at a time. These need to be treated as life-threatening obstacles; be patient and wait for the water to subside.

High winds may bring down trees and branches on the trail and campgrounds. The latter may occasionally be washed away by surf. Flash floods are also possible. Be sure to check the weather forecasts by calling ☎ 961-5582 before setting out. Hiking poles will ease the treacherous final descent into Waimanu Valley and help with stream crossings. All freshwater available along the trail must be filtered or chemically treated before drinking.

Maps

The USGS 1:24,000 maps *Kukuihaele* and *Honokane* cover the trail. However, a pocket-sized photocopy of a more detailed topographic map showing the Muliwai Trail is available free along with camping permits from the DOFAW office in Hilo.

Permits & Regulations

Bishop Estate (☎ 322-5300, fax 322-9446; 78-6831 Ali'i Dr, Suite 232, Kailua-Kona, HI 96740; office open 7:30am-4:30pm Mon-Fri) allows camping at four primitive sites inland from Waipio Beach. Each camper is required to sign a liability waiver and bring along a chemical toilet, but the permits are free. The maximum stay is four days. Apply for a permit at least two weeks in advance, as campsites fill up fast on weekends and in summer. The office is in Keauhou, just south of Kailua-Kona proper, but permits can be mailed with advance notice.

Because Waimanu Valley represents an unaltered Hawaiian freshwater ecosystem, it has been set aside as a national estuarine sanctuary, and the removal of any plant and most aquatic life is forbidden. The DOFAW office in Hilo handles hiking permits and camping reservations for Waimanu Valley. Tent camping is free and allowed for up to six nights; facilities are limited to a few composting outhouses and fire pits. Reservations are taken no more than 30 days in advance.

NEAREST TOWNS & FACILITIES

Honoka'a

This former sugar-plantation town is the largest on the Hamakua Coast. Residents of

Stick to the Trail

Many Waipio Valley residents who are tolerant of visitors trekking down to visit the beach aren't keen on them exploring the valley interior – there are a lot of 'Private Property' and 'Kapu – No Trespassing' signs. The farther back in the valley you go, the more menacing the dogs become, so stick to the trail.

❀ ❀ ❀ ❀ ❀ ❀ ❀ ❀ ❀ ❀ ❀ ❀ ❀

Waipio Valley (you'll know them by their muddy trucks with hounds scrambling around in the back) come 'topside' to resupply here. The **visitor center** (Mamane St) will probably not be staffed when you show up, but feel free to avail yourself of the public toilet out back.

Stock up on groceries at **Taro Junction Natural Foods** (Mamane St; open 10am-5:30pm Mon-Fri, 9am-5pm Sat), just west of the hotel, or **TKS Supermarket** (cnr Mamane & Lehua Sts), which is next to a hardware store selling a few camping supplies.

Places to Stay & Eat The basic **Hotel Honokaa Club** (☎ 775-0678, 800-808-0678; e honokaac@gte.net; Mamane St; dorm beds/singles/doubles $15/20/30, doubles with bath $45-65, double suites $80; reception open 9am-1pm & 4pm-8pm daily) is the only game in town. The cheapest rooms share a shower and toilet at the quieter end of the hotel's plantation-style building.

New Moon Café (Mamane St; meals $3.50-5.50; open 9am-4pm Mon-Fri, 9am-1pm Sat), behind Taro Junction Natural Foods, has a mellow patio. Try the taro burger with an impressive side salad, or chill sipping some kava.

Café Il Mundo (☎ 775-7711; 45-3626A Mamane St; sandwiches $5-8, pizzas $9-17; open 11am-7:30pm daily) does dreamy sandwiches, soups and salads, with fresh pizza slices available before 5pm.

Tex Drive Inn (☎ 775-0598; Hwy 19; meals $5-10; open 5:30am-8:30pm daily) is reason enough to make the drive from Hilo. Its famous *malasadas* (Portuguese pastries made of sweet fried dough, rolled in sugar and served warm) cost 75¢ plain. Oh yes, Tex also serves superb fresh fish sandwiches, burgers and local plate lunches.

Getting There & Away The county public bus, **Hele-On** (☎ 961-8744; office open 7:45am-4:30pm Mon-Fri), offers limited services between Hilo and Honoka'a ($3.75, one hour, weekdays only). The No 31 Honoka'a bus departs from Hilo's Mo'oheau Terminal at 1:30pm, 2:30pm and 4:30pm; early morning buses at 3:45am, 5:25am and

THE BIG ISLAND

5:30am leave from the parking lot just east of the terminal. The No 7 Downtown Hilo bus departs Honoka'a from the downtown parking lot across from the soccer field at 6am, 8:35am, 3:25pm, 5:20pm and 5:30pm.

Kukuihaele

Kukuihaele is the setting-off point for most tours into Waipio Valley, but has no visitor facilities to speak of except for a few shops on the main road.

Last Chance Store (☎ 775-9222; 125 Old Government Hwy; open 9am-3:30pm Mon-Sat) is aptly named; this small grocery store

has snacks, canned chili, beer, water and wine. **Waipi'o Valley Artworks** (☎ 775-0958, 800-492-4746; 48-5416 Kukuihaele Rd; open 8am-5pm daily) sells Tropical Dreams ice cream, inexpensive sandwiches, baked goodies and coffee.

Waipi'o Ridge Vacation Rental (☎ 775-0603; e rlasko3343@aol.com; PO Box 5039, Kukuihaele, HI 96727; double 1-bedroom cottage per day/week $85/$450, double trailer $75/350), poised on the cliff above the valley, has the location of a lifetime with views to match. The funky Airstream trailer has an outside shower and kitchenette.

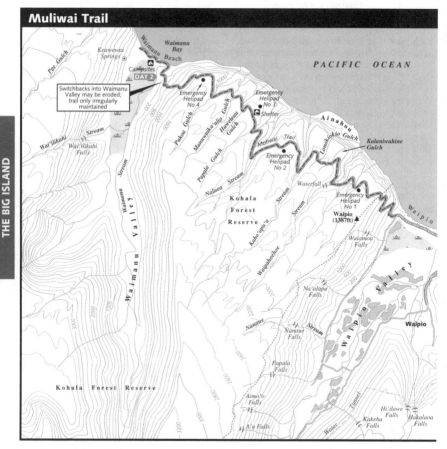

Muliwai Trail

Getting There & Away There is no public transport. Kukuihaele is on a loop road that leaves Hwy 240 before the Waipio Valley Overlook, about a 15-minute drive west of Honoka'a.

GETTING TO/FROM THE HIKE
There is no public transport to the start of the hike at Waipio Valley Overlook, about 9 miles west of Honoka'a at the end of Hwy 240. Vehicles may not be parked at the overlook for more than 24 hours. **Waipi'o Valley Artworks** in Kukuihaele (p104) charges hikers from $7.50 per vehicle for

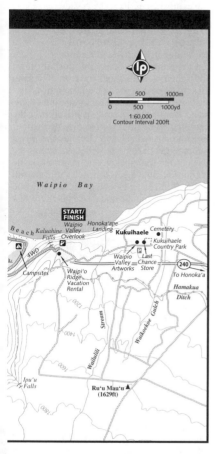

overnight parking in the store's unsecured outdoor lot. It's less than a mile's walk from there up to Hwy 240 and by turning right, to the overlook further west.

THE HIKE
Day 1: Waipio Valley Overlook to Waimanu Valley
6½–8 hours, 9.5 miles (15.3km)
Hwy 240 ends abruptly at the cliffs overlooking Waipio Valley. From the overlook there are glimpses of the rugged coastal cliffs stretching out to the northwest and on the clearest days, even the dark outlines of Maui in the distance. Multiple waterfalls burst from the cliff faces during rainfall, commonly in winter. Start by descending the nearly mile-long, paved sinew of road that leads down into Waipio Valley. It is so steep that it's open only to hikers and 4WD vehicles, and it can be very slippery after rain, especially if you're carrying a heavy pack.

At various points, the valley's interior and the zigzag switchbacks of the Muliwai Trail rising on the valley's far west wall come into view. After only about a half-hour, the road reaches the valley floor. Detour to the left for a chance to see wild horses that graze along the stream; it's a beautiful Hawaiian tableau, with precipitous cliffs as a backdrop. You'll also get a distant view of **Hi'ilawe Falls**, which is Hawaii's highest free-fall waterfall – a sheer drop of more than 1000ft.

Back at the bottom of the road, it's a 10-minute walk to Waipio Beach, but tack on an extra 10 minutes and a pound of mud if it has rained recently. At a small fork, veering right leads up over drier ground. Soon the grey sands of Waipio Beach appear lined with graceful ironwood trees, serving as a barrier for campers against strong winds. Surfers catch wave action at Waipio, but mind the rip currents and if the sea seems too rough, it is. Rogue waves and a treacherous undertow are features of the roiling ocean here.

Walk west along the beach toward the stream mouth for a good view of **Kaluahine Falls**, which cascade down the cliffs to the east. Getting to them is easier said than done, as the intervening coast is made up of loose, ankle-twisting lava. High surf breaking over

THE BIG ISLAND

the uppermost rocks can be very dangerous. Instead, when it's safe ford the stream at its calmest point where it breaks over the sand banks. Cut inland and follow the gently rolling forested path to the far west end of the beach, past wild horses and fishing boats, to the base of the cliffs.

The path turns left below the cliffs, then veers right and ascends under thick forest cover. Laboring up the steep switchbacks on the cliff face, the Muliwai Trail rises over 1200ft in a mile. It is hot and exposed, so try to hike this stretch in the early morning. Eventually the trail moves into ironwood and Norfolk pine forest, becoming carpeted with soft needles. It tops a little knoll, then starts to gently descend, becoming muddy and frequented by mosquitoes. Views of the ocean disappear, but a rushing stream can be heard.

The trail crosses a gulch and ascends past a trail sign for Emergency Helipad No 1 on the *mauka* (toward the mountains, inland) side of the trail. For the next few hours, the trail finds a steady rhythm of wet gulch crossings and ascents back up into drier forest. Some gulches are dry, some wet. A waterfall at the third gulch is a source of freshwater, but it must be filtered or treated before drinking. Mostly the trail is covered in squashed guava, ferns and buzzing gnats, even bees. There are few landmarks along the way, but look for Emergency Helipad No 2 at about the halfway point from Waipio Beach. Later an open-sided **trail shelter** with pit toilets has room enough for a dozen people, but may be littered with trash.

Rest here before making the final difficult descent. Leaving the shelter, hop across three more gulches and pass Emergency Helipad No 4, from where it's less than another mile to Waimanu Valley. Over an elevation loss of 1200ft, this final section of switchbacks starts out innocently enough, with some artificial and natural stone steps set in the mud. However, the trail is poorly maintained and extremely hazardous later. A glimpse of a waterfall on the far side of the valley wall may inspire hikers to press onward. The trail is very narrow, and washed out in parts, with sheer drop-offs hundreds of feet into the ocean and nothing to hold onto apart from

mossy rocks and spiny plants. Dense *hala* (screw pine) leaf litter underfoot hides centipedes and slippery *kukui* nuts. If the descent proves to be impossible, head back to the trail shelter for the night, stopping at one of the stream gulches for water.

Waimanu Valley is a mini-Waipio, less the tourists. A stunning deep valley framed by escarpments, waterfalls and a black-sand beach, on any given day, you'll bask alone among this beauty. From the bottom of the switchbacks, it's a 10-minute walk past the camping regulations signboard to the boulder-strewn beach. When safe, ford the stream to reach the campsites on its western side.

Day 2: Waimanu Valley to Waipio Valley Overlook
6–7½ hours, 9.5 miles (15.3km)

On the return trip, be careful to start off on the right trail. Walking inland from Waimanu Beach, do not veer left on a false trail-of-use that attempts to climb a rocky streambed. Instead keep heading straight inland past the camping regulations sign to pick up the trail again to the switchbacks. It takes about two hours to get past the switchbacks and arrive back at the trail shelter, and about the same amount of time again to reach the waterfall gulch. Refill water here. Exiting the ironwood forest soon after, the trail descends fairly easily back to the floor of Waipio Valley.

Mauna Kea

Duration	7–9 hours
Distance	12 miles (19.3km)
Difficulty	demanding
Start/Finish	Onizuka visitor center
Nearest Town	Hilo (p97)
Transport	private

Summary Climb a palette of cinder cones, passing Hawaiian archaeological sites en route to a cluster of modern astronomical observatories around the summit of Hawaii's highest peak.

High altitude, steep grades and brisk weather all make this hike quite strenuous. Walking on cinders adds marginal difficulty, but there are incredible vistas and strange other-worldly landscapes en route. In fact, Moon Valley is where the Apollo astronauts rehearsed with their lunar rover before journeying to the real moonscape. Marked with wooden posts and cairns, the trail runs roughly parallel to the summit road, but far enough away to feel quite solitary. Wandering alone around majestic cinder cones above the level of the clouds is an unforgettable experience.

The summit of Mauna Kea has the greatest collection of state-of-the-art telescopes on earth. At almost 14,000ft, the summit is above 40% of the earth's atmosphere. The air is typically clear, dry and stable. It's also relatively free of dust and smog. Only the Andes Mountains match Mauna Kea for cloudless nights, although air turbulence in the Andes makes viewing more difficult there.

Officially the Onizuka Center for International Astronomy Visitor Information Station (VIS), the **Onizuka visitor center** (☎ 961-2180; Ⓦ www.ifa.hawaii.edu/info/vis/; open 9am-noon & 1pm-5pm Mon-Fri, 9am-6pm Sat & Sun) at 9300ft was named for Ellison Onizuka, a Big Island native and one of the astronauts who perished in the 1986 Challenger space shuttle disaster.

This excellent educational center has photo displays of the observatories, information on discoveries made from the summit, computer-driven astronomy programs and exhibits on the mountain's history, ecology and geology. There are steaming cups of hot chocolate, instant noodles and freeze-dried astronaut food. Staff also vend books, maps, souvenirs and limited cold-weather gear (hats, gloves, etc). Hours are subject to change, so it's a good idea to call ahead. There is a stargazing program from 6pm to 10pm daily; summit tours start at 1pm Saturday and Sunday.

NATURAL HISTORY

Mauna Kea's lower flanks are open range populated with grazing cattle, which were brought to Hawaii in 1793 by Captain Vancouver. Mouflon (mountain sheep) and feral goats roam freely. It's easy to spot Eurasian skylarks in the grass, and if you're lucky you might see the *io,* a Hawaiian hawk, hovering overhead. Both birds make their home on the grassy mountain slopes, which are also home to the nene (Hawaiian goose), as well as the *palila,* a small yellow-headed honeycreeper that feeds on seeds and lives nowhere else in the world. One of the more predominant invasive plants is mullein, which has soft woolly leaves and shoots up a tall stalk. In spring the stalks get so loaded down with yellow flowers that they bend over. Mullein is not a native plant but was inadvertently brought in by ranchers as a freeloading weed. Endangered silversword, a distant relative of the sunflower, is found at higher elevations.

Plans to build additional observatories at the summit have been met with strong opposition from leading conservation groups and native Hawaiian activists. Environmental protection is paramount here precisely because the mountain is the exclusive home for numerous plants, birds and insects, not to mention its cultural importance to native Hawaiians. The University of Hawaii, which leases land on the summit to different observatories, claims that it is unlimited public access to the summit area that is doing the most environmental damage.

PLANNING

There is no overnight camping on Mauna Kea, so this is strictly a day trip. Afternoon

---

Pu'u Poliahu

Just below Mauna Kea summit is Pu'u Poliahu, home of the goddess of snow. According to legend, Poliahu is more beautiful than her sister Pele. During catfights, Pele would erupt Mauna Kea, then Poliahu would pack it over with ice and snow. Then an angry Pele would erupt again. Back and forth they would go. Interestingly, the legend is metaphorically correct. As recently as 10,000 years ago, there were volcanic eruptions up through glacial ice caps here. Because of its spiritual significance, the hill is off-limits to astronomical domes, so you won't find observatories here.

❀ ❀ ❀ ❀ ❀ ❀ ❀ ❀ ❀ ❀ ❀ ❀ ❀

THE BIG ISLAND

fog and cloud banks that roll in can dim visibility to zero, making cairns and reflector poles on the trail next to impossible to see, so get an early start. It may be tempting to hitch a ride up to the summit and then hike back down, but there's a serious danger of not having enough time to acclimatize before making a strenuous descent.

It's often windy and cold up here, even on sunny mornings. Don't even attempt the hike in foul weather. Be prepared for severe weather conditions anyway, as temperatures can drop well below freezing. Mauna Kea can have snow flurries any time of the year, and winter storms can dump a couple of feet of snow overnight. Dress in layers of warm clothes and bring sunglasses to protect your eyes from UV radiation, particularly if there's snow on the ground. Call ☎ 956-4593 or click to Ⓦ hokukea.soest.hawaii.edu for a mountain weather forecast.

No water is available along the trail, but there are drinking fountains at the Onizuka visitor center.

Maps
The USGS 1:24,000 map *Mauna Kea* covers the trail. Detailed photocopy maps for navigating the summit area are available free from the Onizuka visitor center.

Permits & Regulations
Hunters require a permit, but hikers do not. Fires and overnight camping are not allowed. Inside Mauna Kea Ice Age Natural Area Reserve the injuring, removing or damaging of any plants or animals is strictly prohibited. Motorized vehicles are allowed only on the designated summit road (ie, no off-road driving).

NEAREST TOWN & FACILITIES
See Hilo (p97).

Mauna Kea State Recreation Area
The state recreation area's campground and cabins are near the 35-mile marker on Saddle Rd. Keep in mind that nearby military maneuvers can be noisy, and with an elevation of 6500ft, the area commonly experiences

Warning

The summit air has only about 60% of the oxygen that's available at sea level, and it's not uncommon for visitors to get altitude sickness. Unlike trekking in Nepal, for instance, here visitors can zip up from sea level to nearly 14,000ft by car in just two hours. Even the astronomers who work up here never fully acclimatize and are always oxygen-deprived in the summit's thin air.

Drink plenty of water. Anyone who gets a headache or feels faint or nauseous should promptly head back down the mountain. For information on Acute Mountain Sickness (AMS), see p53. Refrain from smoking and scuba diving for at least two days before making the ascent. Children aged under 16, pregnant women and those with a respiratory condition, or even a cold for that matter, should not go beyond the Onizuka visitor center.

cool days and colder nights. At the time of writing, the state-owned cabins and campground were closed for renovations. Should they reopen, camping and cabin reservations can be made through the Division of State Parks in Hilo.

GETTING TO/FROM THE HIKE
True to its name, Saddle Rd runs between the island's two highest points, with Mauna Kea to the north and Mauna Loa to the south. The 50-mile road passes over large lava flows and climbs through a variety of terrains and climates. Although most car rental contracts prohibit travel on Saddle Rd, it's a paved road straight across. The rental agencies just don't want to be responsible for the towing charge ($500 and up) if your car breaks down on Hawaii's most remote road. There are no gas stations or other facilities along the way, so be sure to start out with a full tank of gas from Hilo.

The unmarked Summit Rd, which climbs up Mauna Kea, begins off Saddle Rd at the 28-mile marker opposite a hunters' check station. From the turnoff, it's a well-paved road

6¼ miles (plus a few thousand feet in elevation) up to the Onizuka visitor center parking lot. Loosen the gas cap first to prevent vapor lock. If you've got a small car, preferably one with a standard transmission, it's probably going to labor a bit. Be sure to drive in low gear on the way back down the mountain and do not ride the brakes. The visitor center is approximately one hour's drive from Hilo or 1½ hours from Kailua-Kona.

THE HIKE

From the Onizuka visitor center parking lot, walk straight uphill along Summit Rd past Hale Pohaku, the buildings where summit observatory scientists reside. Before the road curves to the right, an old jeep track leads off to the left. Start climbing steeply uphill among silversword plants, taking a right at the next two forks. Look on the left for the official trailhead, found near three brown posts, after about 20 minutes (do not veer onto the gravel path off to the right). From now on, the trail continues doggedly upward, while numerous false spur trails only lead back to Summit Rd. The main trail cuts left and crosses over a dry gulch after another 10 minutes. Keep ascending

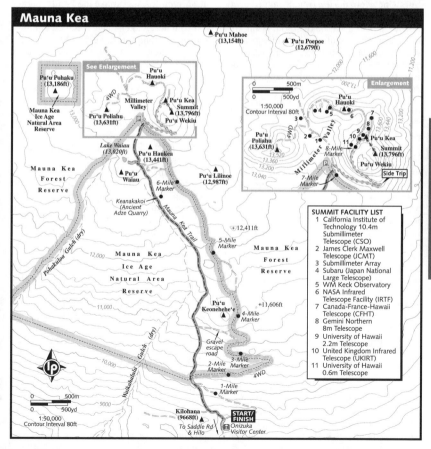

Mauna Kea

Pu'u Mahoe (13,154ft)
Pu'u Poepoe (12,679ft)

Pu'u Pohaku (13,186ft)
Pu'u Hauoki

Mauna Kea Ice Age Natural Area Reserve

See Enlargement

Millimeter Valley

Pu'u Kea Summit (13,796ft)
Pu'u Poliahu (13,631ft)
Pu'u Wekiu

Enlargement

0   500m
0   500yd
1:50,000 Contour Interval 80ft

Pu'u Hauoki
Pu'u Kea

Pu'u Poliahu (13,631ft)

Millimeter Valley

8-Mile Marker
Pu'u Wekiu
Summit (13,796ft)

Side Trip

7-Mile Marker

Lake Waiau (13,020ft)
Pu'u Haukea (13,441ft)

Mauna Kea Forest Reserve

Pu'u Waiau
6-Mile Marker

Pu'u Lilinoe (12,987ft)

Keanakakoi (Ancient Adze Quarry)

+12,411ft

5-Mile Marker

Mauna Kea Ice Age Natural Area Reserve

Mauna Kea Forest Reserve

Pohakuloa Gulch (dry)

12,000

11,000

Pu'u Keonehehe'e

+11,606ft

4-Mile Marker

Gravel escape road

3-Mile Marker
2-Mile Marker

4WD

1-Mile Marker

Kilohana (9668ft)
To Saddle Rd & Hilo

START/ FINISH
Onizuka Visitor Center

Waikahalulu Gulch (dry)

10,000

9000

0   500m
0   500yd
1:50,000 Contour Interval 80ft

SUMMIT FACILITY LIST
1 California Institute of Technology 10.4m Submillimeter Telescope (CSO)
2 James Clerk Maxwell Telescope (JCMT)
3 Submillimeter Array
4 Subaru (Japan National Large Telescope)
5 WM Keck Observatory
6 NASA Infrared Telescope Facility (IRTF)
7 Canada-France-Hawaii Telescope (CFHT)
8 Gemini Northern 8m Telescope
9 University of Hawaii 2.2m Telescope
10 United Kingdom Infrared Telescope (UKIRT)
11 University of Hawaii 0.6m Telescope

THE BIG ISLAND

sharply, with enormous views of Mauna Loa on the left and banks of clouds behind you. Distinct cinder cones perch on the side of Mauna Kea, creating a colorful playground in the sky.

At about an hour, the summit road comes back into view. Remember to take time to acclimatize as you go, with frequent rest breaks if necessary. Vegetation begins to disappear and the path is marked intermittently with red painted poles, sometimes with reflectors. An escape gravel road connects to Summit Rd over to the right, while the hiking trail curves west around a dominant *pu'u* (hill). Underfoot the *a'a* (rough, jagged lava) gives way to soft cinders, but the winds remain intense. Past the two-hour point, the trail starts to ascend more gradually as it weaves among giant cinder cones. After a level traverse over some more *a'a*, the trail rises through white boulders and, far up ahead, the summit of Mauna Kea is visible.

Meanwhile the trail passes into the Mauna Kea Ice Age Natural Area Reserve. There was once a Pleistocene glacier here, and scratchings on rocks from the glacial moraine can still be seen. Entering a broad valley after about three hours, the battering winds die down temporarily. A sharp, short ascent on crumbly soil takes you over a rise. **Keanakakoi**, an ancient adze quarry, comes into view off to the right; look for large piles of bluish-black chips. From this spot, high-quality basalt was quarried by ancient Hawaiians to make tools and weapons that were traded throughout the islands. As this is a protected area, nothing should be removed. The quarry is about two-thirds of the way up the trail.

After a stiff ascent of about a mile, the trail meets another jeep road coming in from the right. Continue straight past the intersection and soon reach a four-way junction, where a 10-minute detour to the left brings you to **Lake Waiau**. This unique alpine lake, sitting inside Pu'u Waiau in a barren and treeless setting, is rather mysterious. At 13,020ft, it's also the third-highest lake in the USA. Set on porous cinder in desert conditions of less than 15 inches of rainfall annually, the lake is only 10ft deep,

yet it's never dry. It's fed by permafrost and meltwater from winter snows, which elsewhere on Mauna Kea quickly evaporate. Hawaiians used to place umbilical cords in the lake to give their babies the strength of the mountain.

Back at the four-way junction, head north and make a final push upward to meet the Summit Rd at an impromptu parking lot. Suddenly the University of Hawaii Observatory and other observatories are visible up on the summit, and straight ahead is **Millimeter Valley**, nicknamed for CalTech's submillimeter telescope. The trail ends here at Summit Rd, just above the 7-mile marker at a hairpin turn.

From here, hikers have a choice of either returning along the same 5-mile-long trail, if the weather and visibility are good, or walking down along the shoulders of Summit Rd, which is faster and easier even though it's two miles longer this way. Below the 5-mile marker, the road leaves the pavement and returns to gravel on its final leg back to the visitor center.

Side Trip: Mauna Kea Summit
2 hours, 3 miles (4.8km)

Few hikers will want to turn back before reaching the summit. Be sure you have enough hours of daylight left. From the hairpin turn described previously, follow the main road up to the right (not the spur road into Millimeter Valley) and for over a mile to the summit observatories. Past the 8-mile marker, where the road forks, veer right and then look for an unofficial trail that starts opposite the University of Hawaii's 2.2m telescope observatory. This trail-of-use descends steeply east, crosses a saddle and scrambles up Pu'u Wekiu to Mauna Kea's true **summit** (13,796ft), marked by a metal pole sticking out of cinders. Given the biting winds, high altitude and extreme cold, most people don't linger long before retracing their steps back to Summit Rd.

Incidentally, taking a left at the earlier fork leads up to the twin **Keck observatories** *(visitor gallery & public restrooms open 10am-4pm Mon-Fri)*, which house the world's most powerful optical and infrared telescopes.

Just west of the two Keck domes is Japan's **Subaru Telescope** *(closed to the public)*, named for the constellation Pleiades. Its 22-ton mirror, reaching 27ft in diameter, is the largest optical mirror in existence. However, most hikers won't have time for this detour.

Captain Cook Monument Trail

Duration	2 hours
Distance	4 miles (6.4km)
Difficulty	easy
Start/Finish	Napo'opo'o Rd
Nearest Towns	Captain Cook (p112), Kainaliu (p112)
Transport	bus

Summary Tramp through tall grasses and over hard-baked fields of *a'a* down to the Captain Cook monument for first-rate snorkeling at Kealakekua Bay beside sacred cliffs.

Admittedly the only hike of any significant length on the Kona coast, the trail mostly follows an old jeep road down to the Captain Cook monument, with a chance to swim (and snorkel) with the tropical fishes in pristine, isolated Kealakekua Bay. The weather here on the leeward coast is dependably hot and sunny, giving those who have been hiking in Hawaii Volcanoes National Park a chance to finally dry out! See Other Hikes (p142) for other short hikes on the Kona side of the island.

HISTORY

British explorer Captain James Cook spent most of a decade exploring and charting the South Pacific before chancing on Hawaii as he searched for a northwest passage to the Atlantic. On January 17, 1779, Cook sailed into Kealakekua Bay on the Big Island, where a thousand canoes sailed to greet him. The tall masts and white sails of Cook's ships – even the way he had sailed clockwise around the island – all fit the legendary descriptions of how the god Lono would reappear. Of course, Cook and his crew were enamored with the islands and their attendant erotic exoticism. The Westerners were received with classic Hawaiian *ho'okipa*, hospitality that includes sharing food, drink, shelter and, in those times, sex.

Leaving on February 4, the English vessels sailed north out of Kealakekua Bay. Off the northwest coast, however, they ran into a storm, and the *Resolution* broke a foremast. When Cook and his crew dropped anchor anew at Kealakekua Bay on February 11, the ruling *ali'i* (chiefs) considered it a bad portent. Things turned ugly when a boat was stolen from Cook's flotilla. The captain blockaded Kealakekua Bay and set off to capture the high chief Kalaniopu'u. Ever the diplomat, Cook intended to hold him hostage until the cutter was returned. Meanwhile, a Hawaiian canoe attempting to sail out of the bay was fired upon by the Englishmen, killing a lesser chief. Word reached the village about his death just as Kalaniopu'u agreed to go with Cook.

Hoping to prevent bloodshed, Cook released Kalaniopu'u, but bedlam uncorked can't be rebottled. Making for his boat, Cook squeezed off some shots, assuming (as had been the case on other Pacific islands), that once trouble started, he could fire his guns and the natives would rapidly disperse. However, the Hawaiians attacked rather than retreated, responding with a volley of stones. More shots rang out, echoing off the cliffs. All hell had broken loose.

The sailors in the boats fired another round as Cook tottered toward them over slippery rocks. The crowd of Hawaiians pressed in and Cook was struck on the head. Stunned by the blow, he staggered into the shallows, where the Hawaiians clubbed and stabbed him to death. Cook's men went on a rampage. They burned a village, beheaded two of their victims and rowed across the bay with the heads on poles. Eventually Kalaniopu'u made a truce and returned the parts of Cook's dismembered body he could find. The Hawaiians placed a *kapu* on the bay.

PLANNING

It's best to do this hike in the early morning when the waters are calmer for snorkeling.

Also the heat is not as overwhelming and there's less of a chance of being caught in one of Kona's afternoon *mauka* showers later on. Bring along a pair of lightweight pants for protection against the heartily overgrown sections of the trail. Don't forget swimwear and snorkeling gear, too. Be sure to carry plenty of extra drinking water, as none is available at the trailhead or along the trail.

Maps
The USGS 1:24,000 map *Honaunau* shows the network of 4WD roads in the area.

NEAREST TOWNS
Captain Cook
Captain Cook is a small, unpretentious town with a few county and state offices, a hotel and a couple of restaurants.

Kealakekua Ranch Center *(Hwy 11)*, a ½-mile south of the Manago Hotel, has a supermarket, cheap eateries and an **Ace Hardware** *(open 10am-8pm daily)* for camping supplies.

Places to Stay & Eat Next to an exotic fruit stand, **Pineapple Park** *(☎ 323-2224, 877-865-2266, fax 323-2086; Ⓦ www.pineapple-park.com; between 110- and 111-mile markers, Mamalahoa Hwy; dorm beds $20, doubles $55-85)* hostel has a guest kitchen and laundry facilities. Campers have access to the kitchen and showers.

Manago Hotel *(☎ 323-2642, fax 323-3451; Ⓦ www.managohotel.com; Mamalahoa Hwy; singles without/with bath $26/44, doubles without/with bath from $29/47)* is a family-run place with absolutely spotless rooms in the vintage building out back, offering unobstructed *lanai* (veranda) views of Kealakekua Bay. The restaurant *(meals under $10; open 7am-9am, 11am-2pm & 5pm-7:30pm Tues-Sun)* is a Japanese version of a meat-and-potatoes eatery. It's not health food, but portions are large and the old-style atmosphere is fun. Pork chops are a speciality.

Pomaikai Farm B&B *(Lucky Farm; ☎ 328-2112, 800-325-6427, fax 328-2255; Ⓦ www.luckyfarm.com; 83-5465 Mamalahoa Hwy;*

B&B singles/doubles from $55/60) overlooks Ke'ei Bay. Casual accommodations include a charmingly rustic converted coffee barn with an outdoor shower. Full breakfasts are a good deal. French is spoken.

Cedar House *(☎/fax 328-8829, ☎ 866-328-8829; Ⓦ www.cedarhouse-hawaii.com; B&B doubles $70-75, with bath $85-95, double 2-bedroom cottage $110)* is perched on a quiet coffee farm 1 mile up from the shopping center. One of the rooms has a kitchenette. The helpful hosts speak fluent German, as well as some French and Cantonese, and serve buffet breakfasts.

Rainbow Plantation B&B *(☎ 323-2393, 800-494-2829, fax 323-9445; Ⓦ www.aloha.net/~konabnb/; Mamalahoa Hwy; B&B doubles from $75)* is also on a working coffee farm situated above Kealakekua Bay. The unique 'Jungle Queen' fishing boat has been converted into a guest cottage, complete with air-conditioning, TV/VCR and *lanai*. All guests share an open gazebo kitchen and hammocks.

Getting There & Away Captain Cook is a 20-minute drive south of Kona on the Mamalahoa Hwy (Hwy 11). From Kona to Hilo, the northern half of the belt road is 92 miles, and the journey takes over two hours nonstop. The southern Kona–Hilo route via South Point (Ka Lae) and Hawaii Volcanoes National Park is 125 miles and takes approximately three hours. Saddle Rd (see Getting to/from the Hike on p108 for Mauna Kea) is another cross-island route.

Hele-On *(☎ 961-8744)*, the county public bus, offers limited services. The No 16 Kailua-Kona bus departs from Hilo's Mo'oheau Terminal at 1.30pm from Monday to Saturday. This bus goes north, stopping all along the Hamakua Coast. It stops at Kona's Lanihau Center and Yano Hall in Captain Cook ($6, 3¾ hours).

Kainaliu & Kealakekua
The small town of Kainaliu, close to Kona, has good eateries. **Evie's Natural Foods** *(☎ 322-0739; 79-7460 Mamalahoa Hwy, Kainaliu; items $3-8; open 8am-7pm Mon-Fri, 9am-5pm Sat & Sun)*, on the *makai*

(ocean) side of Hwy 11, sells organic produce, fruit juices, smoothies, salads and sandwiches.

Aloha Angel Cafe (☎ 322-3383; 79-7384 *Mamalahoa Hwy, Kainaliu; breakfast & lunch $6-13, dinner $14-25; open 8am-3pm & 5pm-9pm daily*), adjoining the Aloha Theater, is undoubtedly the best eatery on the South Kona coast, with a distant ocean view from tables on the *lanai*. Choose from vegetarian dishes and fresh fish specials, fresh-squeezed juices, espresso and heavenly cookies.

Although tiny, Kealakekua is the commercial center for Kona's hill towns. **Island Books** (☎ 322-2006; 79-7360 *Mamalahoa Hwy, Kealakekua*) is a wonderfully well-stocked used bookstore that sells some general maps and Hawaiiana titles aplenty.

Getting There & Away Kainaliu is a 15-minute drive south of Kailua-Kona on the Mamalahoa Hwy (Hwy 11). The **Hele-On** bus between Hilo and Kailua-Kona stops in Kainaliu before reaching Captain Cook (see Getting There & Away p112 for Captain Cook).

GETTING TO/FROM THE HIKE

The trail starts just off the Mamalahoa Hwy (Hwy 11) in the town of Captain Cook.

If you're driving, turn off Hwy 11 south of Captain Cook proper onto Napo'opo'o Rd and go down about 250 yards, where you'll find a dirt road immediately after the second telephone pole on the right. When parking on the shoulder, pay attention to 'No Parking' signs and do not block private driveways.

THE HIKE

A chained-off asphalt road on the *makai* side of the road may look like the trail, but it quickly dead-ends in a field. The unsigned monument trail actually begins further uphill on Napo'opo'o Rd on a dirt

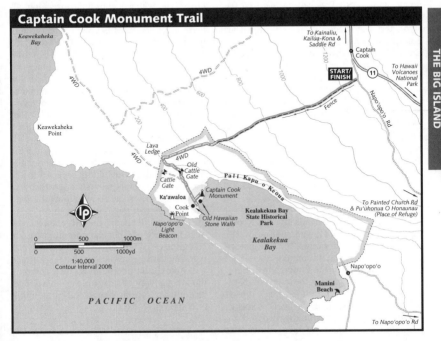

Captain Cook Monument Trail

4WD road. It's not that the trail is particularly steep or uneven, but it's not consistently maintained. At times this can be a jungly path through tall elephant grasses, which scratch up exposed arms and legs. At other times the trail is kept clear by horseback riders.

Start walking down the dirt road and after 200 yards it will fork – stay to the left, which is essentially a continuation of the road you've been walking on. At this point the trail is usually not too overgrown although it has narrowed to single-track width. In most places the trail runs downhill alongside a dilapidated barbed-wire fence. Dense foliage, including papaya, mango and avocado trees, overhangs the trail. When in doubt, stay to the left. The trail gradually gets steeper and rockier, then widens out onto packed dirt. Around the one-mile point, the vegetation changes from tall tufts of grasses to scrubby *koa haole* (shrub). The trail levels out, passing a gate with a 'No Trespassing' sign on the left.

As the way becomes rockier, the trail emerges into vast fields of *a'a* and views of the *pali* arise, while the ocean suddenly seems not so far away. It's unshaded and hot as you trek over lava flows, veering to the left along a broad ledge. The 4WD road descends ever more steeply, but with a partial shade cover of *kiawe* trees, then crosses through a broken-down cattle gate. Straight ahead are views down the coast to Napo'opo'o village. Still going downhill, another jeep road comes in from the *makai* side of the trail; memorize this Y-junction for the return walk, but do not veer to the right.

Flanking either side of the trail as it leaves behind *a'a* and heads straight for the ocean are a few old Hawaiian stone walls. Almost at the water's edge, the trail passes a 'No Camping' sign. A mongoose may well be racing around in the undergrowth here. Then continue right to the edge of Kealakekua Bay. The 'beach' is made up of broken bits of white coral as well as speckled black sand, occasionally crossed by *pahoehoe* (smooth, ropy lava) flows that stretch fingers of lava into aquamarine ocean. After gazing out to sea, with an abandoned light beacon far off to the right, turn around and walk back uphill, looking for a break in the stone wall at the 'No Camping' sign. A short spur trail curves right through the stone walls and in a few minutes reaches the 1874 **monument** marking the spot of Cook's demise.

By slipping into the ocean from the rocks on the left side of the cement dock in front of the monument, the water starts out about 5ft deep and gradually deepens to about 30ft. The cove is protected and usually very calm. Visibility is good, and coral, turtles and fish are abundant. Snorkeling tour boats pull into the bay in the morning, but they generally don't come ashore, and most leave by lunchtime.

Queen's Bath, a little lava pool with brackish spring-fed water, lies at the edge of the cove, a few minutes walk from the Captain Cook Monument in the direction of the cliffs. The water is cool and refreshing, although the mosquitoes can get aggressive here. A few minutes beyond Queen's Bath, the path ends at **Pali Kapu O Keoua,** the 'cliffs sacred to the chief Keoua.' The cliffs' numerous caves were the burial places of Hawaiian royalty, and it's speculated that some of Captain Cook's bones were placed here as well. A few lower caves are accessible, but they don't contain much other than beer cans. All are sacred and should be left undisturbed.

After snorkeling and sunbathing on the rocks, be sure to leave at least an hour before sunset time for hiking back up to the trailhead. The return trip is straightforward, except for the tricky Y-junction described earlier. Keep an eye out for it, and veer to the right, uphill toward the ledge; those who miss the fork and instead continue straight along the coast will be lost shortly. (Several working cattle gates across that 4WD track will quickly let hikers know they're going the wrong way.) Back on the lava ledge, turn away from the ocean and plow uphill to Napo'opo'o Rd.

[Continued on page 120]

ISLANDS OF FIRE: HAWAII'S VOLCANOES

There are some 1500 active volcanoes on earth. Around 95% of these are located on plate edges. The spectacularly volatile 'Ring of Fire' is a series of the world's most active volcanoes (eg, Mt Pinatubo in the Philippines, Mt St Helens in Washington state and Japan's Mt Unzen) around the rim of the Pacific Plate.

So what does this all have to do with Hawaiian volcanoes? Next to nothing, because the volcanoes here fall into that special 5% that are nowhere near the plate margin, which is about 2500 miles away from Hawaii. Instead, these volcanoes are part of the Hawaiian Island-Emperor Seamount chain, created by somewhat mysterious 'hot spots' in the earth's mantle.

The Big Island, once again in a league all of its own, straddles the hot spot and so has active, dormant and extinct volcanoes, while all of the other, older Hawaiian islands have shifted away from the hot spot. Experts estimate that the Big Island is a youthful one million years old, while Kauai is the wizened *kupuna* (elder) of the group at six million years old.

To ancient Hawaiians, volcanoes were a potent source of supernatural power. The mountains engendered myths of the Hawaiian pantheon, provided a spiritual training ground for *kahuna* (priest, healer or sorcerer) and a place where *maka'ainana* (commoners) could bury ancestral bones and umbilical cords, thereby ensuring their family's strength and endurance through the generations.

Adventurous foreign travelers have been drawn to Hawaii's volcanoes for centuries, including literary figures Mark Twain, Jack London and Isabella Bird, and scientific luminaries such as botanist David Douglas and Thomas Jaggar, an innovative volcanologist. Today hikers carry on their traditions of being awed by the sunrise atop Haleakala, summiting the active volcanic peaks of Mauna Kea and Mauna Loa, and trekking through Hawaii Volcanoes National Park, now at the heart of the longest recorded eruption in Hawaiian history.

Origins

The Hawaiian Islands are the tips of massive shield volcanoes, created not by explosions but by a crack in the earth's mantle that has been spewing out molten rock for more than 25 million years. As weak spots in the earth's crust pass over the hot spot, molten lava rises and bursts through, slowly piling up and building underwater mountains. Some of these shield volcanoes finally emerge above the waterline as islands.

Hawaii's hot spot is stationary, but the ocean floor is part of the Pacific Plate, which is moving northwest towards Japan at the rate of about 3 inches per year. (Californians already know this plate by its eastern edge along the jumpy San Andreas Fault.) Every new shield volcano eventually creeps past the hot spot that created it. The farther from the source, the lower the volcanic activity, until the volcano is eventually cut off completely and turns cold.

Once the lava stops, it's a downhill battle. The forces of erosion – wind, rain, waves – slowly wash the volcanoes away. The ocean floor settles and the island essentially crushes itself under its own weight. Thus, the once mountainous Northwestern Hawaiian Islands, the oldest in the Hawaiian chain, are now low, flat atolls that in time will be totally submerged.

Similarly, the islands of Maui County – Maui, Molokai and Lanai – were once joined as a single land mass called Maui Nui (Big Maui). Even the island of Maui itself will eventually be split into two islands, just like when it arose as two separate volcanoes from the ocean floor. But Maui's highest peak, Haleakala, last erupted around 1790, which on the geological clock means it could just be snoozing.

The Big Island, Hawaii's southernmost island, is still in the birthing process. Its most active volcano, Kilauea, is directly over the hot spot. In its latest eruptive phase, which began in 1983 and still continues, Kilauea has managed to pump out more than two billion cubic yards of lava.

Around 20 miles southeast of the Big Island, a new seamount named Loihi has already risen to within 3200ft of the ocean surface and almost 12,500ft on the ocean floor. Some like to imagine the volcano becoming hyperactive and then emerging within a century or two. That's hardly likely, but since the 1996 earthquake swarms in the summit region returned with a vengeance in September 2001, the exact geologic timetable is anybody's guess.

What are the Odds?

Volcanic statistics for the Hawaiian Islands are staggering:

- Highest recorded lava temperature: 2192°F
- Fastest speed at which lava runs downhill: 35 mph
- Height of Haleakala volcano when measured from the ocean floor: 5 miles
- Average number of Big Island earthquakes weekly: 1200
- Longest time Mauna Loa has gone without erupting: 25 years
- Shortest time taken by lava erupting from Mauna Loa to reach the shoreline: 4 hours
- Number of square miles buried under lava in Kilauea's current eruption since 1983: 40.4
- Amount of lava pouring into the sea from Kilauea Caldera: 90,000 gallons per minute, on average
- Years the Hawaiian Island-Emperor Seamount chain has been in the making: 70 million (at least)
- Years until the Loihi Seamount pokes above the ocean surface: 60,000 (at current rate), 10,000 if it gets a move on, but 100,000 if it switches to 'Island time'

Footsteps in the Flow

Although many visitors expect to see lava fountains and dramatic explosions, this is certainly the exception rather than the rule. Hawaii's shield volcanoes lack the explosive gases of more dramatic volcanoes that spew mud, ash or lava into the air. Here lava mostly oozes and creeps along, letting scientists get close to live lava flows in relative safety.

In Hawaii, people generally run to active volcanoes, not away from them. When Pele sends up curtains of fire, Rorschach-type splatterings and flaming lava orbs, cars stream into Hawaii Volcanoes National Park from all directions. Lucky are those hikers who have witnessed a curtain of fire dancing from a fissure or a lava fountain shooting a mile into the sky.

The destructive power of Hawaii's volcanoes can not be underestimated. On the one hand, the Big Island's continuous lava flow means that new earth and black sand are being created daily as lava flows into the sea. On the other hand, there are completely leveled villages, displaced families, spreading forest fires and beaches buried under a blanket of lava. There's a reason why Hawaiians call Pele *ka wahine ai konua*: 'the woman who devours the land.'

Experts at the landmark Hawaii Volcano Observatory (HVO; Ⓦ hvo .wr.usgs.gov), which was founded by Thomas Jaggar in 1912, are able to give some early warnings of impending volcanic events using instrumentation developed atop Kilauea Caldera, such as specialized seismographs and electronic tiltmeters. These can be seen at the next-door Jaggar Museum on the Crater Rim Trail (p131).

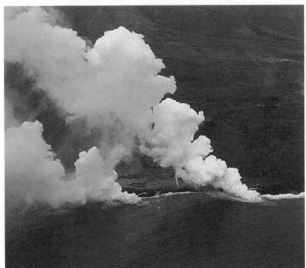

GRAHAM TWEEN

Right: Volcanic steam meets the sea on Hawaii's Big Island

The Language of Lava

Among the most important words in the lava lexicon are *a'a* and *pa-hoehoe*, the two types of lava found here in Hawaii. *A'a* is rough, jagged, clinkery stuff that twists ankles and scrapes up shins; it's often shaded darker brown or jet-black. *Pahoehoe* is a smooth, ropy wave of grayish lava; it can reflect iridescent colors seen close-up, but appears like a lunar landscape from a distance. Lava that starts as *pahoehoe* can cool unevenly, lose gas content and turn into *a'a*. But once *a'a*, always *a'a*. These Hawaiian words have been adopted worldwide as lava classification terms. Aspiring volcanologists should also know the following:

bench – a shelf or step-like area of new land covered by lava flows along the coast, often highly unstable

blowhole – a hole in shoreline lava through which surf spurts up

caldera – bigger than a crater, a caldera can be created by the collapse of underground lava reservoirs or more commonly, when a volcanic vent collapses from the top, leaving a bowl-shaped depression; Haleakala's summit 'crater' is technically a caldera

crater – a volcanic depression smaller than a caldera that can form by explosion or collapse

kipuka – an oasis of land spared by lava flows, where unique species may develop

littoral fountain – an explosion of molten lava, lava bombs and tephra from a lava tube at or below sea level

Pele – goddess of volcanoes and fire

Pele's hair – strands of basalt ejecta spun by the wind into golden, thready glass with a steel wool-type texture

Pele's tears – fast-cooling, basalt ejecta that form droplets of ebony glass

pit crater – a circular crater with steep walls formed when magma is subducted, causing the ground to collapse or sink; Halema'uma'u is a pit crater

pumice – solidified lava foam; some pumice is so light and airy, it floats, and exfoliates naturally

pu'u – hill, cinder cone

reticulate – fragile, honeycomb-like pumice ejecta with glass-like threads

seamount – an underwater mountain; when it breaks the ocean's surface, it becomes a volcano or island

tephra – anything thrown into the air during an eruption

tephra jet – a burst of hydrochloric acid steam, hot water and tephra caused by immense heat where molten lava meets the ocean

tree mold – formed by lava that hardens around a moisture-laden rain-forest tree, before the tree's living tissue burns away

vog – volcanic fog created by sulfur dioxide and other gases; around 2000 tons of vog issue from Kilauea Caldera on an average day, mostly from Pu'u O'o vent

Pele's Power

Mythical understandings intertwine with geological explanations to create a vision of volcanoes that is uniquely Hawaiian. From time immemorial, Hawaiians have respected the power of volcanoes. As ancient Hawaiians had done, contemporary supplicants petition the benevolent side of Madame Pele, the goddess of volcanoes and fire, with chanted prayers, sacred hula (traditional dance) and offerings.

Where did she come from? Legend holds that Pele was born in Tahiti (where the earliest Hawaiians are thought to have immigrated from), but was chased across the Pacific Ocean by her sister Namakaokahai. She ascended as the fiery ruler of the Big Island after a lover's spat with the pig-god Kama-Pua'a and on the summit of Mauna Kea, she did fierce battle with her sister Poliahu, goddess of snow (see the boxed text 'Pu'u Poliahu,' p107).

One of the earliest legends in Puna, the district of the Big Island adjacent to Kilauea's lava flows, dates back to the 14th century. It seems that Kahavari, a young ali'i (chief), was holding a holua (lava sled) contest on the slopes of Kapoho Crater. One of the spectators was a beauty who stepped forward and challenged the ali'i to a race. Kahavari tossed an inferior sled to the woman and charged down the hill, daring her to overcome him. Halfway down, he glanced over his shoulder and found her close behind, racing down atop a wave of molten lava. It was, of course, the volcano goddess who chased Kahavari out to sea, where he narrowly escaped in a canoe. Everyone and everything in Pele's path was buried in the flood of lava.

Equally common are modern stories of Pele as a mysterious woman traveling alone through Puna. Sometimes she's young and attractive, other times she's old and wizened, and often she's seen just before a volcanic eruption. Those who stop and pick her up hitchhiking or show some other kindness are protected. On January 13, 1960, a fountain of fire half a mile long shot up in the midst of a sugarcane field just above Kapoho and a hot springs resort and nearly 100 homes and businesses disappeared beneath the flow. A bizarre phenomenon occurred when the lava flow approached the sea at Cape Kumukahi, which means 'first beginning' in Hawaiian. Within a few feet of the lighthouse, the river of lava parted and circled around the structure, sparing it from destruction. Afterwards rumors circulated of how the lighthouse keeper had offered a meal to an elderly woman who had showed up at his door on the eve of the eruption.

In the 21st century, worship and reverence of Pele are alive and well on the Big Island. The area all around Halema'uma'u Crater, which the goddess calls her home, is dotted with lei (garlands), anthuriums and ho'okupu, sacred offerings wrapped in ti leaves. In modern times she has developed a taste for gin, and you may spy a bottle or two nestled in a fissure. And it's common practice to offer a couple of heavily laden ohelo berry branches to the goddess before partaking of this fruit. It's also completely kapu (forbidden) to take away lava rocks from Hawaii, for to do so risks upsetting the goddess.

[Continued from page 114]

Hawaii Volcanoes National Park

Unique among US national parks, Hawaii Volcanoes National Park (HVNP) contains two active volcanoes and terrain ranging from tropical beaches to the subarctic summit of Mauna Loa, the most massive volcano on earth. It has 140 miles of amazingly varied trails and both drive-up campsites and backcountry camping. The centerpiece of the park is Kilauea Caldera, the sunken center of Kilauea Volcano, the youngest and most active volcano on earth.

The park's landscape is phenomenal, with dozens of craters and cinder cones, hills piled with pumice, and hardened oceans of lava frozen rock-solid on the hillsides. Dotting the lava landscape are rain forest and fern grove oases called *kipuka*, plus newer thickets of green that have taken root in the rugged black rock. These islands provide a protected habitat for a number of native bird species. More than half of the park is kept as wilderness.

The park encompasses about a quarter-million acres of land and it's still growing. In the past 15 years, lava pouring from Kilauea has added more than 500 acres to the Big Island. The current series of eruptions, which is the longest in recorded history, has spewed out more than 2.5 billion cubic yards of new lava. Central to all the action is the Pu'u O'o vent, a smoldering cone in the northeast section of the park. You can often hike to the active lava flow at the end of Chain of Craters Rd (see the boxed text 'Go to the Flow'). For more about Hawaii's amazing volcanoes, see Islands of Fire: Hawaii's Volcanoes (p115).

CLIMATE

Rain, wind and fog typify the rather moody weather up here. Chilly conditions move in fast, and on any given day it can change from hot and dry to cool and soaking in a flash. As a result, many people shiver their way around this park in shorts. Near Kilauea

---

THE BIG ISLAND

Go to the Flow

Giving in to visitor demands, the park service somewhat reluctantly allows people to hike from the end of Chain of Craters Rd to the active lava flow. The park's 24-hour eruption **hotline** (☎ 985-6000) tells what the volcano is doing that day and where to best view the action.

What you'll be able to see depends on current volcanic activity. From the end of Chain of Craters Rd, you may see steam clouds billowing and that's about it. Once the sun is down however, lava tubes on the mountainside usually glow red in the night sky and lava lakes at the top of vents are aflame. If the ceiling of a tube collapses, you can see 'skylights': punctures in the earth's surface that reveal the molten lava below.

Park rangers have marked a trail over hardened lava to a good, though distant, observation point where the lava flows dramatically into the sea. Watch your footing, as there are sharp jags as well as cracks and holes in the brittle surface. During the day, the black lava reflects the sun's heat and the temperature commonly gets into the high 90s (°F); there's no shade along the way. Nighttime offers the most inspiring viewing, but a flashlight is essential for navigating the ankle-wrenching lava trail. The park service also suggests each person carry a minimum of 2L of water and a first-aid kit, and wear long pants and a hat.

While the steam plumes are impressive to see from a distance, they are extremely dangerous to view up close. The explosive clash between seawater and 2100°F molten lava can spray scalding water hundreds of feet into the air and can throw up chunks of lava. The lava crust itself forms in unstable ledges called lava benches, which can collapse into the ocean without warning. Several visitors have been injured, and even killed, by hiking beyond the established safe observation point.

Caldera, temperatures average about 15°F cooler than down on the coast. Even when it's bright and sunny in Hilo, by the time Hwy 11 gains in elevation and reaches Volcano town, the weather may have turned foul. For recorded weather information call ☎ 961-5582.

PLANNING

A custom you are likely to come across on a trail is the piling up of stones, particularly *a'a* into *ahu* (cairns). These cairns help demarcate barely-there trails across volcanic landscapes and other trails in fog and inclement weather; adding to them will help other hikers.

When to Hike

One of the many beauties of HVNP is that it's open 24 hours a day, 365 days a year. It is certainly possible to hike year-round in the park; however, some hikes are best done in certain seasons. Keep in mind that Volcano sees a lot of rainfall, which is possible any time of year, and that visiting during the winter months increases the likelihood that hikers will come away soaked. However, storms rarely make hiking impossible. All of the main hikes in the central Kilauea crater area ringed by Crater Rim Dr can be hiked anytime. The real concern is volcanic activity, which can temporarily close or wipe out certain trails.

What to Bring

The park service considers the following essential to safe hiking: a first-aid kit, a flashlight with extra batteries, a minimum of 4L of water, an extra stash of food, a compass, a mirror (for signaling), complete rain gear, sunscreen and a hat.

Maps

Blame Mother Nature, but topographic maps simply can't keep up with the park's dynamically changing landscape. National Geographic's Trails Illustrated *Hawaii Volcanoes National Park* ($9.95) is a large-format, prefolded, waterproof and rip-resistant topographic hiking map. It covers the most popular hiking and wilderness areas and adds features of special interest, such as campsites and trail distances. However, both this map and the USGS topographic maps recommended for individual hikes later in this chapter are likely to be outdated, especially when it comes to hiking trails in the more active rift zones.

A free full-color visitors guide containing basic driving maps is given out automatically at the park entrance station. While these maps are meant for navigating around by car, they also outline the park's major networks of hiking trails, showing important trailheads, key junctions and distances. Topographic detail is lacking, but it's enough to keep most hikers from getting lost.

Books

The *Road Guide to Hawaii Volcanoes National Park*, by Barbara & Robert Decker, will be particularly helpful for auto junkets. In *Volcano: A Memoir*, Garrett Hongo's poetic prose dances off the page as he rediscovers his birthplace with explorations of mind, body, soul and nature.

Information Sources

While in the immediate vicinity of the park, updates on volcanic eruptions, weather conditions and road closures are available at 530 AM on the radio dial.

The friendly rangers at **Kilauea visitor center** (☎ 985-6017; Ⓦ *www.nps.gov/havo; Crater Rim Dr; admission free; open 7:45am-5pm daily*), near the park entrance, have the latest information on volcanic eruption activity, guided interpretive programs and walks, backcountry trail conditions and road closures. Ask for free trail guide pamphlets and photocopied handouts. The center also contains a small museum and a theater, where a 25-minute film on the geology of Kilauea is played on the hour from 9am to 4pm.

Permits & Fees

The entry fee for Hawaii Volcanoes National Park is $10 per car, or $5 per person arriving on foot, bicycle or motorcycle. Fees are collected at park entry gates and a multiple-entry ticket is good for seven days.

THE BIG ISLAND

Warning

There have been only two known violent explosions from Kilauea, in 1790 and in 1924. Hawaiian volcanoes are seldom violent, and most of the lava that flows from cracks in the rift zones is slow-moving, giving plenty of warning.

Still, fatalities happen. Most recent deaths have resulted from unstable collapsing 'benches' of new land and steam explosions at the edge of the active lava flow near the ocean. Other potential hazards include deep cracks in the earth and thin lava crust, which may mask hollows and unstable lava tubes. Stay on marked trails and take all park warning signs seriously.

Another hazard is the toxic cocktail of sulfuric and hydrochloric acid, as well as minute glass particles, issuing from steam vents. Everyone should take care, but especially those with respiratory and heart conditions, pregnant women and those with infants or young children. At times, 'vog' can spread over the entire park area, depending on which way the winds are blowing. Check with rangers for the latest information.

All hikers and campers are required by federal law to register and obtain a free permit at the Kilauea visitor center, near the park entrance, before heading out. Permits are issued on a first-come, first-served basis, beginning no earlier than noon on the day before your intended hike. There's a three-day limit at each backcountry camping site.

Special Events

Tuesday nights at 7pm, the visitor center hosts **After Dark in the Park** (admission free), a series of talks led by area experts on issues of cultural, historical and geological importance.

The national park sponsors several annual events that become truly special in such an inspired setting. Park entrance fees apply to the following selection of the most popular events:

Annual Dance & Music Concert – this event hosted by the Volcano Art Center presents works by Big Island choreographers, dancers and musicians; last weekend in March.

Na Mea Hawaii Hula Kahiko Series – this series of free outdoor hula performances takes place mainly in summer.

Annual Kilauea Volcano Wilderness Runs – a marathon, and 5- and 10-mile runs (there's also a 5-mile walk) held the last weekend in July.

Aloha Festivals Ka Ho'ola'a O Na Ali'i – this brilliant royal court procession and celebration on the Halema'uma'u Crater rim at the end of August is a must-see.

GETTING THERE & AWAY

From Hilo, it takes about 45 minutes to drive the 29 miles to the park entrance station by heading south on Hwy 11. Drivers should note that the nearest gas is in nearby Volcano town. **Hele-On** (☎ 961-874), the county public bus, offers limited services. The No 23 Kau bus stops at the park visitor center (and at Volcano village) once in each direction Monday to Friday. It leaves the visitor center for Hilo at 8:10am and returns from Hilo's Mo'oheau Terminal at 2:40pm ($2.25, one hour).

GETTING AROUND

There is no public transport within the park.

Crater Rim Dr is a field trip in vulcanology. This amazing 11-mile loop road skirts the rim of Kilauea Caldera and has marked stops at steam vents and smoking crater lookouts. If you take Crater Rim Dr in a counterclockwise direction, you'll start off at the visitor center. Unlike the Chain of Craters Rd, Crater Rim Dr is relatively level, making it a good road for cyclists.

Chain of Craters Rd winds 20 miles down the southern slopes of Kilauea Volcano, ending abruptly at the edge of the most recent lava flow on the Puna Coast. There are a handful of craters that drivers can literally pull up to and peer into along the way. This is the region called the East Rift Zone and it's where all the most recent lava action happens. It's a good paved two-lane road, although there are no services.

Natural forces have rerouted these two main roads in the park more than a few times. Chain of Craters Rd, for example, once connected to Hwys 130 and 137, allowing traffic between the volcano and Hilo via Puna. Flows from Kilauea's east rift cut the link in 1988 and have since buried a 9-mile stretch of the road.

ACCESS TOWNS & FACILITIES

It's feasible to commute to the park from Hilo (p97), or at least stock up on gas, groceries and camping supplies there before driving down to the park or Volcano town.

Kilauea Visitor Center Area

Volcano House *(☎ 967-7321, fax 967-8429; annex doubles $85-95, upper-floor doubles $165-185)* is perched right on the rim of Kilauea Caldera. Although it has an enviable location, not to mention a venerable history, most accommodations do not have crater views. Nevertheless, the small rooms do have a pleasant character, with koa wood furniture, vintage stationery and most importantly, heat. There are no TVs, but the hotel has a terrific game library.

The Volcano House hotel's **dining room** and **snack bar** are the only options for food inside the park, but they are bland and overpriced. Instead warm yourself by the living-room fire, which has been burning for more than 126 years, or order drinks at the hotel's **Uncle George's Lounge** *(open 4:30pm-9pm daily)*. Instant hot chocolate, coffee and tea are also available from the snack bar.

Next door to the visitor center, inside the original Volcano House lodge built in 1877, the **Volcano Art Center** *(☎ 967-7565; W www .volcanoartcenter.org; open 9am-5pm daily)* is a quality arts and crafts gallery. It's home to a nonprofit organization that offers workshops and sponsors *hula kahiko* (ancient-style hula) performances, concerts, plays and other activities. Look for their free monthly publication, the *Volcano Gazette*, for a calendar of local events.

Around the Park

The park has two drive-up campgrounds that are less crowded outside summer. Sites are first-come, first-served. Because of the elevation, nights can be crisp and cool at both. Officially, camping is limited to seven days per campground per month, not to exceed 30 days per year.

Kulanaokuaiki Campground *(Hilina Pali Rd; sites free)*, about 4 miles off Chain of Craters Rd in a remote and peaceful area of the park, is newer and less developed. It has three campsites plus toilets, barbecues and picnic tables, but no water. **Namakani Paio Campground** *(Hwy 11; sites free)*, the park's busiest campground, is about 3 miles west of the visitor center. Tent sites are in a small meadow that offers little privacy, but is surrounded by fragrant eucalyptus trees. There are rest rooms, water, fireplaces and picnic tables.

Namakani Paio Cabins *(bookings at Volcano House ☎ 967-7321; quad cabins $40)* are windowless A-frame plywood palaces at the campground. Each has a double bed, two single bunks and electric lights, but no power outlets or heating; bring a sleeping bag. Showers and toilets are shared. Check-in requires refundable deposits for keys ($12) and linen ($20).

Volcano

In the village of Volcano, a mile east of the park entrance, giant fern trees unfurl, ohia trees droop with red, puffy blossoms and the mist dances among sunbeams. No wonder so many artists and poets reside there.

Information There's a small **visitor information center** *(Volcano Rd; open daily)* out in front of the Thai Thai restaurant. Mostly it has racks of glossy tourist brochures. To catch up on local news, special events and more, check the **information boards** at Volcano's two general stores.

Supplies & Equipment Pickings are slim at both **Volcano Store** and **Kilauea General Store** on the main road. Both carry drinking water, basic supplies, snacks and a few groceries. The Volcano Store has a greater selection and cheaper prices. One or the other is open 5am to 7pm daily.

Places to Stay & Eat Volcano town is blooming with places to stay. Reservations are a must. Check W www.volcanogallery .com for links to B&Bs, vacation rentals and restaurants.

Holo Holo In (☎ 967-7950, fax 967-8025; W www.enable.org/holoholo/; 19-4036 Kalani Honua Rd; dorm beds $15-17; doubles $40) is a small, friendly lodge affiliated with Hostelling International. There's a shared kitchen, laundry facilities and a sauna. Call for reservations after 4:30pm.

Chalet Kilauea Collection (☎ 967-7786, 800-937-7786, fax 967-8660; W www.volcano -hawaii.com; doubles with shared bath $50-70, vacation houses from $140) has various lodgings spread around town, from affordable rooms with shared bath up to exclusive honeymoon suites.

Aloha Junction (☎ 967-7289; 800-967-7286, W www.bbvolcano.com; doubles & suites $60-125) is a 1920s plantation home, tucked behind the post office in the heart of town. Amenities include a Jacuzzi and fireplace.

Volcano Rainforest Retreat (☎ 985-8696, 800-550-8696; W www.volcanoretreat.com; double cottages $95-185) rents three cottages. Each harmonizes functional structure with nature. All prices include breakfast and use of the hot tub nestled among the green.

JP Cafe (19-4005 Haunani Rd; snacks & meals $3-7; open 6:30am-5:30pm Mon-Sat, 9am-5pm Sun), just behind Volcano Store, serves Hawaiian-style breakfasts and hot sandwiches, soups and salads.

Lava Rock Cafe (☎ 967-8526; Old Volcano Rd; meals $6-12; open 7:30am-5pm Mon, 7:30am-9pm Tues-Sat, 7:30am-4pm Sun), behind Kilauea General Store, is the favored breakfast spot in town, but then again, there are not many alternatives. Order the French toast with *lilikoi* (passion-fruit) butter, skip the saimin and burgers.

Kilauea Lodge (☎ 967-7366; Hwy 11; mains $18.50-35; open from 5:30pm daily) has a warm country dining room with a stone fireplace and windows looking onto a fern forest. Expect upmarket mains, such as braised rabbit, venison, Parker Ranch steaks and fresh fish in papaya-ginger sauce, that are worth every penny. Reservations are advised.

Mountain View

Halfway between Hilo and the national park, the village of Mountain View is centered on Hwy 11. **Pineapple Park** (☎/fax 968-8170, 800-865-2266; W www.pineapple -park.com; camping $12, dorm beds $20; doubles $55-85) is a quiet, out-of-the-way hostel. Excellent amenities include a big guest kitchen, laundry facilities, common room with TV/VCR and affordable Internet access. To get here, turn east onto South Kulani Rd after the 13-mile marker, then hang a right onto Pohala St, a left on Pikake St and look for the sign on your right.

Halema'uma'u Loop

Duration	3 hours
Distance	6 miles (9.7km)
Difficulty	easy–moderate
Start/Finish	Kilauea visitor center
Nearest Town	Volcano (p123)
Transport	bus
Summary	Edge on over to Halema'uma'u Crater, a smoking fuming beast that's green around the gills from sulfurous gases and home to Madame Pele, goddess of volcanoes.

Goldilocks would agree that this Halema'uma'u Loop is 'just right.' First of all, it's not too long, and not too short. While it's a well-traveled route, which aids navigation, it's not too busy. Furthermore it's less tiring than the Crater Rim Trail (p131), but offers greater challenges than its rival, the Kilauea Iki Loop (p129). It has impressive displays of volcanism, all giving a sense of the earth's raw power, yet without the choking fumes of more highly active rift zones.

The first section of the trail descends almost 500ft to the floor of Kilauea Caldera and strikes out across the surface of the active volcano, pocked with smoking vents. The trail crosses flow after flow, beginning with one from 1974 and continuing over flows from 1885, 1894, 1921, 1954, 1971 and 1982, each distinguished by a different shade of black. All of the Big Island is Pele's territory, but Halema'uma'u Crater is her home.

THE BIG ISLAND

Ceremonial hula is performed in her honor on the crater's rim, and throughout the year those wishing to appease the goddess leave flowers, bottles of gin and other offerings.

The web of trails around Kilauea Caldera suggests variations for this loop. Perhaps combine the hike with a side trip into Kilauea Iki Crater (p129). Another possibility is to join the Crater Rim Trail (p131) by walking from Halema'uma'u Overlook parking lot straight across Crater Rim Dr on a connector trail for about a ½-mile. Turn left at the Crater Rim Trail junction and hike counter-clockwise around to Thurston Lava Tube and eventually Kilauea visitor center.

NATURAL HISTORY

For at least a hundred years (from 1823, when missionary William Ellis first recorded the sight in writing), Halema'uma'u was a boiling lake of lava that alternately rose and fell, overflowing its banks before receding down the crater slopes, measuring about 1000ft deep at that point.

This fiery lake ensorcelled travelers from all over the world. Some observers compared this liquid inferno to the fires of hell, while others saw primeval creation. Of staring down at it, Mark Twain wrote:

Circles and serpents and streaks of lightning all twined and wreathed and tied together....I have seen Vesuvius since, but it was a mere toy, a child's volcano, a soup kettle, compared to this.

In 1924, seeping water touched off a massive steam explosion, causing boulders and mud to rain down and setting off a lightning storm. When it was over, the crater had doubled in size (about 300ft deep by 3000ft wide) and the lava activity had ceased. The crust has since cooled, although the pungent smell of sulfur persists.

Shortly after breakfast on April 30, 1982, geologists at the Hawaiian Volcano Observatory watched as their seismographs and tiltmeters went haywire, warning of an imminent eruption. The park service quickly closed off Halema'uma'u Trail and cleared hikers from the crater floor. Before noon a

Warning

On any given day the floor of Halema'uma'u Crater sends volcanic gases heavenward, tainting the air all around. The entire area constantly emits volcanic gases, including sulfur dioxide, that lie trapped beneath the summit of Kilauea Caldera. Those who are pregnant, have respiratory ailments or are traveling with small children or babies should not do this hike. When air quality in the caldera area is especially poor, usually due to 'vog' pollution, ask rangers at the visitor center for advice before hiking.

½-mile fissure broke open in the crater and began spewing out a million cubic meters of lava – and nothing since.

PLANNING

Walking across Kilauea Caldera is entirely exposed, making this either a hot, dry hike or chillingly damp. No water is available along the way, but there are drinking fountains near the trailhead at Kilauea visitor center.

Maps & Books

The USGS 1:24,000 map *Kilauea* covers the Halema'uma'u Trail. Ask rangers at the visitor center for a free copy of the Hawaii Natural History Association's *Halema'uma'u Trail Guide* booklet covering geology and natural history, and including illustrations of native flora and fauna.

GETTING TO/FROM THE HIKE

See Getting There & Away (p122).

THE HIKE (see map p126)

From the visitor center, cross over Crater Rim Dr. Then look for a paved path that is off to the right of the Volcano House hotel sign. The trail starts off in *uluhe* (false staghorn) ferns, and almost immediately meets a junction. Continue to the right and down between guardrails and then over some rock steps. Take a left at the next junction. The trail briefly threads through a moist, pretty ohia forest, with tall ferns as well as flowering ginger. Look for giant *hapu'u* (tree

THE BIG ISLAND

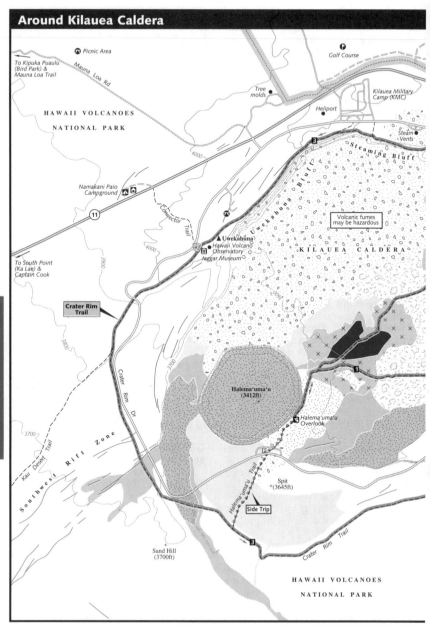

Around Kilauea Caldera

THE BIG ISLAND

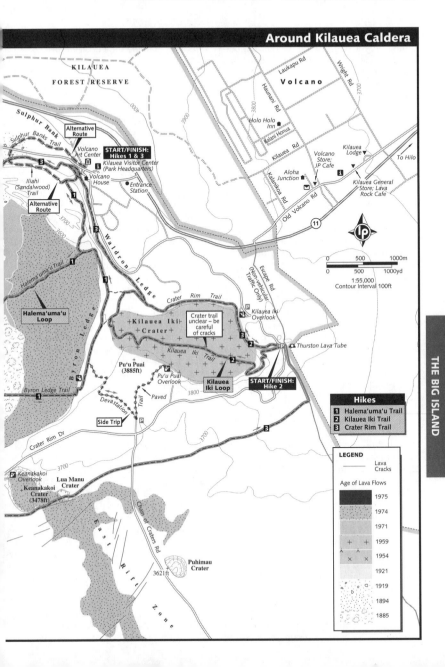

Around Kilauea Caldera

KILAUEA FOREST RESERVE

Volcano

Laukapu Rd

Wright Rd

Haunani Rd

Sulphur Bank

Alternative Route

Sulphur Banks Trail

Volcano Art Center

START/FINISH: Hikes 1 & 3
Kilauea Visitor Center (Park Headquarters)

Volcano House

Entrance Station

Holo Holo Inn

Kalani Honua

Kilauea Rd

Aloha Junction

Kalanikoa Rd

Volcano Store; JP Cafe

Kilauea Lodge

To Hilo

Kilauea General Store; Lava Rock Cafe

Old Volcano Rd

11

Iliahi (Sandalwood) Trail

Alternative Route

Waldron Ledge

Halema'uma'u Trail

Halema'uma'u Loop

Byron Ledge

Crater Rim Trail

Escape Rd (Nonvehicular Traffic Only)

Kilauea Iki Overlook

Kilauea Iki Crater

Crater trail unclear – be careful of cracks

Kilauea Iki Trail

Thurston Lava Tube

Pu'u Puai (3885ft)

Pu'u Puai Overlook

Byron Ledge Trail

Kilauea Iki Loop

START/FINISH: Hike 2

Devastation Trail

Paved

Side Trip

Crater Rim Dr

Keanakakoi Overlook

Lua Manu Crater

Keanakakoi Crater (3478ft)

Chain of Craters Rd

East Rift Zone

Puhimau Crater

3621ft

0   500   1000m
0   500   1000yd

1:55,000
Contour Interval 100ft

Hikes

1 Halema'uma'u Trail
2 Kilauea Iki Trail
3 Crater Rim Trail

LEGEND

Lava
Cracks

Age of Lava Flows

1975
1974
1971
1959
1954
1921
1919
1894
1885

THE BIG ISLAND

ferns) and *amau* ferns, distinguished by having only a single frond. Cooler temperatures prevail as the trail keeps descending and becomes mossy.

At the third junction, about a ½-mile from the visitor center, the trail fork on the left leads to Halema'uma'u Crater and the Byron Ledge Trail. The path gradually slopes down around some boulders. Wild orchids and grasses crowd around as it bottoms out at the crater floor. Veer right to continue toward Halema'uma'u Overlook (the left-hand trail climbs onto Byron Ledge, which is the return route of this loop). While it may be hard to judge where the trail is heading, follow the *ahu* (lava rock cairns) and look for tell-tale lighter shades of grey lava cinders on the beaten path.

Usually the first to colonize new lava flows, ferns and ohia plants can be seen struggling up through cracks in the *pahoehoe*. Watch out for lava cracks in the surface to avoid them. Blistering winds only add to the difficulty of crossing this parched expanse of lava. As the trail makes its way southwest across Kilauea Caldera, veering slightly off to the right, turn around for good views of the Volcano House hotel on Waldron Ledge and also Pu'u Puai cinder cone rising above the trees.

At first the crater terrain is relatively flat, but eventually this gives way to rollicking waves of *pahoehoe* flows and steam vents creep upon the trail. Off to the right, the Hawaii Volcano Observatory and Jaggar Museum stand on the crater rim. The silvery glint of vehicles in the Halema'uma'u Overlook parking lot may be visible ahead. Just before the one-hour point, the trail curves around to the right and climbs through mixed *a'a* and *pahoehoe* atop an outcropping. A sign warns, 'Caution: Thin Crust Area. Stay on Trail.' The trail quickly drops down to an obscure Y-junction.

Do *not* head straight across the intersection. Instead turn sharply right and head toward some distant cairns. From this point, there are many false trails-of-use leading right off to the crater edge. But the views are not as good (ie, only partial) as at the official overlook. After bypassing rainbow-streaked lava and steam vents, the main trail reaches smoking **Halema'uma'u Overlook** (3640ft), which is about 3 miles from the visitor center. Roped-off areas prevent visitors from approaching the rim too closely. When ready, backtrack to the earlier Y-junction, then turn right onto the Byron Ledge Trail.

The trail heads toward a prominent round-topped cinder cone, golden Pu'u Puai, or 'Gushing Hill,' which formed during the 1959 eruption of Kilauea Iki Crater. Closely follow the *ahu* as the trail zigzags over colorful cinder and worn *pahoehoe*. Some of the lava cracks here are over 20ft deep, so you must be careful. Grasses and *pukiawe* berry plants pop up all around. Keep heading for the ledge straight ahead. At its base, a well-camouflaged brown sign reads, 'Byron Ledge Trail.' Some flat rocks for sitting here provide good views across the crater.

As the trail rises onto the ledge, do not short-cut the switchbacks. Look backward to distinguish all of the different lava flows that were hiked over already. The trail passes into partly shaded fern forest, veering left and gently downhill as it becomes increasingly narrow, buggy and overgrown. A guardrail **overlook** offers more spectacular views. Soon the junction with the Devastation Trail (see Side Trip, p129) appears. Turn left to continue on the Byron Ledge Trail by walking north, staying above the west rim of Kilauea Iki Crater.

Birdsong now fills the silence and the damp, cool forest air comes as a relief. Go straight at the next junction, then left at the following junction after that. After passing a bench, the trail starts to descend, then switchbacks down through fern forest. Pause for great views into Kilauea Caldera before the path becomes steeper and rockier. At the bottom, head for a stand of trees on the opposite crater wall, which is only about 300m away. At the intersection with the Halema'uma'u Trail, a sign points up and to the right. The trail climbs back up onto the ledge and returns to the visitor center, now less than ¾-mile away. Turn right at each of the next two signposted intersections. Only some colorful Khalij pheasants may be startled by the presence of hikers along the way.

The University of Hawaii's telescope (left) on the summit of Mauna Kea, the Big Island

Molten lava from Kilauea Volcano, on the Big Island, flows into the Pacific Ocean under a full moon

Waianapanapa State Park, Maui

Sliding Sands Trail in Haleakala crater, Maui

ANN CECIL

ANN CECIL

SHANNON NACE

Cloud-dusted valley, Haleakala National Park, Maui

Side Trip: Devastation Trail
1 hour, 2.2 miles (3.6km)

The Devastation Trail walks through a former rain forest, devastated by cinder and pumice, in the fallout area of the 1959 eruption of Kilauea Iki Crater. This trail gets its name from the dead ohia trees, stripped bare and sun-bleached white, which stand stark against the black landscape. Slowly, ohia trees, *ohelo* berry bushes and ferns have started colonizing the area anew. There are also some tree molds along the way.

By turning right at the Byron Ledge trail junction, a connector path travels through pine forest to a large clearing, then climbs up the devastated hillside. It meanders past spatter cones, and Pele's hair and tears (see the special section Islands of Fire: Hawaii's Volcanoes p115). Look back to see the massive rounded top of Mauna Loa, and on the right, the more pointed Mauna Kea summit. After reaching the parking lot, an asphalt path veers off back to the left. This is officially the start of the Devastation Trail, which ends half a mile later at an **overlook** with educational interpretive signboards. On the return leg of this side trip, keep Pu'u Puai on your right as you descend from the parking lot back to the Byron Ledge Trail junction.

Kilauea Iki Loop

Duration	1½ hours
Distance	4 miles (6.4km)
Difficulty	easy–moderate
Start/Finish	Thurston Lava Tube parking stalls
Nearest Town	Volcano (p123)
Transport	private

Summary Venture into still-steaming Kilauea Iki Crater, an otherworldly landscape that last erupted less than a half-century ago, and view Halema'uma'u crater and Mauna Loa from various bird's-eye overlooks.

Wisps of steam blowing out of lava cracks are an ever-present reminder of the raw natural forces lying inside awesome Kilauea Iki (Little Kilauea) Crater. Recent plumb tests reveal that lava is brewing a mere 230ft beneath the surface. It's an unforgettable hike over earth less than fifty years old. The Kilauea Iki Trail begins near the Thurston Lava Tube, quickly descends through fairy-tale ohia forest, and then cuts across the 1-mile–wide crater, past the main smoking vent. Combining the best of both worlds, this loop then returns via awesome viewpoints over Kilauea Iki Crater.

Who'd want to miss it? Almost no one. A constant stream of vehicular traffic at the Kilauea Iki Overlook is matched only by the number of hikers all making their way across the crater floor at any given time. The trail is extremely popular with everyone from young children to novice hikers to serious lava-cave spelunkers. Ambient traffic noise and other hikers' conversations destroy some of the serenity of the trail. Thankfully just a little rain may drive many other folks away, even as it eases the intense heat of walking over lava and spreads a multitude of rainbows across the crater floor.

It's also possible to do this hike as an extended side trip from either the Halema'uma'u Loop (p124) or Crater Rim Trail (p131).

NATURAL HISTORY
When Kilauea Iki burst open in a fiery inferno in November 1959, the whole crater floor turned into a bubbling lake of molten lava over 400ft deep. A ½-mile–long line of lava fountains reached record heights of 1900ft, lighting the evening sky with a bright orange glow for miles around. At its peak, it gushed out 2 million tons of lava an hour. When the eruption finally settled, a huge expanse of the park southwest of the crater was buried deep in ash. Today crossing the crater could be compared to walking on ice – here, too, there's a lake below the hardened surface, although in this case it's molten magma, not water.

PLANNING
Avoid the crowds by hiking early or late in the day, or when the sky is overcast. Carry

THE BIG ISLAND

enough water, as there is no drinking water available except near the rest rooms at Thurston Lava Tube, opposite the Kilauea Iki trailhead on the east side of Crater Rim Dr.

Maps
The USGS 1:24,000 maps *Kilauea* and *Volcano* cover the Kilauea Iki Crater trails.

GETTING TO/FROM THE HIKE
After driving through the national park entrance station, turn left onto Crater Rim Dr before reaching the visitor center, then drive almost 2 miles to the marked Thurston Lava Tube parking stalls. The trailhead is on the west side of Crater Rim Dr.

There is no public transport, but hikers can connect with this loop from the visitor center via a combination of the Halema'uma'u and Byron Ledge Trails, or a more direct 1-mile section of the Crater Rim Trail, which runs along Waldron Ledge. Either way intersects this loop on the west side of Kilauea Iki Crater; hikers can proceed by taking the second half of the trip before the first (or doing the entire loop in reverse).

THE HIKE (see map p126)
Confusingly, there are actually two marked trailheads for Kilauea Iki. Take the trail that starts at the south edge of the parking stalls. The paved path immediately descends, cutting left and giving way to loose gravel, leaves as well as dirt while dropping through ohia forest that is sprinkled with wild ginger and *hapu'u* ferns. Less than twenty minutes later, the trail reaches the crater floor.

A beaten path marked by *ahu* appears across the vast expanse of grey lava. Strong winds and mist are commonplace in this lunar landscape that pulses with steam (and sometimes rainbows). When it's sunny, there is simply no shade cover to ward off dehydration, so take care not to get burned. Heading generally northwest across the crater floor, you'll find that the path begins moving smoothly over *pahoehoe* in a rhythm that's not taxing. Soft black cinders reveal the

footprints of previous hikers, aiding navigation. Look for *ohelo* berries, ferns and dwarf ohia growing up out of cracks in the lava. If it's not foggy, Mauna Loa can be seen on the horizon.

Don't wander off-trail to explore steaming vents, lava tubes or caves without an experienced guide. Repeated rises and dips become ever more pronounced as the trail draws near to the far crater wall. Pu'u Puai cinder cone is still on the left and Waldron Ledge to the right, but the trail becomes unclear as it emerges into a lava jungle of piled-up *a'a*. Do *not* scramble up the scree hill directly ahead. Instead pick any reasonable path across the crater, veering right when a gaping cave appears directly off to the left. Following other hikers or at least their footprints is the safest bet, but you must be careful of sudden fissures as well as cracks.

Keep heading to the right and ascend the far side of the crater wall by picking up the trail again. It has guardrails and steps that are clearly visible from the crater floor. The trail empties out atop Byron Ledge, the ledge that separates Kilauea Iki from Kilauea Caldera. Turn around for good views of Kilauea Iki Crater and gold-topped Pu'u Puai, which looks much more jagged than when viewed from the Halema'uma'u Trail. After ascending into rain forest, the trail reaches a junction marked by a bench; turn right here. The trail gently wanders through forest on packed dirt and scattered leaves, soon meeting yet another junction. To continue with this loop, turn right onto the Crater Rim Trail, passing another bench. (Note that taking a left turn at either of these last two junctions leads just over a mile back to Volcano House and the visitor center.)

Now it's less than ¾-mile to the **Kilauea Iki Overlook**, delivering views of Kilauea Iki Crater, Kilauea Caldera, Halema'uma'u Crater and Mauna Loa beyond. The trail continues on the opposite side of the parking lot, from where it's only another ½-mile back to Thurston Lava Tube. Descend some steps to emerge at the north end of the parking stalls.

Crater Rim Trail

Duration	4½–5 hours
Distance	12 miles (19.3km)
Difficulty	moderate
Start/Finish	Kilauea visitor center
Nearest Town	Volcano (p123)
Transport	bus

Summary Get up close and personal with endangered flora and fauna, explore native rain forest and solitary cinder deserts, all on a grand-tour hiking loop.

With a variety of views and natural environments unmatched by any of the park's other trails, this long-distance hiking loop runs roughly parallel to Crater Rim Dr. On the north side, the trail skirts the crater rim, while on the south side, it runs outside the paved road. Except for a stretch through the Southwest Rift Zone around Halema'uma'u Crater, the trail remains out of sight of the road. Annoying traffic noise is the exception, rather than the rule.

Because the vehicle road is designed to take in the main sights, you might actually miss a couple of them by hiking the trail, but quick side trips are possible. Also, hikers will gain in other ways by hoofing it. This trail leaves behind almost all of the park's crowds. Another bonus is seeing natural phenomena at close range. Each footstep seems to echo the passing of geologic time, as a collection of dissimilar, but beautiful landscapes roll by like a movie. Lastly, this trail lets you truly appreciate the meaning of changeable weather (okay, so that's not such a bonus).

For those who haven't done so already, nothing compares to hiking inside still-steaming Kilauea Iki Crater, and it only adds another 1½ miles to the Crater Rim loop trail. Divert from the Crater Rim Trail after Thurston Lava Tube and follow the first half of the Kilauea Iki Loop (p129). Cross the crater floor and climb back up onto Byron Ledge, proceeding to the marked junction back at the Crater Rim Trail, then turn left for the last stretch along Waldron Ledge back to the visitor center.

PLANNING

No specialist equipment is necessary for exploring Thurston Lava Tube, which is artificially lit, but spelunkers planning to crawl into the less-explored lava tube at the rear must bring a headlamp with extra batteries. Binoculars are handy for crater overlooks and watching wildlife.

As weather radically varies between different areas (and even from one minute to the next), be prepared for anything from dry, dusty and hot conditions to bone-chilling rain. Contact lens should be traded for glasses because the Kau Desert winds can be gritty. Drinking water is only available at the visitor center, Jaggar Museum and Thurston Lava Tube.

Maps

The USGS 1:24,000 maps *Kilauea* and *Volcano* cover the trail. Note that trail distances on hiking maps and park signboards often disagree, albeit usually just slightly.

GETTING TO/FROM THE HIKE

See Getting There & Away (p122).

From Namakani Paio Campground, you will find that a handy ½-mile connector trail crosses Hwy 11 to the Jaggar Museum, and hikers can also join the Crater Rim Trail there.

THE HIKE (see map p126)

From the visitor center, cross over Crater Rim Dr. Look for a paved path off to the

THE BIG ISLAND

Extreme Steam

Appearing like something from a particularly good *Star Trek* set, Sulphur Bank is one of many areas where Kilauea lets off steam, releasing hundreds of tons of sulfuric gases daily. As the steam reaches the surface, it deposits sulfur around the mouths of the vents, crusting them over with a fluorescent yellow froth. The rotten egg smell is from the hydrogen sulfide wafting from the vents. Other gases in the mix include carbon dioxide and sulfur dioxide. Don't breathe too deeply!

right of the Volcano House hotel sign. The trail starts off in *uluhe* ferns, and almost immediately meets a junction. Continue to the right and down between guardrails and over rock steps. At the next junction, turn right again, marked 'To Steaming Bluffs'. Ohia trees, *hapu'u*, wild ginger and orchid varieties, and tall grasses now crowd the trail, which passes in and out of shade cover accompanied by birdsong. An overlook peeks into Kilauea Caldera and beyond it to the flanks of Mauna Loa.

As the forest thins out even further, fern glades and wisps of steam announce the approach to the bluffs. Just before reaching them, the trail hits a four-way junction with the Iliahi (Sandalwood) Trail coming in from the left and the Sulphur Bank trail heading off to the right. Either of these trails makes for an interesting alternative to the initial segment of the Crater Rim Trail described previously, and without adding much mileage to the overall trip.

For now, continue straight across the intersection. After walking among the steaming cracks, the trail pauses at a windy overlook above the steaming bluffs. Rainwater that sinks into the earth is heated by the hot rocks below and rises back up as steam. Peek into the cracks and chasms beside the trail here to see *ho'okupu* (sacred bundles) left for Pele by past visitors. The trail continues to run parallel to Crater Rim Dr, but far enough away that a wall of foliage blocks traffic noise.

Past the Kilauea Military Camp (KMC) turnoff, views of Halema'uma'u Crater open up. Look for an **interpretive signboard** showing drawings of what Halema'uma'u probably looked like around 1823, based on early maps and accounts, versus what it looked like in 1959. One has to regret not being here two centuries ago when the crater was a lake of fire.

Dirt turns to asphalt on the trail's final ascent of Uwekahuna Bluff up to the summit of Kilauea Caldera. Here stands the **Hawaii Volcano Observatory** (*HVO; closed to the public*). Across the parking lot, the **Jaggar Museum** (☎ 985-6049; admission free; open 8:30am-5pm daily) is worth a visit both for the fine view of Pele's home, the Halema'uma'u Crater, and its educational displays. The museum is named for Dr Thomas A Jaggar, who also founded the observatory next door. Drinking fountains are outside by the public rest rooms. Rejoin the trail at the west end of the parking lot, beyond the tour buses.

After leaving the museum, the trail passes the **Southwest Rift**, where hikers can stop and take a look at the wide fissure slicing across the earth. The rift is essentially one gigantic crack extending from the caldera summit to the coast and out to sea beneath the ocean floor. As trail conditions quickly become exposed and windy, it's 1½ miles to the Kau Desert Trail junction, with nothing but sand, lava and shrubs visible for miles. A rare native plant with green and red leaves, called *a'ali'i,* grows along the way.

Keep hiking straight ahead on the Crater Rim Trail, which drops through tall grasses on cinder track. Ignore (if you can) the noise from Crater Rim Dr as cars snake through the landscape. At last the trail pulls away from the road, marked by cairns again as it passes over dry gullies. It winds up and down through jumbled *a'a*, but is clearly worn through each lava flow. Expect some signposted detours guiding hikers around vents and cracks and straight across a park service road. The smell of sulfurous fumes from Halema'uma'u becomes quite distinct and smoke is visible rising up over the crater's edge. The trail drops abruptly over a soft scree ledge and out across more *pahoehoe* flows dotted by *ahu*; a spur trail to Halema'uma'u Overlook comes in on the left (see Side Trip, p133).

From there the trail rises and falls, while fierce winds will slow down even strong hikers, and vegetation has nearly disappeared apart from stray berry plants. About half an hour past the spur trail junction, the Crater Rim Trail edges up to the south side of multicolored **Keanakakoi Crater**. Signs caution hikers to stay well back from the rim, but the trail passes close enough to the crater to peek inside. Soon the trail passes through an animal-control fence; be sure to close the gate before striking off across the *a'a* field, then back into rain forest. Even here intrusions of lava flows are still evident, but instead of issuing from the crater they push in from the *makai* side of the trail.

As the trail widens out, a pedestrian crossing leads – surprise! surprise! – over Chain of Craters Rd to where an oasis of dense rain forest awaits. Unlike rain forests elsewhere in the world, where most species hug the tree canopy, Hawaiian rain-forest plants and animals live crowded around the forest floor. This makes them more visible, but also more vulnerable to predatory and invasive species. Nevertheless here you will find giant-sized ferns grow taller than human beings, trees are hung with ficus and covered with moss (watch out for falling branches!), and Khalij pheasants rustle in the undergrowth.

You'll likely be accompanied by a soundtrack of birdsong along this walk. The *apapane*, a native honeycreeper, is easy to spot at the upper end of the trail. It has a red body and silvery-white underside and flits from the yellow flowers of the *mamane* tree to the red pom-pom blossoms of the ohia. You may also hear strains of the *omao* (a type of thrush) or the common *amakihi*, another type of honeycreeper whose yellow and green feathers were once used in capes worn by Hawaiian royalty.

Emerging from this beautiful rain forest, the trail passes a solar reflector and meets a 4WD track with grass growing up in the middle, labeled as the 'Escape Road' on maps. Turn sharply left and ascend up the road toward Crater Rim Dr. At the end of the dirt road is another gate that helps protect the native montane rain forest, keeping it free of feral pigs. Use the hiker's pass-through and latch it afterwards.

Almost immediately, detour right to walk through **Thurston Lava Tube**. Lava tubes are formed when the outer crust of a river of lava starts to harden but the liquid lava beneath the surface continues to flow on through. After the flow has drained out, the hard shell remains. Thurston Lava Tube, created between 300 and 500 years ago, is a grand example – its tunnel formation is almost big enough to run a train through. All the organized tours stop here, so it might be loud and crowded inside. Dedicated spelunkers can explore a less disturbed cave that extends back for 334m from the far end of Thurston Lava Tube. But you need the right footwear, a head lamp with extra batteries and you shouldn't go by yourself.

From the rest rooms and drinking fountains, cross Crater Rim Dr to pick up the Crater Rim Trail on the other side. At the north end of the parking stalls, look for a sign reading 'Kilauea Iki Trail, Park Headquarter 2.8 miles'. A paved stairway leads uphill and then walks along the north rim of Kilauea Iki Crater for a ½-mile to **Kilauea Iki Overlook**, where there are views of Pu'u Puai, Halema'uma'u and Mauna Loa. On the far side of the overlook parking lot, the trail descends over lava stone steps, continuing along the crater rim on a gently rolling track.

At the next junction with the Byron Ledge Trail, turn right to continue on the Crater Rim Trail as it cuts across defunct sections of the old Crater Rim Rd, which comes complete with obsolete parking lots, stop signs, picnic tables as well as overlooks from Waldron Ledge. In another mile, the trail passes a three-sided bench shelter before reaching Volcano House. Here behind the hotel is a **historical marker** and coin-operated telescopes. Turn right and cross Crater Rim Dr to return to the visitor center.

Side Trip: Halema'uma'u Crater

½–¾ hour, 1.4 miles (2.3km)

For those who haven't already hiked the Halema'uma'u Trail (p124), a detour to the crater abode of the goddess Pele is a must. It's very straightforward, too, but first read the Warning (p125) regarding hazardous fumes. From the well-marked Halema'uma'u spur trail junction in the Southwest Rift Zone, strike out across the September 1982 lava flow for half a mile. Cross Crater Rim Dr, walk through the overlook parking lot and about ¼-mile later, arrive at the official overlook.

Napau Crater Trail

Duration	5½–7 hours
Distance	16 miles (25.7km)
Difficulty	moderate–demanding
Start/Finish	Mauna Ulu parking lot
Nearest Town	Volcano (p123)
Transport	private

Summary Trek past the gaping maws of the largest craters in Kilauea's East Rift Zone, meander through misty rain forest and reach the heart of an active volcanic eruption, Pu'u O'o vent.

Hikers won't get any closer to the source of the Big Island's newest lava flows than on this trail. Day-trippers will see giant plumes of steam arising from the base of the massive Pu'u O'o vent, while at night fiery red 'skylights' allow glimpses of the molten lava beneath. Further catastrophic activity around the Pu'u O'o vent is inevitable, so this hiking route is vulnerable to change. Don't expect the trip to be without its hazards either, like fragile reticulate lava that suddenly gives way underfoot or choking fumes if the wind blows too hard in the wrong direction. Yet this trip isn't as technically demanding as other Big Island volcanic hikes. All it really takes is willpower and stamina.

NATURAL HISTORY
In 1969 eruptions from Kilauea's east rift began building a new lava shield, which eventually rose 400ft above its surroundings. It was named Mauna Ulu, 'Growing Mountain.' By the time the flow stopped in 1974, it had covered 10,000 acres of parkland and added 200 acres of new land to the coast. It also buried a 12-mile section of Chain of Craters Rd in lava up to 300ft deep.

Then in 1983, the Pu'u O'o vent further east started shooting up lava fountains as Mauna Loa exploded in a separate eruption in the background. These were the first concurrent eruptions in Hawaii in 165 years and hikers on this trail bore witness to the extraordinary event. The most powerful lava fountains shot up almost a mile into the sky.

In 1992 the Pu'u O'o vent erupted once again, forming a lava shield. Although it once measured over 800ft high, the continuing collapse of the cinder cone has created large craters around its base. When a new vent opened on the cone's west flank in May 2002, forest fires broke out all over the park. Nicknamed the 'Mother's Day Flow,' its molten lava reached the Puna Coast in two months. At the time of writing, new lava was still trickling into the ocean not far from the end of Chain of Craters Rd (see the boxed text 'Go to the Flow,' p120).

PLANNING
Check the weather forecast and solicit advice from rangers before setting out. On some days, strong winds blow such choking volcanic fumes down the trail that it's not wise to hike. All backcountry hikers must stop by the Kilauea visitor center before heading out to pick up permits, get eruption updates and read the safety regulations. A minimum of 4L of water per day is essential and no water is available anywhere along the trail. Wearing light-colored clothes reduces your risk of dehydration. Since volcanic activity is often best viewed at night, ask rangers about doing this hike as an overnight backpack and camping near the Napau Crater rim.

Maps
The USGS 1:24,000 maps *Kilauea* and *Volcano* cover the area but not the final section of trail; neither does the park visitors map. All printed map references have likely been outdated by ongoing volcanic activity.

Permits & Regulations
All hikers and campers are required by federal law to register and obtain a free permit at the Kilauea visitor center. Permits are issued on a first-come, first-served basis, beginning no earlier than noon on the day before your intend hike. There's a three-day limit at Napau Crater Campground.

GETTING TO/FROM THE HIKE
There is no public transport to the trailhead. Immediately after driving through the

national park entrance station, turn left onto Crater Rim Dr instead of continuing toward the visitor center. Follow Crater Rim Dr past Thurston Lava Tube and turn left onto Chain of Craters Rd. The Mauna Ulu parking lot turnoff is about 3½ miles further down the road. If you continue down Chain of Craters Rd after your hike, you'll be passing over Mauna Ulu's extensive flows.

THE HIKE

Start from the east end of the parking lot, which has a toilet but no drinking water available. Skirt around some concrete poles and watch for an interpretive signboard on the left, which is the official trailhead.

Initially the Napau Crater Trail follows what was formerly Chain of Craters Rd, before *pahoehoe* lava covered it in 1973–74. There are great examples of pumice and Pele's hair strewn all over the flows. Marked by cairns with reflectors and edged by high piles of *a'a*, the trail wanders under a scraggly forest cover of ohia trees, ferns and berry plants. At the 1-mile mark, a five-minute spur trail switchbacks up to the top of a 150ft cinder cone, **Pu'u Huluhulu** (Hairy Hill), for a look at its fern-filled crater and other steaming vents in the area.

Back on the main trail, wind around the southeast side of Pu'u Huluhulu before diverting right into the thick of old *pahoehoe* flows. Following *ahu* the whole way, the trail climbs in and out of a sunken lava bed before starting to ascend over successive lava shields. Avoid breaking through thin lava crusts by sticking closely to the path demarcated by the cairns. Around 2 miles from the start, the trail draws close to 500-year-old **Mauna Ulu** lava shield, which is still puffing away.

Instead of continuing south, the cairns show the trail making a sharp vee left. Head east, now descending across *pahoehoe* flows toward Makaopuhi Crater. Vegetation, mostly ohia and ferns, has thinned, but on clear days the views are religious: Mauna Loa off to the northwest, Mauna Kea to the north and fire-breathing Pu'u O'o vent straight ahead. After another mile, the trail approaches the south rim of jaw-dropping

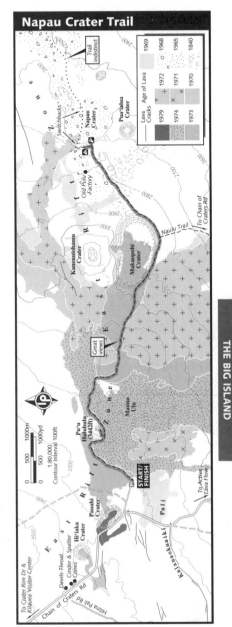

Napau Crater Trail

THE BIG ISLAND

Makaopuhi Crater, which measures 1 mile wide and 500ft deep. The trail parallels the crater rim, providing various overlooks until chunky *a'a* invades from the *makai* side of the trail.

Soon duck into a cool fern forest where new purple fiddlehead ferns look like staffs from a Dr Seuss musical score. Another mile from where the trail enters the forest, the Naulu Trail fork leads right to the Kealakomo parking area on Chain of Craters Rd, but continue straight across this junction to where the trail becomes slippery, with mud, mossy rocks and fallen giant tree ferns, before ascending again and drying out under ohia trees and running across a small *a'a* field where volcanic fumes swirl.

After exiting the fern forest, you'll come to the preserved rock walls of the '*pulu* factory,' an old depository for *pulu,* the reddish-brown silken clusters encasing the coiled fronds of *hapu'u* ferns. The ancient Hawaiians used *pulu* to embalm their dead. In 19th-century industrial times, *pulu* was used as mattress ticking and pillow stuffing, until it was discovered *pulu* turns to dust after a few years. Oops!

Past the '*pulu* factory' fantastic views of the partially collapsed Pu'u O'o cone begin. At the next trail junction, a short spur trail leads to a **lookout** over Napau Crater. Otherwise turn left to reach the primitive **Napau Crater Campground**. Both sites are on a rise that gazes directly on the vent. If you're backpacking, set up camp here before attempting the final 2-mile stretch of trail beyond Napau Crater.

Otherwise pass by the toilet sign and push through tall grasses to emerge onto another field of *a'a.* The cairns here are hard to spot, as they are easily confused with natural piles of lava. A path beaten in the gravel leads right down toward Napau Crater, then the cairns veer left for a short distance atop the rim. Keep an eye out for where the indistinct 'trail' plunges over the crater wall in a daringly steep fashion. Here crumbling switchbacks have been forced onto *a'a* rockslides and intermittent scree. Although relatively short, the switchbacks

are not painless – and they're even more difficult to scale on the way back.

After making this precipitous descent, there's a barely discernible trail snaking across Napau Crater. Cairns are a work-in-progress, but generally lead east across the middle of the crater floor, which last erupted into fountains of lava in January 1997! From this point forward, step lightly and keep as close to the cairns as possible to avoid mishaps when reticulate lava gives way underfoot. On the far eastern side of the crater, there's another set of short, but steep switchbacks ascending the crater wall.

At the time of research, the trail set off relentlessly for another mile northeast toward the base of the massive Pu'u O'o vent. Gigantic lava boulders loom off to the sides of the soft cindery footpath, with steam plumes puffing directly ahead like dragon's breath. Wherever the cairns end near the base of the **Pu'u O'o vent** is the de facto terminus of the trail. Use your best judgment in deciding how closely to approach this extremely active volcanic area. Don't linger too long, to avoid more exposure than necessary to hazardous fumes.

Mauna Iki Trail

Duration	2½ hours
Distance	7 miles (11.3km)
Difficulty	easy
Start/Finish	Hilina Pali Rd
Nearest Town	Volcano (p123)
Transport	private

Summary Enjoy the silence while exploring the vast Kau Desert on a little-used track, which runs over lava fields past twin pit craters and unusual rock outcroppings.

The Kau Desert represents a land of parched beauty and broad horizons. The area's geography and natural features are unique, even within the exceptionally varied environment of the national park itself. A prime joy of this trail is its very lack of foot traffic. It is also wonderfully short, compared to other dull trails in the Kau

Desert network that involve long hauls over hot lava fields. The Mauna Iki path reaches the desert's main highlights without much trouble. There are opportunities to continue beyond the end of trail, if you should feel so inspired.

PLANNING

During periods of prolonged drought, Hilina Pali Rd is subject to closure due to fire-hazard conditions. It's best to hike this trail either in the early morning or late afternoon. That way hikers can avoid the worst midday heat and savor the play of angled sunlight over the desert landscape. There is no water available at the trailhead or anywhere else along the trail. Carry extra water to prevent rapid dehydration.

Maps

The USGS 1:24,000 map *Kau Desert* covers the trail.

GETTING TO/FROM THE HIKE

There is no public transport to the trailhead. Immediately after the national park entrance station, turn left onto Crater Rim Dr before reaching the visitor center, then follow the road past Thurston Lava Tube and turn left onto Chain of Craters Rd. The Hilina Pali Rd turnoff is about 2 miles down Chain of Craters Rd on the west side of the road.

Driving conditions on Hilina Pali Rd can be hazardous due to blind curves, sharp rises and fog. Go slowly, and shortly after Kulanaokuaiki Campground, about 4½ miles from the start of the road, look for a trailhead

sign on the right. Park on the opposite road shoulder, just beyond the sign.

THE HIKE

At the trailhead sign on the west side of Hilina Pali Rd, look for a large *ahu* that signals the start of the trail. From this point, although cairns appear intermittently, the trail is often marked by lines of small stones and sometimes spray-painted arrows. Initially hikers walk over *pahoehoe* dotted with shrubby ohia and other vegetation. Varied colors splash across the lava, from shiny grey to muted brown to metallic red. Look for golden Pele's hair in the undergrowth. After about a mile, the trail passes by some upright spikes of lava encircling a few solitary trees on the left. It's the most noticeable landmark in this otherwise flat terrain.

Keep going over *pahoehoe* flows, but mind the lava crevices and cracks. Another mile or so later at a set of small switch-backs, the trail drops lightly over eroded cliffs onto cinder sands. Incredible views open up here for the first time, so pause before switchbacking down. Hikers can easily pick out isolated natural features in the distance ahead, including double-peaked Pu'u Koae (3250ft) and over to the right, a tawny cinder cone with a rust-colored 'chimney' formation on its top.

At the bottom of the switchbacks, do not turn right or left. Instead look for a line of small rocks pointing out the trail straight ahead. Previous hikers' footprints are preserved in the soft cinders of the trail, making the path more obvious. Fields of brown

THE BIG ISLAND

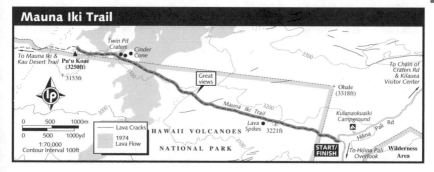

Mauna Iki Trail

a'a stretch off to the right, but the trail continues on grey *pahoehoe*. Some of the lava is unstable and will chip or even break off underfoot, so hike cautiously and stick close to the cairns.

By the time streaks of grey, green and white appear on the ground ahead, it's obvious that the trail is arriving at the **twin pit craters**. Warning signs read, 'Danger Overhanging Edge, Stay Back.' Carefully edge close enough to peer inside the craters. They hide a surprising amount of plant life, including ferns, and a jumble of rainbow-colored rocks. A short trail-of-use leads north to the chimney **cinder cone**. It's an easy scramble up the cone's scree slope, but there's not much to see inside the partly collapsed cone. As the soil is highly unstable, every hiker who climbs it hurries along the cone's erosion. The panoramas from the desert floor are breathtaking enough anyway.

In the vicinity of the twin craters, hikers may see *koae*, a native white-tailed tropic bird. The bird lends its name to **Pu'u Koae**, another cinder cone a ½-mile further west down the trail. This trip turns around here, but those who can't bear to leave the solitude of this arid expanse quite yet can venture further down the trail, turning left at the Kau Desert Trail junction to reach **Mauna Iki** (3032ft) lava shield, about 3 miles from Pu'u Koae.

Hilina Pali

Duration	2 days
Distance	16 miles (25.7km)
Difficulty	moderate–demanding
Start/Finish	end Hilina Pali Rd
Nearest Town	Volcano (p123)
Transport	private

Summary Explore the national park's remote backcountry, with panoramic views, tumbling cliff-side trails, expanses of lava marked only by cairns and camping by a solitary white-sand beach.

Set beneath tall Hilina Pali, this is an arduous day hike or overnight backpacking trip on the Puna Coast. Trail-finding and common-sense survival skills are in order. The reward? A piece of paradise all to yourself at Halape. After all, the Puna Coast area is one of the most untrammeled in the park.

Halape was an idyllic beachfront campground bordered by coconut trees until November 29, 1975, which was when the strongest earthquake in 100 years shook the Big Island. Just before dawn, rock slides from the upper slopes sent most of the 36 campers running toward the sea, where the coastline suddenly sank. As the beach submerged beneath their feet, a series of tsunami swept the campers up, carrying them first out to sea and then coughing them back on shore. Miraculously, only two people died.

The earthquake left a fine sandy cove inland of the former beach, and despite its turbulent past, Halape is still a beautiful spot. Swimming is good in the protected cove, but there are strong currents in the open ocean beyond. Halape is one of only eight Big Island nesting sites for the endangered hawksbill sea turtle, though they haven't been seen around lately. Still, some guidelines to observe include: not setting up tents in areas identified as turtle nesting sites; keeping sites clean of food scraps; and minimizing the use of night lighting, which can disorient the turtles. Hawksbill turtles also nest at the park's Keauhou and Apua Point backcountry camping areas.

There are many possible variations to this hike, but be aware that most of the trails in the Kau Desert and along the Puna Coast are simply not worth hiking. Barren but not beautiful, these extremely tough 'trails' suffer from both a serious lack of water and shade cover, not to mention passing little that's of interest along the way. Trust us on this point! Or at least, try the route recommended here before doing more backcountry exploring on the Puna Coast.

PLANNING

Note that temperatures are cooler in winter (December to March), which is the best time of year to do this hike. During periods of prolonged drought, Hilina Pali Rd is subject to closure due to fire-hazard conditions. For camping overnight, a tent and lightweight sleeping bag are essential because the three-sided Puna Coast trail shelters provide little protection from the wind, heavy rains or the cockroaches and other bugs that crawl over all of the campsites.

Always carry more than enough water, as dehydration quickly occurs when there is no shade cover and lava rocks only reflect and intensify the sun's heat. Ask rangers at Kilauea visitor center about nonpotable water tank levels at various shelters along the coast. Even on a day hike, carry a water filter or chemical treatments to make the catchment water drinkable, if only for emergency use.

Maps

The USGS 1:24,000 maps *Kau Desert* and *Makaopuhi Crater* cover the trail. Be aware that most of the trail is marked only by *ahu* and since there are few other easily distinguished natural features, maps provide only a thumbnail sketch for trail navigation.

GETTING TO/FROM THE HIKE

There is no public transport to the trailhead. Immediately after the national park entrance station, turn left onto Crater Rim Dr before reaching the visitor center, then follow that road past Thurston Lava Tube and turn left onto Chain of Craters Rd. The Hilina Pali Rd turnoff is about 2 miles down Chain of Craters Rd on the west side of the road. Driving conditions on Hilina Pali Rd can be hazardous due to blind curves, sharp rises and fog. Drive slowly, passing Kulanaokuaiki Campground and the Mauna Iki trailhead, to the very end of the road, about 9 miles down from Chain of Craters Rd. Park on the shoulder by the overlook.

THE HIKE
Day 1: Hilina Pali Overlook to Halape

3–5 hours, 8 miles (12.8km)

The route is straightforward at first. Start from the Hilina Pali Overlook, which has

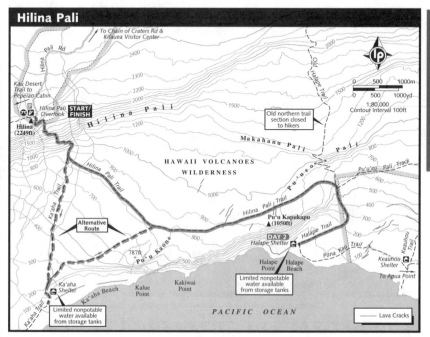

THE BIG ISLAND

Hiking on Mauna Loa

Mauna Loa, the world's most massive active volcano, has erupted more than 18 times in the past century! The last eruption was in March 1984 and lasted 21 days as the lava from the summit crater threatened to overrun Hilo.

The Mauna Loa Trail, a challenging trek starting from inside Hawaii Volcanoes National Park, provides access to the eastern approach of Mauna Loa. It's also possible to summit from the Mauna Loa Weather Observatory, but it's not recommended unless you're acclimatized like an Andean. Because so few hikers attempt this route each year, and most visitors to the islands won't have enough time to devote to Mauna Loa, we've only provided the essential details for trip-planning here.

Planning

The ideal time of year for either hike is between May and October. Even so, snow has certainly been known to fall at the summit in June and overnight temperatures dip below freezing year-round. It's possible to successfully summit in winter, but only during periods of clear weather. Consult the rangers at Kilauea visitor center (see Information Sources p121) about weather conditions before setting out.

On both the Mauna Loa Summit and the Observatory Trails, it's important to acclimatize. Acute Mountain Sickness (AMS) is a danger at these high elevations. Rest frequently and drink plenty of water. If you experience symptoms of AMS (see Altitude Sickness, p53), relief will only come with immediate descent. Hypothermia is another hazard. A good windproof jacket, wool sweater, winter-rated sleeping bag and rain gear are all essential. Sunglasses and sunscreen will provide protection from snow glare and the sun's strong rays that prevail in the thin atmosphere. Bring extra rations, a camp stove and fuel.

Two cabins are available on a first-come, first-served basis on the Mauna Loa Trail and are good places to break the hike. Red Hill cabin has eight bunks with mattresses, and Mauna Loa summit cabin has 12. Any available water (including from both cabin's water tanks) must be boiled, filtered or chemically treated before drinking. There are water holes near Jaggar's Cave and south of the summit cabin.

The road to Mauna Loa, winding past a volcanic cone

Hiking on Mauna Loa

All overnight hikers are required to register and obtain a free permit at the Kilauea visitor center. The visitor center also has the latest information on trail, cabin and water tank conditions. Permits are issued on a first-come, first-served basis, beginning no earlier than noon on the day before your intended hike. For maps, see p121.

Mauna Loa Summit Trail

Constructed by the US Army in the early 20th century, the trail once started from Volcano House inside the park. Today the rugged 19-mile Mauna Loa Trail begins at the end of Mauna Loa Rd, 13½ miles up from Hwy 11 (less than an hour's drive from the visitor center). During periods of prolonged drought, Mauna Loa Rd is subject to closure due to fire-hazard conditions.

Although the 7000ft ascent is gradual, the elevation and arctic conditions at the summit make it a serious hike, for which hikers must be fit and well-equipped. Plan on at least three days, but four will allow for proper acclimatization and time to reach the true summit.

Starting from Mauna Loa Lookout (6662ft), near a picnic pavilion and emergency phone, the trail rises out of an ohia forest and above the tree line, climbing 7.5 miles (12.1km) to **Pu'u Ulaula (Red Hill) cabin** at 10,035ft. This leg of the hike takes four to six hours. From Red Hill there are fine views of Mauna Kea to the north and Maui's venerable Haleakala to the northwest.

It's 11.6 miles (18.7km) and a full day's hike from Red Hill to the summit cabin at 13,250ft. The route is barren, with gaping fissures cleaving the lavascape that includes spatter ramparts and cones. After 9½ miles at Mokuaweoweo Caldera, there's a fork in the trail. To the left, the Cabin Trail (2.1 miles/3.4km) leads up to that night's resting place. For those who absolutely can't push on to the summit cabin, Jaggar's Cave (just beyond the fork to the right), can provide bivouac shelter for a night.

The right fork is the Summit Trail (2.6 miles/4.2km) leading to guess where? At 13,677ft, the Mauna Loa summit has a subarctic climate, and winter snowstorms can last a few days, bringing white-out conditions and snow packs as deep as 9ft. Occasionally, snow falls as low as Red Hill and covers the upper end of the trail. Allow about six hours for the 9.4 miles (15.2km) round-trip from Mauna Loa cabin to the mountain's true summit.

Observatory Trail

This steep, strenuous approach to the Mauna Loa summit starts at the Mauna Loa Weather Observatory (11,150ft). The Observatory is reached along a 19-mile paved spur off Saddle Rd. The narrow, winding road is passable in a standard car, but loosen the gas cap to prevent vapor lock. Park in the lot below the weather station; the equipment used to measure atmospheric conditions is sensitive to vehicle exhaust.

As the Observatory Trail gains over 2500ft in just 6.4 miles (10.3km), hikers must be properly acclimatized and equipped to even think about this trip. Heavy weather conditions (including freezing wind, fog, snow and other unpleasantness) are also considerations in assessing the hike. The Observatory Rd may be closed during winter and during foul weather at other times.

The actual trailhead is about a half mile below the observatory, down a 4WD road. Set out early – either before or with the rising sun – since the trail will take five to seven hours each way. The trail crisscrosses a series of a'a and pahoehoe lava flows and the way is (hopefully) marked frequently with ahu. If there has been recent heavy snowfall, the cairns may be obscured, in which case turn back. After summiting, it's possible to circle around to the other side of Mokuaweoweo Caldera to the Mauna Loa Cabin (4.7 miles), but staying there overnight is dangerous without having had proper time previously to get acclimatized. The Observatory Trail can only be recommended as a day hike for those who are already in top shape.

picnic tables. A path leading off to the right is the Kau Desert Trail to Pepeiao Cabin. Instead turn left onto the Hilina Pali Trail, which gently descends through tall grasses on rubbly *a'a*. Sometimes the lava rolls underfoot, while in other spots it's set hard into the ground like a cobblestone path.

The switchbacks cut into the side of the cliffs begin, gradually becoming steeper but thankfully not narrower. Steep drop-offs on the *makai* side aren't anything to worry about when the trail is in good condition. Hilina Pali means 'cliffs struck by wind'. The switchbacks wind down the cliffs over a mix of clinkery *a'a* and soft dirt, reaching the bottom about an hour or so from the trail start. From this point, carefully follow *ahu* across *pahoehoe* lava flows to the signposted junction with the Ka'aha Trail (see the Alternative Route below).

At the junction, continue on the Hilina Pali Trail toward Halape by following the cairns that lead off to the left and walk southeast toward the coast. In just over another mile, the trail meets another junction, where a spur trail from Ka'aha Shelter comes in from the left. From there, it's another three long miles along the hot Puna Coast, passing shrubby lantana and ohia, the Pu'ueo Pali and Pu'u Kapukapu (1050ft) to finally descend and reach the junction with the Halape Trail. Hikers should turn right here and curve back toward the ocean, reaching **Halape** trail shelter, water tank and the white-sand beach lined by palm trees in just over 1½ miles.

Day 2: Halape to Hilina Pali Overlook

4–6 hours, 8 miles (12.8km)

Retrace your steps back to the Hilina Pali Overlook to complete day two of this hike.

Alternative Route: via Ka'aha Shelter

2 days, 17.8 miles (28.6km)

This slightly longer route detours before reaching Halape to another coastal trail shelter set underneath cliffs by the sea. At the bottom of the switchbacks on the Hilina Pali Trail, follow cairns leading off to the

right from a signposted junction. Walk over intermittent *pahoehoe* and *a'a* lava for about 1½ miles. The trail runs parallel to the cliffs, always gently descending toward the coast. Watch out for thorny weeds that infest hiking boots and socks. About ¼ mile before reaching the shelter, a connector trail to Halape takes off to the left. But first continue straight ahead, jumping down over some *a'a* to reach a windy spot beneath the cliffs at grassy **Ka'aha Shelter**, which has a water tank and toilet. An ocean inlet here has brackish water and high surf, but the setting is scenic. Backtrack to the previous trail junction, turn right and connect with the main route in less than 1½ miles.

Other Hikes

KOHALA COAST
Pololu Valley

East of Hawi, Hwy 270 dead-ends at a viewpoint over the secluded Pololu Valley and its steeply scalloped coastal cliffs. The last islanders left the Pololu Valley in the 1940s, and the slopes are now forest reserve land. A trail down from the lookout only takes about 20 minutes to hike. It's steep, but not overly strenuous and there are seductive vistas throughout; be cautious with footing since much of the trail is packed clay that can be slippery. Cattle and horses roam the valley; a gate at the bottom of the trail keeps them in. The black-sand beach fronting the valley stretches for about a ½-mile. Driftwood collects in great quantities and on rare occasions glass fishing floats get washed up. In winter the surf is usually intimidatingly high, and there can be rip currents year-round.

Mo'okini Heiau

Chants date this temple, where *ali'i* offered human sacrifices to the war god Ku, back to AD 480. Because so few people come this way, there's a good chance this national landmark will be deserted except for the wind and the spirits. In winter it's a fantastic place for observing migrating humpback whales. Turn off Hwy 270 at the 20-mile marker south of Hawi and drive along an access road downhill to Upolu Airport. Park outside the gates. Walk left on a rutted and muddy dirt road that runs parallel to the rugged coast outside the airport fence. After 1½ miles at a fork in the road, a side path leads uphill and left to the

THE BIG ISLAND

heiau. Otherwise, continuing straight ahead for a third of a mile, hikers will reach a low stone enclosure that marks the birthplace of Kamehameha the Great.

Puako Petroglyphs

With more than 3000 petroglyphs, the Puako preserve has one of the largest collections of ancient lava carvings in Hawaii. From Hwy 19 north of Waikoloa Rd, take Mauna Lani Dr and turn right at the rotary, then right again on the beach road immediately before the grounds of The Orchid. From the inland end of the beach parking lot, a well-marked trail leads three-quarters of a mile to the petroglyph field. The human figures drawn in simple linear forms are some of Hawaii's oldest. These petroglyphs are fragile, as the old lava into which they're carved is brittle and cracking, so please do not touch them or walk directly on top of them. Like all petroglyphs in Hawaii, the meaning of the symbols remains enigmatic.

HAWAII VOLCANOES NATIONAL PARK & AROUND
Pu'u Loa Petroglyphs

The marked Pu'u Loa Trail begins on the national park's Chain of Craters Rd, midway between the 16- and 17-mile markers. The trailhead is about a 45-minute drive from Kilauea visitor center. The petroglyph site, which is along an ancient trail that once ran between Kau and Puna, has more than 15,000 drawings – perhaps the greatest concentration of petroglyphs in Hawaii. The easy 1½-mile roundtrip trail ends in a wide field of petroglyphs carved into *pahoehoe*. Please stay on the boardwalk, as walking on the petroglyphs damages them. At the boardwalk's southeastern edge, Pu'u Loa (Long Hill) was the place where Hawaiians buried the umbilical cords of their babies so their children would enjoy long lives. The thousands of dimpled depressions in this petroglyph field were probably pounded out as receptacles for the umbilical cord *(piko)*.

Kipuka Puaulu (Bird Park)

Kipuka Puaulu, a unique sanctuary for native flora and fauna, is about 1½ miles up Mauna Loa Rd, off Hwy 11, about 10 minutes drive west of the national park entrance. A free trail guide may be available at Kilauea visitor center for the gentle mile-long loop trail that runs through a 100-acre oasis of Hawaiian forest. About 400 years ago, a major lava flow from Mauna Loa's northeast rift covered most of the surrounding area, but spared this ecopreserve of rare endemic plants, insects and birds, including the inquisitive *elepaio* (native flycatcher) and three honeycreepers – the *amakihi, apapane* and *i'iwi*. All of these brightly colored birds are sparrow-sized, so bring binoculars. Koa is the largest of the soaring trees here. About midway along the trail is a lava tube, in the dark depths of which a unique species of big-eyed spider was discovered in 1973.

Pu'u O'o Trail

A shorter alternative to the Napau Crater Trail (p134), this unofficial trail-of-use leads to the base of the fuming Pu'u O'o vent from outside the national park boundaries. Before the 20-mile marker on Hwy 11 north of Volcano town, turn east onto S Glenwood Rd and wind through Fern Forest subdivision to the end of the dirt road. Before starting out, check to see if the winds are blowing predominantly toward the trailhead – if that's the case, don't hike, since volcanic fumes can seriously impair breathing. Otherwise park by some junker cars. Beyond the Kahaualea Natural Area Reserve sign a well-beaten footpath wanders for about 4½ miles through lush fern forest, then forges ahead one last mile over lava toward Pu'u O'o vent. Be cautious and exercise common sense when approaching the active rift zone.

South Point (Ka Lae) to Green Sands Beach

One-lane South Point Rd starts out in macadamia-nut farms from between the 69-mile and 70-mile markers on Hwy 11, leading down to Ka Lae, the southernmost point in the USA. Take the right fork near the end and park near the craggy cliffs. Go past archaeological sites and a light beacon, then continue northeast along the coast on any 4WD track. It's a gentle and beautiful hike, though windy. From the boat ramp, at about the halfway point, it's another 2½ miles along a rutted dirt road to the beach. Notice pockets of green sand sparkling in the sun; these are semiprecious olivine crystals chipped from lava cliffs and worn smooth by relentless surf. At the end, veer inland and scramble down some cliffs. Pick a calm day to visit, as during periods of high surf the entire beach can be flooded.

THE BIG ISLAND

Maui

With unsurpassed beaches and a good public trail system, Maui offers hikers the best of both worlds. Snorkel, fins and a bathing suit become backpack essentials on Maui, where you can hit the trail in the morning and surf the pipeline in the afternoon.

Half-day hikes and accessible trails are the staple of this island. Stream hikes swing through the jungle on plank-and-cable suspension bridges in the Waiheʻe Valley and wander up the dusky bamboo forest to a waterfall above Oheo Gulch. Historic King's Highway trails provide different perspectives on an ancient coastline lava road at Hana and La Perouse Bay. Loftier trails overlook native rain forests in the misty West Maui Mountains and penetrate the cool, dark forests of Polipoli.

Haleakala National Park reserves the greatest spectacle for big-adventure seekers, where a cabin-to-cabin backpack explores unforgettable scenes inside a massive, volcanic crater.

HISTORY

Early islanders lived in independent districts around Hana, Wailuku and Lahaina until the 16th century, when Piʻilani, the road-building chief of Hana, conquered the island to become Maui's first ruler. The chiefdom ended in 1795 when Maui was captured by Kamehameha the Great, who used the island to stage subsequent invasions of Oahu, Molokai and Lanai. After establishing sovereignty over the main Hawaiian Islands (except Kauai), Kamehameha sited his royal court at Lahaina.

A friendly visit by French explorer Jean François de Galaup La Perouse in 1786 is the first recorded Western contact. Protestant missionaries in 1820 became the first Western settlers, and whalers soon followed to make Lahaina a bawdy port of call. The 1870s drew investors and foreign laborers to the sugar industry. Tourism discovered Maui's world-class beaches in the 1960s and it has boomed as a resort mecca ever since.

Highlights

KARL LEHMANN

Waiheʻe Ridge Trail, West Maui Mountains

- Delighting in the rickety thrill of Waiheʻe Valley's (p149) undulating plank-and-cable suspension bridges

- Warming up around a woodstove in a snug cabin tucked inside Haleakala's (p155) awesome volcanic crater

- Watching waves break against tropical *pali* (sea cliffs) on Waianapanapa State Park's ancient Piʻilani Trail (p165)

NATURAL HISTORY

During the last Ice Age, Maui was joined with Molokai, Lanai and Kahoʻolawe as part of a bigger land mass called Maui Nui. Two islands in one, Maui consists of two distinct volcanoes, the Haleakala massif (topped by Puʻu Ulaula, 10,023ft) and the older West Maui Mountains (Puʻu Kukui, 5788ft), united by a flat, fertile isthmus. Rain forests and waterfalls fill the lush

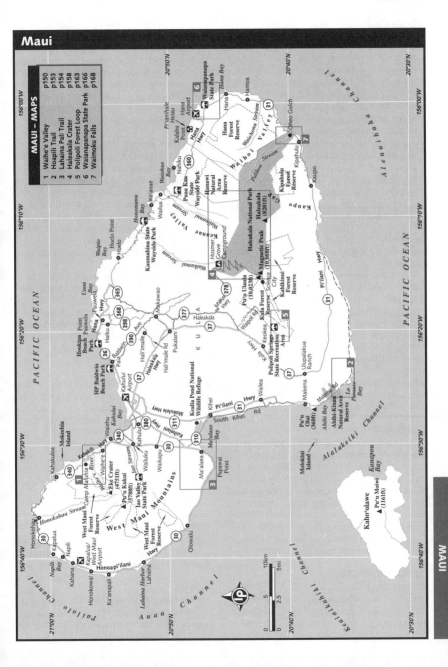

Maui

MAUI – MAPS	
1 Waihe'e Valley	p150
2 Hoapili Trail	p153
3 Lahaina Pali Trail	p154
4 Haleakala Crater	p158
5 Polipoli Forest Loop	p163
6 Waianapanapa State Park	p166
7 Waimoku Falls	p168

Hiking the King's Highway

Maui was once circled by an ancient coastal road known as the *alaloa* (long road) or King's Highway. Many of Maui's modern highways reference Chief Pi'ilani, who initiated this project in the early 16th century. His son, Kiha'a Pi'ilani, brought it to completion in 1561. Hikers can follow in the footsteps of the ancient *ali'i* (chiefs) on the Hoapili and Pi'ilani (Waianapanapa State Park) Trails, two spectacular segments of highway built over lava flows. The Lahaina Pali Trail, built later in the early 1800s, also became part of the *alaloa*.

eastern valleys of both mountains, and the south-facing slopes are characterized by dry rangeland.

The rare, alien silversword is unique to the Haleakala crater, and the volcano's shrubland provides habitat for Hawaii's endangered nene. Also endangered are at least six native Maui birds (mostly honeycreepers) that are found almost nowhere else in the world, including the Maui parrotbill and the cinnamon-colored *po'ouli*, which quite amazingly wasn't discovered until 1973, when it was sighted by a group of University of Hawaii students working in a secluded area of the Hana rain forest.

CLIMATE
The wettest months are from December to March. Mountainous, eastern coastlines around Hana and Waihe'e Valley catch the most rain – up to 300 inches annually in places. South-facing regions are sunny and dry. Constant clouds hovering around the 5000ft to 7000ft elevations lift only briefly each morning, keeping forests cool and wet.

Call ☎ 877-5111 to hear the latest weather or visit ⓦ www.prh.noaa.gov/pr/hnl.

INFORMATION
When to Hike
Under normal circumstances all of Maui's trails can be hiked year-round, although some times are more ideal than others. Rain brings dangerous flash floods and trail closures to Waihe'e Valley and Oheo Gulch. Haleakala is popular in summer, but a dry spell can mean no water in the cabin tanks. The hot Hoapili and Lahaina Pali Trails are best saved for winter months and cloudy days. Mornings are the only chance for a break in the clouds for mountain hikes such as Waihe'e Ridge and Polipoli.

What to Bring
Islanders love camping but they are certainly no mountaineers. Hence lightweight backpacking equipment and freeze-dried meals are not available here. Equipment can't be rented, so bring all your gear from home. Maui's only overnighter features trailside cabins stocked with propane stoves, cookware and padded bunks. If you arrange to stay in these you'll be able to leave some items behind.

Butane cartridges (such as Camping Gaz) are hard to find on Maui, and to save hassles you may wish to bring a different type of stove. For butane check Sports Authority in Kahului first and then try **West Maui Sports** (☎ 661-6252; *1287 Front St, Lahaina; open 8am-8pm Mon-Sat, 8am-6pm Sun)* in Lahaina.

Maps
Trail maps range from poor to nonexistent. Topographic hiking maps are only available for Haleakala National Park. USGS topographic maps can't be purchased on Maui and don't always show the trails.

One of the best regional maps is the *Maui Recreation Map*, a 1:100,000 combination shaded relief map and guide to public trails, parks and campgrounds. Free copies are available from the Division of State Parks counter in Wailuku.

Free road maps are abundant on Maui. If yours seems inadequate try the University of Hawaii's topographic *Map of Maui* or Nelles' *Maui, Molokai, Lanai.*

Books
Ancient Sites of Maui, Molokai and Lanai, by Van James, provides interesting archaeological insights into landmarks along the trails and around the island.

Information Sources

Most trails on Maui are maintained by **Na Ala Hele** (☎ 873-3508; W www.hawaii trails.org), which offers little beyond general on-line trail information and can answer questions by phone. A safety brochure, a few trail guides and the *Maui Recreation Map* are available from the Division of State Parks office in Wailuku.

Maui has no staffed tourist office, but you can order an official vacation planner from the business office of **Maui Visitors Bureau** (☎ 800-525-6284; W www.visitmaui .com; 1727 Wili Pa Loop, Wailuku, HI 96793) and there's a big brochure rack at airport arrivals.

Budget accommodations in private cottages and B&Bs is pretty inconspicuous, and often booked through vacation rental agencies. **Ho'okipa Haven** (☎ 579-8282; W www.hookipahaven.com; PO Box 791658, Paia, Maui, HI 96779) is a good place to start looking for affordable places around Paia, Haiku and Makawao.

Permits

Permits are required if you want to hike in the Waihe'e Valley and to stay overnight inside Haleakala crater (see those sections for details).

Camping permits and cabin reservations for Waianapanapa and Polipoli State Parks can be obtained in person or by mail from the Division of State Parks office in Wailuku. The rule-ridden application process (forget about driving straight to the park) is made easier by downloading the paperwork off the website (W www.state.hi.us/dlnr/dsp /maui). State park camping reservations can also be made at state park offices on any island. The maximum length of stay at any state park is five nights a month. Campsites cost $5 per night. You can inquire about availability for specific dates by calling ☎ 587-0300 on Oahu between 8am and 3:30pm on weekdays.

GATEWAYS
Kahului

Maui does business in centrally located Kahului, the island's commercial hub and home of the international airport. Most only stay long enough to buy discount groceries and supplies before driving off to the resorts.

Supplies & Equipment Stock up on groceries at **Grocery Outlet** (☎ 893-0337; 380 Dairy Rd; open 8am-9pm Mon-Sat, 8am-7pm Sun), **Kmart** (☎ 871-8553; 424 Dairy Rd; open 7am-11pm daily) or **Wal-Mart** (☎ 871-7820; 1011 Pakaula St; open 6am-11pm daily).

The mammoth **Costco** (☎ 877-5241; 540 Haleakala Hwy; open 11am-8:30pm Mon-Fri, 9:30am-6pm Sat, 10am-6pm Sun) is cheap for bulk foods and gas, but to shop there you must buy an annual membership ($45).

The biggest (but still limited) selection of camping equipment is available at **Sports Authority** (☎ 871-2558; 270 Dairy Rd; open 9am-9:30pm Mon-Sat, 9am-7pm Sun). Liquid stove fuel (such as Coleman) and propane are common in grocery and hardware stores.

If you are looking for maps or books try **Waldenbooks** (☎ 871-6112; Queen Ka'ahumanu Center, Ka'ahumanu Ave; open 9:30am-9pm Mon-Sat, 10am-5pm Sun) or **Borders** (☎ 877-6160; Maui Marketplace, 270 Dairy Rd; open 9am-10pm Sun-Thur, 9am-11pm Fri & Sat). Smaller book selections are often found in souvenir shops, such as the **Whaler's General Store** and **ABC Store** chains.

Places to Stay Unless you have a peculiar fondness for old motor lodges there's little reason to stay overnight in Kahului. Rooms cost as much as a resort, so most people just head straight for the beach. For cheaper places check out hostels in nearby Wailuku (p148).

Maui Beach Hotel (☎ 888-649-3222; W www.castleresorts.com/MBH/; 100 Ka'ahumanu Ave; doubles from $120) is a pleasant full-service motel with a free airport shuttle, an on-site restaurant and indoor pool.

Maui Seaside Hotel (☎ 877-3311, 800-560-5552; W www.sand-seaside.com; 100 Ka'ahumanu Ave; doubles from $119) is like a Hawaiian version of Motel 6, only older and with free *mai tais* in the lobby.

Places to Eat For meals under $7 you just can't beat the **food court** at Queen Ka'ahumanu Center on Ka'ahumanu Ave. The in-store deli at **Down to Earth Natural Foods** (☎ 877-2661; *305 Dairy Rd; open 7am-9pm Mon-Sat, 8am-8pm Sun*) sells fresh salads and hot entrees.

Ba Le (☎ 877-2400; *Maui Marketplace, 270 Dairy Rd; meals $8; open 9am-9pm Mon-Sat, 9am-7pm Sun*) is good for inexpensive French-Vietnamese meals.

Aloha Grill (☎ 893-0263; *Maui Marketplace, 270 Dairy Rd; meals $7; open 8am-9pm Mon-Sat, 8am-7pm Sun*) takes diners back to the 1950s with a vast burger menu that includes plenty of vegetarian choices.

Mañana Garage (☎ 873-0220; *33 Lono Ave; lunch $7-13, dinner $16-26; open 11am-2pm Mon-Fri, 5:30-9pm daily*) is a good place to splurge on spicy Latin-inspired creations from Cuba, the Caribbean and South America. It's very popular and reservations are recommended.

Getting There & Away Direct flights to Maui's Kahului International Airport are available from mainland cities on the west coast, though most flights connect through Honolulu. **Hawaiian Airlines** (☎ 800-882-8811; W *www.hawaiianair.com*) and **Aloha Airlines** (☎ 800-432-7117; W *www.alohaair lines.com*) are the main domestic and inter-island carriers, with additional services provided by **Delta** (☎ 800-221-1212; W *www .delta.com*), **United** (☎ 800-241-6522; W *www .ual.com*) and **Air Canada** (☎ 888-247-2262; W *www.aircanada.ca*).

Local buses operated by **Holo Ka'a Public Transit** (☎ 879-2828; W *www.ankina tours.com; fares $1-5*) serve Wailuku and Kahului (Central Maui); Kihei and Wilea (South Maui); and Kapalua, Ka'anapali and Lahaina (West Maui). All three areas are linked to one another via connecting buses to Ma'alaea. There is no airport bus.

To get to trailheads you can join a hostel tour (see Wailuku, below) or you'll need a car. Most national car rental agencies have branches near the airport. It's fashionable among budget and long-term visitors to go 'local' by renting an older model car at a discount rate. **Word of Mouth Rent A Car** (☎ 877-2436, 800-533-5929; W *www.maui rentacar.com; 150 Hana Hwy*) rents reliable

Nissan sedans from $133 per week (tax is included).

For a cab call **Islandwide Taxi** (☎ 874-8294) or **Maui Central Cab** (☎ 244-7278).

Wailuku

Gateway to the West Maui Mountains, this plain government town next to Kahului features Maui's only hostels and is close to hikes in Waihe'e Valley.

Information A safety brochure, a few trail guides and the *Maui Recreation Map*, as well as state park camping permits and cabin reservations, are available from the **Division of State Parks** (☎ 984-8109; W *www .state.hi.us/dlnr/dsp/maui; 54 S High St, Room 101; open 7:45am-4:30pm Mon-Fri, phone hours 8am-3:30pm Mon-Fri*).

Although not a tourist office, you can pick up an official vacation planner from the business office of **Maui Visitors Bureau** (☎ 800-525-6284; W *www.visitmaui.com; 1727 Wili Pa Loop*).

Places to Stay & Eat Remarkable value for clean, comfortable hostel rooms, **Aloha Windsurfers' Hotel** (☎ 249-0206, 800-249-1421; W *www.accommodations-maui.com; 167 N Market St; dorm beds $22, singles $42-49, doubles $46-56*) provides breakfast, airport pick-up, activities and off-street parking. The hostel also rents cars.

Banana Bungalow Hostel (☎ 800-846-7835; W *www.mauihostel.com; 310 N Market St; dorm beds $17.50, singles/doubles/triples $32/40/50*) is a mattress-on-the-floor type place that makes up for its lapses in cleanliness with a friendly young crowd. Perks include free airport pick-up and activities.

Old Wailuku Inn (☎ 244-5897, 800-305-4899; W *www.mauiinn.com; 2199 Kahookele St; doubles $120-180*) is an elegant 1920s home that was a wedding gift from a wealthy banker to his new daughter-in-law. Shaded by trees and very private, this regal building has been beautifully restored.

Buy groceries at **Ooka Supermarket** (*E Main St*). Grab a trail sandwich from **Subway** (☎ 244-9999; *1955 Main St; open 9am-9pm daily*) on your way through town.

Cafe Marc Aurel (☎ 244-0852; 28 N Market St; lunch $5; open 7am-6pm Mon-Fri, 7am-1pm Sat) has scrumptious French pastries and gourmet sandwiches.

Saeng's Thai Cuisine (☎ 244-1567; 2119 Vineyard St; entrees $7.50-13; open 11am-2:30pm Mon-Fri & 5pm-9:30pm daily) serves great Thai food in an intimate setting with partial outdoor seating in a garden.

Getting There & Away Wailuku is 2 miles west of Kahului via Hwy 32, and is reached from the south on Honoapi'ilani Hwy (Hwy 30). Advance arrangements are necessary for airport pick-up or car rental through local hostels.

If you don't have a car, it's still possible to get to a few hikes by joining hostel tours.

Waihe'e Valley

Duration	2–2½ hours
Distance	4 miles (6.4km)
Difficulty	moderate
Start/Finish	Waihe'e Valley Rd
Nearest Towns	Wailuku (p148)
Transport	private

Summary Cross two thrilling suspension bridges on an easygoing stream hike to a popular swimming hole in the West Maui Mountains.

Plank-and-cable suspension bridges over a jungle stream make Waihe'e Valley (also known as the Swinging Bridges Trail) one of the most fun and popular hikes on Maui. Flowering vines drape the emerald jungle, fringed with ti and wild ginger, as the trail leads through banyan trees, bamboo and ripe guava. The watershed is privately owned, its cascading river tapped by irrigation projects that divert water to plantations on the central plains. A cooling plunge awaits upstream where the river pools behind a dam. Passage is granted to hikers by permit.

PLANNING

Pack a bathing suit for a dip in the freshwater pool at the end. The trail is an especially popular place on summer weekends.

Car break-ins are common, so carry all valuables and leave car doors unlocked.

Map
The USGS 1:24,000 map *Wailuku* covers the area but does not show the trail.

Permits
Due to potential flash floods, permits are required from **Wailuku Agribusiness** (☎ 244-9570; Hwy 30, Waikapu; open 7am-3:30pm Mon-Fri). They are issued free of charge, but only when no rain is forecast. Call ahead for weather conditions and directions to their office, a few miles south of Wailuku.

GETTING TO/FROM THE HIKE
Waihe'e Valley is 4½ miles northwest of Wailuku. Follow Kahekili Hwy (Hwy 340) 1 mile past Waihe'e and turn left onto paved Waihe'e Valley Rd. Drive uphill past houses for 0.4 mile and find parking in a vacant lot on the right. The hike technically begins another 100yd past the T-junction down a sketchy dirt road, but it's often muddy and there's no room to park.

THE HIKE (see map p150)
Small farms fill the lower portion of Waihe'e Valley with plots of taro and banana, and it feels like you've stumbled into Maui's backyard. The hike is unsigned and follows a maintenance road for the first ½ mile before becoming a trail. Just stick to the obvious route and avoid the 'No Trespassing' signs.

Head uphill past houses on Waihe'e Valley Rd to the T-junction and turn right down a dirt lane, sidestepping chickens and the crumpled husks of dead cars. A gated maintenance road leads to the right over a dry streambed and off into forest, veering left at

MAUI

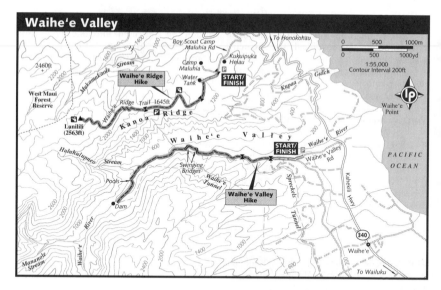

Waihe'e Valley

a post to approach the valley as a flat walk beside cane. After a low hill the road levels out west along an irrigation ditch and reaches a metal gate, about ½ mile from the start. The hike resumes up the valley on a forested path above the Waihe'e River, its waters empty into ditches and tunnels running alongside the trail.

Quiet waters appear through banyan trees after the next ½ mile, where the trail dips down to the river. Slung across the rocky riverbed is the first high-flying **plank-and-cable suspension bridge** – not death-defying, but enough to take your breath away. After a brief touchdown, a trickier bridge, with an even longer span and a few missing planks, comes next.

Cascades fill the river on the way to the third crossing, where the trail rock-hops on boulders and goes through jungle past guava, ginger and bamboo. Tranquil pools encountered ¾ mile from the swinging bridges make an inviting place to linger before climbing the last ¼ mile to the end. Proceed across the river and follow a steep path to an old irrigation ditch, which you then follow to reach the **dam**. Stunt diving into the pool from a rope swing is a popular pastime here.

When you've finished your swim, retrace your steps to return to Waihe'e Valley Rd.

Waihe'e Ridge

Duration	3 hours
Distance	4½ miles (7.2km)
Difficulty	moderate
Start/Finish	Boy Scout Camp Maluhia Rd
Nearest Town	Wailuku (p148)
Transport	private

Summary A lofty ridgeline hike with misty views of the West Maui Mountains.

Splendid views of steep mountains backing the lush Waihe'e Valley are just rewards for this 1500ft climb up a showery ridge in the West Maui Mountains. Native wet forest plants thrive along the muddy Waihe'e Ridge Trail, which rises halfway up the mountain to the Lanilili peak. Clouds seldom rise from the summit above at Pu'u Kukui (5788ft) – which is Maui's wettest point – and heavy rains fill the surrounding slopes with rain forest and streaming white waterfalls.

MAUI

PLANNING

This misty trail is best hiked on a clear, dry day. Morning is the most ideal time to catch a break in the clouds.

Car break-ins are evident here; carry all valuables and leave car doors unlocked to avoid costly damage.

Map & Books

The USGS 1:24,000 map *Wailuku* covers the area, but the trail is not shown. However, the trail is well-signed and a map is not essential.

Native trailside plants are identified in the *Waihe'e Ridge Trail Native Plant Guide* brochure, free from the Division of State Parks office in Wailuku.

GETTING TO/FROM THE HIKE

The Waihe'e Ridge trailhead is 7 miles northwest of Wailuku off Kahekili Hwy (Hwy 340), near Boy Scout Camp Maluhia. Continue a winding 2½ miles past Waihe'e to a signed left turn, after the 6-mile marker, for paved Boy Scout Camp Maluhia Rd. Drive 1 mile above the ocean to the end of this steep road and park in the designated area by the gate.

THE HIKE (see map p150)

The Waihe'e Ridge Trail begins amid pasture at a gated road, vaults straight up a concrete road and follows arrows pointing left into forest. Pass through a stile at the next cattle gate, to continue climbing through introduced stands of Cook pine and paperbark eucalyptus. Darker forest after the ½-mile marker shades the two long switchbacks to Kanoa Ridge. Pause midway to glance at a waterfall in the adjacent Makamakaole Valley.

The ridgeline scenery opens with a picture-perfect **viewpoint** at a bench perched above Waihe'e Valley. Directly ahead is Kahului Bay. Waterfalls spill down the mountain high up the valley, with helicopters swarming in for a closer look. Sharing the airspace is the quieter *apapane,* a small native red bird that darts between ohia trees growing along the ridge.

A gentle ascent over meadow crosses a wire fence and quickens to steep, shrubby switchbacks past the 1-mile mark. Steps hasten the end of the next steady ½ mile climb as the trail levels behind a wooded slope and dips through a broad swampy saddle. Continue upwards on more switchbacks to complete the final grasp for **Lanilili** (2563ft), topped by a solitary picnic table. There are panoramic views over deep-pleated valleys and out to sea.

Finish by climbing back down the mountain on the same route.

Hoapili Trail

Duration	2–2½ hours
Distance	4 miles (6.4 km)
Difficulty	moderate
Start/Finish	La Perouse Bay
Nearest Town	Kihei (p152)
Transport	private

Summary A short hike along an ancient road over jagged lava goes to a secluded ocean oasis at Kanaio beach.

One of two King's Highway routes, the Hoapili Trail is a remnant of an ancient coastline road, and spans miles of empty lava fields from La Perouse Bay to the Pi'ilani Hwy (Hwy 31). Lava that spilled from Haleakala only 200 years ago erased the original path, and it was rebuilt (1824–40) as this curious cinder road under governor Hoapili.

A restored portion of the trail ventures into this volcanic wilderness to find spectacular ocean scenery in jagged black coves and blue-green waters. Spinner dolphins swim right offshore.

The bay once held a sizable fishing village that may have been settled as early as 1100. Ancient ruins along this coastline have been untouched by archaeologists, and there is currently a push to have the area to Kanaloa Point preserved as a national park. Allow extra time to explore archaeological sites at either end.

PLANNING

Winter months, mornings and cloudy days are the best times to hike the hot, black lava.

MAUI

Rough footing makes sturdy hiking boots necessary. Car break-ins are common, so carry all valuables and leave car doors unlocked to avoid costly damage.

Maps

The USGS 1:24,000 map *Makena* shows the route.

NEAREST TOWN & FACILITIES

Tasty plate meals with fresh fruit and grilled sweet potatoes make the **Makena Grill** *(lunch plates $7)* lunch wagon, a few miles from the trailhead on Makena Rd, a tempting stop.

Kihei

Sunny Kihei, a commercialized beach town on Maui's 'south' shore, is popular for affordable condos and broad sandy beaches.

Places to Stay Condos line Kihei Rd on both sides, representing all price ranges and views. Most expect a three-night stay and/or charge a cleaning fee. For an extensive list of local properties call ☎ 800-221-6118 to order the free *Maui Accommodations Guide*, or browse photos of condos on-line (w www.mauiaccommodations.com).

Wailana Kai *(☎ 891-1626, 866-891-1626; w www.wailanakai.com; 34 Wailana Pl; double 1-bedroom units $75-90, quad 2-bedroom units $90-110)* is a smaller, two-story complex with well-maintained apartment units at reasonable prices.

Kihei Kai Nani *(☎ 879-9088, 800-473-1493; w www.kiheikainani.com; 2495 S Kihei Rd; double 1-bedroom units low/peak season $79/99)* has 180 comfortably furnished units with plenty of personal touches (some with ocean views) in a low-rise opposite Kamaole Beach II.

Two Mermaids on the Sunny Side of Maui B&B *(☎ 874-8687, 800-598-9550; w www.twomermaids.com; 2840 Umalu Pl; double suites from $110)* is a garden-like retreat in a modern home away from Kihei Rd. Rooms have kitchens, bathrooms – and oh yeah, acoustic guitars.

Aston Maui Lu Resort *(☎ 879-5991, 800-922-7866; w www.astonhotels.com; 575 S Kihei Rd; doubles from $108)* offers discounts of roughly 25% for on-line reservations. If your heart is set on a beachfront hotel, try this palm-fringed one.

Places to Eat Prowl the strip malls for take-out joints and supermarkets along Kihei Rd. Get organic groceries and fresh salads from **Hawaiian Moons Natural Foods** *(☎ 875-4356; Kamaole Beach Center, 2411 S Kihei Rd; open 8am-9pm Mon-Sat, 8am-7pm Sun)*. A fruit smoothie from **South Beach Smoothies** *(1455 S Kihei Rd; open 8am-4pm Mon-Fri, 9am-2pm Sat)* makes a refreshing follow-up to any hike.

Kihei Caffe *(☎ 879-2230; 1945 Kihei Rd; meals $6-10; open 5am-8:30pm Mon-Fri, 5am-3pm Sat & Sun)*, opposite Kalama Beach Park, is Kihei's sunniest breakfast spot, with salads and sandwiches served throughout the day.

Pita Paradise *(☎ 875-7679; Kalama Village, 1913 S Kihei Rd; meals $7-13; open 11am-9:30pm Mon-Sat)* features satisfying Mediterranean-style pita sandwiches and kabobs with ample veggies and outdoor seating.

Maui Tacos *(☎ 879-5005; Kamaole Beach Center, 2411 S Kihei Rd; meals under $7; open 9am-9pm daily)* is a delicious Hawaiian-based chain with a fresh twist on Mexican take-out.

Getting There & Away Kihei is 12 miles south of Kahului on Hwy 311. Pi'ilani Hwy (Hwy 31) connects Kihei to West Maui via Ma'alaea.

GETTING TO/FROM THE HIKE

The trailhead at La Perouse Bay is 11 miles south of Kihei at the end of Makena Rd. Follow Pi'ilani Hwy (Hwy 31) past Wailea to the end of the highway, and continue south along the coastline for 7 miles on narrow and winding Makena Rd. The pavement ends in cinders at La Perouse Bay, where the road continues as a 4WD track. Venture right over the lava and park by the beach.

THE HIKE

Hawaiians once made homes amid this jumble of lava at the ancient fishing village of Keone'o'io. An interpretive sign near the

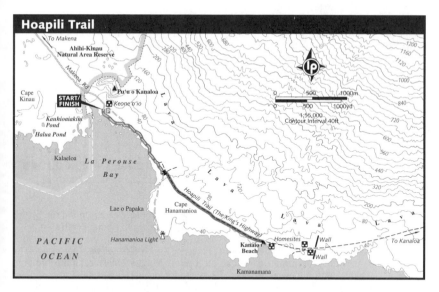

Hoapili Trail

(Map labels:) To Makena · Ahihi-Kinau Natural Area Reserve · Makena Rd · Cape Kinau · START/FINISH · Pu'u o Kanaloa · Keone'o'io · Kauhioaiakini Pond · Halua Pond · Kalaeloa · La Perouse Bay · Lae o Papaka · Cape Hanamanioa · Hanamanioa Light · Hoapili Trail (The King's Highway) · PACIFIC OCEAN · Lava · Kanaio Beach · Homesites · Wall · Wall · Kamanamana · To Kanaloa · 1:55,000 Contour Interval 40ft

road depicts some of the **ruins** found among the *a'a* (rough lava). The first mile to the beginning of the King's Highway is on a 4WD road that continues south past the bay.

Starting at the beach, briefly swing by the bay on a dirt track that veers left to rejoin the main cinder road. Continue right, drifting back to the shore on what is now a lazy dirt road that winds through small, shady coves fringed with *kiawe* (a member of the mesquite family). The road departs the shore and forks left toward a barbed wire fence, straightening over cinders past a long rock wall. At the foot of a cinder hill turn left through the wall and venture across the lava to the signed Hoapili Trail. The trail sign puts Kanaio Beach at 2 miles, but you've already come halfway. Proceed right to take up the King's Highway.

Leveled, curbed and evenly graded, this 4ft wide cinder expressway is still plenty tough going as it cuts an unwavering path across Cape Hanamanioa. An immense sea of jagged black *a'a* dominates the scenery for most of the way until the trail crests to a view of the ocean. **Kanaio Beach** stands out as a shady oasis ahead, at a clump of seaside *kiawe*. A driftwood swing on the

beach is a lovely spot to catch the ocean breeze before turning back.

The trail beyond the beach is unmaintained and hard to follow. South along the beach are nearby **hale ruins** (ancient Hawaiian homesites), and the shoreline leads to sea cliffs and white coral pebble coves. More ruins await discovery by those with the energy to continue to another ½ mile down the trail.

Lahaina Pali Trail

Duration	3–4 hours
Distance	5 miles (8km)
Difficulty	demanding
Start/Finish	West Lahaina Pali Trailhead
Nearest Towns	Kihei (p152), Wailuku (p148)
Transport	private

Summary A grueling 1600ft climb up arid canyons on a historic bridle trail with ocean views, and good places to watch whales in winter and spring.

Lahaina means 'cruel sun,' and is an apt description of what lies in store on this hot, rocky trail over a dry sea cliff. To get around this *pali* (cliff), travelers once had to swim, paddle or climb. The Lahaina Pali Trail, built in the 1800s, made the trip a little easier, but it went down in history as a treacherous journey. Bandits no longer hide behind rocks waiting to ambush travelers, but it still holds its reputation as a tough climb.

This up-and-back hike, beginning from the west trailhead at Ukumehame, winds up the cliff to an ocean viewpoint atop Kealaloloa Ridge. From the summit the trail descends northeast to Ma'alaea, but the scenery becomes industrial and it's best to turn back at the top. Follow up with an ocean swim at the beach park across the highway.

PLANNING

The trail is too hot to enjoy under full sun. Winter months, early morning hours and cloudy days are the best times to hike. Humpback whales can be viewed offshore from mid-November to April.

Map & Books

The USGS 1:24,000 map *Ma'alaea* covers the area but does not show the trail.

For a narrative of the hike, pick up a copy of the free *Maui History and Lore from the Lahaina Pali Trail* brochure from the Division of State Parks counter in Wailuku. The guide contains descriptions corresponding to numbered posts along the trail. A drawing on the back cover of the trail guide is the only map that shows this hike.

NEAREST TOWNS & FACILITIES

See Kihei (p152) and Wailuku (p148).

Olowalu

A private beachside campground run by the Episcopal Church, **Camp Pecusa** (☎ 661-4303; W *www.maui.net/~norm/pecusa.html;* *Honoapi'ilani Hwy; tent sites per person $6*) is one of Maui's nicest camping options. Amenities include picnic tables, solar shower and dressing area, a clothesline and utility

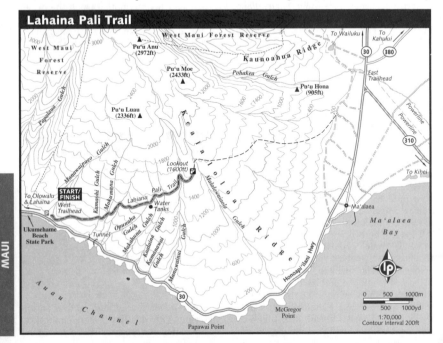

sinks. Reservations aren't taken but space is usually available. Check-in is by 5pm, and stays are limited to seven nights. A cabin facility is available for organized groups.

Nearby **Olowalu General Store** *(Honoapi'ilani Hwy)* has limited groceries, and there are **supermarkets** and **restaurants** in trendy Lahaina, 6 miles further northwest.

Getting There & Away Olowalu is 17 miles southwest of Kahului and 3 miles northwest of the trailhead, at a fairly rocky blip between wayside beach parks along Honoapi'ilani Hwy (Hwy 30). A blue 'Camp Pecusa' sign marks the turn-off to the campground between mileposts 14 and 15.

GETTING TO/FROM THE HIKE

The west Lahaina Pali trailhead on Honoapi'ilani Hwy (Hwy 30) is 10 miles west of Kihei and 11 miles southwest of Wailuku. There's nothing obvious to mark it, and it comes up suddenly just west of the tunnel at the bottom of the cliff. Pull off the highway to the right at the first spot of shoulder to find the signed dirt parking area under the *kiawe* trees.

End-to-end hikers can go look for the tricky east trailhead at the Kihei junction on Hwy 30, north of Ma'alaea. Scan the shoulder carefully south of the ditch between Hwys 380 and 310 for a small brown and yellow Na Ala Hele sign (run over at the time of writing).

THE HIKE

The hike begins at a plaque with an explanation of the trail's significance to early island travel. A short dirt path leads up to an old cliff road built to replace the trail. Hike right along the road and turn left onto the rough and rocky trail, which rises east above the highway. A tunnel appears below at ½ mile, and there's a spot of shade around the bluff at Kamaohi Gulch. Ocean views are the only thing good about the next 0.9-mile rocky climb up steep cliffs to Opunaha Gulch. Concrete water tanks visible below begin a gentler ascent over the next ½ mile of boulder-strewn prairies and gulches. Gorgeous canyon scenery culminates as the

trail enters **Manawainui Gulch**, a long, deep canyon with a welcome rest under a solitary *wiliwili* tree.

The trail leaves this last gulch, taking in a huge view across the ocean to Haleakala, Kaho'olawe and Lanai. The rocky slope becomes pasture on the way to the well-signed **summit** (1600ft) at 2½ miles, at the top of a broad, rocky plain where there's a panoramic view encompassing the ocean around Haleakala and Ma'alaea Bay.

The trail continues another 3 miles to Ma'alaea, but it's really more enjoyable to turn back here and go jump in the ocean down by the west trailhead.

Haleakala Crater

Duration	4 days
Distance	19.3 miles (32km)
Difficulty	moderate–demanding
Start	Haleakala Visitors Center
Finish	Halemau'u Trailhead
Nearest Towns	Kahului (p147), Hali'imaile (p159)
Transport	private
Summary	An unforgettable cabin-to-cabin backpack explores another world of cinder hills and lava inside Haleakala's desolate, 3000ft-deep crater.

Haleakala National Park, one of Hawaii's two national parks, stretches from the spectacular summit of the Haleakala volcano down to the pretty waterfall pools of Oheo Gulch. There are separate entrances to both sections of the park, but no passage between them. This hike concentrates on the volcano summit region, while Oheo Gulch is covered in the Waimoku Falls hike (p167).

The summit of the Haleakala volcano (which peaks at 10,023ft and is Maui's tallest mountain) is occupied by an awesome cavity filled with cinder cones and shifting clouds. At 7½ miles long and 3000ft deep, this striking depression is a geological wonder. A paved road from Central Maui goes straight up to the top, a popular spot to view the sunrise. Two wilderness

MAUI

trails reach the crater floor from the summit, connecting to a 27-mile trail system featuring Maui's most spectacular hiking. If the scenery doesn't take your breath away the thin air surely will, with trail elevations ranging between 7000ft and 10,000ft.

This classic multiday backpack showcases Haleakala's many moods – stark cinder desert, lava-filled valleys and alpine shrubland. The tour begins at the summit on the Sliding Sands Trail and returns on the Halemau'u Trail, stopping at rustic backcountry cabins from the Civilian Conservation Corps (CCC) era along the way. Spending a night at all three cabins makes a leisurely four-day trip, although experienced hikers can complete it quite easily in three. Camping is not permitted at Kapalaoa, and if you don't have cabin reservations you'll need to hike 10 miles to reach the first day's camp at rainy Paliku.

Short side trails cut across the crater floor between the Sliding Sands and Halemau'u Trails, making it easy to adjust the itinerary for fewer days. Those with the urge to 'do it all in one day' have the chance on a long, one-way trip through Haleakala crater (see the boxed text 'Haleakala Crater Day Hike').

NATURAL HISTORY

Haleakala began as a prehistoric shield volcano that, in a series of eruptions, billowed its way out of the ocean to at least 13,000ft. Wind, water and possibly glaciers scooped out Ke'anae Valley (Ko'olau Gap) and Kaupo Gap, which formed the so-called 'crater' where they met at the summit (real volcanic craters or calderas are caused by explosion or collapse rather than erosion). Relatively recent eruptions from dozens of fiery vents filled this valley with heaps of red and ochre cinders, and sent floods of lava oozing in all directions. Still considered active, Haleakala last erupted in 1790 near Makena.

Ecologies include barren cinder desert, shrubland and forests. Silversword, one of the few plants to thrive inside the crater, once covered the slopes in silvery globes but was nearly picked to extinction by early

Haleakala Crater Day Hike

Maui's most spectacular day hike traverses Haleakala's 3000ft-deep crater on an eight hour, 10.8 mile one-way trip over crimson cinders and black lava. Scenes from all over the crater are condensed on this strenuous hike from the summit to the Halemau'u trailhead. A 2800ft descent from the summit to Holua Cabin journeys past vibrant cinder cones, rough a'a and gardens of silversword. The hike exits the crater up a 1400ft cliff.

Water at Holua Cabin is not fit for drinking and day hikers should carry 3L. This hike is very popular, and hostel guests staying in Wailuku may be able to ride up on a hostel tour.

The first stage of the day hike follows Day 1 (p159) of the Haleakala crater hike from the visitors center 3.8 miles along the Sliding Sands Trail to the first trail junction. Turn left here and follow the unnamed shortcut 1.6 miles to the Halemau'u Trail (see Alternative Route: via Ka Moa o Pele, p160). At the Halemau'u Trail junction head left for 1.6 miles to Holua Cabin, following the last section of the Day 3 (p161) description. The final 3.8-mile stage of the day hike from Holua Cabin to the finish at Halemau'u trailhead follows the Day 4 (p162) description.

❀ ❀ ❀ ❀ ❀ ❀ ❀ ❀ ❀ ❀ ❀ ❀ ❀

visitors who used them for parade floats and lobbed them down the crater for sport. Nene, the friendly Hawaiian goose, is also making a comeback here, but is still endangered. The geese often hang around cabins in hopes of seeing visitors, but *do not* give in to their begging. Feeding the geese tames them and draws them out of the wilderness to become the hapless victims of passing cars.

PLANNING
When to Hike

Trails are open year round. The summer weather is the most favorable and the best time to catch the showy silversword in bloom. The rainiest months are December to May. You'll improve your chances for cabin reservations, however, by avoiding summer months and weekends.

MAUI

What to Bring

Come prepared for changeable weather and cold temperatures (which average 65°F during the day and 45°F at night in summer, and 15°F cooler in winter). Hypothermia is a concern and it's important to carry raingear and warm clothing at all times. Also come prepared for sun – at high altitudes it's easy to get scorched. Sturdy boots are essential for hiking rough lava. Bees and wasps are hazards at some cabins, so carrying a bee sting kit is recommended.

The only water is the untreated supply at the three backcountry cabins. During drought it is sometimes not available and you will have to pack it in (allow 3L per person per day). Call the park headquarters to check.

Cabins are equipped with a propane stove and fuel, woodstove, cookware (removed during droughts) and padded bunks. Those intending to use the cabins should bring candles, plus kindling and fire starters for coaxing flame out of the stubborn fire logs.

Maps

Two waterproof trail topographic maps, the Trails Illustrated 1:25,000 *Haleakala National Park* and the Earthwalk Press 1:24,000 *Haleakala National Park Recreation Map*, cover the entire park. The Trails Illustrated map is more current.

Information Sources

Maps, books, information and backcountry permits are available at the **Haleakala**

House of the Sun

The legendary 'House of the Sun,' Haleakala is where the trickster demigod Maui hid to catch the fiery orb. Atop this very volcano Maui lassoed the sun with ropes braided from his sister's hair, refusing to let go even as the sun begged for mercy. Not until the sun agreed to slow down its daily race across the sky and thereby bathe the Hawaiian islands in more hours of glorious sunlight, did Maui release his Herculean hold.

National Park headquarters (☎ 572-9306; ⓦ www.nps.gov/hale; Haleakala Crater Rd; open 8am-4pm daily), located 1 mile above the park entrance near Hosmer Grove. There's also **Haleakala Visitor Center** (open 6am-3pm, from 6.30am in winter) near the summit. The center has displays on geological and volcanic evolution and a recording explaining what you see on the crater floor. The center also offers short natural and cultural history talks (around 15 to 20 minutes) at 9:30am, 10:30am and 11:30am daily.

Permits & Regulations

The entry fee for Haleakala National Park is $10 per car, or $5 per person arriving on foot, bicycle or motorcycle. However, while the park never closes the pay booth is only open from before dawn until, usually, sunset. The entry fee is valid for seven days and is also good for the Waimoku Falls hike (p167).

Backcountry permits must be picked up in person from the park headquarters before any overnight trip. Stays are limited to three nights, with a two-night limit at any one site. Maximum group size is 12. Open fires are not allowed. Camping is permitted only at Paliku and Holua, and restrictions may be placed on Paliku to protect nesting nene. Feeding the nene is prohibited.

Reservations are required to stay in the cabins, which are booked to one party at a time through a monthly lottery. Cost is $40 per night for up to six people, and $80 for seven to 12. Requests are accepted by mail or in person, and must be received at least 90 days before your trip. List your dates (with alternatives) and cabins in order of visit in a letter addressed to: Haleakala National Park, PO Box 369, Makawao, HI 96768. If you miss the lottery window (or don't hear back) there's still a chance for unfilled vacancies and cancellations. Phone the **park headquarters** (☎ 572-9306) between 1pm and 3pm daily to check availability (have a credit card ready). The cabin at Paliku is your best choice if you can only pick one.

Guided Hikes

Park rangers lead guided hikes in the area, including a three-hour, 3-mile 'Walk on the

Haleakala Crater

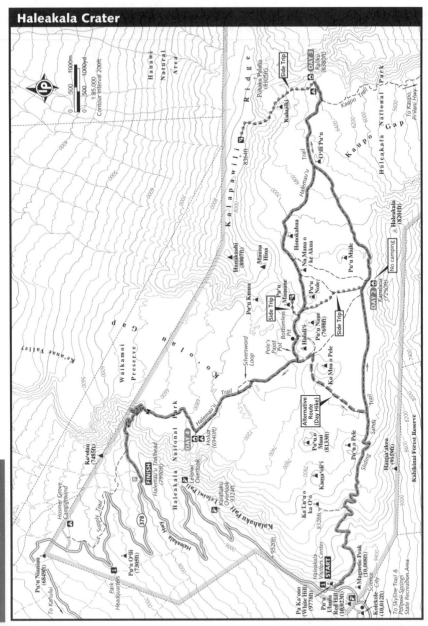

Wet Side' hike into Waikamoi Preserve. Adjoining the park, the 5230-acre preserve contains native koa and ohia rain forest and is habitat for Hawaiian forest birds, including a number or rare and endangered species. The guided hikes leave from Hosmer Grove campground at 9am on Monday and Thursday. **The Nature Conservancy** *(TNC; ☎ 572-7849)*, which manages Waikamoi Preserve, also offers guided hikes into the preserve.

NEAREST TOWN & FACILITIES

See Kahului (p147).

Hali'imaile

In the pineapple fields, Hali'imaile is a quiet countryside retreat at the foot of Haleakala and is right off the Haleakala Hwy.

Places to Stay & Eat Friendly **Peace of Maui** *(☎ 572-5045, 888-475-5045; W www .peaceofmaui.com; 1290 Hali'imaile Rd; singles/doubles $40/45, double cottage $85)* offers six comfortable guest rooms on the ground level of a modern country home. Guests share a bathroom, kitchen and the morning crop of fresh-picked fruit. There's also a detached one-bedroom cottage. There's no minimum stay.

Just down the road is Maui's best restaurant, which bears the unlikely name **Hali'imaile General Store** *(☎ 572-2666; 900 Hali'imaile Rd; lunch $9-15, dinner entrees $22-40; open 11am-2:30pm Mon-Fri, 5:30-9:30pm daily)*.

Getting There & Away Hali'imaile is 10 miles southeast of Kahului, off the Haleakala Hwy (Hwy 37) on Hali'imaile Rd.

Kula

The nearest food and lodging to Haleakala National Park is at the junctions of Hwys 377 and 378, in the Kula region.

Prominent **Kula Lodge & Restaurant** *(☎ 878-1535, 800-233-1535; W www.kula lodge.com; Hwy 377; chalets $110-165; restaurant open 6:30am-9pm daily)* offers homey lodge rooms at elevated prices. Avoid the fine-dining type restaurant, food is better across the road at **Kula Sandalwoods Restaurant** *(☎ 878-3523; Hwy 377; meals $7-12; open 6:30am-2pm Mon-Sat, 7am-noon Sun)*, good for breakfast and lunch.

Right at the Kula junction is **Sunrise Market & Protea Farm** *(Hwys 377 & 378; open 8am-4pm daily)*, a small store with sandwiches and fruit salads.

Hosmer Grove Campground

Forested Hosmer Grove Campground hovers just below the 7000ft level with free campsites off the crater road near the park headquarters. It's often cold and rainy, but after a few days of wilderness camping the free firewood, sheltered eating area and drinkable water all seem like huge luxuries. Sites fill on a first-come, first-served basis and there's a three-night limit.

GETTING TO/FROM THE HIKE

The hike begins at 9740ft from the summit visitors center, about 1½ hours from Kahului. The Haleakala Hwy leads southeast from Kahului as Hwy 37 and continues beyond Pukalani as Hwy 377. At Kula turn left onto Hwy 378 (Haleakala Crater Rd). It's another 11 miles to the park entrance and then 10 miles to the summit. Expect heavy traffic during sunrise hours, and be alert to oncoming cyclists.

The hike ends 6 miles back down the road from the visitors center at the Halemau'u trailhead.

Unless you have two cars, hitchhiking is unavoidable. As National Park Service (NPS) staff will tell you, it's easy to catch a lift up to the summit before or after the hike from the designated hitchhiking area along the park road near Halemau'u. If you're uncomfortable sticking your thumb out, try approaching visitors at park headquarters to arrange a car drop.

THE HIKE
Day 1: Haleakala Visitors Center to Kapalaoa Cabin

3–4 hours, 5.7 miles, 2500ft descent
'Sliding sands' sounds like you're in for a big spill down the crater, but the trail is surprisingly gentle. The name refers to noticeable piles of black sand heaped up beneath the

MAUI

Warning

Visitors rarely experience altitude sickness, or Acute Mountain Sickness (AMS), at Haleakala summit. An exception is those who have been scuba diving in the past 24 hours, so plan to do your Haleakala trip before any dives. Children, pregnant women and those in generally poor health are also susceptible. If you experience dizziness, sudden headaches, confusion and difficult breathing, make sure you descend immediately. See Altitude (p52) for more information on AMS.

Hypothermia poses a danger to visitors unprepared for unexpected weather changes and high altitude rain. All hikers should carry raingear and extra clothing.

crumbling crater wall. To find the Sliding Sands trailhead, turn your back on the visitors center and head towards the road, looking for a dirt and gravel path that swings left behind Pa Ka'oao (White Hill) and drops straight down the *pali*. A long chain of craters and frozen rivers of lava form the stark, multicolor spectacle that lasts all the way to the crater floor. Long, gentle switchbacks over the first 2 miles give way to a rockier terrain as hikers pass a turn for red-rimmed **Ka Lu'u o ka O'o** (8326ft). A lone *mamane* tree offers the next shade another 1.8 miles below, where the trail flattens at a trammeled junction. The left fork steals day hikers 3½ miles north to Holua (see Alternative Route: via Ka Moa o Pele, below).

For Kapalaoa continue straight on the Sliding Sands Trail, which takes off across the black cinder desert. Heaps of red on black cinders loom large over the final 1.9 miles to **Kapalaoa Cabin** (7250ft), tucked beneath a cliff. An outdoor picnic table and pit toilet are nearby. Water is behind the cabin and must be treated. Camping is prohibited here, and those without cabin reservations must complete the hike for Day 2 to reach the camp at Paliku, another 3.4 miles east.

If you finish the day early, you can explore the heart of the crater along an easy tie to the Halemau'u Trail (see Side Trip: The Cinder Desert, below).

Alternative Route: via Ka Moa o Pele
1 hour, 1.6 miles
Day hikers leave the Sliding Sands Trail at the first trail junction and fork left for Holua. The route skirts the rugged west edge of the cinder desert on an unnamed tie trail around red and black **Ka Moa o Pele**. A left turn over a saddle at a four-way intersection is the shortest distance to the Halemau'u Trail. The straight path hooks up to the Halemau'u Trail via a ½ mile detour around Halali'i, visiting the 65ft-deep **Kawilinau** (bottomless pit) and a colorful passage known as **Pele's Paint Pot** (see Day 3, p161).

Side Trip: The Cinder Desert
1½–2½ hours, 2.2 miles
Those staying at Kapalaoa cabin have the afternoon or next morning to explore the heart of the crater on this easy shortcut to the Halemau'u Trail. Cache your pack at the cabin and backtrack (west) 100yd to a signed side trail for Halemau'u and Holua. Untrammeled black sand dappled with red cinders and silverswords unfolds over an otherworldly 1.1 miles on this path between Pu'u Naue and Pu'u Nole. This is a good place to look for **lava bombs**, pieces of molten lava that hardened after being expelled from volcanic vents.

Opportunities for further exploration await at the junction with the Halemau'u Trail, where a nearby signed but unmaintained path scrambles up red cinders to a sweeping view of the crater and Ko'olua Gap. Or head a ½ mile west on the Halemau'u Trail to preview the 65ft-deep 'bottomless' pit en route to a colorful area known as Pele's Paint Pot (see Day 3, p161).

The quickest way back to Kapalaoa is to backtrack, but if time permits it's also possible to make a loop on a longer 1.6 miles tie around Pu'u Naue.

Day 2: Kapalaoa Cabin to Paliku Cabin
2½–3 hours, 3.4 miles, 970ft descent
Yesterday's barren cinder landscape soon fades to memory as the Sliding Sands Trail

Dusk at the lower pools of Oheo Gulch, Kipahulu, Maui

KARL LEHMANN

Black-sand beach in Waianapanapa State Park, Maui

LINDA CHING

Plank-and-cable suspension bridge in the Waihe'e Valley, Maui

View of topside Molokai from Kalaupapa Peninsula's mule trail

Nightlife in Haleakala Crater

Haleakala is one of the few national parks with backcountry wilderness cabins, which were built in 1927 by the CCC. They're kept cozy with Irish-built Waterford wood stoves, airlifted in by helicopter. NPS staff perform maintenance on horseback and replenish the fire logs, packed in by mule.

Darkness falls quickly in the crater. So how do you pass the long evening without resorting to carving your initials upon the furniture? It helps to plan some entertainment. Some suggestions:

- Cook up a romantic candlelight dinner. Be sure to completely pack out leftovers and scraps.

- Stargazing, if it's clear. A map of the night sky is available from the park headquarters. Bring a warm hat and gloves.

- Play cards – each cabin comes with at least one deck.

- Pen some postcards, or bring a portable book light and a novel.

- Break out the ukuleles for a Hawaiian sing-along. Browse souvenir shops for songbooks. Don't be shy – there's no one around to hear.

moves east toward grass and scrub. In no time hikers are picking over jagged *a'a* lava on an otherwise easy descent to Paliku. A sliver of blue soon fills the horizon with ocean as the trail clinks on black cinders across the head of **Kaupo Gap**. A break from rough footing comes after 2 miles at vegetated O'ili Pu'u, which offers the first shade since Kapalaoa.

At this point the Sliding Sands Trail converges with the Halemau'u Trail, which leads east down a flow of syrupy *pahoehoe* (smooth, ropy lava). Past O'ili Pu'u the crater begins to show its rainier side, and when clouds aren't blowing up Kaupo Gap the view extends across the ocean to the Big Island. The berries of woody plants like *pukiawe*, *pilo* and *kukaenene* provide food

for nene and other shrubland birds, and it's not uncommon to startle a pheasant or chukar along this stretch. At 1.1 miles bypass the Kaupo Trail on the right for the last shrubby ¼ mile to **Paliku Cabin** (6380ft), on a plain beneath a high cliff.

Water here must be treated. A brown message board left of the cabin points uphill to **campsites** hidden in the wet grass. A path behind the cabin leads up to the toilet, and there's an NPS ranger cabin down on the right.

Side Trip: Kalapawili Ridge

3½–4 hours, 4.6 miles, 2000ft ascent

A difficult 2000ft ascent up the cliff behind Paliku Cabin is rewarded with big views down to Hana and Kaupo Gap. A brown sign uphill from the camper's water spigot marks the start of this unmaintained trail, which rises steeply up rocky shrubland to Kalapawili Ridge. Use caution on this tough and tricky route, which no longer appears on most maps.

Day 3: Paliku Cabin to Holua Cabin

4 hours, 6.3 miles, 900ft ascent, 260ft descent

Begin the day by retracing the Halemau'u Trail 1.3 miles to O'ili Pu'u, a gradual 300ft ascent. Bypass the Sliding Sands Trail and continue right on the Halemau'u Trail for Holua. A hot, rugged climb alternates between black sand and *a'a* as it heads up a gap between two lava flows, before swinging up past Honokahua. Hues shift from brown to vermilion, and lava levels to black sand as the trail regains the cinder desert through a valley of basalt spires. Rest comes about halfway to Holua at a spot of shade behind pointy Na Mana o ke Akua, near a signed shortcut for Kapalaoa.

Volcanic scenery culminates over the next 1.3 miles as hikers cross the divide to Ko'olau Gap. After the next signed path for Kapalaoa (where the Side Trip: The Cinder Desert, p160, joins), a nearby signed, but unmaintained, path on the right scrambles up red cinders to a sweeping view of the crater and Ko'olau Gap. The Halemau'u

MAUI

Trail veers right over a black and red saddle and drops to yet another junction past Pu'u Naue (7698ft). A railing points out the upcoming **Kawilinau** (bottomless pit), a red-orange vent that the NPS figures to be 65ft deep, but ancients believed went all the way to the ocean. Wind and color intensifies around the last cone, Halali'i, which spends itself in splashes of crimson, tan, orange and ochre through a colorful passage known as **Pele's Paint Pot**.

The Halemau'u Trail reaches a final junction at the end of the divide and plunges north all the way across a gusty lava flow that fills Ko'olau Gap. Day hikers from the Sliding Sands Trail should enter here from the left (see Alternative Route: via Ka Moa o Pele, p160). Wind-blasted *a'a* forms quite interesting contortions along a flat sandy corridor that crests a red cinder hill in 0.7 mile. The **Silversword Loop** detours right here on a side path through patches of silversword before rejoining the main trail in 0.3 mile. Tall bluffs are approached over cinders and shrubland as the trail presses down across the gap for the last 0.9 mile to Holua.

A picnic table and toilet make **Holua Cabin** (6940ft) a popular rest stop for day hikers. Water here must be treated. Gorgeous **campsites** perched atop a rocky bluff on the left have their own water supply and toilet.

Day 4: Holua Cabin to Halemau'u Trailhead

2–3 hours, 3.8 miles, 1400ft ascent

The first downhill mile of the Halemau'u Trail warms up for the steep exit to the park road by dropping left over lava and crossing a flat plain to a gate at the foot of a cliff. Short, well-graded switchbacks scale 1400ft on the final 2.8 miles up the crater wall to absolutely incredible views overlooking both Holua and Keanae Valley. Hana town appears below on the right as the trail leaves the rim and straightens west over native shrubland. The climbing continues all the way to the end at the Halemau'u Trailhead (7990ft), which is 0.7 mile past the supply trail.

Polipoli Forest Loop

Duration	2½–3 hours
Distance	4.9 miles (7.9km)
Difficulty	moderate
Start/Finish	Polipoli Springs State Recreation Area
Nearest Town	Kahului (p147)
Transport	private

Summary   A calming deep-woods hike at Polipoli Springs State Recreation Area loops through the amazingly cool, dark Kula Forest Reserve.

A dense redwood forest plopped down on tropical Maui, the Polipoli Springs State Recreation Area in the remote Kula Forest Reserve offers peaceful walking on a quiet network of nature trails. Hawaii's Division of Forestry and the CCC planted these viewless stands of pine, cedar and redwood during the conservation efforts of the 1920s and 1930s. Polipoli is a perfect place to find solitude and the cooling woods can be a pleasant change from the island's tropical humidity. However, it's nothing extraordinary and since it takes a 4WD or high-clearance vehicle to get there, vacationers with short itineraries can safely save this one for another trip.

PLANNING

Kula Forest Reserve trails pass through hunting areas, so stay on marked trails. Bright clothing does nicely in a pinch for blaze orange. Polipoli is best hiked in the morning, before clouds move in with mist and rain. Carry raingear and dress for cooler temperatures.

Maps

An inset map of Kula Forest Reserve trails appears on the *Maui Recreation Map*, but the free *Recreational Trails of the Kula Forest Reserve* is easier to cram in your pocket. Both are available from the Division of State Parks in Wailuku.

NEAREST TOWN & FACILITIES

See Kahului (p147) and Kula (p159).

Polipoli Campground & Cabin

Cold, damp weather keeps most visitors away from Polipoli's primitive trailhead **campground** *(tent sites $5)* and **cabin** *($45)*, used mainly by scouts and hunters. Amenities include picnic shelters and a flush toilet. Obtain permits in Wailuku through the Division of State Parks.

GETTING TO/FROM THE HIKE

Polipoli Springs State Recreation Area is 28 miles southeast of Kahului, deep in the Kula Forest Reserve at the end of Waipoli Rd. The last 4 miles or so over gravel are rough and require a 4WD or high-clearance vehicle.

From Kahului take the Haleakala Hwy to Pukalani, instead of continuing on Hwy 377 to Kula, stay right on Hwy 37, which becomes the Kula Hwy and continues through the upcountry vicinity of Kula. Turn left after 6 miles onto Hwy 377 and take the first right onto one-lane Waipoli Rd, which rises on steep switchbacks. The pavement ends after 5½ miles at around 6400ft and the road continues on a rough dirt and gravel ridge. Be alert for stray cattle. A signed fork past the 8-mile marker leads

right down to Polipoli, a wooded picnic area and park at the end of the road.

THE HIKE

A wood-carved map behind the picnic shelters orients hikers to the Kula's well-signed network of nature trails. The Polipoli Trail leaves the park at 6200ft and contours south through deadfall forest for 0.6 mile to intercept the Haleakala Ridge Trail. Turn right here. Monterey pine and cedar give

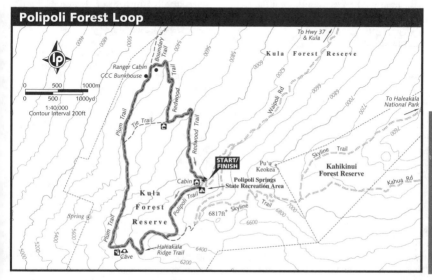

Polipoli Forest Loop

way to eucalyptus as the trail loses 200ft down a windy ridge over the next 0.9 mile to the Plum Trail. Halfway down on the left is a signed path to a small **cave** and a view of sunny south Maui.

The Plum Trail picks up at the end of the Haleakala Ridge Trail and swings north for a downhill stroll across a heavily wooded slope. Spots of plum and other deciduous trees provide breaks from the dark forest monotony that lasts well beyond the first 1.1 miles to the Tie Trail (a shortcut back to the park). Continue straight on the Plum Trail another 0.6 mile to the ruins of a **CCC bunkhouse** (5300ft).

Just ahead in a patch of hydrangeas the Plum Trail becomes the Boundary Trail and steams straight to other hunting units. Complete the loop to Polipoli by turning right up the Redwood Trail, passing another dilapidated structure that once served as a **ranger cabin**. Port Orford cedar and redwoods fill the mix of shaggy conifers shading the final 1.7 miles and 900ft climb to the park. Another **shelter** appears at the Tie Trail after ½ mile. The trail arrives back at Polipoli in a clearing near the **cabin**. Follow a gravel drive left toward the yellow gate to finish on the park road with the parking lot on the right.

Hana

The one word 'Hana' names a slumbering rural outpost in East Maui, Hawaii's most picturesque highway and an ancient, jungle-filled land jurisdiction. Visited mainly for the long scenic drive, the Hana Hwy snakes along the coast via lush tropical rain forests, plunging waterfalls and hidden freshwater pools to isolated Hana town.

Trails in two nearby parks – Waianapanapa State Park and Haleakala National Park's Kipahulu (Oheo Gulch) section – await exploration on foot. If you just can't wait to stretch your legs, pull on over to one of many roadside paths leading to gardens and waterfalls along the way. Blue Pool, a favorite for a waterfall that streams into a seaside pool, is located just outside Hana at the end of Ulaino Rd. Although most make

the tiring drive in one day, Hana really deserves to be done overnight.

CLIMATE
Heavy rainfall – up to 300 inches annually – fills the lush coastline with waterfalls and rain forests. Hana town is drier, with 83 inches of annual rainfall and plenty of sunshine between bursts of mist.

PLANNING
Crowds peak in the early afternoon (it takes a long time to drive out here), leaving the mornings a pleasantly quiet time to hike.

There's virtually nothing between Paia and Hana, so be sure to fill the tank and buy groceries and supplies in either Kahului or Paia on your way out. Campers headed for Kipahulu (Oheo Gulch) should remember to bring water – fill up at Waianapanapa State Park if you forget.

Check brochure racks for the *Hana Visitors Guide* (W *www.hanamaui.com*), which contains accommodations listings and a helpful map.

ACCESS TOWN & FACILITIES
Hana
A handful of tin-roofed shacks and small shops make up Hana town, an outpost for services in East Maui.

Supplies & Equipment Hana's two small stores, the **Hana Ranch Store** (☎ 248-8261; *Hana Ranch Center; open 7am-7pm daily*) and **Hasegawa General Store** (☎ 248-8231; *5165 Hana Hwy; open 7am-7pm Mon-Sat, 8am-6pm Sun*), offer limited goods at ridiculous prices. The only gas is the **Chevron Station** (*open until around 6:30pm*) on the highway at the south end of town; expect to pay more than in larger towns.

Places to Stay & Eat For simple guest rooms in a modern home try **Joe's Place** (☎ 248-7033; W *www.joesrentals.com, 4870 Uakea Rd; doubles without/with bathroom $45/ 55*), with a shared kitchen and common area.

Hana Accommodations (☎ 248-7868, 800-228-4262, fax 248-8240; W *www.hana -maui.com; PO Box 249, Hana, HI 96713;*

doubles from $75) rents about a dozen private houses on the lush Hana coast. All have cooking facilities and are about 10 minutes out of town.

Aloha Cottages *(☎ 248-8420; Keawa Place; double studios/quad 2-bedroom cottages from $65/85)* is quite close to Hotel Hana-Maui. All of the units are pretty straightforward and none has a phone, but messages are taken.

The best meals are your own camp cooking or picnic lunch. Budget-priced plate meals and burgers are served out snack windows at **Hana Ranch Restaurant** *(☎ 248-8255; Hana Ranch Center; meals under $7)* off Hana Hwy (skip the dining room) and at **Tutu's Snackbar** *(☎ 248-8224; Hana Beach Park; meals $6; open 8am-4pm at least Mon-Thur)* on Hana Bay.

Getting There & Away The Hana Hwy leads east from Kahului as Hwy 36 and arrives in Hana town as Hwy 360. Allow roughly three hours to navigate the 53 miles of hairpin turns to Hana town. Driving at night is not advised.

While the whole point is to drive to Hana, it is also possible to fly. Small prop planes touch down at Hana's single runway airport, 4 miles northwest of town. **Paragon Air** *(☎ 244-3356, 866-946-4744; W www .paragon-air.com)* provides connections to other Maui airports (Kahului and Kapalua), Molokai and Lanai. **Pacific Wings** *(☎ 873-0877, 888-575-4546; W www.pacificwings .com)* flies daily from Kahului and Honolulu. At the Hana airport, **Dollar** *(☎ 248-8237)* rents cars from $48 per day; reservations required.

Waianapanapa State Park

Idyllic seaside cabins at Waianapanapa State Park *(Hana Hwy; tent sites $5, quad cabins $45)*, 3 miles northwest of Hana, are the best excuse to stay overnight in the area. Each of the 12 cabins comes fully furnished with kitchen, bedding, towels and hot showers, and has electricity. A grassy picnic area near the park's busy beach serves double-duty as a campground – fine after the crowds go home. Camping facilities

> ### Warning
>
> Don't get bit by dengue fever. East Maui is under a health alert for this disease, spread by the Asian tiger mosquito. Wear long-sleeved clothing and use a DEET-containing repellent to prevent bites. Symptoms include sudden fever accompanied by severe headache, muscle pain, nausea and vomiting. See Dengue Fever (p55) for more information.

include rest rooms and an outdoor beach shower. Permits for camping or cabins must be obtained in advance in person or by mail from the Division of State Parks office in Wailuku, and stays are limited to five nights. Early reservations are recommended for cabins.

Waianapanapa State Park

Duration	2½–3 hours
Distance	4 miles (9.6km)
Difficulty	moderate
Start/Finish	Waianapanapa State Park picnic area
Nearest Town	Hana (p164)
Transport	private

Summary A beautiful balmy cliff walk overlooking crashing surf, rock arches and blowholes from an ancient lava trail on the Hana coast.

From Waianapanapa State Park, hikers can follow in the footsteps of ancient Hawaiians on a scenic lava trail that leads both north and south along the rugged Hana coast. One of two King's Highway trails, the Pi'ilani Trail is a remnant of an ancient road that once circled the entire island (see the boxed text 'Hiking the King's Highway', p146). It's quite different in character from the big lava road at La Perouse Bay, and travels a footpath over exposed lava sea cliffs overgrown with *naupaka* (native beach plant with clusters of white flowers) and *hala* (screw pine).

MAUI

This down-and-back hike on the longer, more scenic southbound trail leads past a *heiau* (ancient Hawaiian temple) to a black cobble beach outside Hana. North on the same trail, towards the airport, are burial sites and caves.

PLANNING

The park gets busy on weekends. Wear sturdy boots for hiking over sharp lava.

Maps

The USGS 1:24,000 map *Hana* shows the route.

NEAREST TOWN & FACILITIES

See Hana (p164) and Waianapanapa State Park (p165).

GETTING TO/FROM THE HIKE

Waianapanapa State Park is 3 miles northwest of Hana. From Kahului, turn left off the Hana Hwy at the state park sign about

½ mile past the Hana airport turn-off, and fork left to the picnic area above the black-sand beach.

THE HIKE

The hike starts on a paved path overlooking a black-sand beach. Almond trees shade the way right through the grassy camping area and past the beach access trail. Heavy surf occasionally pounds the bay below, signed for hazardous swimming conditions.

A signed dirt path for Hana (3 miles) continues south, leaves the bay at a blowhole and heads along the shore. Mats of low-growing *naupaka* soften a lava field on the way past the housekeeping cabins, which are set amid dense groves of *hala*. At a dirt road the path leads left through rough *a'a* to take up the rocky sea cliffs past a blowhole. Hikers clamber over a natural arch **footbridge** and step down a low cliff to avoid breaking waves. A stepping-stone path – a trademark of the original King's Highway –

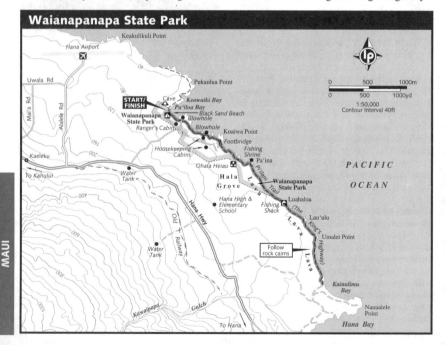

Hawaiian *Heiau*

Rectangular rock platforms similar to the one along the Pi'ilani Trail at Waianapanapa are the foundations of ancient Hawaiian temples called *heiau*. An enclosure built around the perimeter contained wooden images of gods, stone altars, prayer towers and grass huts.

Heiau ranged in purpose from agriculture to healing. The Ohala Heiau along Pi'ilani is of the Hale o Lono, or agricultural type.

Luakini, temples associated with the war god Ku, were used for human sacrifice. A fine example of this type is the mammoth and multitiered Pi'ilanihale Heiau, located a few miles west of Hana at **Kahanu Gardens** (☎ 248-8912; Ulaino Rd; admission $10; open 10am-2pm Mon-Fri).

Little is known about *heiau* rituals, which were fading by the time Europeans arrived. Hikers should ensure they respect these sacred sites by not climbing onto the platforms or walls.

❀ ❀ ❀ ❀ ❀ ❀ ❀ ❀ ❀ ❀ ❀ ❀ ❀

leads the rest of the way past spires and tidepools to **Ohala Heiau** at 0.7 mile. A path on the right beyond the wall will take you in for a closer look. And a **fishing shrine** up ahead on the left affords a good view south of basalt cliffs that are lined up all the way down to Hana.

Hala and ironwood encroaches the shoreline past the *heiau*. Round stones continue to mark the way across lava and a grassy clearing, fading briefly on the way over a rugged sea cliff. A dirt road comes in from the right as the trail arrives at Luahaloa, a ledge with a small **fishing shack**. Inland stands of ironwood heighten the beauty of the scenic last mile of cliff-top walking to Kaimalimu Bay. A trail through familiar *a'a* is soon led by rock cairns over a smoother flow of flat *pahoehoe*. Stepping stones hasten the approach to the bay ahead, as the trail dips down a shrubby ravine to a quiet black cobble **beach**. The bay marks the turning point of the hike. Dirt roads lead another mile from here south up to sleepy Hana.

Waimoku Falls

Duration	2 hours
Distance	4 miles (6.4km)
Difficulty	moderate
Start/Finish	Kipahulu Visitors Center
Nearest Town	Hana (p164)
Transport	private

Summary An up-and-back hike along a stream discovers hidden pools and dark bamboo forests, and climbs to a 400ft waterfall above Oheo Gulch.

Kipahulu, 10 miles south of Hana, is the turning point for most Hana Hwy drivers, and the site is thronged with tourists cooling off in Oheo Gulch's pretty tiered pools, the reward for the long drive. Crowds are thinner upstream along the Pipiwai Trail, which gains 900ft in elevation along a basalt gorge to Waimoku Falls. Not to be missed is the unforgettable boardwalk through dark corridors of tall bamboo, which grows so dense light barely enters.

Kipahulu was once the site of a large Hawaiian settlement, and is littered with over 700 surveyed ruins. Popular Oheo Gulch was misnomered 'Seven Sacred Pools' in a hotelier's attempt to drum up business for his Hana luxury hotel. There are more pools than seven, and while not sacred they are inarguably among Maui's most beloved swimming holes. A businessman bought the property in the 1960s but abandoned his plans to build a trophy home in favor of preservation interests. Oheo Gulch, together with a TNC biological reserve in neighboring Kipahulu Valley, were added to Haleakala National Park in 1969.

Information is available at the trailhead from the **Kipahulu Visitors Center** (☎ 248-7375; open 9am-5pm daily). Call ahead for a schedule of ranger-led hikes.

PLANNING
In flash flood conditions the trail may be closed. For the most solitude, take advantage of the primitive campground and explore Kipahulu in the morning.

MAUI

Warning

Rocks and debris swept over Waimoku Falls makes the pool below unsafe for swimming. Also, dangerous flash floods may strike without warning and are especially dangerous to hikers who venture off the trail to explore hidden pools. Save time for a swim after the hike in Oheo Gulch's pretty pools beneath the highway bridge.

There is no drinking water at Kipahulu, so bring enough for the hike. Because of falling rocks, the water beneath Waimoku Falls is unsafe for swimming. Bring a towel and bathing suit to join the hoards for a refreshing post-hike dip in the nearby Oheo Gulch pools. There may be other trailside pools, but water access is pretty limited. Carry protection against mosquitoes.

Maps
This hike is easy enough without a map. The trail is covered by the Trails Illustrated 1:25,000 map *Haleakala National Park*.

Permits
The $10 per car national park entry fee (good for seven days) is waived with a valid pass from Haleakala summit. Otherwise pay at the Kipahulu Visitors Center.

NEAREST TOWN & FACILITIES
See Hana (p164). Three miles before the Kipahulu Visitors Center you'll pass **Seven Pools Smoothies** (smoothies $5), open if you're lucky.

Kipahulu Campground
This primitive campground provides pleasant trailhead camping with semisecluded sites featuring picnic tables and grills set along the edge of a field next to the sea. It's located down a dirt access road from the visitors center parking lot. There's no water and camping is free with park entry.

GETTING TO/FROM THE HIKE
Haleakala National Park's Kipahulu Visitors Center is at Oheo Gulch, 10 miles southwest of Hana on Hwy 31. The drive takes 20 to 45 minutes from Hana. The trail is not nearly so bad as the crammed visitors center parking lot leads you to expect, since most head straight for the pools.

From the Kipahulu Campground, hike north across cane fields and go left up the hill to join the trail below the highway.

THE HIKE
Towel-toting tourists streaming down a path left of the busy visitors center lead the way to Oheo Gulch. Follow them past the signboard, but ignore the lower pools for now and fork left to get back up to the highway. A trail sign points across the road to the Pipiwai Trail, a steep dirt path that follows the gulch 2 miles and 900ft upstream. Palikea Stream pounds through the gorge on the right, but there's not much to see in the dusty first ½ mile until the vegetation breaks for a view of **Makahiku Falls**, plunging 184ft into the gulch. A pretty **pool** at the

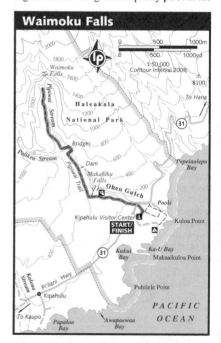

Hiking Lanai

West across the channel from Maui is Lanai, the island that pineapple left behind. Scarcely developed and 98% privately owned, activity now centers on two exclusive resorts. Celebrities and executives hell-bent on privacy visit this remote island to play golf and get away from everyone else.

Visiting Lanai can be expensive, and for all it's done to find new life as an adventure destination there aren't any hikes worth a special trip. The much-touted Munro Trail – really a 10-mile ridgeline dirt road – is a much better off-road experience than a hike (trust us, we tried it). Views across the channel *are* nice, but anywhere else this would be the kind of place you'd take mom and dad's car to make out on a Saturday night.

Should you ever find yourself passing time on Lanai, try the Koloiki Ridge Hike (5 mile roundtrip), which visits the prettiest part of the Munro Trail to a view overlooking Maunalei Gulch on a designated hiking trail. The hike begins behind The Lodge at Koele. Information and a free trail map are available from The Lodge at Koele concierge desk (☎ 565-7300).

top of this waterfall is accessed a short distance ahead on an unmarked path leading down to the right. Water overflows the pool to feed the waterfall, and swimmers should take care to stay away from the edge.

In the next ½ mile the trail goes through a gate, climbs past a banyan tree and winds up a grove of ripe guava. A pair of **bridges** crisscross the gorge 1 mile above the road, where stone steps reach a boardwalk for the last level mile through bamboo. Civilization once reached these dark corridors, forgotten by daylight, and the ruins of old taro fields are hidden in the overgrowth.

Hikers emerge to a rocky clearing at the base of **Waimoku Falls**, which plunges 400ft in a single stream over a sheer cliff. Signs warn against swimming, so turn back down the trail to finish with a dip in the Oheo Gulch pools.

Other Hikes

Waiakoa Loop Trail
This pleasant 3-mile, partial-loop through native scrub forest in the Kula Forest Reserve offers good views of the West Maui Mountains. It's part of the same trail network as the Polipoli Forest Loop, only not as dark and the trailhead on the lower, paved portion of Waipoli Rd can be reached without 4WD. The trail begins as a road near the hunter's check station (5.4 miles from Hwy 377) and rises slightly for ¾ mile to a gate where it loops. Fork right uphill to grassland and good views, bypassing the Upper Waiohuli Trail. The trail loses 500ft to forest and switchbacks up to return via the fork on the left. Refer to the *Maui Recreation Map* for information.

Skyline Trail
Most hikers are so eager to explore the scenery inside Haleakala's crater (p155) that they completely fail to notice the little-used Skyline Trail, which follows the barren southwest spine of Haleakala to the Polipoli Springs State Recreation Area. This cinder-covered maintenance road begins at 9750ft near the Haleakala summit at Science City (a private astronomical observatory that is off-limits to visitors), and passes nearly a dozen cinder cones and island views on a steep descent into scrub forest. At 6½ miles it meets Waipoli Rd, and continues to Polipoli via the Haleakala Ridge and Polipoli trails. Hiked one-way it's 7½ miles with a 3500ft descent. Getting back to the car is problematic, and because the trailheads are hours apart this hike is really only feasible if you can arrange for a friend with a 4WD or high-clearance vehicle to pick you up from remote Polipoli. Visitors are infrequent, so do not count on catching a lift out. Refer to the *Maui Recreation Map* for information.

MAUI

Molokai

Rural and relaxed, Molokai enjoys a reputation as the most Hawaiian island. Roughly half its residents are of Hawaiian ancestry, and inhabitants are practiced hula dancers and ukulele-playing aunties who keep close ties to their cultural roots and traditional ways. *Aloha aina* (love of the land) runs deep on Molokai, which has spurned big tourism in favor of preserving itself as the last holdout of old Hawaii. Development is sparse, with beautiful tropical scenery unmarred by sprawling beach resorts or high-rise hotels.

Molokai's less-beaten paths lead to rich natural areas and cultural treasures. Hikes visit Hawaii's largest native rain forest, the world's tallest sea cliffs and one of the state's last free-flowing streams. Traveled on foot, Molokai's famed mule trail plunges down an ocean cliff to a former leprosy colony preserved as a tough history lesson in society's great inhumanity. Wind-scoured dunes occupy another distant corner with remnants of an ancient era concealed in the sands of one of Hawaii's last untouched beaches.

Molokai makes a great getaway from modern life, or the hikes can be done as an easy day trip from Honolulu or Maui. Access to these remote areas requires advance planning and spending some extra money for permits and transport.

HISTORY

Molokai is the legendary island child of the moon goddess Hina. Its first inhabitants were early Marqueseans who landed their canoes at Halawa Bay. Powerful *kahuna* (priests or sorcerers) trained at an elite Molokai school succeeded in protecting the island from invaders for centuries; in fact, they were said to have been able to simply pray their enemies to death. Due to internal dissent, Molokai's chiefs eventually lost control of the island during the 18th century. Oahu, Maui and the Big Island all took turns ruling it until 1795, when Molokai was united into the Hawaiian sovereignty under Kamehameha the Great.

Highlights

Kamakou, Molokai's highest point

- Plunging 1600ft down a sea cliff to Kalaupapa (p175), a former leprosy colony with stirring scenery and a troubled past

- Probing a deep, ancient jungle at Kamakou (p179), Hawaii's largest native forest

- Finding haunting scenery and untrammeled sands at Mo'omomi (p181), a fragile coastline preserve

In modern times Molokai was reputedly the favorite island of Kamehameha V, who left as his legacy the now decommissioned leprosy colony at Kalaupapa and a royal coconut grove. In the 1850s Kamehameha V established Molokai Ranch, a now foreign-owned entity comprising one-third of the island. Cattle ranching, honey production and pineapple farming provided livelihoods in large-scale agriculture until the bottom dropped out of the pineapple market in the 1970s. *Paniolo* (cowboys) still ride the range, but their numbers have dwindled. Resistant to big tourism, Molokai has since struggled to develop a viable substitute, and despite emerging cottage industries in coffee beans and macadamia nuts, many still survive by hunting, fishing and farming dry homesteads.

NATURAL HISTORY

Molokai consists of two volcanic mountains joined together by a short plain. Plunging sea cliffs along the island's north shore are the world's tallest, created when the north half of the East Molokai volcano suddenly collapsed into the sea. The remaining caldera eroded into inaccessible valleys that today harbor Hawaii's largest native rain forest as well as one of the state's last wild streams.

Livestock introduced in the 1850s overgrazed much of the island into an arid badland of ruddy gulches and thorny *kiawe* (a relation of the mesquite). In the 1930s Molokai, like many islands, was reforested by the Civilian Conservation Corps (CCC), which planted eucalyptus, ironwood and Norfolk Island pine to stop erosion and protect watersheds. Ohia lehua dominates Molokai's last patch of native rain forest in the higher elevations, and provides habitat for the *apapane* or red honeycreeper.

The axis deer that run free in Molokai are descendants of eight deer sent from India in 1868 as a gift to Kamehameha V. Feral pigs, introduced by the early Polynesian settlers, still roam the upper wetland forests, and feral goats inhabit the steep canyons and valley rims. All three wreak havoc on the environment and are hunted game animals.

Endangered green sea turtles nest on Molokai's undisturbed beaches, and humpback whales spend winters in the waters between Molokai, Lanai, and Maui.

Today's native waterbirds include the common moorhen, Hawaiian coot and blacknecked stilt, which are all endangered. The Hawaiian owl can be found along the inland shore.

CLIMATE

Lowland temperatures average 84°F in summer and 78°F in winter, and annual rainfall is about 26 inches. The west half of the island is dry and ranch-like, and the mountainous east half is wetter and more lushly vegetated. Mist is a prominent feature of Molokai's high-elevation cliffs, which capture the rainfall that feeds streams and bogs inside the island's cloud covered rain forest.

INFORMATION
Maps

The only trail maps for Molokai are the free, photocopied preserve maps available from the Nature Conservancy (see Information Sources, below). USGS topographic maps cannot be purchased anywhere on the island. For roadmaps try Nelles' *Maui, Molokai, Lanai* or the University of Hawaii's *Molokai-Lanai*.

Information Sources

For island information contact the friendly **Molokai Visitors Association** (☎ 553-3876, 800-800-6367; Ⓦ *www.molokai-hawaii.com; PO Box 960, Kaunakakai, HI 96748)*. Remote beach hideaways are scattered throughout the island, and the condo and vacation-home listings in the association's free *Molokai Visitors Association Directory* are a good starting point for planning an extended stay. Or visit the Molokai Resorts' handy website (Ⓦ *www.molokairesorts.com)* to comparison shop accommodations online. There's also good travel information at Ⓦ www.visitmolokai.com.

Terrible dirt roads impede both the Mo'omomi and Kamakou Preserves, and visitors planning to visit these fragile areas should first contact the **Nature Conservancy** *(TNC; ☎ 553-5236; Ⓦ www.nature.org/hawaii; PO Box 220 Kualapu'u, HI 96757; open 7:30am-3pm Mon-Fri)*. Often the best way of getting to these preserves is to join one of the Nature Conservancy's guided hikes (members/nonmembers $10/25), which occur monthly and book up fast. Reserve at least one month in advance. Participants meet at the airport, making it easy to fly in for the day from other islands.

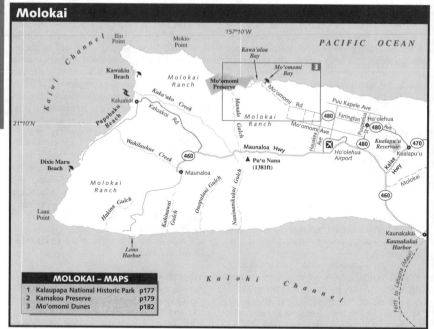

Molokai

PACIFIC OCEAN

Ilio Point
Mokio Point
Kawa'aloa Bay
Mo'omomi Bay   **3**
Kawakiu Beach
Molokai Ranch
Mo'omomi Preserve
Kaka'ako Creek
Mo'omomi Rd
Puu Kapele Ave
Kaluakoi
Kaluakoi Rd
480 Farrington Ho'olehua
Papohaku Beach
Molokai Ranch
Mo'omomi Ave   **480** Ave
Wahilauhue Creek
460
Maunaloa Hwy
480
Kualapu'u Reservoir   **470**
Dixie Maru Beach
▲ Pu'u Nana (1381ft)
Ho'olehua Airport
Kualapu'u
Molokai Ranch
Maunaloa
Hakina Gulch
Kahinawai Gulch
Onopolani Gulch
Naninanikukui Gulch
460
Laau Point
Molokai
Lono Harbor
Kaunakakai
Kaunakakai Harbor
K a l o h i   C h a n n e l
Ferry to Lahaina (Maui)

MOLOKAI – MAPS	
1 Kalaupapa National Historic Park	p177
2 Kamakou Preserve	p179
3 Mo'omomi Dunes	p182

Place Names

Topside refers to the main part of Molokai from the perspective of those living on the Kalaupapa Peninsula, which looks up at a range of impenetrable cliffs.

GATEWAY & FACILITIES
Kaunakakai

Centrally located along the island's south shore, Kaunakakai serves as the commercial center for the entire island. Few services exist outside of Kaunakakai, and other 'towns' are mainly clumps of plantation homes alongside the road.

A wharf built in the 1920s for shipping pineapples, upgraded Kaunakakai from a sleepy fishing village to the island's main town. Today people mainly visit this dusty farm town to buy groceries and gas. Many shops are closed Sunday.

Information The friendly **Molokai Visitors Association** (☎ 553-3876, 800-800-6367;

w *www.molokai-hawaii.com; Suite 700, Kamoi Professional Bldg, Kamoi St; open 8am-4:30pm Mon-Fri)* has useful information on accommodations, events and attractions as well as transportation.

Get your county camping permits from the **Department of Parks & Recreation** (☎ 553-3204; *Mitchell Paole Center, cnr Ala Malama & Ainoa Sts; open 8am-4pm Mon-Fri).*

Supplies & Equipment Ala Malama St has two **grocery stores**. Behind Kalama's gas station is **Outpost Natural Foods** (☎ 553-3377; *70 Makaena Place; open 9am-6pm Mon-Thur, 9am-4pm Fri, 9am-5pm Sun),* which lives up to its name with meager shelves of natural food items.

Basic camping equipment, Coleman fuel, propane, and local maps and books can be purchased at **Molokai Fish & Dive** (☎ 553-5926; *Ala Malama St; open 8am-6pm Mon-Sat, 8am-2pm Sun).* Maps and books on local topics can also be found at **Molokai**

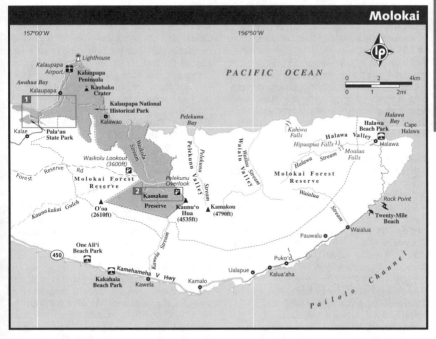

Molokai

PACIFIC OCEAN

Drugs (☎ 553-5313; 28 Kamoi St; open 8:45am-5:45pm Mon-Sat), next to the tourist office. A lot of equipment hassles can be spared by renting. **Molokai Rentals & Tours** (☎ 553-5663, 800-553-9071; W www.molokai -rentals .com) offers a two-person gear package for $20/80 a day/week. Campers can fill a jug with filtered water (gallon 65c) from the vending machine behind **Kamoi Snack-N-Go** (Kamoi St).

Places to Stay No one hangs around Kaunakakai. The closest places to stay are within a few miles east on the Kamehameha V Hwy (Hwy 450).

County-run **One Ali'i Beach Park** (Kamehameha V Hwy; tent sites per person $3), 3 miles east of Kaunakakai, is the closest campground – if spending the night on the highway shoulder is your idea of a campout. Obtain camping permits from Kaunakakai's Department of Parks & Recreation office.

Hotel Molokai (☎ 553-5347, 800-367-5004; W www.hotelmolokai.com; Kamehameha V Hwy; doubles $85-135, quads $125-140), 1½ miles east of town, really is a place that time forgot. Luckily someone noticed before it was too late, and renovated this 1960s motor lodge into a nostalgic oceanside hideaway, complete with poolside restaurant and bar. 'Garden view' rooms are preferable over the cheapest rooms, which neighbor the septic tank.

B&Bs offer a tropical getaway at good value. The Molokai variety is essentially a small, country vacation rental with a kitchen and full complement of rooms.

Ka Hale Mala B&B (☎ 553-9009; W www .molokai-bnb.com; Kamehameha V Hwy; doubles without/with breakfast $70/80), 5 miles east of Kaunakakai, means 'garden house,' which hints at the tropical surroundings of this spacious ground-level apartment. In the morning hikers can fuel up on a home-grown, gourmet breakfast on the *lanai* (veranda). Happily there's no minimum stay. Credit cards are not accepted.

Kamalo Plantation Bed & Breakfast (☎ 558-8236; W www.molokai.com/kamalo/; Kamehameha V Hwy; doubles $85) is 10 miles east of Kaunakakai in Kamalo. The small cottage here makes a cozy plantation paradise for two, where every day starts with fruit and a loaf of bread. There is a two-night minimum stay and cash payments only; traveler's checks OK.

Places to Eat Restaurants are scarce outside of Kaunakakai, so either grab a bite while you're in town or stock up on groceries for cooking your own meals.

Fill your pack with bread and pastries from Hawaii's famed **Kanemitsu's Bakery** (☎ 553-5855; Ala Malama St; open 5:30am-6:30pm daily) or grab a sandwich from **Subway** (130 Kamehameha V Hwy; open 8am-8pm Sun-Thur, 8am-9pm Fri & Sat) and hit the trail.

Molokai Pizza Cafe (☎ 553-3288; 15 Kaunakakai Place; pizza slices $2.50, pies $5-13, pasta $7.50-9; lunch & dinner daily), at the wharf turnoff, is popular for pizza and pasta, and also good for deli sandwiches, burgers and chicken dinners.

Kamuela's Grill (☎ 553-4286; Ala Malama St; meals $4-8; open 7am-9pm Mon-Sat, 7am-3pm Sun) is also inexpensive, with plate meals, sandwiches and saimin (Hawaiian version of Japanese noodle soup).

Campers Beware

Progress has yet to land at Molokai's airport, where checked luggage and carry-ons are all still searched by hand. Regardless of how many baggage scanners you've eluded already, campers flying into Molokai can expect to have camp stoves or fuel bottles (yes, even empty ones) confiscated by airport security when it comes time to leave. If you'd rather not part with such items either don't bring them or travel by ferry. For places that rent or sell stoves on Molokai, see Supplies & Equipment (p172).

✿ ✿ ✿ ✿ ✿ ✿ ✿ ✿ ✿ ✿

The beachfront restaurant at **Hotel Molokai** (☎ 553-5347; breakfast & lunch $5-10, dinner $12.50-17.50; open daily) makes a perfect conclusion (or beginning) to a long day on the trail. If the menu is out of your range you can still knock back a few mai tais and watch the sun sink into the ocean at the palm-fringed bar.

Getting There & Away Kaunakakai is linked to other islands by air and ferry. While flying is generally faster and easier, no one comes to Molokai seeking speed and convenience – especially when the ferry promises so much adventure!

Hawaiian Airlines (☎ 800-882-8811, Oahu ☎ 838-1555; W www.hawaiianair.com) and **Island Air** (☎ 800-652-6541; W www.islandair.com) serve Molokai's Ho'olehua Airport, 6 miles northeast of Kaunakakai. Most flights connect through Honolulu; Island Air flies direct to Maui.

If you don't mind small planes (or want more scenery), you can shop commuter airlines for cheaper fares. **Molokai Air Shuttle** (☎ 567-6847, Oahu ☎ 545-4988) has the cheapest flight to Honolulu ($70 roundtrip). **Paragon Air** (☎ 866-946-4744, Maui ☎ 244-3356; W www.paragon-air.com) has flights from Maui (Kahului $93 roundtrip, Kapalua $103 and Hana $136) and Lanai (Lanai City $130 roundtrip). **Pacific Wings** (☎ 567-6814, 888-575-4546, Maui ☎ 873-0877; W www.pacificwings.com) offers scheduled service from Maui (Kahului $145 roundtrip) and Honolulu ($147 roundtrip).

See Travel Facts (p218) for more information on discount flight coupons, domestic and interisland flights, and commuter airlines. In Kaunakakai, interisland flight coupons can be purchased at **Friendly Isle Travel** (☎ 553-5337; 64 Ala Malama St; open 8am-5pm Mon-Fri). Credit cards are not accepted.

If you want to travel by ferry, **Island Marine** (☎ 800-275-6969; W www.molokaiferry.com) operates the service between Maui (Lahaina) and Kaunakakai ($42.40 one-way, 1½ hours); call for reservations. Currently the boat leaves Lahaina at 6:30am on Monday, Wednesday, Friday and Saturday, and 5:15pm daily. Departures from Kaunakakai are at 5:30am Monday to Saturday, 2:30pm on Monday, Wednesday, Friday and Saturday, and 3pm on Sunday. For most hikes the layover in Kaunakakai is too short to make a day trip by ferry. However, the ferry can be a day trip option for the Kalaupapa hike using a hike-fly package (see Getting to/from the Hike, p178, for details).

Cars rent for around $40 with discounts in winter months. There are a relatively limited number of vehicles available, so don't count on strolling up to the rental counter without a reservation or there may not be anything left. **Budget** (☎ 800-527-0700) and **Dollar** (☎ 567-6156, 800-800-4000) rent cars at the airport. In Kaunakakai, **Island Kine Auto Rental** (☎ 553-5242, 866-527-7368; w www.molokai-car-rental.com) offers free customer pick-up and also rents 4WD jeeps ($65).

For shuttle services call **Molokai Off-Road Tours & Taxi** (☎ 553-3369) or **Molokai Outdoors** (☎ 553-4477, 877-553-4477).

Pala'au State Park

Ten miles north of Kaunakakai, Kalae Hwy ends at this park overlooking the Kalaupapa Peninsula. This wooded headland adjacent to Kalaupapa National Historic Park is the closest you can get to the peninsula by car, and is the starting point for the mule trail providing the only land access.

A grove of ironwood and eucalyptus shelters a pleasant, sometimes rainy **campground** (☎ 567-6923; tent sites $5), well situated for hikers headed down to Kalaupapa the next day. Unsigned and invisible from the highway, sites have picnic tables and fire pits, and are found down a driveway just past the picnic shelter. Water is nonpotable, so bring it from town. There's a maximum five-night stay. Pick up the required camping permit from the caretaker's residence, next to the mule-ride stables, when you arrive. For advance permits contact the **Division of State Parks** (Oahu ☎ 587-0300, Maui ☎ 984-8109) offices on Oahu or Maui.

Just downhill from the park, near the junction of Hwys 470 and 480 (Farrington Ave), is **Kamuela's Cookhouse** (☎ 567-9655; Farrington Ave, Kualapu'u; breakfast & lunch $4-7; open 7am-3pm Mon-Sat), which serves the island's best breakfast out of a cheery plantation house. Also along this road is a small **grocery store** (Farrington Ave, Kualapu'u; closed Sun).

Kalaupapa National Historic Park

Duration	2½–3 hours
Distance	6 miles (9.6km)
Difficulty	moderate–demanding
Start/Finish	Pala'au State Park entrance
Nearest Town	Kaunakakai (p172)
Transport	private

Summary A dizzying 1600ft descent of a sheer sea cliff to visit a once-forbidden leprosy colony set amid Molokai's most spectacular scenery.

Protruding from the island's precipitous north shore, in ancient times the flat Kalaupapa Peninsula was favored by Molokai chiefs for surfing and was a popular resting spot for seafaring canoes. Imprisoned behind 3000ft cliffs and inaccessible by road, this isolated peninsula received worldwide fame for the leprosy colony that operated here until 1969. Still inhabited (residents are no longer contagious), the settlement is preserved as a unique historic park.

Most visitors only peer down on Kalaupapa from Pala'au State Park. But breathtaking scenery rewards the intrepid few who follow the supply trail down a 1600ft sea cliff to explore the leftover town below. This idyllic, self-contained hamlet is somewhat of a marvel (modern life still managed to find its way down here) and there are great views of Molokai's towering north shore *pali* (cliffs), the world's tallest sea cliffs.

Access to Kalaupapa is restricted and requires joining a guided tour. Hiking time is one hour down and 1½ hours up, but combined with the tour it takes a full day. Those daunted by the idea of climbing back up have an option to fly out from the Kalaupapa airport.

From Pala'au State Park, hikers can preview the settlement (or gaze down to where they've been) from the nearby Kalaupapa Overlook, at the end of the park road. Interpretive plaques identify landmarks and explain Kalaupapa's history as a leprosy colony.

Damien of Molokai

Hawaii's most venerated hero, Father Damien sacrificed his life to serve those exiled to the Molokai leprosy colony at Kalaupapa. Born in 1840 on a small farm in Belgium as Joseph DeVeuster, Fr Damien joined the Congregation of Sacred Hearts in 1859. He arrived in Hawaii as a missionary in 1864, and after being ordained a priest on Oahu was sent off to the Big Island to preach Christianity.

Meanwhile at Kalaupapa, missionaries had built a chapel, but because the disease was so feared the settlement had no resident priest. Fr Damien volunteered for the job in 1873. His order originally planned to provide priests on a rotating basis, but Damien wrote back that he wanted to stay.

Fr Damien's initial efforts to restore dignity focused on providing proper funerals. Cemetery fences were put up to protect graves from wild animals. He built coffins, founded a burial association to look after ceremonies and organized musicians to play for funeral processions. Medical care and other facilities were almost nonexistent, and he was soon very busy caring for the sick and helping residents build homes, farms and roads. When he needed a break he scaled the cliffs behind the peninsula (today's trail had not been built yet) to deliver sacraments and build churches on topside Molokai (violating Hawaii's isolation law).

His inspiring bravery drew relief efforts as more brothers and priests came to help out. A group of nuns arrived in 1888 to establish a home for girls. Fr Damien eventually contracted leprosy, but continued to work up to his death in 1889. In 1995 he was beatified by Pope John Paul II and is now a candidate for sainthood.

Left of the overlook a short path leads through ironwood to Kauleonanahoa (Penis of Nanahoa), a phallic-shaped rock. Reputedly women who bring offerings of lei and dollar bills and spend the night here will return home pregnant, but apparently there is no danger in just going to have a look.

HISTORY

Naturally isolated by ocean and cliffs, the peninsula was selected as the site of a leprosy settlement, established under King Kamehameha V in 1865. Introduced to Hawaii in the 1830s, leprosy had by the 1860s become an incurable epidemic affecting one out of 50 Hawaiians. Isolation became public policy for containing this fearsome disease. From 1866 to 1969, over 8000 Hawaiians were ripped from their families and shipped across the sea from Honolulu, forever banished to this colony of sick and dying people.

Early residents suffered inhumane conditions, and were abandoned here without shelter, clean water or any means of supporting themselves. Fr Damien arrived in 1873 and worked tirelessly to make improvements (see the boxed text, 'Damien of Molokai'). His efforts galvanized worldwide concern for these unfortunate sufferers and helped pioneer important medical advancements. Cures that emerged out of the 1940s eventually brought an end to isolation laws in 1969. Outpatient treatment is used to control leprosy today. No longer contagious, the last of Kalaupapa's aging residents remain here by choice, free to come and go as they wish.

Prior to becoming a leprosy colony, native Hawaiians occupied the peninsula for 900 to 1000 years, as evidenced by a vast number of undisturbed ruins. Protection for this tremendous archaeological resource was another reason Kalaupapa was declared a national historic park in 1980.

NATURAL HISTORY

A late addition to the island, the peninsula was formed long after the north half of the East Molokai volcano slumped into the ocean, leaving behind a bank of sheer cliffs.

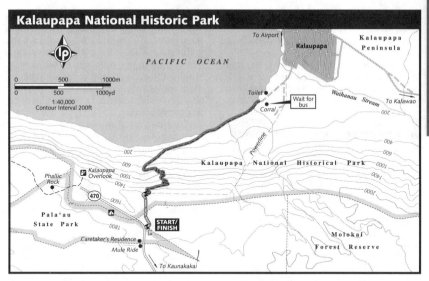

The peninsula was tacked on by Kauhako Crater, a volcano that emerged from the ocean to build a flat plain against the shore.

PLANNING

Kalaupapa is administered jointly by the National Park Service (NPS) and the Hawaii Department of Health. For general park information contact **Kalaupapa National Historic Park** (☎ *567-6802*; W *www.nps.gov/kala/*; *PO Box 2222, Kalaupapa, HI 96742*) or pick up a free NPS history brochure at the Molokai Visitors Association office in Kaunakakai.

When to Hike

Plan to start hiking by 8am in order to meet up with the tour, which leaves from the bottom of the *pali* at 9:45am. An early start will also put you ahead of the mule train, which hits the trail around 8:30am. Visitors are returned to the trail at 1:50pm for the hike out. The trail may not be hiked on Sunday.

What to Bring

Bring enough cash for the tour ($30), lunch and a raincoat. The trail is often slick and muddy, so wear sturdy shoes.

Maps & Books

The USGS 1:25,000 map *Kaunakakai* provides good detail of the peninsula, but is not really necessary for this hike. There is just one route down and up – step off the trail and you certainly won't be needing a map anyway.

Histories of Kalaupapa and biographies of Fr Damien are popular subjects on Molokai. You'll find them in the settlement's small bookshop and in stores around Kaunakakai.

Permits & Regulations

Law requires that all visitors to Kalaupapa obtain a permit from the Hawaii State Department of Health. Although this is medically unnecessary, the law is kept on the books to protect the privacy of the remaining residents.

What this really means is that hikers must sign-up in advance for a four-hour bus tour through **Damien Tours** (☎ *567-6171*). The permit isn't anything tangible, but once you have a reservation you are authorized to hike in. The tour begins at the end of the trail from the bottom of the *pali*. You'll sign in and pay ($30) the driver upon boarding.

MOLOKAI

Visitors are kept on a short leash within the settlement itself (no wandering off by yourself) but nobody bothers you along the trail.

Tours run Monday to Saturday. Reservations are required and children under 16 are not allowed. Camping is prohibited within the park, as is taking pictures of the residents.

NEAREST TOWNS & FACILITIES

See Kaunakakai (p172) and Pala'au State Park (p175).

The trailhead in Pala'au State Park is 9 miles north of Kaunakakai on Kalae Hwy, a mile below the overlook. The hike begins at a gated dirt road marked 'no unauthorized persons' near milepost five. A parking pull-off appears on the right, just past the mule stables.

From Maui, the $229 hike-fly package through **Island Marine** (☎ 800-275-6969; W www.molokaiferry.com) offers a way for hikers to day trip by ferry. Passengers hike down to Kalaupapa for the tour and then fly topside to Ho'olehua Airport for ground transport all the way back to the ferry. The trip, which runs Monday, Wednesday, Friday as well as Saturday, includes all transportation, tour reservations and, conveniently, a sack lunch.

It's also possible to organize your own flight out from the Kalaupapa Airport, which is served by **Paragon Air** (☎ 808-244-3356, 866-946-4744; W www.paragon-air .com). A topside flight to Ho'olehua Airport costs $43, while an interisland flight to Maui or Lanai will cost you somewhere around $80.

THE HIKE (see map p177)

It wasn't until the early 1900s that someone finally built this 3-mile mule trail as a supply route to the settlement. Before then the peninsula was accessible only by sea, with Fr Damien periodically sneaking off to other parts of Molokai by scaling the cliffs behind the town. The trail is still traveled by mule today, only now the mules carry tourists and most supplies come by air or barge.

A dirt road leads the way beneath ironwood and eucalyptus. Although a sign forbids entry, hikers may proceed past the cattle gate if they have tour reservations. The track drops gently past a meadow to reach NPS signs at another gate, a replacement for the original locked model put here to enforce the quarantine between patients and everyone else.

After one last 'no trespassing' sign the path narrows and breaks out onto a slippery, cliff-hung ledge that unwinds in 26 switchbacks to the ocean below. You can count your way down the numbered posts as you go. Shrubs obscure the peninsula for almost all of the way. An outstanding view past turn No 10 reveals the settlement in striking detail. Roads, houses, airport runways and a lighthouse all unfold below. Behind the town lies Kauhako Crater, which is a less obvious landmark topped by a white cross.

The trail comes off the *pali* in forest, leveling after the last switchback to an ambling ½-mile walk along a palm-fringed shore. A small footbridge hastens hikers towards the end of the trail at a field just outside the settlement. Head right for the bleachers by the corral to wait for the tour.

On tour, visitors are driven around the well-ordered town site aboard a funky old school bus. If it all seems like paradise, consider this balmy town was actually the settlement's administrative headquarters, *kapu* (forbidden) to patients who were forced to live in the rainy Kalawao District to the east. **Fr Damien's church** is pretty much all that remains of this original settlement area, visited next. At the end of this road is a quiet **park** where the tour stops for lunch, with ample time given for gazing at the magnificent, 3600ft north shore *pali* shrouded in mist.

After lunch the tour drives back to the trailhead and drops off hikers for the steep climb up. If the trail seems difficult, imagine what it must've been like in Fr Damien's day when there was no trail and he had to scale the cliffs behind Kalaupapa town.

Kamakou Preserve

Duration	2 hours
Distance	3 miles (4.8km)
Difficulty	easy–moderate
Start/Finish	end Molokai Forest Reserve Rd
Nearest Town	Kaunakakai (p172)
Transport	private

Summary A short boardwalk through lush rain forest visits an ancient bog en route to a dramatic view of the Pelekunu Valley, encompassed by 4000ft cliffs.

A short walk back to an ancient time, the 2774-acre Kamakou Preserve offers a last glimpse of what Hawaii looked like centuries ago. With most of Hawaii's native forests lost to overgrazing and shortsighted forest practices, this tropical wilderness endures on a remote slope of Kamakou (4961ft), Molokai's highest point. The 1½-mile Pepeopae Trail explores endemic plants and an ancient bog, finishing up just below the island's summit atop the Pelekunu Overlook for a stunning view of the wild, deep-cut Pelekunu Valley.

NATURAL HISTORY

Underlying Kamakou's forested slopes are the ancient remains of the East Molokai volcano, its deep, crumbling caldera given over to the remarkable Pelekunu Valley. In 1982 TNC established rights to manage a small patch of this native rain forest as a nature preserve in a conservation deal cinched with Molokai Ranch. A few years later TNC purchased neighboring land in the inaccessible Pelekunu Valley, which shelters one of Hawaii's last untamed streams.

Of the 250 native plant species found here, 90% are endemic to Hawaii. The wood, leaves and flowers of many were gathered by native Hawaiians and used for a variety of traditional purposes. Blossoms of ohia lehua sustain the *apapane*, a red honeycreeper that flutters in the wind around the Pelekunu Overlook. Naturalists often visit with high hopes of spotting the elusive Hawaiian happyfaced spider, its small, yellow body marked by a bright red grin. Islanders frequent the forest to hunt pig and deer.

PLANNING

The preserve is managed by **TNC** (☎ 553-5236; W *www.nature.org/hawaii; PO Box 220 Kualapu'u, HI 96757; open 7:30am-3pm Mon-Fri*) and is open to public access. Permits are not required, but visitors should check conditions before heading up. While the trail is hikeable year-round, it is often wet; any amount of rainfall can turn the road into an impassible mess.

Even when dry, the road requires a 4WD and is difficult to negotiate. Visitors should not attempt to drive, but should plan to visit the preserve by getting onto one of TNC's guided hikes (members/nonmembers $10/25), held monthly on the first Saturday. Knowledgeable volunteers do an excellent job explaining the natural and cultural significance of rain forest plants, and participants

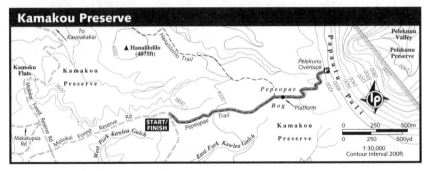

tend to be studied naturalists. On the downside the pace may seem slow to those who don't have a strong interest in ecology. The hikes fill months ahead, so reserve early.

Wear long pants to protect legs from cuts and scrapes from vegetation. Carry raingear and expect to get wet whether it's raining or not. A field guide comes in handy for identifying the preserve's many native rain forest plants. Boots should be thoroughly scrubbed of dirt to prevent accidentally introducing non-native plants.

Maps & Books

A map, directions and full-color guide to flora and fauna are included in the *Pepeopae Boardwalk Trail Guide*, available from the TNC office. The USGS 1:25,000 *Molokai East* is the only topographic map, but because the trail was built in stages it still shows the route ending at Pepeopae Bog.

NEAREST TOWNS & FACILITIES

See Kaunakakai (p172). A poorly maintained campground at Waikolu Lookout (8 miles from Hwy 460) lies just outside the preserve boundary, but unless you're a pig hunter there's really no reason to stay here. Camping is prohibited within the preserve.

GETTING TO/FROM THE HIKE

It's not always possible to get to the trail near the end of 10-mile Molokai Forest Reserve Rd (also called 'Forestry Road'). Dirt the entire way, the road requires a 4WD vehicle and plenty of off-road driving experience. Driving it is not recommended for visitors, who are better off getting a lift up to the trailhead on the tour. In unsafe conditions the road may be closed, check with the TNC office in Kualapu'u.

Molokai Forest Reserve Rd heads east from the Maunaloa Hwy (Hwy 460) at the Homelani Cemetery turnoff, 3.4 miles north of Kaunakakai. The road passes Waikolu Lookout before crossing into the preserve for the last 2.2 miles of treacherous slopes and axle-deep mud. A small brown post marks the trail near the road's end. Allow at least an hour to reach the trailhead from the highway.

Getting to Kamakou

Getting to the Kamakou Preserve is half the adventure. The Molokai Forest Reserve Rd not only makes for an exciting drive, but it also has some interesting sites to explore along the way:

4 miles – the CCC helped to reforest Molokai's lower elevation slopes in the 1930s. Here the road reaches an old CCC barrack and **woodcarvers shop**. TNC uses the barracks to host researchers and volunteers. Visitors are welcome to stop by to check out the whimsical carvings.

6.7 miles – a green railing marks the **sandalwood measuring pit**, a grassy depression dug by enslaved commoners for measuring ship loads of sandalwood in the early 1800s. Many died during the harvesting of this wood, which was carried down to the harbor for export to the Orient.

8 miles – arrive at **Waikolu Lookout** (3735ft), a stunning coastal viewpoint over a deep, forested valley.

final 2.2 miles – the road enters the preserve and becomes a giant mudhole. Warnings crackle over the CB. Knuckles turn white as your rig thrashes through ruts and up slippery slopes.

✿ ✿ ✿ ✿ ✿ ✿ ✿ ✿ ✿ ✿ ✿ ✿ ✿

THE HIKE (see map p179)

Starting at the brown post, the first narrow planks of the Pepeopae Trail quickly disappear into vegetation and enter a damp scrub forest. Wooden boards push end-to-end through the fern-filled undergrowth past *puahanui*, a Hawaiian hydrangea; lacy *wawaeiole*, a type of club moss; and *painiu*, or silver lily, with long flat leaves. Many of these plants have been gathered by Hawaiians for centuries, and serve important medicinal and household purposes in addition to use in traditional leis. Crowned by red blossoms, the wood from the scrawny-looking ohia lehua, found only in Hawaii, was once harvested for building homes, canoes, spears and religious carvings. Versatile *hapu'u*, a tall, endemic tree fern, finds function as roof thatch, mattress stuffing and fish nets. *Pukiawe*, a short shrub with small pinkish berries, was indispensable to Hawaiian chiefs who burned it before making public appearances; it was believed the smoke temporarily erased the chiefs' godliness, lifting the *kapu* (taboo) that prevented them from mingling with commoners.

Trees grow taller and the forest gets wetter as the trail gradually gains elevation. A ½-mile track opens to 10,000 year-old **Pepeopae Bog**, veiled in a timeless grey mist. Clusters of crimson plants are actually the familiar ohia lehua, stunted to the height of small shrubs by the acidic soil.

Cross the bog and keep right at a junction to a small viewing platform. From here the trail continues uphill and returns to dark forest, where keen eyes may spot lanky lobelia. Dense vegetation fills a winding ravine on the final steep, sodden trek to the overlook. It takes careful footing to stay balanced on the slippery planks ahead. Don't step off, or you'll sink knee-deep in the saturated soil. At 1½ miles the trail meets sky, ending on a grassy ledge with a sweeping view at **Pelekunu Overlook**. Cascading streams etched this deep valley through the eroded remains of a volcanic crater. Sit back and savor the scenery before turning back.

Mo'omomi Dunes

Duration	4½ hours
Distance	8 miles (13km)
Difficulty	moderate–demanding
Start/Finish	Mo'omomi Rd
Nearest Town	Kaunakakai (p172)
Transport	private

Summary A long trek across rangeland to an untrammeled coastal dunes preserve noted for rare plants, endangered shorebirds and archaeological secrets.

A wilderness beach and unique geology highlight this lonely shoreline walk along Mo'omomi Preserve, one of the last undis-

turbed coastal dune areas in Hawaii. Lowly vegetated mounds shape this desert-like landscape, distinguished by fragile ecology and prehistoric findings. In ancient times Hawaiians from Molokai's north and west valleys summered here to catch fish and quarry basalt stones for adzes. Today this desolate area is protected by TNC for the rare coastal plants and the nesting habitat the dunes provide to endangered green sea turtles. The preserve also holds scientific interest, with fossilized bones found here leading to the discovery of several prehistoric birds.

The prettiest part of the hike is the established TNC trail, which starts atop Kaiehu Point and traces the rugged preserve edge to a pristine wilderness beach. However, you'll

Treading Lightly at Mo'omomi

Mo'omomi Preserve is an extremely fragile area requiring special protection from overuse. To help minimize impact, visitors are strongly encouraged to join a TNC tour.

Hikers should observe the following guidelines:

- Check in with TNC for conditions. Calling at least two to three months ahead increases your chance of getting on the tour.
- Stay on the marked trail, sticking to the beaches below the vegetation line. Many grasses and low-lying plants are rare and easily damaged by careless feet. Don't venture out across the open dunes.
- Tread with care across sandstone area to avoid damaging lithified plant casts.
- Do not pick plants or collect natural objects, including fossils, bones, rocks or coral.
- Do not dig anything up. Tampering with archaeological sites and removing artifacts is prohibited.
- Pack out your litter and carry out as much beach debris as you can.
- Swimming is discouraged due to heavy surf. Camping is prohibited, with exception given to local anglers by permit (contact the TNC office).

✿ ✿ ✿ ✿ ✿ ✿ ✿ ✿ ✿ ✿ ✿

spend most of the hike just getting to the preserve boundary, approached by a long, tiring walk over arid rangeland on a dirt road to Kawaʻaloa Bay. The terrain is mostly level and some route-finding is necessary. Guided hikes led monthly by TNC make it possible for a shorter, 2-mile hike beginning from inside the preserve.

PLANNING

Moʻomomi Preserve is managed by **TNC** (☎ 553-5236; W *www.nature.org/hawaii*; PO Box 220 Kualapuʻu, HI 96757; open 7:30am-3pm Mon-Fri) through a cooperative agreement with Molokai Ranch. To help minimize impact visitors are encouraged to join the guided hike (members/nonmembers $10/25), held monthly on the fourth Saturday. Hikers benefit from getting to start right at the preserve trailhead, eliminating the long walk in along Moʻomomi Rd. The hike meets at the airport, so if you fly in for the day you won't need a car. Reservations fill months in advance (February and March are most coveted).

Visitors are also allowed to walk into the preserve on their own. The way in is unmarked, so be sure to stop by the TNC office to check in and grab a map. A snug-fitting sun hat is essential for this hike, which is hot and windy, with no shade along the way.

Maps & Books

Moʻomomi, West Molokai: A Coastal Treasure, by Hannah Will Johnstone, makes a good plant guide and is required reading for learning about Moʻomomi's fragile ecology and archeological finds. Copies are found in shops around Kaunakakai (TNC doesn't sell it).

A free preserve map available from TNC is essentially a photocopy of an older USGS 1:24,000 map *Molokai Airport*, marked to show the trail. The route is mostly unsigned, so don't head out without one.

Permits & Regulations

Regulations are stated simply on a sign at the end of Farrington Ave – 'Love this land.' See also the boxed text 'Treading Lightly at Moʻomomi' (p181).

GETTING TO/FROM THE HIKE

The preserve trail starts atop Kaiehu Point above Kawaʻaloa Bay, but because the road to it is washed out hikers can start walking

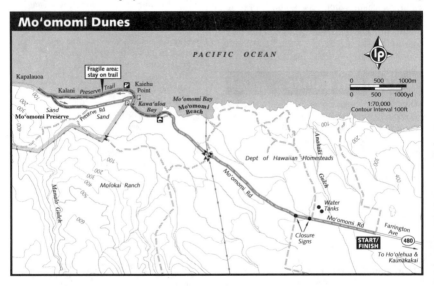

anywhere past the end of Farrington Ave, 3 miles west of Hoʻolehua. From Kaunakakai, head toward the airport and turn right after 6 miles onto Hwy 480. Turn left at the stop sign onto Farrington Ave and drive until the pavement bites the dust and becomes a red dirt road (Moʻomomi Rd).

Stay on good terms with your car rental company by parking here and continuing along Moʻomomi Rd on foot. On a dry day it's conceivable for an ordinary passenger car to venture another rutted mile to the first or second closure signs, but don't attempt to go any further without 4WD. Moʻomomi Rd worsens ahead and is closed at a locked gate.

THE HIKE
Beginning at the parched plots of Hawaiian homesteads, the long walk to the preserve follows Moʻomomi Rd for 3 miles to Kawaʻaloa Bay. Green and orange road closure signs, appearing at 0.8 miles and 1 mile, direct motorists to use side roads for access to Moʻomomi Beach. Don't confuse these signs for the way to dunes. Keep straight at all turns, continuing onward past the water tanks towards the sandy horizon. The road ahead reaches for ocean, and goes blazing across the range in a bright red ribbon that's intercepted at 2.2 miles by a barbed-wire fence at the Molokai Ranch boundary. Avoid the road leading off to the right. On the left you'll see two consecutive cattle gates about 20 yards apart, separated by another gated road coming in from the south. Climb over the two gates to finish hiking the washed-out road to a littered beach at Kawaʻaloa Bay.

A more spectacular shoreline awaits in the preserve just beyond the bay. Traverse the beach and follow the arrowed fence posts up the rocky ledge to Kaiehu Point. Here you'll meet the end of the preserve road used by TNC. The mile-long preserve trail begins a few steps past the second parking area. Leave the road for a signed path

that heads right (north) across a meadow to a rocky **sandstone beach**. Wiry green mats of rare, ground-loving plants lie humped along the shoreline and a fine view extends east to Kaluapapa's distant lighthouse.

From here it's important to stick closely to the trail, which leads west along the sandy dunes to gradually rockier terrain. Tubular-shaped rocks littering a sandstone outcropping are actually the remains of lithified plant casts, an unusual geologic feature formed when the roots and stems of an ancient forest reacted with sand and water over hundreds of years and slowly turned to cement.

Signs fade as the trail veers inland, drops over a low dune and vanishes in the sand. Search the brush on the right to pick up the subtle path that tunnels under *kiawe*. The trail resumes as a vague, sandy walk behind a dune, eventually ending after 1 mile at a deserted beach near a sandstone cliff.

The return route varies slightly as trail signs lead hikers in a loop back to the trailhead via the grassy preserve road. From Kaiehu Point retrace your steps down to the bay and back up Moʻomomi Rd.

Other Hikes

Halawa Valley
Older guidebooks often recommend this gorgeous streamside hike up the lush Halawa Valley to two waterfalls. As the site of Molokai's earliest settlement, the valley is strewn with the remains of ancient *heiau* (temples), *hale* (house) sites and burial grounds. Land disputes have since closed the trail to public access, and now hiking is only allowed with a guide. Starting 27 miles (1½ hours) east of Kaunakakai from Halawa Bay, the trail hacks through taro fields and mango groves for 1½ miles to 250ft Moalua Falls at a swimmable pool. The 500ft Hipuapua Falls is just upstream. A couple of bridgeless stream crossings and rough terrain make it moderately difficult. To find a guide contact the **Molokai Visitors Association** (☎ 808-553-3876, 800-800-6367; W *www.molokai-hawai.com*) in Kaunakakai.

Kauai

If you want to revel in some of the lushest scenery on earth, Kauai is an unbeatable destination – the island is so richly green that it's nicknamed the 'Garden Island.' Ever since Elvis made it famous in *Blue Hawaii,* Kauai has been a prime destination for honeymooners looking for that perfect paradisiacal setting. It's also a perennial favorite of backpackers, who are hot to hit its challenging trails and take advantage of some of the best beachside campgrounds in all of Hawaii.

Kauai is less developed than other major islands like Oahu, and most of its interior is made up of mountainous forest reserve. Moviemakers looking for scenery bordering on fantasy have often found it in Kauai. The classic films *South Pacific* and *Raiders of the Lost Ark* were both filmed on Kauai's North Shore. The remote Honopu Valley on the Na Pali Coast was the jungle home of King Kong, while both the Hanapepe and Lawai Valleys served as locations for Steven Spielberg's *Jurassic Park.*

HISTORY

Kauai was never conquered by invaders from another Hawaiian island, and its history is one of autonomy. Kaumuali'i was the last chief to reign over an independent Kauai. Although he was a shrewd leader and Kauai's warriors were fierce, it was allegedly the power of *kahuna* (priests) that protected them. When Kamehameha the Great, who had conquered all the other islands, sailed from Oahu toward Kauai in 1796 with an armada of war canoes, a mysterious storm suddenly kicked up at sea, compelling him to turn back to Oahu, and he never reached Kauai's shores.

In 1804 Kamehameha and his warriors again massed on the shores of Oahu, ready to attack Kauai. However, on the eve of the invasion, an epidemic of what was probably cholera struck the island of Oahu, decimating the would-be invaders and forcing yet another delay. In 1810 the two *ali'i nui*

Highlights

ANN CECIL

Sunset over the Na Pali Coast

- Trekking along the dramatic cliffs of the Na Pali Coast (p188)

- Rolling by cinematic views on the Powerline Trail (p199) and atop Kuilau Ridge (p197)

- Exploring the 'Grand Canyon of the Pacific' on the Kukui and Canyon Trails (p206)

- Spying varied bird life in Alakai Swamp (p214) and along cliff-top lookouts into ancient valleys

(high chiefs) reached an agreement that ceded the island of Kauai to the kingdom of Hawai'i. It was essentially a truce, and Kaumuali'i never fully accepted Kamehameha's ultimate authority.

When Kamehameha I died in 1819 he was succeeded by his son Liholiho, who didn't trust Kaumuali'i's loyalties any more than his father had. Liholiho set off for

Kauai in a luxury schooner purchased from Western sandalwood traders. After tricking Kaumuali'i into going for a cruise, Liholiho kidnapped him and took him to Oahu, where Kaumuali'i was forced to marry Kamehameha's widow, Ka'ahumanu. In the grand scheme of royal design, this served to bring Kaumuali'i into the fold. When Kaumuali'i passed away in 1824 so too did the kingdom of Kauai.

NATURAL HISTORY

Kauai is the oldest of the main Hawaiian islands. Over time, heavy rains have eroded deep valleys, while pounding waves and falling sea levels have cut steep cliffs. The island was settled most intensively along river valleys near the coast, such as Waimea and Hanalei. Even valleys that were difficult to reach, like Kalalau on the Na Pali Coast, had sizable settlements. When winter seas prevented canoes from landing on the shore, trails down precipitous ridges and rope ladders provided access.

Kauai's central volcanic peak, Mt Waialeale (5148ft), is quite possibly the wettest place on earth and feeds seven rivers, including Hawaii's only navigable one. On a

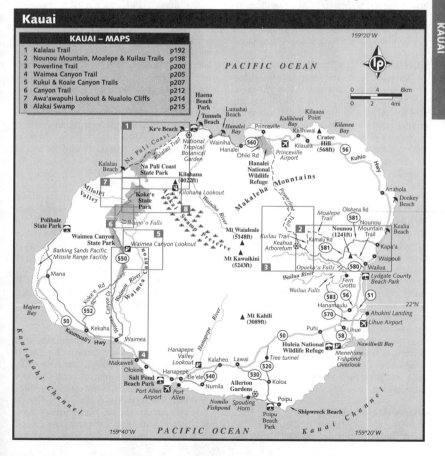

Kauai

KAUAI – MAPS	
1 Kalalau Trail	p192
2 Nounou Mountain, Moalepe & Kuilau Trails	p198
3 Powerline Trail	p200
4 Waimea Canyon Trail	p205
5 Kukui & Koaie Canyon Trails	p207
6 Canyon Trail	p212
7 Awa'awapuhi Lookout & Nualolo Cliffs	p214
8 Alakai Swamp	p215

plateau below Mt Waialeale where clouds and mist rarely lift sits the Alakai Swamp, supporting a unique ecosystem where trees grow knee high and rare native birds thrive. A deep north–south rift slices through the western side of the island, creating the immense Waimea Canyon. The North Shore and Na Pali (literally 'The Cliffs') Coast are lush regions, with waterfalls, beautiful beaches and stream-fed valleys.

The most powerful hurricane to hit Hawaii in over a century was Hurricane Iniki in 1992. Packing gusts of 165mph, Iniki felled thousands of trees, washed away beachfront and damaged over half of the buildings on Kauai, yet only two people perished. Some native koa forests were demolished and a few native bird species have since disappeared.

CLIMATE

At Kalalau Beach the temperature seldom drops below 60°F, while a few thousand feet above, at Koke'e State Park, it dips into the 30s on winter nights. Kauai's average annual rainfall is about 40 inches, but the variances across the island are extreme. Waimea, on the southwest coast, averages 21 inches, while Hanalei, in the north, averages 85 inches. For recorded forecasts call ☎ 245-6001.

INFORMATION
When to Hike

In midwinter it's quite possible to have fairly continuous downpours for a week at a time. Then again, it might be all blue skies and calm seas. Kauai's famous red soil turns to slippery clay when it rains, making some trails excruciatingly difficult if not impossible. A summer visit to the island virtually guarantees dry weather, but it's also peak season for ecotourism. Reserve all accommodations, car rental, camping and hiking permits at least a few weeks, if not months, in advance. For more advice, see the 'Planning' sections for individual hikes later in this chapter.

Maps & Books

The free *Kauai, Island of Discovery* is a good illustrated pocket map that's available

---

Safety in Numbers

Women travelers are advised not to hike or camp alone on Kauai. Organized group outings with the Sierra Club's **Kauai Group** (Ⓦ *www.hi.sierraclub.org; nonmember donation $5*) are an excellent way to connect with other hikers. Other hiker hangouts are Haena Beach Park outside Hanalei, the hostels in Kapa'a and Koke'e Museum in Koke'e State Park.

---

in the many racks of tourist brochures at Lihue airport.

A free foldout topographical map of Kauai, which shows in detail the island's network of trails, is available from the Division of Forestry & Wildlife (DOFAW) office in Lihue.

The Birds of Kauai by Jim Denny is a full-color guide to many of the island's most common and also its rarest avian species. Other specialized titles about Kauai's unique history and wildlife are available from island bookstores, museums and botanical gardens.

Information Sources

Kauai's main newspaper, the *Garden Island* (Ⓦ www.kauaiworld.com), publishes a community calendar with details on organized hikes, volunteer workdays in natural areas and at historical sites, cultural events, public lectures and more. Channel 3 on cable TV features visitor information programs. Kauai's community radio stations, KKCR (90.9 FM) and KKCU (91.9 FM), broadcast local news, weather and events.

Getting Around

Kauai has a limited public bus service and, while this connects most towns on the island, it won't take you out to major trailheads. Consequently, renting a car (usually upon arrival in Lihue) is almost essential for exploring the island in depth.

If you plan to use the **Kauai Bus** (☎ 241-6410; 7am-5pm Mon-Sat) extensively, keep in mind that there's no service at all on

Sunday or holidays and oversized backpacks are not allowed on board. All public buses are white with a green sugarcane motif. Two main routes operate from Lihue north to Hanalei and west to Kekaha. Weekday shuttles loop around Lihue and up to Kapa'a. The adult fare is $1.50 per ride on all routes (bring exact change); there's also a $15 monthly pass. Schedules are available from bus drivers and at public libraries.

GATEWAY
Lihue
The former plantation town of Lihue is the county capital and the arrival point of all visitors to Kauai. Virtually all county and state offices are in Lihue and the town is home to the island's main shopping centers. Simply put, if you have business to do in Kauai, you go to Lihue. Although it can bustle a bit during the week, on weekends it's a real sleeper.

Information Visitors will find well-stocked racks loaded with activity and accommodations brochures, as well as Kauai's free tourist magazines, in the airport baggage claim area.

The **Kauai Visitors Bureau** (☎ 245-3971; ⓦ www.kauaivisitorsbureau.org; 4334 Rice St, Suite 101; open 8am-4:30pm) isn't really set up for walk-in traffic, but there's a helpful hotline (☎ 800-262-1400; open 5am-5pm Mon-Fri, 6am-2pm Sat) that can answer visitor-related questions about Kauai.

Sharing an office, the **Division of Forestry & Wildlife** (DOFAW; ☎ 274-3433; 3060 Eiwa St, Room 306; open 8am-4pm Mon-Fri) has free topographical maps of Kauai, while the **Division of State Parks** (☎ 274-3444; 3060 Eiwa St, Room 306; open 8am-3:30pm Mon-Fri) issues hiking and camping permits for state parks.

Camping permits for county parks are available at the **Division of Parks & Recreation** (☎ 241-6660; Lihue Civic Center, cnr Kaumuali'i & Kuhio Hwys; open 8am-4:15pm Mon-Fri)

USGS topographic maps are sold at the **Kauai Museum** (☎ 245-6931; 4428 Rice St; open 9am-4pm Mon-Fri, 10am-4pm Sat), which also has books on Hawaiian flora and fauna, culture and history.

Borders Books & Music Café (☎ 246-0862; Kukui Grove Center, 4303 Nawiliwili Rd; open 9am-10pm Mon-Thur, 11am-11pm Fri, 9am-11pm Sat & 9am-8pm Sun) is Kauai's biggest bookstore and sells driving maps.

Supplies & Equipment Kauai's largest shopping complex is the **Kukui Grove Center** (☎ 245-7784; 3-2600 Kaumuali'i Hwy, cnr Nawiliwili Rd; open daily). It has a **Big Kmart** (☎ 245-7742; open 6am-10pm Sun-Thur, 6am-11pm Fri-Sat) that sells cheap camping and outdoor gear. Elsewhere try **Ace Hardware** (☎ 245-4091; 4100 Rice St; open 7am-7pm daily) or **Wal-Mart** (☎ 246-1599, 3-3300 Kuhio Hwy; open 6am-11pm daily) for basic supplies. **Big Save Market** (☎ 245-6571; Hardy St, cnr Kuhio Hwy; open 7am-11pm daily) is the town's central grocery store. There's a **Star Market** (☎ 245-7777; open 6am-11pm daily) at the Kukui Grove Center.

Places to Stay & Eat Visitors won't want to spend more than a couple of nights here. However, Lihue does have some great, down-to-earth restaurants serving a local crowd.

Motel Lani (☎ 245-2965; 4240 Rice St; standard/deluxe doubles $34/52) is a family-run place and Lihue's best budget choice, although it sits at a busy intersection. All rooms have bath and air-con. There's a two-day minimum stay or a $2 surcharge.

Tip Top Motel, Cafe & Bakery (☎ 245-2333, fax 246-8988; ⓔ tiptop@aloha.net; 3173 Akahi St; doubles $45) is another cinder-block structure. Rooms are basic, with twin beds and air-con, but they do have TV and bath. Guests gather at the no-fuss coffee shop and sushi bar.

Garden Island Inn (☎ 245-7227, 800-648-0154, fax 245-7603; ⓦ www.gardenisland inn.com; 3445 Wilcox Rd; 1st-/2nd-/3rd-floor doubles from $65/85/95) is a family-owned hotel with rooms that are compact but tidy, with TV, ceiling fans, minirefrigerator and microwave. The hotel is near an industrial area and at the side of a rather busy road, but it's within walking distance of Kalapaki Beach.

KAUAI

Hamura Saimin (☎ 245-3271; 2956 Kress St; meals around $3.75-6.50; open 10am-10pm daily), in central Lihue, is a throwback to an older Kauai, serving bowls of freshly made saimin (a Hawaiian version of the Japanese noodle soup ramen) and tasty skewers of barbecued chicken or beef. There are no tables, just a winding bar where visitors and locals rub elbows as they slurp from steaming hot bowls.

Fish Express (☎ 245-9918; 3343 Kuhio Hwy; lunch special $7.25; deli open 10am-7pm Mon-Sat, 10am-5pm Sun, grill hours 10am-3pm Mon-Fri), just south of Wilcox Memorial Hospital, makes superb take-out. Try the fish of the day, perhaps grilled with passion-orange sauce or blackened, served with rice and green salad. Tasty *poke* (bite-sized, marinated raw fish) is sold by the pound.

Nueva España (☎ 632-0513; Anchor Cove Mall, Nawiliwili Rd; breakfast & lunch $6-10, dinner mains around $13; open 8am-9pm daily), just opposite the Garden Island Inn, serves authentic Mexican food, including a tantalizing *mole* (savoury chili sauce with mixed spices and chocolate). Enjoy it on the outdoor deck.

Wild Bill's (☎ 245-9085; Kukui Grove Center, Nawiliwili Rd; sandwiches & salads $6-8, pizzas $12-17; usually open 6:30am-11pm Mon-Sat, 9am-11pm Sun) has kick-ass coffee and overstuffed salads, sandwiches and exotically flavored pizza. It's next to Borders bookstore.

Getting There & Away All scheduled passenger flights to Kauai land at Lihue airport. See Getting Around (p225) in the Travel Facts chapter for details on domestic and interisland flights, commuter airlines and discount flight coupons.

Mokihana Travel Service (☎ 245-5338; Lihue Plaza, 3016 Umi St, Suite 3; open 8am-5pm Mon-Fri, 8am-noon Sat), in downtown Lihue, sells interisland flight coupons at reasonable prices.

The Kauai Bus does not stop at Lihue airport. Taxis can be picked up curbside, just outside the baggage claim area. Expect to pay about $10 into central Lihue, $24 to Kapa'a and at least $70 to Haena. Car rental

booths line the opposite side of the road. **Rent-a-Wreck** (☎ 632-0741; e rentawreck.kauai@verizon.net; Harbor Mall, Suite 112A, 3501 Rice St; closed Sun) offers free pickups from the airport.

In Lihue, all Kauai Bus services north to Hanalei and west to Kekaha stop at the Big Save Market on the northeast side of the Lihue Civic Center and also at the First Hawaiian Bank at the Kukui Grove Center. There is no service on Sunday or holidays. Another local bus runs between Lihue's shopping centers once an hour from 8am to 3:40pm on weekdays, making additional stops at Wal-Mart, Ace Hardware and the Garden Island Inn.

Kalalau Trail

Duration	2 days
Distance	22 miles (35.4km)
Difficulty	demanding
Start/Finish	Ke'e Beach
Nearest Towns	Hanalei (p189), Haena (p190)
Transport	private

Summary A heartbreaking trail, both beautiful and brutal, along the valleys of Kauai's famous Na Pali Coast, past hidden waterfalls, wild beaches and visions of traditional Hawaii.

By reputation Kalalau is Hawaii's premier backpacking trail. Here, it's quite common to come across hikers who have trekked in Nepal or climbed to Machu Picchu. The Na Pali Coast is similarly spectacular, a place of singular, rugged beauty, stretching for 22 miles between Ke'e Beach in the north and, at the opposite end of the island's coastal highway, Polihale State Park in the west. In Hawaiian, *na pali* means simply 'the cliffs.' Indeed, these are Hawaii's grandest.

The Na Pali valleys, with limited accessibility and abundant fertility, have long been a natural refuge for people wanting to escape. In ancient Hawaii, these deep river valleys once contained sizable settlements. Precarious trails led from the upland Koke'e area down to the valley floors along the Na Pali Coast. In some places, footholds were gouged into cliffs, and in others rope ladders were used. These trails no longer exist, and the valleys themselves were abandoned by the close of the 19th century.

Only the wild and remote Hanakapiai, Hanakoa and Kalalau Valleys can still be reached on foot, solely along the coastal Kalalau Trail. This trail basically follows the same ancient route used by the Hawaiians who once lived in these north coast valleys. It runs along high sea cliffs and winds through lush valleys before finally ending below the steep fluted *pali* of Kalalau. The scenery is exquisite, with sheer green cliffs dropping into brilliant turquoise waters.

Although not Hawaii's most technically challenging trail, the Kalalau Trail has eroded switchbacks, scree slopes and multiple stream crossings, all of which can be risky. The trail's popularity can be more of a curse than a blessing, as thousands of hikers each year take a severe toll on the environment, causing soil erosion, contributing to the loss of native plant and bird life and leaving trashed-out campgrounds that pollute waterways. Please help preserve this paradise by hiking responsibly.

The classic Na Pali backpacking trip involves hiking all the way into Kalalau Valley on the first day, camping at Kalalau Beach for two nights, then hiking back out the third day. Some hikers break the journey by camping at Hanakapiai Valley first. If the campground at Hanakoa Valley ever reopens, consider taking advantage of it. Hanakoa Valley is ideally situated more than halfway to Kalalau, but before the most challenging part of the trail (much better approached after a full night's rest). The first 2 miles of the hike make for a popular day hike, especially with a side trip up to Hanakapiai Falls (p193), and hiking permits are not required for those going only as far as Hanakapiai Valley. Otherwise the most distance you can reasonably expect to cover on a day-hike is just beyond Hanakoa Valley.

PLANNING
When to Hike
In winter, there are generally only a few people at any one time hiking all the way in to Kalalau Valley, but the trail is heavily trodden in summer. As it's a popular hike for islanders as well as visitors, weekends tend to see the most use. Always check the weather forecast (☎ 245-6001) before heading out. If storms are predicted for the North Shore, consider putting off this trip, since hiking can be extremely muddy and slippery during rain. Successive days of bad weather are more likely in winter than summer.

What to Bring
You can count on there being at least a few places along the trail to collect fresh water, although it must always be filtered, boiled or chemically treated. Hiking poles or even a stout walking stick may prove invaluable.

Maps
The USGS 1:24,000 map *Haena* covers the trail. The color 1:50,000 *Recreation Map of Eastern Kauai* also covers the trail in topographic detail; it's available free from the DOFAW office in Lihue. A foldout *Kalalau Trail* pamphlet, which shows mile-markers and hiking advice on a basic topographic map, is available free from the Division of State Parks in Lihue.

Permits & Regulations
The trail is within Na Pali Coast State Park. A permit is officially required to continue on the Kalalau Trail beyond Hanakapiai. Camping is currently allowed in Hanakapiai and Kalalau valleys, and is limited to five nights in total. The trail's third valley, Hanakoa, was closed to campers at press time, but may reopen. Day-use hiking and camping permits are available for $10 per person per day from the Division of State Parks in Lihue or state park offices on any island. During the busy summer period of May to September, Na Pali Coast campgrounds are often completely booked up many months ahead, so apply for your permit as far in advance as possible (up to one year is allowed).

NEAREST TOWNS & FACILITIES
Hanalei
Backed by lofty mountains and fronted by a lovely bay, there's no real development of

KAUAI

Warning

Accidents are not unknown on the Kalalau Trail. Most casualties are the result of people trying to ford swollen streams, walking after dark on cliff-edge trails, or swimming in treacherous surf. In places the trail runs along steep cliffs and can narrow to little more than a foot in width, which some people can find unnerving. However, hikers accustomed to high-country trails generally enjoy the hike and don't consider it unduly hazardous. Don't try to climb the cliffs, which are composed of loose and crumbly rocks, and don't camp directly beneath them, as goats commonly dislodge stones that tumble down the cliff walls.

any kind in Hanalei. Take away the telephone poles and asphalt road, and this is how the North Shore has looked for centuries.

Supplies & Equipment In Ching Young Village shopping center, **Big Save Market** *(open 7am-9pm daily)* is the town's grocery store. **Hanalei Health Food** *(Ching Young Village, 5-5190 Kuhio Hwy; open 8:30am-8pm daily)* sells a few organic vegetables, quick-prep grains and other health food items.

Pedal & Paddle *(☎ 826-9069; Ching Young Village; open 9am-6pm daily)* rents two-person tents for $12/35 a day/week, backpacks for $5/20 and sleeping bags, sleeping pads or trail stoves for $3/10 each. The knowledgeable staff also sell miscellaneous supplies, including rain gear, freeze-dried food and maps.

Kayak Kauai *(☎ 826-9844, 800-437-3507; Kuhio Hwy; open 8am-5:30pm daily, until 8pm in summer)* rents two-person tents or backpacks for $8/32 a day/week, camping stoves or sleeping bags for $6/24 and sleeping pads or daypacks for $4/16.

Places to Stay & Eat Camping is allowed on Friday, Saturday and holidays with a county permit at **Hanalei Blackpot Park**, which has a grassy area, showers, rest rooms and a long beach shaded by ironwood trees. Permits are sold at the Division of Parks & Recreation in Lihue.

Hanalei Taro & Juice Company *(open 10am-5pm Tues-Sun)* serves up vegetarian or turkey sandwiches on taro buns ($6) that make a nice meal, and the taro *mochi* dessert at just 50¢ is a treat not to be missed. In the same parking lot adjacent to Kayak Kauai are **Wishing Well Shave Ice** and **Hanalei Taro Farmers Market**, a produce truck selling fresh fruit and vegetables.

Hanalei Gourmet *(☎ 826-2524; Hanalei Center; sandwiches $7-9, meals $11-20; open 8am-10pm daily)* offers live music nightly. A delightful deli at the side vends pasta salads, bread and sandwich meats over the counter.

Neide's Salsa Samba *(☎ 826-1851; dishes $8-14; open 11:30am-2:30pm & 5:30pm-9pm daily)*, a little owner-run restaurant west of the Hanalei Center, has a quiet veranda where diners can linger over excellent Mexican and Brazilian fare.

Postcards Café *(☎ 826-1191; breakfast $6-10, dinner $15-25; open 8am-11am & 6pm-9:30pm daily)* tends to be overpriced, but the setting is engaging and the food fresh. It serves seafood dishes but otherwise the menu is vegetarian, with a healthy blend of Asian and local influences.

Getting There & Away Coming from Lihue via Princeville, after the Hanalei Bridge, the Kuhio Hwy (Hwy 560 – the continuation of Hwy 56 west of Princeville) runs parallel to the Hanalei River. For a mile before Hanalei village the road is a pastoral scene of taro patches and grassland. The **Kauai Bus** *(☎ 261-6410)* goes between Lihue and Hanalei ($1.50, 1¼ hours), stopping in Wailua and Kapa'a. There are seven buses per weekday, but only four departures on Saturday in either direction; there is no service on Sunday.

Haena

County-run **Haena Beach Park** *(before the 9-mile marker, Kuhio Hwy)*, which is just over 1 mile east of Ke'e Beach, has covered picnic tables, campsites, rest rooms, drinking water and showers. Many hikers like to use it as a base before starting the Kalalau Trail. Permits cost $3 per adult per night.

Limahuli Garden

Most of Limahuli, the last valley before the start of the Na Pali Coast, is still lush, virgin forest. The National Tropical Botanical Garden, a nonprofit organization that preserves and propagates rare native plants, owns 1000 acres of Limahuli Valley.

Limahuli Garden (☎ 826-1053; admission $10; open 9:30am-4pm Tues-Fri & Sun) contains collections of Hawaiian ethnobotanical and medicinal plants and other endangered native species. There are also ancient stone terraces planted with taro. A ¾-mile loop trail winds through the most interesting parts of the garden, and for the cost of admission visitors can make a self-guided walking tour. The garden is on the *mauka* (inland) side of the highway, just before the stream that marks the Haena State Park boundary.

Apply at the Division of Parks & Recreation in Lihue.

Kauai YMCA-Camp Naue (☎ 826-6419; before the 8-mile marker, Kuhio Hwy; campsites per person $10, bunks $12) has simple beachside bunkhouses and tent camping. There are hot showers, but the kitchen is reserved for large groups only. The Y doesn't accept reservations, yet you should still call ahead, as there are specific check-in policies and the camp is only open to individual travelers on a space-available basis.

Getting There & Away There is no bus service beyond Hanalei. From Haena Beach Park, it's just over 1 mile to the trailhead.

GETTING TO/FROM THE HIKE

There's space for parking at Ke'e Beach, right at the trailhead. Unfortunately, break-ins to cars left overnight are all too common. Some people advise leaving cars unlocked to prevent smashed windows and locks. It's generally safer to park at the campground at Haena Beach Park. Whatever you do, don't leave valuables in a locked car.

Another possibility is to store everything in Hanalei and take a taxi to the trailhead.

Kayak Kauai (☎ 826-9844) in Hanalei lets hikers park their cars in the shop's lot for $5 a day and stores backpacks or suitcases for $4 a day. **North Shore Cab** (☎ 639-7829) charges about $20 for a taxi from Hanalei to Ke'e Beach. Another option is the **Wainiha General Store** (☎ 826-6251) in Wainiha, en route to Ke'e Beach, which stores bags for $3 a day.

THE HIKE (see map p192)
Day 1: Ke'e Beach to Kalalau Valley
6–9 hours, 11 miles (17.7km)

Because average hiking times vary quite a bit, as everyone proceeds at a much different pace, it is helpful to think of the trail as divided into three parts: Ke'e Beach to Hanakapiai Valley (2 miles); Hanakapiai to Hanakoa Valley (4 miles); and Hanakoa to Kalalau Valley (5 miles).

Early morning is a good time to be heading west on the first segment from Ke'e Beach to Hanakapiai Valley, with the sun at your back, starting inland from the parking lot at a large signboard. Just ¼ mile up the trail, look for a fine view of Ke'e Beach and the surrounding reef. The trail weaves steeply through *hala* (screw pine) and ohia trees, as well as ti plants, and then back out to clearings with fine coastal views. There are purple orchids, wildflowers and a couple of tiny Zen-like waterfalls en route. The black nuts embedded in the clay are *kukui* (candlenut), polished smooth by hiking boots.

After ½ mile, the trail gets its first view of the Na Pali Coast. The trail ascends pretty steadily for another ½ mile, then starts to dip under soft-needled ironwoods and through stream gulches. Some rocks are quite slippery and the trail can be muddy, even where logs have been set to prevent erosion. A black-and-yellow striped tsunami pole marker appears just before the trail at last reaches Hanakapiai Valley, then fords the stream.

Hanakapiai has a sandy beach in the summer. In the winter, the sand washes out, and it becomes a beach of boulders, some of them sparkling with tiny olivine crystals. The western side of the beach has a small

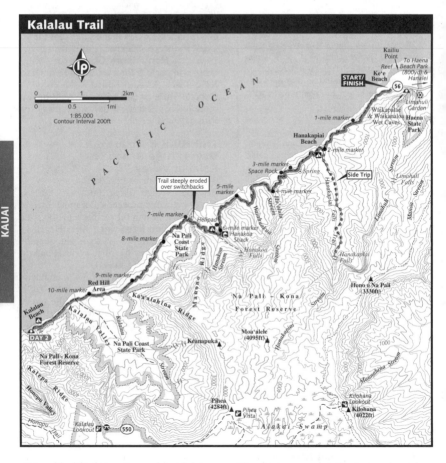

Kalalau Trail

cave with dripping water and a miniature fern grotto. The ocean is dangerous here, with unpredictable rip currents year-round. Hanakapiai Beach is nearly unmatched for the number of drownings on Kauai.

There are various **campsites**, some of which are near the shore with views, while others sit inland under guava trees. For day-hikers it may well make more sense to head up the valley to Hanakapiai Falls (p193) than it does to continue along the coastal trail to Hanakoa.

Otherwise, on the 4-mile trail from Hanakapiai Valley to Hanakoa Valley, just 10 minutes up past the tsunami marker, there's a nice view of Hanakapiai Beach, but from there the trail goes into bush, and the next coastal view is not for another mile. The switchbacks here are well cut, but also hot and exposed, and gain 800ft in elevation. Craggy cliffs begin to tower overhead and the trail leads over an outcropping of black rocks where rivulets of water tumble over the cliff face into a pool. Beyond this the trail keeps ascending past the 3-mile marker. This final section of the switchbacks over rocks and mud can be fairly brutal, and the grade is steep. Soon the trail reaches its

Coastal views from the Kalalau Trail, Kauai

Hanakoa Stream along the Kalalau Trail, Kauai

Limahuli Garden in Haena, Kauai

Late afternoon at Waimea Canyon, Kauai

Sunset over the Na Pali Coast, Kauai

Sunset over Kalalau Valley, Koke'e State Park, Kauai

highest point at **Space Rock**, a prominent boulder overlooking the coast. A lot of hikers stop to rest here.

The trail then passes through several minivalleys within the greater Ho'olulu Valley, winding from each waterfall gulch out to another ridge nose and back in, then on through Waiahuakua Valley. Both are 'hanging valleys' where the streams tumble off the cliffs directly into the sea, instead of flowing into outlets at broad beaches. Old Hawaiian stone terraces announce the trail's entrance into Hanakoa Valley, passing a helipad and hunting shack.

The valley is lovely and Hanakoa Stream has pools perfect for swimming. There's a waterfall about ½ mile up the valley, but it's rough getting up there as the path is overgrown. The valley was formerly settled by farmers who grew taro and coffee, both of which still grow wild. Most hikers rest a while here.

From Hanakoa Valley to Kalalau Valley is the most difficult part of the trail, although without question the most beautiful. Make sure you have at least three hours of daylight left. There are some very narrow and steep stretches, so make sure all gear is properly packed and be cautious about footing. About a mile out of Hanakoa, ascending past coffee shrubs and ti plants, the trail reaches the coast again and begins to get fantastic views of Na Pali's jagged edges. At the red-dirt switchbacks, there's incredible erosion due to salt sea spray and sparse rainfall as well as to the feral goats that consume the vegetation.

For the next few miles, the trail winds in and out of gulches, some dry and some with fast-flowing streams that need to be crossed, past sisal grasses, lantana and guava trees. A little past the halfway mark from Hanakoa Valley, hikers get their first view into Kalalau Valley. Another eroded section of trail before the 10-mile marker is called Red Hill, for obvious reasons. After sliding down the red-dirt scree, cross over Kalalau Stream and start down the final mile of track into Kalalau Valley.

The large valley has a beach, a *heiau* (temple) site, some ancient *hale* (house) sites and some interesting caves that are sometimes dry enough to sleep in during the summer. Valley terraces where Hawaiians cultivated taro until 1920 are now largely overgrown with ornamental Java plum, and edible guava and passionfruit. Look for papaya trees and medicinal *noni* (Indian mulberry) growing here. Feral goats scurry up and down the crumbly cliffs and drink from the stream. An easy 2-mile trail leads back into the valley past wild ginger to a **pool** in Kalalau Stream where there's a natural water slide. If you have a quick hand, you might try your luck at catching some of the prawns that live in the stream. Back at Kalalau Beach, rangers occasionally swoop in unexpectedly by helicopter to check camping permits; those without permits are forced to hike back out immediately.

Side Trip: Hanakapiai Falls
2½–4 hours, 4 miles (6.4km)
Because of some tricky rock crossings, the trail from Hanakapiai Beach to Hanakapiai Falls is rougher than the walk from Ke'e Beach. Due to the possibility of flash floods in the narrow valley, the hike should only be done in fair weather. There are unmaintained trails on both sides of the stream, but the main route heads up the western side. About 50 yards up, there are old stone walls and guava trees. There are also some big old mango trees along the way. Ten minutes (200 yards) up from the trailhead, thickets of green bamboo are interspersed with eucalyptus. Also along the trail is the site of an old coffee mill, though all that remains is a little of the chimney, and a few stream crossings. **Hanakapiai Falls** is spectacular, with a wide pool gentle enough for swimming. Directly under the falls, the cascading water forces you back from the rock face – a warning from nature, as rocks can fall from the top. It's a beautiful lush valley, though it's not very sunny.

Day 2: Kalalau Valley to Ke'e Beach
6–9 hours, 11 miles (17.7km)
Returning to Ke'e Beach essentially means retracing your steps along the trail from

KAUAI

Kalalau Valley. Some hikers do choose to spend another night in the valley before hiking out.

East Kauai

East Kauai covers the coastal region north of Lihue to the start of the North Shore around Kilauea. The 3-mile stretch of the Kuhio Hwy (Hwy 56) from Wailua to Kapa'a is largely a scattering of shopping centers, restaurants, hotels and condos. Most of its sights are clustered around the Wailua River. This is the only navigable river in Hawaii, and is popular for riverboat tours and kayaking. Wailua was once the site of Kauai's royal court, with seven sacred *heiau* running from the mouth of the river up to the top of Mt Waialeale. All date back to the early period of Tahitian settlement.

PLANNING

All of these trails can be hiked year-round. When it's rainy along the Na Pali Coast or up in West Kauai's mountainous state parks, hiking here may be the only option.

Maps

The color 1:50,000 *Recreation Map of Eastern Kauai* covers all of these trails, including access roads. It's available free from the DOFAW office in Lihue.

GETTING THERE & AROUND

The **Kauai Bus** (☎ 241-6410) heads north from Lihue to Hanalei, stopping along the way in Wailua and Kapa'a. It does not go to the trailheads.

Taxi companies serving the Lihue-Kapa'a area include **Akiko's Taxi** (☎ 822-7588). Otherwise the only option for getting around, except by car, is to rent a bicycle.

Kauai Cycle and Tour (☎ 821-2115; 1379 Kuhio Hwy, Kapa'a; open 9am-6pm Mon-Fri, 9am-4pm Sat) rents 18-speed cruisers for $15/75 a day/ week and quality mountain bikes with front suspension for $20/95 a day/week, with full suspension for $35/150. Being a dedicated cycle shop, its bikes are among the best maintained.

Kayak Kauai (☎ 822-9179, 800-437-4507; Coconut Marketplace, Kuhio Hwy, Wailua), in the shopping center's south parking lot, rents mountain bikes for $20/75 a day/week and beach cruisers for $10/35.

ACCESS TOWNS
Wailua

This town doesn't really have a center. The Coconut Plantation resort fronts a ½-mile-long beach partially shaded by ironwood trees. Occasionally Hawaiian monk seals can be seen basking on the shore. The large field between the Kauai Coconut Beach Resort and the Kauai Coast Resort at the Beachboy is popular with golden plovers and other migratory birds.

Coconut Marketplace (4-484 Kuhio Hwy; open 9am-9pm Mon-Sat, 10am-6pm Sun) is the resort's shopping center and has a handful of eateries. **Trailmates** shoe store sells Tevas and other sport sandals.

Places to Stay & Eat If you don't feel any need to be on the beach, the following B&Bs represent some of the best value on Kauai. All are within a mile or so of the intersection of Hwys 581 and 580, west of the Kuhio Hwy.

Rosewood B&B (☎ 822-5216, fax 822-5478; W www.rosewoodkauai.com; 872 Kamalu Rd; bunkhouse dorm beds $40-50, doubles with bath & double studio apartments $85, double cottages $105-150) surrounds a beautifully restored century-old plantation home.

Magic Sunrise Hawaii (☎ 821-9847, fax 823-8542; W www.magicsunrisehawaii.com; Royal Dr; doubles $50-60, double suite $85, quad 2-bedroom cottage $120), a delight-fully serene place run by a Swiss mother and daughter, has quite a New Age flavor. All guests have kitchen access and there's a pool.

Inn Paradise (☎ 822-2542; e mcinch@ aloha.net; 6381 Makana Rd; studio $70, 1-/2-bedroom units $85/90) has Persian carpets, rattan furnishings and Hawaiiana wall prints. All guests share a *lanai* (veranda) with a view of pasture and mountains.

Caffe Coco (☎ 822-7990; 4-369 Kuhio Hwy; lighter fare $3.50-12, platter meals $16-21; open 5pm-9pm Tues-Sun), just north of the Kuamo'o Rd (Hwy 580) intersection, has an espresso bar, art gallery and live music nightly. On the island-style menu are chef-inspired dreams, like Moroccan-spiced *ahi* (yellowfin tuna) with banana chutney or silver noodle salads.

Korean Bar-B-Q (4-356 Kuhio Hwy; combo plates around $7; open 10am-9pm Wed-Mon, 4:30pm-9pm Tues) has good Korean take-out food at honest prices. Across the road, **Aussie Tim's Texas Barbeque** (☎ 822-0300; 4-361 Kuhio Hwy; meals $8-15) serves up slow-cooked meats with side dishes like potato salad and jalapeño cheese cornbread.

Getting There & Away The **Kauai Bus** (☎ 241-6410) stops in Wailua at the Coconut Marketplace, with weekday services approximately hourly to Lihue ($1.50, 20 minutes) and Kapa'a ($1.50, 10 minutes). Buses to Hanalei ($1.50, one hour) are less frequent. On Saturday, there are only four buses in each direction. There's no service on Sunday.

Waipouli

Waipouli is the mile-long commercial strip between Coconut Plantation and Kapa'a. At the Kauai Village shopping center, **Kauai Heritage Center** (☎ 821-2070; 4-831 Kuhio Hwy; open 10am-6pm Mon-Fri, 10am-4pm Sat) displays and teaches traditional Hawaiian crafts and culture.

Kauai Village has the greatest concentration of eateries. **Papaya's Natural Foods & Café** (☎ 823-0190; Kauai Village, Kuhio Hwy; open 9am-8pm daily, café closes 7pm) is an excellent health food store, serving whole-

some salads, sandwiches and simple meals. Although it's take-out style, there are tables in the courtyard where you can relax and eat. **Safeway** (open 24 hours) supermarket has a deli counter with fried chicken and salads, a bakery and a fish counter with un-beatable sesame-*ahi* poke. Also try **Ba Le** (snacks & meals $3-8; open daily) for Vietnamese *pho* (noodle soup) and stuffed French bread sandwiches.

Further north, the Kapa'a Shopping Center has a **Big Save Market** (4-1105 Kuhio Hwy; open 7am-11pm daily) and an **Ace Hardware** (☎ 822-7751; open 7am-7pm daily) with limited camping supplies.

Coconuts Island Style Bar & Grill (☎ 823-8777; 4-919 Kuhio Hwy; most mains $15-25; open 4pm-10pm Mon-Sat) is East Kauai's liveliest restaurant, with consistently mouth-watering fusion food, like Thai curry pasta or salmon glazed with *lilikoi* (passionfruit) and coconut. Even the hipster Tiki lounge decor is enticing.

Getting There & Away The **Kauai Bus** (☎ 241-6410) southbound from Hanalei ($1.50, 45 to 60 minutes) stops at the Kapa'a Big Save Market and Safeway in the Kauai Village shopping center, en route to Lihue ($1.50, 25 minutes). Weekday departures are hourly, but there are only four buses on Saturday, and no service Sunday.

Kapa'a

Kapa'a is an endearing old plantation town with an easily walkable commercial center that is half-local, half-tourist oriented. It's probably the best place for budget-minded travelers to be based.

Information Maps are sold at the small **Waldenbooks** (☎ 822-7749; Kauai Village, 4-831 Kuhio Hwy). **Tin Can Mailman** (☎ 822-3009; Kinipopo Shopping Village, 4-356 Kuhio Hwy; usually open 10:30am-4pm daily), a used bookstore specializing in Hawaiiana titles, keeps a few local maps on hand.

Places to Stay & Eat The rather re-laxed hostel-style **Kauai Beach House** ☎ 822-3424; W www.kauai-blue-lagoon.com;

4-1552 Kuhio Hwy; dormitory singles/doubles $23/35, doubles $50) has a fine oceanfront location, but it's a work in progress so don't expect things to be too refined.

Kauai International Hostel (☎ 823-6142; W www.hostels.com/kauaihostel/; 4532 Lehua St; dorm beds $20, doubles $50) has been through some ups and downs over the years, and gets mixed reviews.

KK Bed & Bath (☎ 822-7348, 800-615-6211 ext 32; W www.kkbedbath.com; 4486 Kauwila St; singles/doubles/triples $35/50/60) is a short walk from the beach. It consists of two units, each with a private bath, refrigerator, TV, phone and ceiling fans, in a converted storehouse.

Mahina's Guest House (☎ 823-9364; W www.mahinas.com; rooms with shared bath $55-90), a quiet, casual home near the beach, provides accommodations for women travelers. Guests share kitchen facilities.

Hotel Coral Reef (☎ 822-4481, 800-843-4659, fax 822-7705; 4-1516 Kuhio Hwy; doubles $60-90) is a small, family-run hotel that serves continental breakfast. Rooms in the seaside building are a bit larger and have oceanview *lanai*.

Pono Market (4-1300 Kuhio Hwy; plate lunches $6; open 7am-7pm Mon-Thur & Sat, 7am-8pm Fri), a small food store with a deli counter, is the place to get traditional Hawaiian fare, local-style.

Beezers (☎ 822-4411; 4-1380 Kuhio Hwy; snacks $3-7.50; open 11am-10pm daily) is an old-fashioned ice-cream shop brimming with a nostalgic decor. A retro menu includes sloppy joes and pastrami sandwiches.

Mermaids Café (☎ 821-2026; 4-1384 Kuhio Hwy; meals $8-10; open 11am-9pm daily) is little more than a kitchen and a handful of sidewalk café tables, but the island-style and pan-Asian wraps, salads and noodle plates rival those at some of Kauai's top restaurants. Next door is **Blossoming Lotus Cafe**, featuring vegan and organic fare.

Getting There & Away The **Kauai Bus** (☎ 241-6410) stops on the outskirts of Kapa'a at the public library and Pono Kai resort on its way from Lihue ($1.50, 30 minutes) to Hanalei ($1.50, 45 to 60 minutes). Southbound buses from Hanalei to Lihue stop at Kojima Store and a bus stop opposite the Pono Kai resort. On weekdays, buses to Lihue are more frequent than to Hanalei. On Saturday, there are only four buses in each direction. There's no service on Sunday.

Nounou Mountain East Trail

Duration	1½–2 hours
Distance	3.5 miles (5.6km)
Difficulty	easy
Start/Finish	Haleilio Rd
Nearest Towns	Kapa'a (p195), Waipouli (p195), Wailua (p194)
Transport	private
Summary	Stroll up a verdant ridge, pausing among native Hawaiian plants, bird life and ocean vistas, to a high viewpoint atop the fabled Sleeping Giant.

From a marked viewpoint just north of the Waipouli Complex on the Kuhio Hwy (Hwy 56) look for the outline of the 'Sleeping Giant' atop Nounou Ridge. According to legend, the local giant fell asleep on this hillside near the banks of the Wailua River after eating too much *poi* at a *luau*. His *menehune* friends tried to awaken him by throwing stones. But the stones bounced from the giant's full belly into his open mouth. As the stones lodged in the giant's throat, he choked in his sleep and turned into rock. Now he rests eternally, stretched out on the ridge with his head in Wailua and his feet in Kapa'a.

A few popular hiking trails climb up the Sleeping Giant to a summit on the giant's upper chest, affording views of both the east coast and the highland valleys. The eastern approach ascends more gradually and since it's more exposed, the views are better. At an elevation of 1241 ft, the giant's forehead is the highest point on the ridge.

PLANNING

No water is available along the trail.

KAUAI

Maps

The color 1:50,000 *Recreation Map of Eastern Kauai* covers the trail.

GETTING TO/FROM THE HIKE

There is no bus service to the trailhead. From Wailua's Coconut Marketplace, which is the nearest bus stop, walk ½ mile south on the Kuhio Hwy (Hwy 56). Turn inland onto Haleilio Rd, which for those driving from Lihue is the first traffic light after passing Kuamo'o Rd (Hwy 580). The trail begins at a parking lot just over a mile up Haleilio Rd in the Wailua Houselots neighborhood.

THE HIKE (see map p198)

From the parking lot, which is marked with a Na Ala Hele trailhead sign, climb to the right over an embankment. The forest trail is scattered with leaf litter and surrounded by ironwood, guava and swamp mahogany trees. Some boulders obstruct the path as it switchbacks upward, gaining in elevation and revealing views over the Wailua Houselots, fertile fields and the wide ocean.

Shortly after the ½-mile marker, the path emerges out of the shade cover. Be sure to keep on the switchbacks, and do not follow false trails-of-use. As it sidles alongside the ridge, the trail descends for a short distance before wrapping around to where the 1-mile marker appears. The trail is still ascending moderately with views, then crossing back and forth over the ridge. In dense forest now, *hala* (pandanus) crowds the trail with its stalky prop roots. Suddenly an eroded section obscures the switchbacks, but offers wide vistas and a minor challenge for hikers.

A few minutes below the summit, the eastern and western trails merge on the ridge. Continue up over tree roots to the left, passing by ti plants. On the summit is a picnic table shelter that offers protection from rain. Passing showers can create some incredible valley rainbows. To the west, there's a 180-degree view of Wailua and the Makaleha Mountains. Below, to the east, are Kapa'a and the Wailua River. To the right of the riverboat docks, Malae Heiau appears as a dark green square in the midst of an abandoned cane field.

From the south side of the picnic area, the trail continues. About 100 yards later, after crossing a narrow saddle, there's a rocky area of boulders to be scrambled before reaching a perch for perfect views. The ridge continues up the giant's chin. Size up the precarious trail-of-use carefully. It's steep, and loose rocks are inevitable. When ready, backtrack to the picnic table, and at the trail junction turn right onto the eastern trail, which descends back to the trailhead.

Alternative Route: Nounou Mountain West Trail

1–1½ hours, 3 miles (4.8km)

Promising a more peaceful, yet rigorous climb up Sleeping Giant, the mountain's western side is a shady forest of tall trees and moss-covered stones. West of Wailua, this 3-mile trail starts on Kamalu Rd (Hwy 581) near house No 1068, just over a mile north of Kuamo'o Rd (Hwy 580). Walk through a metal gate and up along a small cattle pasture to the trailhead. Drivers can access the trail at the end of Lokelani Rd, which is off Kamalu Rd a bit farther north. Right after the Norfolk pines begin, veer left at the fork. The trail passes through thick strawberry guava bushes that can grow up to 15ft high, in places creating a canopied, tunnel-like effect. A few minutes below the summit, the eastern and western trails merge on the ridge.

Moalepe & Kuilau Trails

Duration	3 hours
Distance	9 miles (14.5km)
Difficulty	easy
Start/Finish	Olohena Rd
Nearest Towns	Wailua (p194), Waipouli (p195), Kapa'a (p195)
Transport	private

Summary Take twin forest trails to the top of rolling Kuilau Ridge for jaw-dropping lookouts over lush valleys and misty mountains.

For the effort, the Moalepe and Kuilau Trails are some of the most visually rewarding on the island. It's possible to do either trail on

KAUAI

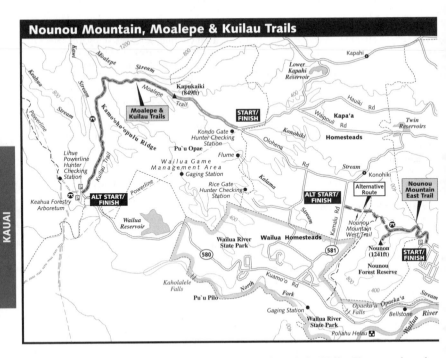

Nounou Mountain, Moalepe & Kuilau Trails

its own, but most hikers won't want to stop halfway since the views just keep improving, especially at each successive high point.

Ambitious hikers can connect with the Powerline Trail (p199) halfway through this hike by turning right out of the Kuilau Trail parking lot and walking down Kuamo'o Rd (Hwy 580) into Keahua Arboretum.

PLANNING

After heavy rains, some sections of trail can be slippery, muddy and boggy. Carry enough water, as none is available along either trail segment.

Maps

The color 1:50,000 *Recreation Map of Eastern Kauai* covers the trail.

GETTING TO/FROM THE HIKE

There is no bus service to the trailhead. From downtown Kapa'a, turn inland onto Kukui St and then right onto Olohena Rd (Hwy 581).

Drive through the Wailua Homesteads to the end of Olohena Rd, where it meets Waipouli Rd. Park on the road shoulder here.

To do this hike in the reverse direction, take the Kuhio Hwy (Hwy 56) to Wailua and follow Kuamo'o Rd (Hwy 580) inland for about 6 miles. Just before entering the Keahua Arboretum and crossing the stream, look for the marked Kuilau Ridge trailhead and a few parking stalls on the right. There is no bus service to the arboretum.

THE HIKE

At the end of Olohena Rd, look for the Na Ala Hele trailhead sign at the start of the Moalepe Trail. Walk past the yellow gate and a hunter checking station mailbox. The trail begins as a wide dirt road in a right-of-way lease through pasture in the Wailua Game Management Area. The road gently climbs between fenced-in private property, passing ferns, *hau* (hibiscus trees) with heart-shaped leaves and eucalyptus trees.

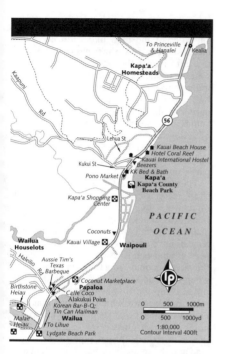

To Princeville
& Hanalei
Kealia
Kapa'a
Homesteads
Kaapuni
Rd
56
Lehua St
Kauai Beach House
Hotel Coral Reef
Kauai International Hostel
Beezers
Kukui St
KK Bed & Bath
Pono Market
Kapa'a
Kapa'a County
Beach Park
Kapa'a Shopping
Center
PACIFIC
OCEAN
Coconuts
Wailua
Houselots
Kauai Village
Waipouli
Haleilio Rd
Aussie Tim's
Texas
Barbeque
Coconut Marketplace
Birthstone
Heiau
Papaloa
Caffe Coco
Alakukui Point
Korean Bar-B-Q;
Tin Can Mailman
Malae
Heiau
Wailua
To Lihue
Lydgate Beach Park
0   500   1000m
0   500   1000yd
1:80,000
Contour Interval 400ft

KAUAI

Ridge to enjoy 360-degre_
next ½ mile, the trail reveals
most beautiful vistas along the entir_
Accompanied by ferns, it rises to a grassy
knoll where there's a **picnic table shelter**
with a view of sacred Mt Waialeale.

Then it's a short, pleasant walk along the
ridge top to where the Kuilau Trail starts to
gently drop again. This moist, grassy footpath leads in just over a mile down toward
Keahua Arboretum. Birdsong comes from
the dense native vegetation, which includes
koa, ohia lehua, guava trees, thickets of ti
and wild thimbleberries. Views of the mountains to the west are spoiled only slightly by
powerlines. When the Kuilau Ridge trailhead
parking stalls come into view at the bottom
of the hill, turn around to start the return leg.

The views on the return trip are very different. Retrace your steps to the picnic table,
and in about a half-hour you will reach the
wooden bridge at the trail junction. If you go
left at the connection with the Moalepe
Trail, you'll come to another viewpoint after
about 10 minutes. Otherwise follow the trail
back to Olohena Rd, being certain not to
veer off the dirt road or hunting trails-
of-use. Please clean off hiking boots and
poles before leaving the area to avoid
spreading seeds of Koster's curse, an invasive plant that chokes out native vegetation.

Look for waterfall cascades on the cliffs up
ahead in the distance. After about a mile,
the road curves to the left, with the high-
peaked Makahela Mountains soaring on the
right and the ocean far behind.

As it widens out and becomes windy, the
road rolls through *uluhe* (false staghorn
ferns), sometimes marked by poles with reflectors. Past the 2-mile marker, the trail
heads uphill to the left over a very rutted,
muddy section of road where trails-of-use
on the road's high shoulders avoid the bog-
giest bits. Soon the trail becomes a footpath
and passes into shady groves of ironwood
and guava. A lovely tree tunnel of papery-
barked acacia ends at a vague junction.

Curve right onto the wider path and start
working gently downhill. In the upper
reaches, the lush, fern-covered hillsides provide broad vistas of the mountains. The
Moalepe Trail ends at a wooden pedestrian
bridge. On the other side, pick up the Kuilau
Trail, which climbs up onto **Kamo'oho'opulu**

Powerline Trail

Duration	3–3½ hours
Distance	8 miles (12.9km)
Difficulty	moderate
Start/Finish	Keahua Forestry Arboretum
Nearest Towns	Wailua (p194), Waipouli (p195), Kapa'a (p195)
Transport	private

Summary Follow an old maintenance road as
it jogs up and over fern-covered hillsides to
head-spinning viewpoints over Kauai's interior
mountains, including sacred Mt Waialeale.

In the 1930s, electric transmission lines were
run along the mountains, and a 13-mile maintenance route now known as the Powerline

rail was created. There is occasional talk of turning it into a real inland road connecting Princeville to Wailua, but environmental concerns make it unlikely this will happen anytime soon. Although hikers will occasionally share the trail with noisy motorbikes and hunters' trucks and endure highly eroded, rutted sections of road, it's all worth it for the cloud-piercing views. While it's possible to hike the trail all the way to its other end outside Princeville, it's the southern half that's most rewarding.

PLANNING

After heavy rains, some sections of the trail can be slippery, muddy and boggy. Hiking poles or a walking stick may be helpful. Carry enough water, as none is available along the trail.

Maps

The color 1:50,000 *Recreation Map of Eastern Kauai* covers the trail.

GETTING TO/FROM THE HIKE

From the Kuhio Hwy (Hwy 56), turn inland onto Kuamo'o Rd (Hwy 580) around the 6-mile marker just north of the Wailua River. Drive west past the junction with Kamalu Rd (Hwy 581) and continue straight ahead another 4 miles to enter Keahua Arboretum. Cross the stream and proceed uphill on a bumpy dirt road for another few minutes to the marked trailhead on the right.

THE HIKE

The trail begins from a hunter checking station mailbox and heads abruptly uphill on a rocky road under deep, dark shade cover. It soon passes an overgrown fork and continues straight ahead, passing telephone poles and emerging into sunlight. Over to the left are broad views of the Makaleha Mountains, and the triangular peak of Mt Kawaikini often shrouded in clouds. Look for native *hau* trees and their papery yellow blossoms with blood-colored centers.

The powerlines cross overhead to roughly parallel the right side of the trail. For almost the next mile, the road rises and falls granting intermittent views of the ocean to the

right. *Uluhe* ferns overhang the deeply cut sides of the road like vertically hung meadows. The powerlines pass back over to the left side of the trail, where there are some majestic mountain views. Ignore any trails-of-use that veer off toward the powerline poles. When the road itself finally curves to the left, the ascent suddenly becomes much steeper. Look behind for views of valleys carpeted with green and the distant ocean. Next the road curves back to the right, but avoid an obscure spur trail that's partly overgrown with grass.

Then the road establishes a pattern of short, steep ascents followed by level and often water-logged stretches. The powerlines cross back over to the right, and a distant waterfall in a valley is visible. Mt Kawaikini continues to appear and disappear around bends in the road. Eventually the way becomes much steeper and even when the road is dry, it's very eroded and rutted. Atop the first major rise is a power relay station, past which the road makes a giant switchback and keeps going up. At the point at which grass starts to grow again, there's a rusted upright pipe on the right side and the grade becomes more gradual.

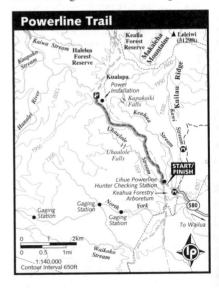

The powerlines close back in on the trail as the road veers to the left. After about 1½ hours of hiking, a fenced-in power installation with two drum-shaped cylinders hooked to either side of a tall pole appears. It's the only landmark. Valleys drop away to the right and ocean vistas play upon the eyes, as the powerlines once again cross overhead to the left of the trail. Hike uphill toward the tower and satellite dishes to arrive at a natural **lookout** at the trail's highest point.

Although the trail continues another 6 miles or so toward Princeville, the views really don't get any better, especially once the 4WD road flattens out and becomes dull walking. Most hunting activity takes place directly up ahead. So instead, backtrack from the lookout, veering left onto the most steeply eroded part of the road. Be careful of any slippery slopes with elephantine ruts on the long descent back to Keahua Arboretum.

Waimea Canyon State Park

Waimea Canyon is nicknamed the 'Grand Canyon of the Pacific.' This may sound like promotional hype, but it's not a bad description. Although it's smaller and 200 million years younger than the famous Arizona canyon, Waimea Canyon is certainly grand. The canyon's colorful gorge is cut into lava and 3657ft deep. The river that runs through it is 19½ miles long, Kauai's longest. All in all, it seems incredible that such an immense canyon could be tucked inside such a small island.

The view of the canyon from above is usually a bit hazy. The best time to view it is a sunny day after it's been raining heavily – at such times, the earth's a deeper red and waterfalls cascade throughout the canyon, providing unbeatable scenery. Of the many viewpoints along Waimea Canyon Dr (Hwy 550), don't skip **Waimea Canyon Lookout**, which is clearly signposted north of the 10-mile marker and offers sweeping views from a perch of 3400ft. The prominent

canyon running in an easterly direction off Waimea Canyon is Koaie Canyon.

Not only are the views fascinating, but so is the area's geology. The canyon runs along an ancient fault line where lava pushed downward to the sea. The west canyon walls are taller, thinner and more eroded, while the eastern wall was formed by thick, layered masses of lava flows. This contrast is most theatrically apparent while hiking along the canyon floor.

PLANNING

Waimea Canyon is not the place to explore on rainy days, when red-dirt trails quickly turn into slides and river fords can swell to impassable. Winter sees more storms than summer, but it's possible to hike these trails on good-weather days year-round. Ensure that you know what time sunset is and start back early to avoid losing too much daylight in the depths of the canyon. All of these backcountry trails are extremely remote, so hike carefully and preferably with a companion. Any available freshwater along the trails must be filtered or otherwise treated before drinking.

Maps

The color 1:50,000 *Recreation Map of Western Kauai* covers all of the state park trails, including access roads. The map is available free from the DOFAW office in Lihue.

GETTING AROUND

There is no bus service into the state park or to any of the trailheads. There are two options for driving. Beautiful Waimea Canyon Dr (Hwy 550) twists its way up from downtown Waimea, traveling over 6 miles to the state park's southern boundary. Koke'e Rd (Hwy 552), which ascends from central Kekaha, also has scenic views, but not of the canyon. Eventually it merges with Waimea Canyon Dr, which continues north toward Koke'e State Park.

ACCESS TOWNS & FACILITIES
Waimea

Waimea (which means 'reddish water') was the site of an ancient Hawaiian settlement.

Warning

During weekends and holidays, all of these trails are fairly heavily used by pig hunters. Hunting season signs are usually quite clearly posted at trailheads or along the trails. Because accidents do happen, try to avoid hiking on days when there's hunting activity. See Hunting Accidents (p60) for additional safety precautions hikers can take.

It was here on January 19, 1778, that Captain Cook first came ashore on the Hawaiian Islands. Later the first wave of 19th-century missionaries to Hawaii also selected Waimea as a landing site, not long after Russian Fort Elizabeth, sitting above the east bank of the river, was abandoned in 1817.

Today, Waimea remains the biggest settlement in West Kauai, but has an engaging small-town character and wooden buildings with false fronts. The dominant structure by the square is the neoclassical First Hawaiian Bank building, dating from 1929. The Waimea Theatre (c. 1938), built in Art Deco style and recently renovated, is another place worth a look – or, even better, swing by at night and enjoy a movie (call ☎ 338-0282).

Information At the start of Waimea Canyon Dr, **West Kauai Technology & Visitors Center** (☎ 338-1332; 9565 Kaumuali'i Hwy; open 9am-4pm Mon-Fri, 9am-1pm Sat) is certainly worth stopping by both for its historical displays and racks of brochures, maps and events flyers. Volunteers lead two-hour walking tours of the town at 9:30am Monday; reservations are preferred. The walk is free, but donations are appreciated.

Supplies & Equipment Both of the town's grocery stores, **Big Save Market** (Kaumuali'i Hwy, cnr Menehune Rd; open 6am-10pm Mon-Sat, 6am-9pm Sun) and **Ishihara Market** (9894 Kaumuali'i Hwy; open 6am-8:30pm Mon-Fri, 7am-8:30pm Sat & Sun), sell bakery goods, deli fare and sundry items. **Westside Sporting Goods** (☎ 338-1411; 9681 Kaumuali'i Hwy; open 9:30am-5:30pm Mon-Fri, 9:30am-4:30pm Sat) stocks camping and hiking supplies, including fleece sleeping bags ($15), camp-stove fuel, *tabi* (reef-walking sandals) and first-aid kits.

Places to Stay & Eat Two blocks south of the highway and within view of the ocean, **Inn Waimea** (☎ 338-0031, fax 338-1814; [W] innwaimea.com; 4469 Halepule Rd; doubles/suites $70/95) combines historic character with modern comforts. Rooms and suites each have private bath, ceiling fans, a refrigerator, TV and phone.

Jo-Jo's Shave Ice (9740 Kaumuali'i Hwy; shave ice $2-3; open 10am-5pm or later daily) makes superb shave ice in 60 tantalizing tropical flavors. The *lilikoi*/guava/mango combination with a scoop of mac nut ice cream is hands-down the local favorite.

Pacific Pizza & Deli (☎ 338-1020; 9852 Kaumuali'i Hwy; calzones, wraps & sandwiches around $5, pizzas $8-20; open 11am-9pm daily), adjacent to Wrangler's steakhouse, serves up freshly made, piping hot calzones and pizzas. The gourmet 'Pacific' version of either comes with basil pesto, delectable calamari, faux crab and sun-dried tomatoes.

Kauai Shrimp Depot (Kaumuali'i Hwy; ½lb shrimp order $10.50; open 11am-6pm Mon-Sat), at the west end of town, cooks 'em up either beer-battered, Thai-style or coated in garlic and olive oil, all with boiled red potatoes or steamed rice on the side.

Waimea Brewing Company (☎ 338-9733; 9400 Kaumuali'i Hwy; dishes $8-15; restaurant open 11am-9pm daily, bar open until 11pm Fri & Sat), at Waimea Plantation Cottages, lays claim to being the westernmost microbrewery in the USA. Pricey pub fare, such as fish and chips or barbecued chicken sandwiches, ain't great, but it's a social place. There's often live music in the evenings.

Getting There & Away The **Kauai Bus** (☎ 241-6410) stops at the First Hawaiian Bank and the Waimea Ball Field on the way to Kekaha ($1.50, 15 minutes). Buses bound for Lihue ($1.50, 50 minutes) stop at Ishihara Market. Departures are roughly every two hours on weekdays, but there are only four buses in either direction on Saturday. Buses do not operate on Sunday.

Kekaha

Kekaha has great beaches, or rather it has one long glorious stretch of sand. Ni'ihau and its offshore island, Lehua, are visible from the highway. And so is the town's most dominant feature, the old sugar mill.

A few blocks inland from the beach, Kekaha Rd runs parallel to the highway. **Traveler's Den** *(8240 Kekaha Rd; open 8am-9pm Mon-Sat, 8am-8pm Sun)*, a small grocery store beside the post office, has a few camping supplies and a Hawaiian-style deli selling *poi, poke* and baked goods.

Places to Stay & Eat Kekaha has a surprising number of vacation rental properties. Most owners list vacation rental homes and apartments on the Internet. A quick Web search should turn up enticing options for as little as $75 per night.

Mindy's *(☎ 337-9275; e mindys@hgea.org; 8842 Kekaha Rd; 1-bedroom apartment $55-85)* is often booked. The upper-story apartment has a full kitchen and deck. Although not near the beach, the place is modern and comfortable, with ceiling fans and cable TV/VCR.

Obsessions Cafe *(☎ 337-2224; Waimea Canyon Plaza, cnr Kekaha & Koke'e Rds; snacks from $4; open 8:30am-6pm Mon-Fri, 6:30am-2pm Sat & Sun)* is a great little place in Kekaha's main shopping center. Everything is homemade, the salads are homegrown and even the coffee here comes from the owner's 5-acre coffee patch.

Getting There & Away The **Kauai Bus** *(☎ 241-6410)* makes several stops along Elepaio Rd, just inland from the highway and parallel to Kekaha Rd. Buses to and from Lihue ($1.50, 65 minutes) stop in Waimea ($1.50, 15 minutes). Departures are roughly every two hours on weekdays, but there are only four buses inbound and outbound on Saturday. Buses do not operate on Sunday.

Polihale State Park Campground

Polihale is near-desert. At the very end of the vast beach is Polihale Cliff, marking the western end of the Na Pali Coast. With miles of untamed ocean and a beautiful white-sand beach, it's a magnificent sight, but strong rip currents make the waters treacherous for swimming. Camping is allowed by permit for up to five nights within a 30-day period; sites cost $5 per night. The main camping area by the picnic pavilion has rest rooms, drinking water and outdoor showers. Farther down, other camping areas are in the dunes just above the beach amid thorny *kiawe* trees. Permits are issued by the Division of State Parks in Lihue.

Getting There & Away Polihale State Park is about 5 miles from the Barking Sands military base, a short drive west of Kekaha along the Kaumuali'i Hwy. Turn left ¾ mile north of the base entrance onto a wide dirt road that passes through abandoned sugarcane fields. The road is a bit bumpy but passable in a standard car. To get to the state park facilities, continue about a mile past a large spreading tree in the middle of the road and turn left at the picnic pavilion on the *makai* (seaward) side.

A Little Menehune Mystery

Kauai was probably settled between AD 500 and 700 by Polynesians who migrated from the Marquesas Islands. While Hawaiian lore makes no direct references to the Marquesan culture, Kauai is often referred to as the home of a race of little people called *menehune*. Legend after legend tells of happy, Disney-like elves coming down from the mountains to produce great engineering works in stone.

It seems likely that when the first wave of Tahitians arrived about AD 1000, they conquered and subjugated the Marquesans, forcing them to build the temples, irrigation ditches and fishponds now attributed to the *menehune*. The Tahitian term for 'outcast' is *manahune* and the diminutive social status the Marquesans had in the eyes of their conquerors may have given rise to tales of a dwarf-size race. While the stonework remains, the true identity of Kauai's 'little people' is lost.

Waimea Canyon Trail

Duration	5–6 hours
Distance	14 miles (22.5km)
Difficulty	easy–moderate
Start/Finish	end of Menehune Rd
Nearest Towns	Waimea (p201), Kekaha (p203)
Transport	private
Summary	Inspect the natural wonders of Kauai's grand canyon from down below, traveling on an old cane haul road, and splash across eight cooling river fords.

This canyon trail, which is 8 miles long, runs north from the town of Waimea all the way to Wiliwili Camp, at the junction with the Kukui and Koaie Canyon Trails. Unlike those other two trails, the Waimea Canyon Trail is mostly level and poses few challenges (although the last mile to Wiliwili Camp is not recommended). However, the Waimea trail's up-close-and-personal views deep into the canyon really are unmatched. You'll find that much of this trail is along a 4WD road that leads to a hydroelectric power station.

PLANNING

Note that while there's public access along the route, the trail passes over private property, so no camping is allowed en route. There are a number of broad river fords, making the trail best considered only during periods of dry weather. Flash floods are also possible. If the water reaches above your knees, turn back. Pack a lightweight pair of *tabi,* reef walkers or sport sandals to make crossings easier.

Maps

The color 1:50,000 *Recreation Map of Western Kauai* covers the trail.

GETTING TO/FROM THE HIKE

The trail starts outside downtown Waimea. At the Big Save Market, turn north onto Menehune Rd and follow it north past Waimea's famous Menehune Ditch to where the pavement ends after about 2½ miles.

You'll find a gravel pull-off on the right. Be sure to watch out for posted 'No Parking' signs.

THE HIKE

Walk down the west bank and ford the river below Menehune Rd, picking up the trail on the other side. Walk left along the road past the hunter checking station and around a gate that blocks unauthorized motor vehicle access. In the next ¾ mile, the road fords the river twice, becoming muddier and entering a forest of swamp mahogany, eucalyptus and *kukui* trees, as well as some Java plum trees. Soon the canyon outcroppings come into view.

Each ford is wider than the last, and the fourth river crossing is no exception. Back on the true left bank of the river, continue along the main road, ignoring a side road that diverts back over the river toward some private houses. Instead keep going straight, passing over an irrigation pipe covered by wooden slats. The fifth ford comes at around the 2-mile point, and has sinking sandbanks on either side, although the water is shallower.

Abruptly after passing through a gate, the road goes sharply uphill and becomes extremely rocky. There are views of grassy canyon walls off to the left. Guava and cactus fill out the landscape. After making a stiff climb, take note of an irrigation ditch approaching from the right. Continue walking alongside the ditch on an exposed stretch of trail. Where the ditch flows through a tunnel hewn out of solid rock, follow the road around to the left. You'll find that the dusty red-dirt road ascends past a broken-down fence enclosure, then gently descends back under shade cover at about the 3-mile point.

As the road levels out, some big views open up, particularly of the red rock of the canyon walls. From here the trail becomes gentle and pastoral, lined by tall stalky grasses and feral sugarcane. The sloping sides of the east canyon wall and its jet-black outcroppings are covered in greenery. At a makeshift bench under a tree on the left, pause to look around at banana plants, berries and taro. Be sure to keep walking straight along the road, which will take you past another ditch tunnel blasted through rock.

Watch for a sluice on the right around the 4-mile point. Do not take the trail-of-use straight alongside the ditch, but instead follow tire tracks down toward the river on the left. The trail hops across a couple of streamlets in dense forest cover. Views of the canyon become more lush and full as the trail quickly drops back down to the river for the sixth ford. If you pause briefly mid-crossing you can gaze in both directions along the very impressive canyon walls.

Now on the left bank of the river, continue to the seventh river ford. Keep following the 4WD tracks made by cane hauling trucks, past awesome evidence of geological handiwork, and around the 6-mile point, make the last river ford. At the **Mauka Powerhouse**, a dam and cable bridge stretch across the river. Stay on the west bank and continue past some ramshackle-looking buildings, rock-hopping over a likely flooded part of the trail outside a chain-link fence. Look for a yellow hunting notice up ahead. Soon a footpath appears and the way becomes more clear. Watch out for rockfall as the trail passes underneath the overhanging red cliffs of the canyon's west wall, hemmed in on the right by the river.

From this point, it's over another mile to Wiliwili Camp, but the track deteriorates into a buggy, wet and claustrophobic experience. The trail is not hard to follow, as it stays on the west side of the river (do not ford it again and ignore false spur trails). But there's no reward in forging ahead except to explore further on the Koaie Canyon Trail (p206). For most people, this is already far enough for one day.

On the return trip from the powerhouse dam to Menehune Rd, the trail divides neatly into thirds, with the first part ending after three river crossings, the second part after descending the rocky road by the gate, and the last after passing the hunter checking station and over the initial river ford.

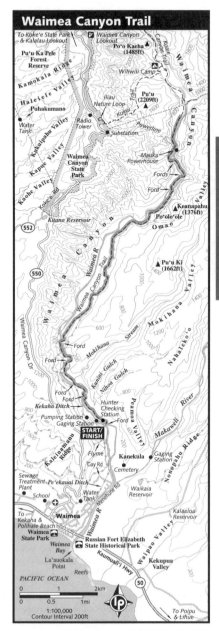

KAUAI

Kukui & Koaie Canyon Trails

Duration	6½–8 hours
Distance	12.2 miles (19.7km)
Difficulty	moderate–demanding
Start/Finish	Waimea Canyon Dr (Hwy 550)
Nearest Towns	Waimea (p201), Kekaha (p203)
Transport	private

Summary Dive into Waimea Canyon, starting in a preserve of endangered Hawaiian *iliau* plants, then skid down red-dirt hills to the banks of Hawaii's longest river and explore a peaceful side canyon.

The Kukui Trail makes a steep 2000ft descent down the western side of Waimea Canyon, 2½ miles to the Waimea River. The trail begins on a segment of the Iliau Nature Loop, worth visiting in its own right. Part of the endangered Hawaiian silversword alliance, Kauai's beautiful *iliau* plants have delicate green leaves radiating from the top of a pole-like stalk. Flowering only in their last year of life, *iliau* are found growing here around the rim of Waimea Canyon.

At the bottom of the canyon, the Koaie Canyon Trail makes a short traverse along a sheer rock face above the river. Old stone remains of *heiau* and *hale,* beautiful scenery and solitude are some of the trail's joys. The canyon's fertile soil once supported an ancient Hawaiian settlement, and the long-abandoned remains of a *heiau* and some *hale* sites are still discernable. The trail starts from a river crossing north of Wiliwili Camp (where the Kukui Trail ends) and gently runs for 3 miles along the southern side of Koaie Canyon past backcountry camps mostly used by hunters. These camps make convenient landmarks as turning points for hikers wanting a shorter walk. There are some good swimming spots along the way and also at the end of the trail, near Lonomea Camp.

PLANNING

All freshwater found along the trail needs to be treated before drinking. Hiking poles or a stout walking stick will help ease the descent into the canyon. Don't hike during stormy weather, or just after heavy rains. Wait until the eroded sections of the trail can dry out before hiking. There is only one river ford near the beginning of the Koaie Canyon Trail, but it can swell to impassable during heavy rains. Don't cross if the water is moving too fast or it's more than knee-deep. A lightweight pair of sandals, *tabi* or reef walkers will help, but aren't strictly necessary. Note flash floods are possible on the canyon floor.

Maps

The color 1:50,000 *Recreation Map of Western Kauai* and the USGS 1:24,000 map *Waimea Canyon* both cover the trails.

Permits & Regulations

Backcountry camping is limited to four nights in the canyon within a 30-day period. Camping permits are free, but need to be picked up from the DOFAW office in Lihue.

GETTING TO/FROM THE HIKE

The joint trailhead for the Kukui Trail and Iliau Nature Loop comes up shortly before the 9-mile marker on Waimea Canyon Dr. Park on the west road shoulder uphill from the trailhead.

THE HIKE

Enter on the Iliau Nature Loop trail, turning right and continuing down past a bench with a scenic view. The Kukui Trail officially starts just beyond it at a hunter checking station on the right. It passes a picnic table before starting its switchback descent through forest, entering archery Hunting Unit K. Koa, silk oak and ohia trees overarch the footpath, with maybe a *lilikoi* vine or two growing alongside. At first the way is not overly steep. Because much of it is so exposed, the trail tends to dry out quickly here, even after rain.

From this point onward, keep a sharp eye out for the switchback turns during the descent. When in doubt about where the trail actually is, stick with the more level forks and ignore the steeply rutted bits going down the deepest gashes in the canyon wall. If the going starts to feel too precipitous, it probably is; backtracking to the last switchback junction may be the best option. There are also tempting places to perch on canyon outcroppings, but unstable, crumbly soil makes it dangerous to do so.

Around the ½-mile marker are some washed-away sections of trail that may well require some light, quick steps to safely cross the scree. Past the eroded traverse the switchbacks resume as the descent steepens and the trail enters Hunting Unit B. Only short-cut the switchbacks if they look much

safer than the main route. Views of the river canyon open up from the **bench** around the 1-mile mark.

Continue sharply switchbacking, the trail still in the vicinity of *iliau* and an unnamed tree-topped *pu'u* (a hill, marked '2209' on topographic maps) with a big gash in its side prominent. Do not veer toward hill 2209. Instead keep it on the right and where the trail abruptly stops its descent for a moment, look for a small sign directing hikers to turn left. Then with hill 2209 at your back, hike down through deeply rutted and colorful dirt, curving right to start slowly

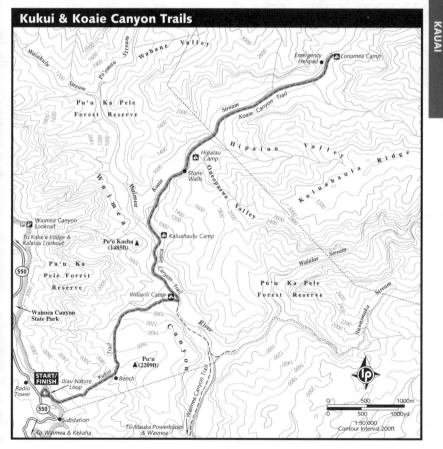

Kukui & Koaie Canyon Trails

KAUAI

picking out a path down over a severely eroded soil slope, meanwhile losing at least 500 feet in elevation. At the 1½-mile mark, the trail is still descending as if it's heading for the opposite canyon wall, and a distinctive butte, Po'o Kaeha, is visible down below. Do not veer right into the forest before reaching the bottom of the steep slope, where there's a broken pole sticking up and a rock covered with graffiti.

About an hour from the start, the trail enters thick forest and tree roots form natural steps going downhill. It requires minor boulder-hopping in parts. The first of the forested switchbacks are the steepest, gradually easing as the path travels downhill and becomes overgrown and scratchy in parts. *Kukui* nuts crunch and swivel underfoot. After pushing through a section of sisal grasses, the path shortly rises and falls once again over boulders. As the sounds of rushing river water become clearly audible, the picnic shelter and toilet of **Wiliwili Camp** come into view. From here, it's only a few more steps to the river itself and a signposted junction with both the Waimea Canyon and Koaie Canyon Trails.

Overnight camping is allowed at Wiliwili Camp although it's mostly used by hunters and may be filled with trash. The camp has an open-air picnic shelter and pit toilet, but there are no other facilities.

A few steps from Wiliwili Camp, the Kukui Trail intersects with a wide dirt road before meeting the river. Follow this road north across a small streambed, then uphill on switchbacks before turning left and heading along the canyon wall, with beautiful views of the river below. At an indistinct junction, stay on the right-hand lower path, which is filled with small rocks that roll underfoot. Growing in the canyon's shade are giant fan-like ferns, and beautiful red cliffs can be seen stretching out in front. Ignore any false spur trails that divert right down to the river. Soon there's a little plank across a stream (test it before trusting it).

The trail narrows to only foot width as it edges along a slippery, mossy rock face above the river. After only a minute or so, the rocks dry out and the going gets easier. When the trail rejoins the old dirt road, it quickly descends back to the river, then crosses over it. The ford is not especially wide, and sometimes it's possible to boulder-hop across it. On the other bank, which is lined by elegant umbrella grass, turn left (north) and walk along an extremely rutted road to **Kaluahaulu Camp**, marked by another picnic table shelter and pit toilet.

All three backcountry camps on the Koaie Canyon Trail are part of the forest reserve system. Although the camps have open-air picnic shelters and toilets, there are no other facilities, and all freshwater needs to be treated before drinking. Staying overnight is not an inviting option, however, considering the amount of trash other campers leave behind.

Beyond the camp, the trail continues as a single track. Po'o Keaha, a striking-looking butte also seen from the Kukui Trail, rises up directly on the left. Inundated with leaf litter, the trail widens out but grows fainter. Be sure to stay on the east bank of the river and do not cross it, even when trails-of-use seem to suggest doing so. A Na Ala Hele trailhead sign signals the start of the Koaie Canyon Trail. Initially it's overgrown and some minor bushwhacking may be required. Spongy, loose soil on the sides of the path can conceal steep drop-offs, so watch your step.

Follow the gently rolling trail underneath the east canyon wall, as *kukui* nuts bounce around underfoot. At about 2 miles from Wiliwili Camp, the trail meets a couple of **stone walls**. Sisal grasses and guava line the rest of the way to **Hipalau Camp**, reached after about an hour of hiking. Making noises as you hike will most likely scare away any wild pigs that may be wandering around, snuffling in the trash. Beyond Hipalau Camp the trail becomes indistinct, but generally keep heading north. Look for an orange-pointed stake at the point where the path becomes visible again, scrambling up over large boulders. Do not veer off toward the river, but continue ascending at approximately the same point midway between the canyon walls and the river.

Becoming ever more steep, the trail has now entered Koaie Canyon, judging by the red-rock walls rising to the left. Although made up of crumbly soil in parts, the trail is not unnerving by any means. In many places it appears to become lost in forest clearings, often hidden by leaf litter and covered in mud. Just head straight across any such clearing and pick up the trail heading upslope on the other side by keeping to the mid-level below the ridge, but not too close to the river. Many of these clearings have interesting old Hawaiian stone walls.

About a ½-hour's hike from Hipalau Camp, grand views of the canyon reward the perseverance of hikers. A stake on the right is labeled '2¼', which is the approximate distance from the official Na Ala Hele trail sign north of Kaluahaulu Camp. Entering a deep forest corridor, the path drags through spider webs, hops across a small stream and passes a circular stone enclosure near the 2½-mile marker stake. In just another ½ mile the trail empties out at **Lonomea Camp**. However, the most rewarding views come just before the end of the trail by the **emergency helipad**, a grassy area that's perfect for picnicking (no camping) or simply gazing at the river and a small waterfall. When ready, retrace your steps back to the Na Ala Hele trailhead sign, then the first river crossing and Wiliwili Camp.

Be sure to conserve enough water for the remainder of the trip from here, which is uphill all the way. Start back early enough not to be caught in fading daylight, which departs the canyon long before sunset. At the first trail junction atop the canyon wall, turn right for a short detour on the Iliau Nature Loop, which has a few readable interpretive signs and labeled plants. Guided by trail markers, the path treads over red dirt to meet a bench that rewards hikers with a topnotch vista of Waimea Canyon. After heavy rainfall, waterfalls explode down the sheer rock walls across the gorge.

Koke'e State Park

Sprawling Koke'e State Park is the starting point for about 45 miles of trails, some maintained by the Division of State Parks, others by the DOFAW.

Koke'e (pronounced ko-**kay**-ay) was once joined to the remote Kalalau Valley on the Na Pali Coast by a very steep ancient Hawaiian trail that ran down the cliffs. At the end of the park's only paved road is the Kalalau Lookout, a coastal overlook that's among the most breathtaking in all Hawaii. Many of the state park's trails also enjoy excellent vantage points into Kalalau Valley and even more isolated valleys along the Na Pali Coast.

Kauai boasts the largest number of extant native bird species in Hawaii, and many of them are found here. Native forest birds are concentrated at remote Alakai Swamp. Not only is the swamp inhospitable to exotic species, but due to its high elevation, it is one of the few places in Hawaii where mosquitoes, which transmit avian diseases, do not flourish.

Incidentally, the chickens that congregate in the museum's parking lot are not the common garden variety but *moa,* or red junglefowl. Early Polynesian settlers brought *moa* to Hawaii, and they were once common on all the main islands, but are now prolific only on Kauai. Not shy of people, these splendidly colored birds are always asking for handouts.

PLANNING
When to Hike
Even when the sun is blazing over Waimea on the coast, conditions up here in the mountains can be overcast. It's often wet and chilly, especially in the early morning and at night, which is not surprising given the high elevations and proximity to Mt Waialeale, the wettest spot on earth. The helpful staff at Koke'e Museum (☎ 335-9975) can give real-time mountain weather reports when hikers nicely ask them to look outside the museum's front door. For recorded islandwide forecasts call ☎ 245-6001.

What to Bring
Hiking poles or a walking stick will help, especially after heavy rains when the park's steep trails become extremely slick. Always bring rain gear and a fleece or wool sweater; layers of warm clothes can be very necessary at these elevations. It's smart to keep a

KAUAI

change of dry clothes and shoes back at the car for after hiking in the rain. After changing, stuff any wet items into a separate plastic garbage bag, as Kauai's famous red dirt can permanently stain just about everything it comes into contact with.

Maps

The color 1:50,000 *Recreation Map of Western Kauai* covers all of the state park trails, including access roads. The map is available free from the DOFAW office in Lihue. Basic trail guides with sketch maps or photocopies of topographic maps are sold at the Koke'e Museum.

Information Sources

Learn about Kauai's ecology and natural history at the **Koke'e Museum** (☎ 335-9975; *admission by donation $1; open 10am-4pm daily*), just off Waimea Canyon Dr, next to Koke'e Lodge. Some good quality handicrafts, an extensive selection of Hawaiiana books, field guides and inexpensive trail maps are also for sale.

Although the ranger station in Koke'e hasn't been open for years, the museum staff can provide assistance, including basic information on current trail conditions. Outside the museum is a good information board with a trail system map.

On summer weekends, trained interpretive volunteers lead 'Wonder Walks' for a nominal donation of $3. Call the museum for schedules and reservations. Also ask at the museum for the brochure to the short nature trail out back. The brochure, which can be borrowed free or purchased for $1.50, offers interpretive information corresponding to the trail's numbered plants and trees, many of them native Hawaiian species.

GETTING THERE & AROUND

This park's boundary starts on Waimea Canyon Dr beyond the Pu'u Hinahina Lookout. After the 15-mile marker, you'll pass park cabins, Koke'e Lodge, a museum and a campground one after the other. A 4WD vehicle will come in handy, providing easier access to some hiking trails. Most 4WD roads can still be navigated by hikers

Warning

Pig and goat hunters use some of these trails during hunting season. Try to avoid hiking on days when there's hunting activity. See Hunting Accidents (p60) for more safety precautions hikers can take.

if they're willing to make the long and often steep slogs required.

ACCESS TOWNS & FACILITIES

See Waimea (p201) and Kekaha (p203).

Inside the Park

If you're staying in the cabins or campgrounds, be sure to bring ample provisions, as the nearest stores (and gas station) are in Waimea, 15 miles away.

Places to Stay & Eat At an elevation of 4000ft, the nights here are crisp and cool. This is sleeping-bag-and-warm-clothing country.

The most accessible camping area is **Koke'e State Park campground**, north of the meadow, just a few minutes' walk from Koke'e Museum. The sites are in an uncrowded grassy area beside the woods and have picnic tables, drinking water, rest rooms and showers. Camping is allowed for up to five nights, but permits cost $5 per site and must be obtained before arriving in Koke'e. Apply at the Division of State Parks in Lihue, or at state park offices on other islands.

If you want to go farther off the main track, **Kawaikoi Camp** and **Sugi Grove Camp** are about 4 miles east of Koke'e Lodge, off the 4WD Camp 10-Mohihi Rd in the forest reserve adjacent to the state park. Each campground has pit toilets, picnic shelters and fire pits. You'll need to carry in your own water or treat the stream water before drinking it. These forest reserve campgrounds have a three-night maximum stay and also require camping permits obtained (free) in advance. Apply at the DOFAW office in Lihue.

The 12 cabins in Koke'e State Park are run by **Koke'e Lodge** (☎ 335-6061; *PO Box 819, Waimea, HI 96796; studio/2-bedroom* cabins *$35/45)*. Each cabin has one double and four twin beds, and a kitchen equipped with a refrigerator and oven, as well as linens, blankets, a hot-water shower and a woodstove. The 2-bedroom cabins are newer than the studio cabins. All are often booked up well in advance, but cancellations do occur, and you can occasionally get a cabin at the last moment. State park rules do limit stays to five days. Koke'e Lodge's **canteen** *(simple fare $3.50-7; open 9am-3:30pm daily, gift shop closes at 4pm)* is the only place to eat north of Waimea. It serves elementary breakfasts, salads, soups and deli sandwiches. The gift shop stocks snacks and a few canned food items.

YWCA Camp Sloggett *(Kumuwela Rd;* [W] *www.campingkauai.com; tent sites per person $10, bunkhouse beds $20, group lodge weekdays/weekends from $50/80)* lies ½ mile east of the park museum down a rutted dirt road that's usually passable in a standard car. Guests must provide their own bedding for the bunkhouse, but there's a kitchenette and bathrooms with hot showers. Tent campers have a barbecue pit for cooking and use of the showers and toilets in the bunkhouse. For the bunkhouse and tent sites, call the caretaker (☎ 335-6060) for availability. Bookings for the lodge are made through the **YWCA** *(☎ 245-5959; 3094 Elua St, Lihue, HI 96766)*.

Canyon Trail

Duration	1½–2 hours
Distance	5.2 miles (8.4km)
Difficulty	easy
Start/Finish	Halemanu Rd
Nearest Towns	Waimea (p201), Kekaha (p203)
Transport	private

Summary Achieve spectacular viewpoints over Waimea Canyon and visit a lush waterfall, all for minimal effort and with scenery equal to Koke'e State Park's most demanding trails.

Even though it's not within the boundaries of Waimea Canyon State Park, this trail gives beautiful overlooks into the canyon itself from atop the western wall and passes through native Hawaiian forest on the way to Waipo'o Falls. Admittedly the route is simple and short, but it's still definitely worth doing, even for those who have already spent time hiking in Waimea Canyon. The perspective is different from up here, with wider vistas and varied scenery.

PLANNING
No drinking water is available along the trail. After heavy rains, the stream feeding Waipo'o Falls may be impassable. Do not attempt to cross the stream when the water reaches above knee-level or is flowing powerfully over the canyon rim.

Maps
The color 1:50,000 *Recreation Map of Western Kauai* covers the trail.

GETTING TO/FROM THE HIKE
The starting point for several scenic hikes, Halemanu Rd is just north of the 14-mile marker on Waimea Canyon Dr. Whether or not the road is passable in a non-4WD vehicle often depends on whether it's been raining recently. Keep in mind that the clay roads provide no traction when wet, and even if you're able to drive a car in, should it begin to rain driving out can be another matter! Instead park on the west shoulder of Waimea Canyon Dr, opposite Halemanu Rd, and then walk down.

THE HIKE (see map p212)
Starting from the highway, walk down Halemanu Rd for just over ½ mile, passing under some koa trees, until reaching a well-signed junction. Veer to the right and continue to the next fork in the road, keeping Halemanu Stream on the left and ignoring a hunting trail-of-use on the right. Leave the road by turning right onto the footpath that's signposted for both the Canyon and Cliff Trails.

At the next trail junction, the Cliff Trail takes off to the right and wanders for less than ¼ mile uphill to the **Cliff Viewpoint**; at the far end of the green-painted guardrails are the very best, and windiest, views of the

KAUAI

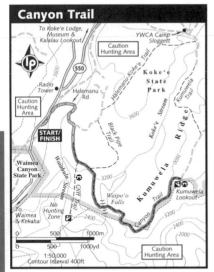

Canyon Trail

To Koke'e Lodge,
Museum &
Kalalau Lookout
YWCA Camp
Sloggett
Caution
Hunting Area
Radio
Tower
Halemanu
Rd
Koke'e
State
Park
Caution
Hunting
Area
START/
FINISH
Black Pipe Trail
Waimea
Canyon
State Park
Kumuwela Ridge
Koke'e Stream
Waipo'o
Falls
Kumuwela
Lookout
No
Hunting
Zone
Canyon Trail
To
Waimea
& Kekaha
Caution
Hunting Area
0   500   1000m
0   1000yd
1:50,000
Contour Interval 400ft

canyon. There's a good chance of spotting feral goats scrambling along the canyon walls.

When ready, backtrack to the previous junction and turn right onto the Canyon Trail, which now descends though more koa and blackberry plants and through a gully by an old irrigation ditch, which was once used to supply sugarcane fields in the canyon far below. It's easy to miss the obscure junction with Black Pipe Trail, past which the Canyon Trail keeps descending past *iliahi* (Hawaiian sandalwood) to the edge of Waimea Canyon.

The trail then runs parallel to the canyon rim over some very eroded, bare sections of rocks and red soil. Strong winds seem to threaten to blow the wildlife right over the canyon walls, so be sure to anchor every step carefully. Views are tremendous from this point, but don't venture too close to the walls, as the soil is not entirely stable.

Just shy of the one-hour point, the Canyon Trail veers away from the rim into another gulch en route to **Waipo'o Falls**. A sign may still be standing, identifying 'Falls No 1', also called 'Ginger Pool' for obvious reasons. Further along is 'Falls No 2' and it

may be tricky to cross, as Koke'e Stream plummets over the canyon walls here. If the water levels and speed look menacing, turn around here.

Otherwise, after hopping boulders across the stream, the trail clambers onto Kumuwela Ridge and has a reunion with the canyon rim for more breathtaking views. The trail ends at **Kumuwela Lookout** with views down the canyon to the Pacific Ocean far beyond. There's a picnic table from which to take it all in before turning around and backtracking to Halemanu Rd.

Those who can't stand backtracking the entire way can detour from the Canyon Trail onto the Black Pipe Trail for a gentle rolling ½-mile walk through *iliau* plants and other native vegetation, eventually emptying out onto Halemanu Rd. After turning left, it's less than a mile's walk back up the dirt road to the highway, past the earlier signed junction with the Cliff and Canyon Trails.

Awa'awapuhi Lookout & Nualolo Cliffs

Duration	2½–3 hours
Distance	7 miles (11.3km)
Difficulty	easy–moderate
Start/Finish	Waimea Canyon Dr (Hwy 550)
Nearest Towns	Waimea (p201), Kekaha (p203)
Transport	private

Summary Wander through native Hawaiian plants to extraordinary viewpoints over the remotest valleys of the Na Pali Coast, and then drop by a small cascade on the Nualolo Cliffs.

The Awa'awapuhi Trail goes out to the very edge of sheer cliffs, allowing you to peer down into valleys that are otherwise accessible only by boat. Awa'awapuhi means 'valley of ginger', and *kahili*, a pretty yellow ginger, can be seen along the way. The trail descends 1600ft, ending at steep and spectacular *pali* overlooking Awa'awapuhi and Nualolo Valleys. Wild goats, prolific in the North Shore valleys, are readily spotted along the cliff walls. The goats actually have no natural predators in Hawaii, and their unchecked numbers have caused a fair amount of ecological damage.

PLANNING

After heavy rain, these trails become quite slick, especially along the alternative route (described at the end of this hike), which is an all-day adventure. Hiking poles or a walking stick will help. Carry plenty of water, as there's none along the way. Edible plants along the trail include blackberries, thimbleberries, guava and *lilikoi*. Although identifying-number signs are just visible for various other trailside plants, at the time of research the trail guide brochure was no longer available from the museum.

Maps

The color 1:50,000 *Recreation Map of Western Kauai* covers all the trails. The USGS 1:24,000 map quadrangles *Makaha Point* and *Haena* cover the Awa'awapuhi, Nualolo Cliffs and Nualolo Trails.

GETTING TO/FROM THE HIKE

The trailhead for the Awa'awapuhi Trail begins at a parking area just after the 17-mile marker on Waimea Canyon Dr, two miles up from Koke'e Lodge and the museum.

THE HIKE (see map p214)

The Awa'awapuhi Trail starts off atop Ka-unuohua Ridge, descending in an ohia forest. About ½ mile down, the forest becomes drier, and koa mixes in with the ohia. The path widens out, becoming very muddy in spots, and gains partial ocean views around the 1½-mile marker. If weather conditions at the trailhead were foggy or rainy, there's a chance of walking out from underneath the clouds and escaping the weather soon. Some viewpoints look *makai* into lush valleys over Honopu Ridge, with the sharply eroded *pali* dropping away below the trail.

Before the 2-mile marker, the trail dries out and curves around the ridge past rocks and low-lying shrubs, such as *a'ali'i* with sticky foliage and *pukiawe* berries. Shade cover is intermittent here, revealing on the

left steep *pali* covered with red dirt and segments of the narrow Nualolo Cliffs Trail snaking out among them. Shortly after the 2½-mile marker is a jaw-dropping **viewpoint** right at the level of the clouds, with hardly anything to distinguish between the blue of the sky and the ocean on sunny days. Choppers can be heard overhead.

From there the trail turns left, and cuts back into the forest, becoming overgrown in some parts. Be careful of steep drop-offs as the trail runs right along the side of a ridge. At the next trail junction, a little short of the 3-mile mark, the Nualolo Cliffs Trail comes in on the left. Although the painted arrows may be misleading, turn right here to reach the vista point, **Awa'awapuhi Lookout**, in just another ¼ mile. The views into Awa'awapuhi Valley straight ahead, and Nualolo Valley off to the left, are quite simply awesome. A few renegades may walk past the guardrails and continue exploring along the very top of the cliffs, but it's very dangerous due to high winds and unstable soil. Some people have even fallen to their deaths here.

When ready, walk back to the trail junction and turn right for a short detour on the Nualolo Cliffs Trail. After just 15 minutes of switchbacking down a narrow footpath, the trail meets a pretty little waterfall in the back of the valley. It's possible to continue along the Nualolo Cliffs Trail by crossing the stream below the waterfall (see the Alternative Route, below), but this trip turns around here. Back at the trail junction, turn right onto the Awa'awapuhi Trail and follow it steadily uphill for just under 3 miles back to Waimea Canyon Dr.

Alternative Route: Nualolo Trail
5–6 hours, 11 miles (17.7km)

The Awa'awapuhi and Nualolo Trails are linked by the Nualolo Cliffs Trail. Experienced (or very ambitious) hikers can combine the three trails to make a strenuous day hike of about 9 miles, then either hitch a ride or walk an additional 2 miles along Waimea Canyon Dr back to the start. The Nualolo Cliffs Trail connects at the Nualolo Trail near the 3¼-mile mark and at the Awa'awapuhi Trail a little short of the 3-mile mark.

KAUAI

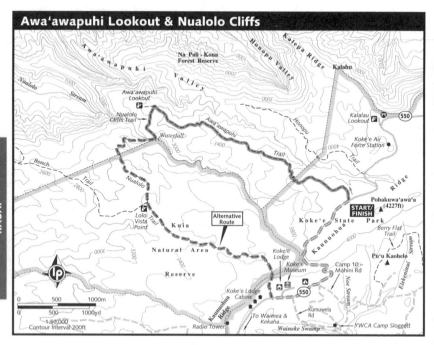

Awa'awapuhi Lookout & Nualolo Cliffs

As numerous warning signs point out, the Nualolo Cliffs Trail contains narrow and washed-out sections. Hikers do proceed at their own risk here. Most descend first on the steep Nualolo Trail, then make their way across the Nualolo Cliffs and ascend on the more gradual Awa'awapuhi Trail. It's possible to do the hike in the reverse direction, continuing on the Nualolo Cliffs Trail beyond the waterfall described earlier, but be prepared for unbelievably exhausting ascents near the end.

The 3¾-mile Nualolo Trail starts between the cabins and Koke'e Lodge off Waimea Canyon Dr. The trail begins in cool upland forest including banana *poka* and redwoods, and descends 1500ft, ending after a badly eroded stretch with a fine view from **Lolo Vista Point**, a lookout on the valley rim. There's a USGS survey marker at the lookout, at an elevation of 2234ft. After turning onto the Nualolo Cliffs Trail, hikers contour above the valley for less than 2 miles,

passing the waterfall, to where the trail meets the Awa'awapuhi Trail at a junction just uphill from the lookout.

Alakai Swamp

Duration	4–5 hours
Distance	8 miles (12.9km)
Difficulty	moderate
Start/Finish	Kalalau Lookout
Nearest Towns	Waimea (p201), Kekaha (p203)
Transport	private

Summary Enjoy a feast for the eyes – of rare bird and plant life, breathtaking lookouts and more – while traversing a boardwalk through one of Hawaii's rarest natural preserves.

Many native and endemic Hawaiian bird species now exist solely on Kauai, the only island that's yet free of the mongoose, an introduced mammal that preys on the eggs of ground-nesting birds. More than a few of these rare birds inhabit the Alakai Swamp. The Alakai Swamp Preserve is inaccessible enough that even invasive plants haven't been able to choke out the endemic swamp vegetation, and native bird species still have a stronghold. Parts of the swamp receive so little sunlight that moss grows thick and fat on all sides of the trees. Most people that get to this swamp see it from a helicopter, but it's far better to explore the extensive network of trails from eye level.

An alternative start/finish point for this hike (see Alternative Start/Finish: Alakai Swamp Trailhead, p216) cuts out strenuous sections of the Pihea Trail.

PLANNING

The Alakai Swamp is often shrouded in fog and rain. Come prepared to get wet (ie, bring rain gear). Although a boardwalk has been constructed through much of the swamp, lightweight gaiters may certainly still be useful. Be sure to carry enough water, as any available freshwater along the trail must be filtered or otherwise treated before drinking.

Maps

The color 1:50,000 *Recreation Map of Western Kauai* covers the trail. The USGS 1:24,000 map *Haena* covers the entire swamp area.

GETTING TO/FROM THE HIKE

This hike starts from the Kalalau Lookout parking lot, near the 18-mile marker at the end of Waimea Canyon Dr, about 3 miles past Koke'e Lodge and the museum.

THE HIKE

From the parking lot walk out to the **Kalalau Lookout**, where from a height of 4000ft, hikers can look deep into the green depths of the valley and straight out to the sea. Notice the cone-shaped pinnacles along the valley walls. One legend says that rain has sculpted the cliffs into the shapes of the proud chiefs who are buried in the mountains.

Walk back to Waimea Canyon Dr and turn left. Now closed to vehicular traffic, the paved road continues east 1 mile to **Pu'u o Kila Lookout**, where it dead-ends at a parking lot. This is the last leg of the aborted Koke'e–Haena Hwy, which would have linked Koke'e with the North Shore,

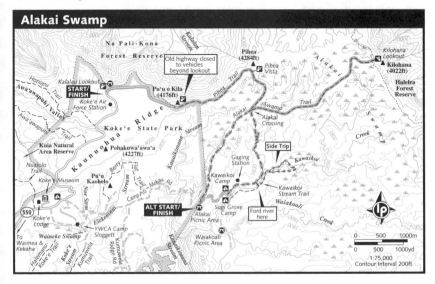

thus creating a circle-island road. One look at the cliffs at the end of the road, and you'll understand why the scheme was scrapped.

From this lookout, you can enjoy another grand view into Kalalau Valley and catch glimpses inland of the Alakai Swamp Preserve. A sign here points to sacred Mt Waialeale. The Pihea Trail starts from this lookout and combines coastal views with an opportunity to see some of the Alakai wilderness. It climbs the ridge straight ahead and runs along what was to be the road. The beginning of the trail was graded in the 1950s, before plans to make this the last leg of the circle-island road were abandoned. Nowadays much of this road has become steeply eroded, but is still wide enough to be manageable on foot.

The first mile of the trail runs along the ridge, offering fine views into Kalalau Valley, before coming to the small fork for **Pihea Vista**, a viewpoint that requires a steep scramble to reach. The Pihea Trail then turns inland through wetland forest and, at about 1¾ miles, arrives at aptly-named **Alakai Crossing**. At this fairy-tale intersection deep in the damp, spooky forest, four boardwalks leading in different directions meet in the middle of nowhere.

Taking a hard left, the trail continues for 2 miles through rain forest and exposed bogs filled with ferns, perfectly blossoming ohia and old telephone poles before reaching **Kilohana Lookout**, perched on the rim of Wainiha Pali. If it's not overcast – and that's a big 'if' considering this is near the wettest place on earth – hikers will be rewarded with a sweeping view of the Wainiha and Hanalei Valleys to the north. While most of the swamp trail has been spanned with boardwalks, this can still be extremely wet and slippery, and in places you can expect to have to slog through mud and even rock-hop across a stream before reaching the lookout, which is the turn-around point for this trip.

Alternative Start/Finish: Alakai Swamp Trailhead
2½–3½ hours, 8 miles (12.9km)
With a 4WD vehicle, it's possible to drive down Camp 10–Mohihi Rd to the main Alakai Swamp trailhead after about 3½ miles by turning left at the major junctions. Doing this cuts out the most strenuous sections of the Pihea Trail described in the earlier hike, substituting instead a gentle stroll on a grassy ridge and over boardwalks through the swamp to Alakai Crossing. From here continue straight (heading east) to Kilohana Lookout. On the return from the lookout, detour at Alakai Crossing by turning left and staying on the Pihea Trail until Kawaikoi Camp, then walk back up Mohihi Road to the starting point. Overall, the total distance is about the same, but with far less elevation gain or loss. See the Side Trip: Kawaikoi Stream Trail (below) for details of a deviation along this route.

Side Trip: Kawaikoi Stream Trail
1½–2 hours, 4 miles (6.4km)
On the way back from Kilohana Lookout, those who can't quite bear to leave this beautiful area yet, or who want to seek additional chances for bird-watching, can detour at Alakai Crossing. Turn left (south) onto the Pihea Trail, which moves through native rain forest dappled with sunlight and brilliantly colored mosses, low-lying ferns and ti plants. The boardwalk descends, then ends at a makeshift log bench, from where the trail continues as a grassy footpath that later switchbacks down toward Kawaikoi Stream.

The temperature drops and so does the elevation. After passing through a number of muddy gullies and then up over tree roots, the trail reaches a picnic shelter on the left. Shortly thereafter a sign points out the stream ford to the Kawaikoi Stream Trail on the far bank, which beckons with bird song and, in spring, the licorice scent of Kauai's inedible *mokihana* berries. (Do not touch or pick the berries, since the juice can cause skin blistering.) Should you choose to detour here, the stream's loop trail will add another 2 miles to this side trip.

Continuing straight ahead on the Pihea Trail, the footpath becomes boggy around stands of invasive strawberry guava, then dries out again. About 2 miles from Alakai Crossing, the trail comes out at **Kawaikoi**

Camp. Walk straight across the grassy campground and exit through the gate, turning right onto Camp 10–Mohihi Rd, a dirt 4WD road. It's a ¾-mile walk uphill to the signposted Alakai Swamp Trail and picnic area. Turn right here to reach the official Alakai Swamp trailhead, beyond which a footpath descends through a shady tree tunnel, then gently rolls up and down through a bog of stunted ohia and other plants. Just as things get very muddy, the trail rejoins the boardwalk and arrives back at Alakai Crossing just over a mile later. Turn left to rejoin the Pihea Trail on its way back to Kalalau Lookout.

Other Hikes

NORTH SHORE
Hanalei–Okoleho Trail

If this 5-mile round-trip trail's steep grades alone don't induce a heart attack, its views – of the verdant North Shore peaks, Hanalei Bay and Kilauaea Lighthouse – just might. Coming from Lihue via Princeville, follow the Kuhio Hwy (Hwy 560), then take a left after the Hanalei Bridge and follow Okihi Rd for about ½ mile to a dirt parking lot opposite a footbridge. Cross over the bridge and enter a confusing network of trails-of-use. Basically, the trail turns right at the first two forks (left turns go to bird-watching overlooks of the pond inside Hanalei National Wildlife Refuge). Before a gate marked 'Unauthorized Entry Prohibited', turn left up the dirt 4WD road, which later becomes a forest path; from that point, it's another 1¾ miles of impossibly steep scrambling to reach a final viewpoint framed by ti plants. Allow around 1½ hours each way.

KOKE'E STATE PARK
Kawaikoi Stream Trail

This scenic mountain stream trail of almost 3 miles round-trip begins between the Sugi Grove and Kawaikoi campgrounds, off Camp 10–Mohihi Rd. It starts out following the southern side of Kawaikoi Stream, then makes a lollipop loop by climbing to the right, then swinging back around to ford the stream twice, all the while passing a variety of native plants, with a few boardwalks. If the stream is running high, don't take the crossings. Camp 10–Mohihi Rd begins up past the Koke'e Museum on the east side of Waimea Canyon Dr. Like many of the dirt roads in Koke'e, when it's dry, it can accommodate ordinary cars, at least part way. However, on those occasions when the road is really wet and rutted, even 4WD vehicles can have difficulty.

Halemanu–Koke'e Trail

A little farther down Halemanu Rd past the Canyon Trail (p211) is the start of the sweet little Halemanu–Koke'e Trail. Signs of recovery from devastating Hurricane Iniki in 1992 are evident. This easy 1¼-mile (each way) nature trail passes through a native forest of koa and ohia trees that provide a habitat for native birds, including the *i'iwi, apapane, amakihi* and *elepaio*. One of the common plants found on this trail is banana *poka,* a member of the passionfruit family and a serious invasive pest. It has pretty pink flowers, but it drapes the forest with its vines and chokes out less aggressive native plants. The trail ends near YWCA Camp Sloggett, about ½ mile downhill from Koke'e Lodge.

Travel Facts

TOURIST OFFICES
Local Tourist Offices
The administrative office of the **Hawaii Visitors and Convention Bureau** *(HVCB; ☎ 923-1811, 800-464-2924; ⓦ www.gohawaii.com)* can mail general information and has a helpful telephone service. Oriented to short-term vacationers and conventioneers, HVCB visitor information offices are found on Oahu, the Big Island, Maui and Kauai, but usually the same brochures and tourists maps are available at the airports.

Tourist Offices Abroad
HVCB changes its overseas agents frequently. The following are the current addresses for HVCB representatives abroad.

Australia (☎ 02-9955-2619, fax 02-9955-2171, ⓔ rlane@thesalesteam.com.au) c/o The Sales Team, 97-103 Pacific Hwy, Suite 602A, North Sydney, NSW 2060

Canada (☎ 604-669-6691, fax 604-669-6075, ⓔ compre@intergate.bc.ca) c/o Comprehensive Travel Industry Services, 1260 Hornby St, Suite 104, Vancouver, BC V6Z 1W2

Germany (☎ 180-223-040, fax 610-236-6611, ⓔ hawaii@noblekom.de) noble kommunikation GmbH, Luisenstrasse 7, 63263 Neu-Isenberg

Hong Kong (☎ 2524-1361, fax 2524-9560, ⓔ pacamltd@netvigator.com) c/o Pacam Ltd, 10/F Tung Ming Building, 40 Des Voeux Rd Central, Room 1003, Hong Kong SAR

New Zealand (☎ 9-977-2234, fax 9-977-2236, ⓔ darragh@walwor.co.nz) c/o Walshes World, Level 6, 18 Shortland Street, Private Bag 92136, Auckland

UK (☎ 020-8941-4009, fax 020-8941-4001, ⓔ jblissett@hvcb.org) c/o Box 208, Sunbury-on-Thames, Middlesex TW16 5RJ

VISAS & DOCUMENTS
Passports
Your passport must be valid for at least six months after your intended stay in the USA. Technically Canadians don't need a passport if they are arriving from another destination within the western hemisphere, but they do need official proof of Canadian citizenship with photo ID.

Visas
Visas are not required for citizens of the EU, Australia and New Zealand for visits up to 90 days. For other eligible countries and details of the visa waiver program, check with the **Bureau of Citizenship and Immigration Services** *(ⓦ www.immigration.gov)*.

All other travelers, for example South African nationals, will need a visitor visa. Visas can be obtained at most US consulates overseas; there is a nonrefundable $100 application fee. Those planning to travel through other countries before arriving in the USA are generally better off applying for their US visa while they are still in their home country, rather than while on the road.

If you want to stay in the USA longer than the date stamped on your passport, only certain classes of visa can be extended. Contact the **Honolulu District Office** *(☎ 532-2701; 595 Ala Moana Blvd, Honolulu) before* the stamped date.

Onward Tickets
A round-trip ticket that is non-refundable in the US is required to enter the country.

Travel Insurance
Buy a policy that generously covers you for medical expenses, theft or loss of luggage and tickets, and for cancellation of and delays in your travel arrangements. It may be worth taking out cover for the cost of rescue. Check that your policy doesn't exclude hiking as a dangerous activity.

Buy travel insurance as early as possible to ensure you'll be compensated for any unforeseen accidents or delays. If items are lost or stolen get a police report immediately – otherwise your insurer might not pay up.

Driving License & Permits
With very few exceptions, you can legally drive in the USA as long as you have a valid

Copies

All important documents (passport, credit cards, travel insurance policy, driver's license etc) should be photocopied before you leave home. Leave one copy at home and keep another with you, separate from the originals.

Another way of storing your travel documents is with Lonely Planet's free on-line Travel Vault. Create your vault at [W] www .ekno.lonelyplanet.com.

❀ ❀ ❀ ❀ ❀ ❀ ❀ ❀ ❀ ❀ ❀ ❀ ❀

driver's license issued by your home country. If your license is not written in English, you may be required to show an international driving permit; a translation of the license may also prove helpful.

Travel Discounts

Flashing your under-26 youth card or student identification may get you slight concessions at attractions, cultural events or live performances. Members of the American Automobile Association (AAA) and associated automobile clubs can get substantial discounts on car rental and airfares, as can members of the American Association of Retired Persons (AARP) and its affiliates. Senior citizens (usually those aged 65 and older) usually qualify for good discounts on transportation and hotel accommodations, as well as entry to museums, tourist attractions and cinemas. You may be asked to show proof of age, so carry photo ID with you.

EMBASSIES & CONSULATES
US Embassies

For other US diplomatic representation abroad, click to [W] usembassy.state.gov for links.

Australia (☎ 02-6214-5600, [W] usembassy -australia.state.gov) Moonah Place, Yarralumla, ACT 2600
Canada (☎ 613-238-5335, [W] www.usembassy canada.gov) 490 Sussex Dr, Ottawa, Ontario K1N 1G8
France (☎ 01 43 12 22 22, [W] www.amb-usa.fr) 2 Ave Gabriel, 75008 Paris

Germany (☎ 030-8305-0, [W] www.usembassy.de) Neustädtische Kirchstrasse 4-5,10117 Berlin
Ireland (☎ 1-668-8777) 42 Elgin Rd, Dublin 4
Israel (☎ 3-519-7410, [W] www.usembassy -israel.org.il) 41 Hayarkon St, Tel Aviv POB 26180
Italy (☎ 06-4674-1, [W] www.usembassy.it) Via Vittorio Veneto 119/A, 00187 Roma
Japan (☎ 03-3224-5000, [W] usembassy.state .gov/tokyo/) 1-10-5 Akasaka, Minato-ku, Tokyo 107-8420
Mexico (☎ 55-5080-2000, [W] www.usembassy -mexico.gov) Paseo de la Reforma 305, Colonia Cuauhtemoc 06500 Mexico, D.F.
Netherlands (☎ 70-310-9209, [W] www.usemb.nl) Lange Voorhout 102, 2514 EJ The Hague
New Zealand (☎ 4-462-6000, [W] wellington .usembassy.gov) 29 Fitzherbert Terrace, PO Box 1190, Thorndon, Wellington
Singapore (☎ 6476-9100, [W] singapore.usembassy .gov) 27 Napier Rd, Singapore 258508
Spain (☎ 91-587-2200, [W] www.embusa.es) Calle Serrano 75, 28006 Madrid
Switzerland (☎ 31-357-7011, [W] www.us -embassy.ch) Jubiläumstrasse 93, 3001 Bern
UK (☎ 020-7499-9000, [W] www.usembassy .org.uk) 24 Grosvenor Square, London W1A 1AE

Consulates in Hawaii

The following consulates and diplomatic representatives are in Honolulu.

Australia (☎ 524-5050, fax 531-5142) 1000 Bishop St, Penthouse Suite
Denmark (☎ 844-2028, fax 852-6778) 285 Sand Island Access Rd
Germany (☎ 946-3819) 252 Paoa Place, Suite 4-1
Italy (☎ 531-2277) c/o Law Offices, 735 Bishop St, Suite 201
Netherlands (☎ 531-6897, fax 531-6895, [e] honolulu@ncla.org) 745 Fort Street Mall, Suite 702
New Zealand (☎ 543-7900, fax 543-7523) c/o Hawaiian Electric Industries Inc, 900 Richards St, Suite 414
Norway (☎ 593-1240, fax 373-2187) 5323 Kalanianaole Hwy
Sweden (☎ 528-4777, fax 523-1888) 737 Bishop St, Suite 2600

CUSTOMS

Each visitor can import 1L of liquor, 200 cigarettes and 100 cigars (provided they are not Cuban), but you must be at least 21 years old to possess the liquor, and 18 years old for the cigarettes and cigars. Each traveler is also permitted to bring up to $100 worth of gift items into the US duty-free.

There are restrictions on taking most fresh fruits and plants into Hawaii to prevent the spread of pests and disease, and customs officials are militant. If you are found to be carrying such items, expect them to be confiscated and to run the risk of being fined.

MONEY

Most Americans do not carry large amounts of cash for everyday use, relying instead on a mix of credit cards, ATMs and direct debit cards. Numerous ATMs are linked to the international Cirrus, Plus and Maestro networks, but expect a surcharge of about $1.50 per transaction. Gas stations, convenience stores and fast-food joints may not accept bills over $20. Personal checks are rarely accepted unless they are drawn on a Hawaiian bank account.

In case of an emergency, it's quickest and easiest to have money wired via **Western Union** (☎ 800-325-6000; Ⓦ www.western union.com), which has several outlets in Hawaii, or Thomas Cook's **MoneyGram** (☎ 800-287-7362; Ⓦ www.thomascook.com), which has an office at Honolulu airport. A $1000 transfer should cost around $75 and take no more than 15 minutes.

Exchange Rates

A good currency converter is Ⓦ www.oanda .com. At the time of going to print, exchange rates were:

country	unit		US dollar
Australia	A$1	=	$0.65
Canada	C$1	=	$0.73
euro zone	€1	=	$1.17
Japan	¥100	=	$0.83
New Zealand	NZ$1	=	$0.57
United Kingdom	UK£1	=	$1.63

Exchanging Money

Cash ATM withdrawals at banks usually guarantee the best currency exchange rates.

Many ATMs also give cash advances using credit cards such as Visa, MasterCard or American Express, generally for a 3% or $5 minimum fee.

Banks offer better rates on exchanging foreign currency or traveler's checks than most exchange bureaus. Both are found at Honolulu airport and all the main tourist areas. Some hotels and souvenir shops handle foreign exchange services, but rates aren't likely to be good.

You can save yourself the hassle and fees involved by purchasing Visa, American Express or Thomas Cook traveler's checks in US currency before departure. Then you can use them just like cash almost anywhere on the islands. American Express and Thomas Cook cash their own traveler's checks fee-free at branch offices, including in Honolulu.

On the Hike

Hikers won't be able to spend much money while on the trail. It's a good idea to carry petty cash 'just in case' and for small expenses before *and* after hiking (such as national park entry fees, camping permits, hot meals, a beer etc).

Costs

What it costs to travel in Hawaii depends largely on when you choose to visit and how much comfort you require. Renting a car is likely to be the major expense at any time of year. Accommodations rates rise during peak tourist season (mid-December to early April) and possibly also during summer vacation (June to August).

Most everyday items cost approximately 25% more than on the US mainland, although prices really do vary from island to island.

A typical daily budget might include:

item/service	cost ($)
campsite (per person)	5
youth hostel	20
meal at budget restaurant	10
compact car rental per day	30
gallon of unleaded petrol	1.80

Tipping & Bargaining

Tip restaurant servers 15% to 20%, except for outrageously rude service. If the restaurant automatically adds a 'service charge' (usually for groups of six or more), do not double-tip. Bartenders get at least $1 for one or two drinks, 15% when buying a round. Give taxi drivers 10% of the fare, rounding up to the nearest dollar. Skycaps and bellhops get $1 to $2 per item; housekeepers at better hotels are tipped $1 to $2 per day.

Taxes

The state of Hawaii imposes a 4.17% sales tax on almost everything, including food. Another 7.24% room tax brings the total surcharge on most accommodations to 11.41%. An additional $3-a-day 'road use' tax applies to car rentals.

Unless otherwise stated, prices in this guidebook do not include applicable taxes.

POST & COMMUNICATIONS
Post

The **United States Postal Service** (USPS; ☎ 800-275-8777, TTY ☎ 877-877-7833; w www.usps.gov) is reliable and inexpensive. Mail delivery to and from the Hawaiian Islands can take a little longer than on the US mainland. Call the toll-free number to find out the nearest post office branch location and opening hours. Hotel concierges, convenience stores and supermarkets sell stamps (usually for a little more than face value).

Postal Rates At the time of writing, 1st-class mail within the US is 37¢ for letters up to 1oz (23¢ each additional ounce) and 21¢ for postcards. International airmail rates are 80¢ for a 1oz letter and 70¢ for a postcard; both 20¢ less to either Canada or Mexico. Aerograms cost 70¢.

Receiving Mail You can have poste restante mail sent to you c/o General Delivery at many post offices in Hawaii. General delivery mail is usually held for up to 30 days.

To pick up your mail in Honolulu, have it addressed to:

YOUR FAMILY NAME, First Name
c/o General Delivery, Main Post Office
3600 Aolele St, Honolulu, HI 96820

Telephone

The telephone code for all of Hawaii is ☎ 808. Only dial the code when calling from one island to another, or when calling Hawaii from outside the state.

Public payphones are either coin- or card-operated; some also accept credit cards. An untimed local call costs between $0.35 and $0.50. Emergency ☎ 911 calls and toll-free numbers (those that begin ☎ 800, ☎ 877, ☎ 888 etc) are free. You can find payphones at beach parks, hotel lobbies and convenience shops, as well as a few campgrounds and trailheads.

Beware that many condos and hotels add a service charge of 50¢ to $1 for each local or toll-free call made from room phones, plus hefty surcharges for long-distance and international calls.

Phonecards Lonely Planet's ekno communication card, specifically aimed at travelers, provides competitive international calls (avoid using it for local calls), messaging services and free email. Visit w www.ekno.lonelyplanet.com for information on joining and accessing the service.

Prepaid phonecards are available at convenience stores, supermarkets and pharmacies. The key is to read all of the fine print *before* buying any card; those that advertise the cheapest per-minute rates may charge hefty connection fees (especially from payphones) and hide miscellaneous surcharges.

Useful Numbers	
Emergency	☎ 911
Directory Assistance	☎ 411
Toll-Free Directory Assistance	
	☎ 1-800-555-1212
Operator Assistance	☎ 0
International Operator Assistance	☎ 00
National Weather Service	
see Weather Information p42	

Cards sold by major telecommunication companies like AT&T may actually offer better deals and more reliable service than fly-by-night companies.

Cell Phones The USA uses a variety of cell phone (mobile phone) systems, 99% of which are incompatible with the standard used throughout Europe, Asia and Africa. Visitors from abroad should check with their own cellular service provider about using cell phones in Hawaii, as sometimes calls are routed internationally. US mainland travelers should beware of exorbitant roaming surcharges. (Either way, it becomes very expensive for a 'local' call.)

Hawaii's mobile telephone network has surprisingly good coverage across Oahu and the other main islands, but it remains extremely patchy (often nonexistent) in parts of the backcountry. If you have trouble accessing the network, try moving a short way along the slope to improve reception. Please remember that many people find cell phones intrusive on the trail, so make your calls discreetly.

Email & Internet Access
Most public libraries provide free Internet access. A Hawaii public library card (a visitor's card costs $10 for three months, or $25 for five years) is required. You may also be required to sign up for time slots (usually limited to less than an hour) in advance, or be subject to limited walk-in availability.

Cybercafés exist in cities and larger towns, and typically charge around $6 per hour for fast connections. Some hostels and B&Bs also offer Internet access.

TIME
Hawaii Standard Time is 10 hours behind GMT. When it's noon in Hawaii, it's 2pm in Los Angeles, 5pm in New York, 10pm in London, 7am the next day in Tokyo, 8am the next day in Sydney and 10am the next day in Auckland.

As Hawaii does not observe Daylight Saving Time, the time difference is one hour greater during those months when other places *are* observing Daylight Saving Time, for example, in the rest of North America from the first Sunday in April to the last Sunday in October.

BUSINESS HOURS
Typical office hours are 8:30am to 4:30pm Monday to Friday. Retail shops are usually open 10am to 6pm Monday to Saturday, noon to 5pm on Sunday. Some gas stations, pharmacies, grocery and convenience stores in major cities are open 24 hours, but those that sell liquor may only legally do so between 6am and 11pm daily. In smaller towns, all services (including restaurants and gas stations) may close quite early, sometimes before 5pm.

Banks are usually open 8:30am to 4pm Monday to Thursday, closing around 5pm or 6pm on Friday. Bank branches inside supermarkets keep longer hours, typically 10am to 7pm weekdays and 10am to 4pm weekends. Post offices tend to keep regular office hours, but main postal branches stay open later on weekdays and also Saturday morning.

Banks, schools and government offices (including post offices) are closed on major holidays, when public transit, museums and other services opt for a Sunday schedule. Private businesses and restaurants may also close on Independence Day, Thanksgiving, Christmas and New Year's Day.

PUBLIC HOLIDAYS
Holidays falling on a weekend are usually observed the following Monday. Major 2004 public holidays in Hawaii are:

New Year's Day January 1
Dr Martin Luther King Jr Day January 19
Presidents' Day February 16
Prince Jonah Kuhio Kalanianaole Day March 26
Good Friday April 9
Memorial Day May 31
King Kamehameha Day June 11
Independence Day July 4
Statehood Day August 15
Labor Day September 6
Veterans Day November 11
Thanksgiving November 25
Christmas Day December 25

Getting There & Away

Almost all visitors to Hawaii arrive by air. Oahu is a major hub and an intermediate stop on many flights between the US mainland and Asia, Australia, New Zealand and the South Pacific. Passengers on these routes can usually make a free stopover in Honolulu, from where interisland flights fan out to Neighbor Islands (the main Hawaiian Islands apart from Oahu).

AIR
Airports & Airlines
Virtually all international flights, and the vast majority of domestic flights, arrive at Honolulu International Airport. Some direct international and domestic flights land at Kona and Hilo, both on the Big Island, and Kahului (Maui). A few domestic airlines schedule flights to Lihue (Kauai). Interisland flights arrive and depart from all of Hawaii's airports, although smaller airfields may only be used by private and charter flights.

airport	code	number
Honolulu	HNL	☎ 836-6413
Kona (Keahole)	KOA	☎ 329-3423
Hilo	ITO	☎ 934-5840
Lihue	LIH	☎ 246-1440
Kahului	OGG	☎ 872-3830
Molokai (Ho'olehua)	MKK	☎ 567-6361

Major airlines include US-based carriers with domestic and international services, as well as foreign airlines that fly to the USA. Charter airlines also fly to Hawaii from within the USA.

The major airlines include:

Air Canada (Ⓦ www.aircanada.com)
Air France (Ⓦ www.airfrance.com)
Air New Zealand (Ⓦ www.airnz.co.nz)
All Nippon Air (Ⓦ www.fly-ana.com)
Aloha Airlines (Ⓦ www.alohaairlines.com)
American Airlines (Ⓦ www.aa.com)
American Trans Air (Ⓦ www.ata.com)
Continental (Ⓦ www.continental.com)
Delta (Ⓦ www.delta.com)

Warning

The information in this chapter is particularly vulnerable to change: prices for international travel are volatile, routes are introduced and canceled, schedules change, special deals come and go, and rules and visa requirements are amended. You should check directly with the airline or a travel agent to make sure you understand how a fare (and ticket you may buy) works and be aware of security requirements for international travel.

The upshot of this is that you should get opinions, quotes and advice from as many airlines and travel agents as possible before you part with your hard-earned cash. The details given in this section should be regarded as pointers and are not a substitute for your own careful, up-to-date research.

Hawaiian Airlines (Ⓦ www.hawaiianair.com)
Japan Airlines (Ⓦ www.japanair.com)
Korean Air (Ⓦ www.koreanair.com)
Northwest Airlines (Ⓦ www.nwa.com)
Polynesian Airlines (Ⓦ www.polynesianairlines .co.nz)
Qantas (Ⓦ www.qantas.com.au)
United Airlines (Ⓦ www.ual.com)

Departure Tax
All taxes and security fees for US airports are normally included in the price of tickets when you buy them, whether they're purchased in the USA or abroad. There are no additional departure taxes to pay when leaving Hawaii.

US Mainland
Competition is high among domestic and international airlines flying to Honolulu. However, only a few airlines and charter-flight companies fly directly to the Neighbor Islands, and at any given time any of them could be offering the cheapest fares.

Hawaiian Airlines and Aloha Airlines have daily nonstop flights to Honolulu, mainly departing West Coast cities. For those flying from other parts of the US, it may be cheaper to buy two separate tickets – one to the West Coast with a low-fare carrier such

Best-Value Air Tickets

For short-term travel, it's usually cheaper to travel midweek and to take advantage of short-lived promotional offers. Return tickets usually work out cheaper than two one-ways.

Booking through a travel agent or via airlines' websites is generally the cheapest way to get tickets. However, while online ticket sales are fine for a simple one-way or return trip on specified dates, they're no substitute for a travel agent who is familiar with special deals and can offer all kinds of advice.

Buying tickets with a credit card should mean you get a refund if you don't get what you paid for. Go through a licensed travel agent, who should be covered by an industry guarantee scheme.

Whatever your choice, make sure you take out travel insurance (p218).

❁ ❁ ❁ ❁ ❁ ❁ ❁ ❁ ❁ ❁ ❁ ❁ ❁

as Southwest Airlines, and then another ticket to Hawaii.

A few charter airlines, such as American Trans Air (ATA), fly direct from the West Coast to Hawaii. Fares are competitive, but there are only a few scheduled flights per week. Package tour companies sometimes offer the best airfare deals, even if you don't want to buy the whole 'package' (including hotel accommodations, car rental etc). Try **Sun Trips** (☎ 800-786-8747; w www.suntrips .com) or **Pleasant Hawaiian Holidays** (☎ 800-742-9244; w www.2hawaii.com).

A Space-Available FlightPass from **Air Tech** (☎ 212-219-7000; w www.airtech.com) is surely the cheapest way to fly between the US West Coast and Hawaii. If you provide a two- to four-day travel window, Air Tech just about guarantees you a seat.

Canada

Air Canada flies to Honolulu from Vancouver, Calgary, Toronto and Montreal. Many of its lowest fares are only available for online bookings. Charter flight companies and ticket consolidators offer competitive deals, especially for steeply discounted flights from Montreal.

The UK & Continental Europe

From Europe, most travelers to Hawaii fly west via New York, Chicago or Los Angeles. If stopping off in Asia appeals to you, consider going in the reverse direction with a Round-the-World (RTW) ticket.

Australia, New Zealand & South Pacific

Qantas flies direct to Honolulu from Sydney or Melbourne. Other international carriers along these routes include Air Canada, American Airlines and United Airlines. No airline currently offers attractive fares between Auckland and Honolulu. Qantas has direct flights between Hawaii and Fiji. Hawaiian Airlines has flights to Tahiti.

Circle Pacific itineraries allow you to swing through parts of Asia and the Pacific, making several stops along the way. The only catch is that you must travel in the same circular direction with the same partnered airlines. There's typically a maximum stay of six months. Air New Zealand's Circle Pacific Escapade fare, offered in conjunction with Singapore Airlines, allows unlimited stops as long as you don't travel more than 22,000 miles.

Asia

Hawaii is a top destination for Japanese tourists. Japan Airlines (JAL) flies direct to Honolulu from Tokyo, Osaka and other gateways. Excursion fares vary with the departing city and the season. Discount fares to Honolulu with All Nippon Airways (ANA) cost almost half as much, matching the best fares offered by US-based competitors Northwest Airlines and United Airlines. From elsewhere around Asia, other

Cheap Seats

Because interisland flights (see Air, p225, under Getting Around) can work out to be so inexpensive, travelers might save hundreds of dollars by booking their flight from home only as far as Honolulu and then taking an interisland flight for the final leg of their trip.

❁ ❁ ❁ ❁ ❁ ❁ ❁ ❁ ❁ ❁ ❁ ❁ ❁

Baggage Restrictions

Airlines impose tight restrictions on carry-on baggage. No sharp implements of any kind are allowed onto the plane, so pack items such as pocket knives, camping cutlery, hiking poles and first-aid kits into your checked luggage.

If you're carrying a camping stove you should remember that airlines also ban liquid fuels and gas cartridges from all baggage, both check-through and carry-on. Empty all fuel bottles and buy what you need at your destination. Note US airport security may confiscate reusable fuel canisters (even if they are empty).

major international carriers include Korean Air and China Airlines.

SEA

Most private yachts weighing anchor in Hawaii do so in Honolulu before visiting the South Pacific. Experienced crew looking to sail between Hawaii and the US mainland or the South Pacific can try one of the following websites:

Boatcrew (W www.boatcrew.net)
Latitude 38 (W www.latitude38.com)
San Francisco Sailing (W www.sfsailing.com)

Getting Around

AIR
Domestic Air Services

Interisland air travel is competitive in Hawaii. Flights between Neighbor Islands may involve connections or a stop in Honolulu. The major interisland carriers are **Hawaiian Airlines** (Oahu ☎ 838-1555, Neighbor Islands ☎ 800-882-8811, US mainland & Canada ☎ 800-367-5320; W www.hawaiianair.com) and **Aloha Airlines** (Oahu ☎ 484-1111, Hilo & Kona ☎ 935-5771, Maui ☎ 244-9071, Kauai ☎ 245-3691, US mainland & Canada 800-367-5250; W www.alohaairlines.com). Both offer discounts for advance and online bookings. Always ask what other new promotions are being offered.

Interisland flights quite often have empty seats. If you ask the agent at the gate to fly stand-by on the next available flight, chances are you'll get a seat. The flip side of this convenient phenomenon is that a few interisland flights end up being canceled each day, so stay flexible.

Commuter Airlines An affiliate of Aloha Airlines, **Island Air** (☎ 484-2222, Neighbor Islands 800-652-6541, US mainland & Canada ☎ 800-323-3345; W www.islandair.com) offers the most extensive schedule of commuter flights, serving Hawaii's smaller airports using prop planes. Book flights either directly or through Aloha Airlines.

Other commuter airlines, sometimes consisting of just a single plane, frequently come and go in Hawaii. Keep in mind that schedules are a bit elastic – if there aren't advance bookings for a flight, the flight is often canceled. Call in advance before making any definite plans.

Flight Coupons You can often save money by paying for flights with discounted interisland flight coupons, which currently cost around $75, depending on for which airline (Hawaiian, Aloha or Island Air). One of the many advantages of using flight coupons is that there are no penalties for changing the date or time of your flight reservation, as long as seats are still available. Just make your flight reservation as you normally would and inform the airline representative that you'll be paying with a coupon. You don't have to be a Hawaii resident to qualify.

Flight coupons are sold by most travel agencies, as well as at supermarkets and convenience stores. Hawaiian Airlines sells its coupons from Bank of Hawaii ATMs, one of which can be found in the interisland terminal at Honolulu Airport. You will need to use your PIN number along with your credit card (Visa or MasterCard). Hawaiian and Aloha each sell coupon booklets containing six interisland flight tickets at all of their airport ticket counters in Hawaii. Usually these can be used by any number of people on any flight without restrictions.

BUS

Oahu has an award-winning public transportation system, but local bus services on the Big Island, Maui and Kauai are only really useful for getting around between major towns and/or resort areas. Hikers who rely on public transportation face frustrating limitations, as few routes directly serve trailheads.

CAR & MOTORCYCLE

Having your own set of wheels is almost indispensable for travel around the Neighbor Islands and off-the-beaten-path areas of Oahu. Trailheads are generally accessible by conventional cars, although 4WD vehicles may sometimes be preferable, especially when roads are quite muddy or unmaintained gravel. Unfortunately there is no car transportation between islands and there are no longer any multi-island car rental deals.

Rental rates range from $25 to $45 per day and $140 to $200 per week, more in peak season; there's a $3-per-day state road tax. Nationwide rental car companies found at island airports include **Alamo** (☎ 800-462-5266), **Avis** (☎ 800-230-4898), **Budget** (☎ 800-527-0700), **Dollar** (☎ 800-800-4000), **Hertz** (☎ 800-654-3131), **National** (☎ 800-328-4567) and **Thrifty** (☎ 800-847-4389). Keep in mind that no one rents to drivers under 21 and many refuse to rent to (or tack on hefty surcharges for) drivers under 25.

The **American Automobile Association** (AAA; Oahu ☎ 593-2221, Neighbor Islands ☎ 800-736-2886; W www.aaa-hawaii.com) has an office in Honolulu that gives out travel advice and free road maps to members. The AAA also provides **emergency roadside service** (☎ 800-222-4357). AAA has reciprocal agreements with other motoring associations, such as the Canadian Automobile Association (CAA) and the Royal Automobile Club of Victoria (RACV) in Australia, so bring your membership card from home.

Road Rules

The minimum age for driving a car in Hawaii is 18 years. If you're under the age of 25,

you should call the car rental agencies in advance to check their policies regarding age restrictions and surcharges.

The minimum age for renting motorcycles is usually 21 years; you will need to show a valid motorcycle license. The minimum age for renting a scooter or moped (scooters are OK at highway speeds, while mopeds are only for around town) is 16 years.

As with the rest of the USA, driving is on the right-hand side of the road. Speed limits are posted *and* enforced. Drivers at a red light can turn right after coming to a full stop and yielding to oncoming traffic, unless there's a sign prohibiting the turn. Stay alert for one-lane bridge crossings: one direction of traffic usually has the right of way while the other must obey the posted yield sign.

The crime of driving while intoxicated (DWI) is legally defined as having a blood alcohol level of greater than 0.08%. Hawaii also requires the use of seat belts for drivers and front-seat passengers. There are no helmet laws for motorcyclists in Hawaii.

BICYCLE

Cyclists in Hawaii face a number of challenges: blistering heat, narrow one-lane highways, traffic jams along the coast, inland mountains and the same persistent crosswinds that so delight windsurfers. The stunning scenery may entice hard-core cyclists, but casual riders hoping to use a bike as a primary source of transportation may not find it feasible. Although Hawaii has been slow to adopt cycle-friendly traits, a few island roads now include bike lanes. Cycling maps, which are available from bicycle rental and repair shops, outline mountain biking trails and recommend highway routes, including helpful elevation, wind and distance charts.

HITCHING

Hitching is never safe in any country and we don't recommend it. Travelers who decide to hitch should understand that they are taking a small but potentially serious risk. People who do choose to hitch will be safer if they travel in pairs and let someone know where they are planning to go. Women traveling alone should be extremely cautious about hitching anywhere.

Hitchhiking is illegal in Hawaii, but that hardly stops anyone. Police will generally look the other way if you hide your thumb until they cruise past. It's easier to get cars to stop along highways where traffic isn't too heavy, so walk as far out of town as possible. On backcountry roads around trailheads, a kindly local or passing tourist may pick you up – eventually.

BOAT

The only interisland passenger ferry services depart Maui's Lahaina Harbor for Molokai and Lanai.

TAXI

All of Hawaii's main islands have taxis. Rates vary, as they're set by each county, but average about $10 per 5 miles. Except at major airports, hotels and resorts, or around the Honolulu-Waikiki area, you'll usually need to call for a cab instead of just flagging one down on the street.

Glossary

a'a – rough, jagged lava

AAA – American Automobile Association, also called 'Triple A'; an auto club

a'ali'i – narrow-leafed shrub with red seed pods, the fruit is used for *lei*-making

AARP – American Association of Retired Persons

adobo – meat, usually chicken or pork, stewed in vinegar, garlic and soy sauce

adze – sharp hewing tool made of stone

ahi – yellowfin tuna

ahinahina – silversword (plant)

ahu – stone *cairn*; altar, shrine

ahupua'a – traditional land division, usually wedge-shaped and extending from the mountains to the sea

aina – land

akia – shrub with small yellow flowers and red berries, which can be toxic

aku – bonito or skipjack tuna

akua – god, spirit, idol

ala – road, path, trail

alala – Hawaiian crow

ali'i – chief, royalty

aloha – traditional greeting meaning love, welcome, goodbye

ama'ama – mullet (fish)

amakihi – small common native yellow-green bird

AMS – Acute Mountain Sickness

anuenue – rainbow

apapane – native Hawaiian honeycreeper that is bright red

ATM – automatic teller machine

au – marlin

aumakua – ancestral spirit helper

awa – milkfish; see also *kava*

backcountry – anywhere away from roads or other major infrastructure

backpack – multiday hike requiring full camping gear

backtrack – to return via the approach route

basalt – common dense igneous rock, dark-gray to black in color

bench – shelf or step-like area of often unstable land, often along coastal areas covered by lava flows

blowhole – hole in shoreline lava through which surf spurts up

bouldering – hopping from one rock to the next; climbing boulders or small outcrops

cairn – pile or stack of rocks marking a route or trail junction

caldera – big crater resulting from the collapse of underground lava reservoirs

CCC – Civilian Conservation Corps, a 1930s-era federal work program

contour – to *sidle* around a hill at approximately the same altitude (or contour level); a map line connecting land points with the same elevation; see also *traverse*

crack seed – dried fruit or seed snack food, can be sour, salty or sweet

DLNR – Department of Land & Natural Resources

DOCARE – Division of Conservation & Resource Enforcement

DOFAW – Division of Forestry & Wildlife

elepaio – native flycatcher

ford – to cross a river by wading

GPS – global positioning system; an electronic, satellite-based network that allows for a calculation of position and elevation using a handheld receiver/decoder

graded – leveled (as in a road or trail)

gulch – narrow ravine cut by a river or stream

hala – screw pine or pandanus, the leaves *(lauhala)* are used in weaving mats and baskets

hale – house, dwelling

haole – Caucasian person, literally 'without breath'

hapa – half; person of mixed blood

hau – indigenous lowland hibiscus tree

haupia – coconut tapioca pudding

Hawaii Nei – all the Hawaiian Islands, as distinguished from the Big Island of Hawaii

heiau – ancient Hawaiian temple

HI – abbreviation for Hawaii

Hina – Polynesian goddess, wife of Ku and mother of Maui

holoholo – to walk, drive, visit or ramble around for pleasure

holua – an ancient Hawaiian sled or sled course

honu – green sea turtle

honuea – Hawksbill sea turtle

ho'oilo – winter

ho'okipa – hospitality; the act of visiting

ho'okupu – offerings of sacred bundles

HTMC – Hawaiian Trail & Mountain Club

hui – social group, club, organization

hula – traditional Hawaiian dance

hula halau – *hula* school or group

hula kahiko – ancient *hula* performed with *mele* and percussive instruments

humhumnukunukuapua'a – rectangular triggerfish, Hawaii's state fish

i'iwi – bright red native forest bird with a salmon-colored beak

iliahi – Hawaiian sandalwood

ili'ili – stones; Hawaiian hot stone therapy

imu – underground earthen oven used in traditional *luau* cooking

kaena akoko – pale-green leafed plant that grows on boulder slopes

kahuna – wise person, commonly a priest, healer or sorcerer

kahuna lapa'au – herbalist healers

kahuna nui – high priest

kai – saltwater

kalo – see *taro*

kama'aina – native-born Hawaiian, long-time resident; literally 'child of the land'

kanaka – human being, man, person (usually of Hawaiian descent)

Kanaloa – one of the four main Hawaiian gods, ruler of the dead

kane/Kane – man; the name of one of the four main Hawaiian gods

kapu – taboo, part of strict ancient Hawaiian social system; also meaning 'Keep Out' or 'No Trespassing'

kau – summer

kaunaoa – parasite plant that looks like orange fishing line

kava – mildly narcotic drink made from the roots of *Piper methysticum*, a pepper shrub

keiki – child, children

kiawe – thorny-branched relative of the mesquite tree introduced to Hawaii in the 1820s, now very common

ki'i – image, statue

kipuka – area of land spared when lava flows around it; oasis

ko – sugarcane

koa – native hardwood tree often used in woodworking of furniture and crafts

koae – white-tailed tropic bird

koa haole – an invasive shrub with elongated brown seed pods, used as cattle fodder

kokio keokeo – white-flowered hibiscus tree

kokua – help, cooperation; 'Please Kokua' on a trash can is a subtle way of saying 'Don't litter'

kona – leeward; leeward wind

kopiko – white-flowering coffee tree

Ku – Polynesian god of war, farming and fishing; husband of Hina

kukui – candlenut tree, Hawaii's official state tree, the oily nuts of which were once burned in lamps

kupuna – grandparent, respected elder

lama – Hawaiian persimmon

lanai – veranda, porch

laulau – bundled package; pork or beef with salted fish, wrapped in leaves and steamed

lei – garland, usually of flowers, but also of leaves, shells, kukui nuts or feathers

lilikoi – passionfruit

limu – seaweed

loco moco – fried egg, hamburger patty and brown gravy served over rice

lomi – to rub or soften; *lomi* salmon is raw, diced salmon marinated with tomatoes and onions

Lono – Polynesian god of harvest, agriculture, fertility and peace

luakini – type of *heiau* dedicated to the war god Ku and once used for human sacrifice

luau – traditional Hawaiian feast

mahalo – thank you

maile – native plant with olive-looking fruit and leathery leaves, often used for *lei*

makaha – sluice gate, used to regulate the level of water in a traditional Hawaiian fishpond

makahiki – ancient Hawaiian harvest festival with games held in honor of Lono

makai – toward the sea

malasada – Portuguese fried dough served warm, similar to a doughnut

malihini – newcomer, visitor

Maui – son of Hina, trickster god-hero who performed feats of strength

Maui Nui – literally 'Big Maui,' referring to the ancient island group of Maui, Kaho-'olawe, Lanai and Molokai, which today comprise Maui County

mauka – toward the mountains, inland

mauna – mountain

mele – song, chant

menehune – the 'little people' who according to legend built many of Hawaii's fishponds and *heiau*

moa – red jungle fowl

moana – ocean, open sea

mu'umu'u – long, loose-fitting dress introduced by the missionaries

Na Ala Hele – Hawaii's public trails and access program

naupaka – beach plant with clusters of white flowers

Neighbor Islands – main Hawaiian Islands, apart from Oahu

nene – native goose, Hawaii's state bird

niu – coconut palm

NOAA – National Oceanic and Atmospheric Administration, for weather forecasts

noni – Indian mulberry with yellow, stinky fruit that is used medicinally

NPS – National Park Service

ohana – family, extended family

ohelo – low-growing native shrub with edible red berries favored by *nene*

ohia lehua – native tree with tufted, feathery red flowers

opihi – tiny, limpet shells

pahoehoe – smooth, ropy lava

pali – cliff

paniolo – Hawaiian cowboy

pau – finished, no more; *pau hana* means quitting time

pau-o-Hi'iaka – vine with blue flowers

Pele – goddess of fire and volcanoes

piko – navel, umbilical cord

pipikaula – salted, dried beef that is served broiled

PKO – Protect Kaho'olawe Ohana; activist movement established in the 1970s to preserve Kaho'olawe as a sanctuary of Hawaiian culture

pohaku – rock

pohuehue – beach morning glory

poi – gooey paste made from *taro* root, a staple of the Hawaiian diet

poke – pronounced '**poh**-kay'; bite-sized, raw fish marinated in ginger, seaweed, soy sauce, oil, sea salt and chili pepper

Poliahu – goddess of snow

pueo – native short-eared owl

pull-off/pull-out – roadside parking area

pulu – silken clusters encasing coiled tree fern fronds

pupu – snack food, hors d'oeuvres; shells

pu'u – hill, cinder cone

saimin – Hawaiian version of Japanese noodle soup *(ramen)*

scree – slippery and loose, weathered rock fragments covering a slope

sidle – to cut along a slope; to *contour*; see also *traverse*

spur – small branch of a main trail

tabi – Japanese split-toed shoes, used for reef-walking

taro – plant with green heart-shaped leaves; cultivated in Hawaii for its edible rootstock, which is mashed to make *poi*

ti – common native plant, its long shiny leaves are used for wrapping food and making *hula* skirts

timberline, tree line – uppermost level to which tree cover extends on a mountainside

TNC – The Nature Conservancy

traverse – to cut along a slope (sometimes also along a ridge); see also *sidle* and *contour*

udon – thick Japanese noodles

ulu – breadfruit

uluhe – false staghorn fern

USGS – United States Geological Survey; national cartographic association

wahine – woman

wailele – waterfall

wikiwiki – hurry, quick

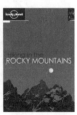

Lonely Planet Guides by Region

Lonely Planet is known worldwide for publishing practical, reliable and no-nonsense travel information in our guides and on our Web site. The Lonely Planet list covers just about every accessible part of the world. Currently there are 16 series: Travel guides, Shoestring guides, Condensed guides, Phrasebooks, Read This First, Healthy Travel, Walking guides, Cycling guides, Watching Wildlife guides, Pisces Diving & Snorkeling guides, City Maps, Road Atlases, Out to Eat, World Food, Journeys travel literature and Pictorials.

AFRICA Africa on a shoestring • Botswana • Cairo • Cairo City Map • Cape Town • Cape Town City Map • East Africa • Egypt • Egyptian Arabic phrasebook • Ethiopia, Eritrea & Djibouti • Ethiopian Amharic phrasebook • The Gambia & Senegal • Healthy Travel Africa • Kenya • Malawi • Morocco • Moroccan Arabic phrasebook • Mozambique • Namibia • Read This First: Africa • South Africa, Lesotho & Swaziland • Southern Africa • Southern Africa Road Atlas • Swahili phrasebook • Tanzania, Zanzibar & Pemba • Trekking in East Africa • Tunisia • Watching Wildlife East Africa • Watching Wildlife Southern Africa • West Africa • World Food Morocco • Zambia • Zimbabwe, Botswana & Namibia
Travel Literature: Mali Blues: Traveling to an African Beat • The Rainbird: A Central African Journey • Songs to an African Sunset: A Zimbabwean Story

AUSTRALIA & THE PACIFIC Aboriginal Australia & the Torres Strait Islands •Auckland • Australia • Australian phrasebook • Australia Road Atlas • Cycling Australia • Cycling New Zealand • Fiji • Fijian phrasebook • Healthy Travel Australia, NZ & the Pacific • Islands of Australia's Great Barrier Reef • Melbourne • Melbourne City Map • Micronesia • New Caledonia • New South Wales • New Zealand • Northern Territory • Outback Australia • Out to Eat – Melbourne • Out to Eat – Sydney • Papua New Guinea • Pidgin phrasebook • Queensland • Rarotonga & the Cook Islands • Samoa • Solomon Islands • South Australia • South Pacific • South Pacific phrasebook • Sydney • Sydney City Map • Sydney Condensed • Tahiti & French Polynesia • Tasmania • Tonga • Tramping in New Zealand • Vanuatu • Victoria • Walking in Australia • Watching Wildlife Australia • Western Australia
Travel Literature: Islands in the Clouds: Travels in the Highlands of New Guinea • Kiwi Tracks: A New Zealand Journey • Sean & David's Long Drive

CENTRAL AMERICA & THE CARIBBEAN Bahamas, Turks & Caicos • Baja California • Belize, Guatemala & Yucatán • Bermuda • Central America on a shoestring • Costa Rica • Costa Rica Spanish phrasebook • Cuba • Cycling Cuba • Dominican Republic & Haiti • Eastern Caribbean • Guatemala • Havana • Healthy Travel Central & South America • Jamaica • Mexico • Mexico City • Panama • Puerto Rico • Read This First: Central & South America • Virgin Islands • World Food Caribbean • World Food Mexico • Yucatán
Travel Literature: Green Dreams: Travels in Central America

EUROPE Amsterdam • Amsterdam City Map • Amsterdam Condensed • Andalucía • Athens • Austria • Baltic States phrasebook • Barcelona • Barcelona City Map • Belgium & Luxembourg • Berlin • Berlin City Map • Britain • British phrasebook • Brussels, Bruges & Antwerp • Brussels City Map • Budapest • Budapest City Map • Canary Islands • Catalunya & the Costa Brava • Central Europe • Central Europe phrasebook • Copenhagen • Corfu & the Ionians • Corsica • Crete • Crete Condensed • Croatia • Cycling Britain • Cycling France • Cyprus • Czech & Slovak Republics • Czech phrasebook • Denmark • Dublin • Dublin City Map • Dublin Condensed • Eastern Europe • Eastern Europe phrasebook • Edinburgh • Edinburgh City Map • England • Estonia, Latvia & Lithuania • Europe on a shoestring • Europe phrasebook • Finland • Florence • Florence City Map • France • Frankfurt City Map • Frankfurt Condensed • French phrasebook • Georgia, Armenia & Azerbaijan • Germany • German phrasebook • Greece • Greek Islands • Greek phrasebook • Hungary • Iceland, Greenland & the Faroe Islands • Ireland • Italian phrasebook • Italy • Kraków • Lisbon • The Loire • London • London City Map • London Condensed • Madrid • Madrid City Map • Malta • Mediterranean Europe • Milan, Turin & Genoa • Moscow • Munich • Netherlands • Normandy • Norway • Out to Eat – London • Out to Eat – Paris • Paris • Paris City Map • Paris Condensed • Poland • Polish phrasebook • Portugal • Portuguese phrasebook • Prague • Prague City Map • Provence & the Côte d'Azur • Read This First: Europe • Rhodes & the Dodecanese • Romania & Moldova • Rome • Rome City Map • Rome Condensed • Russia, Ukraine & Belarus • Russian phrasebook • Scandinavian & Baltic Europe • Scandinavian phrasebook • Scotland • Sicily • Slovenia • South-West France • Spain • Spanish phrasebook • Stockholm • St Petersburg • St Petersburg City Map • Sweden • Switzerland • Tuscany • Ukrainian phrasebook • Venice • Vienna • Wales • Walking in Britain • Walking in France • Walking in Ireland • Walking in Italy • Walking in Scotland • Walking in Spain • Walking in Switzerland • Western Europe • World Food France • World Food Greece • World Food Ireland • World Food Italy • World Food Spain **Travel Literature:** After Yugoslavia • Love and War in the Apennines • The Olive Grove: Travels in Greece • On the Shores of the Mediterranean • Round Ireland in Low Gear • A Small Place in Italy

Lonely Planet Mail Order

Lonely Planet products are distributed worldwide. They are also available by mail order from Lonely Planet, so if you have difficulty finding a title please write to us. North and South American residents should write to 150 Linden St, Oakland, CA 94607, USA; European and African residents should write to 72-82 Rosebery Ave, London, EC1R 4RW, UK; and residents of other countries to Locked Bag 1, Footscray, Victoria 3011, Australia.

INDIAN SUBCONTINENT & THE INDIAN OCEAN Bangladesh • Bengali phrasebook • Bhutan • Delhi • Goa • Healthy Travel Asia & India • Hindi & Urdu phrasebook • India • India & Bangladesh City Map • Indian Himalaya • Karakoram Highway • Kathmandu City Map • Kerala • Madagascar • Maldives • Mauritius, Réunion & Seychelles • Mumbai (Bombay) • Nepal • Nepali phrasebook • North India • Pakistan • Rajasthan • Read This First: Asia & India • South India • Sri Lanka • Sri Lanka phrasebook • Tibet • Tibetan phrasebook • Trekking in the Indian Himalaya • Trekking in the Karakoram & Hindukush • Trekking in the Nepal Himalaya • World Food India **Travel Literature**: The Age of Kali: Indian Travels and Encounters • Hello Goodnight: A Life of Goa • In Rajasthan • Maverick in Madagascar • A Season in Heaven: True Tales from the Road to Kathmandu • Shopping for Buddhas • A Short Walk in the Hindu Kush • Slowly Down the Ganges

MIDDLE EAST & CENTRAL ASIA Bahrain, Kuwait & Qatar • Central Asia • Central Asia phrasebook • Dubai • Farsi (Persian) phrasebook • Hebrew phrasebook • Iran • Israel & the Palestinian Territories • Istanbul • Istanbul City Map • Istanbul to Cairo • Istanbul to Kathmandu • Jerusalem • Jerusalem City Map • Jordan • Lebanon • Middle East • Oman & the United Arab Emirates • Syria • Turkey • Turkish phrasebook • World Food Turkey • Yemen **Travel Literature**: Black on Black: Iran Revisited • Breaking Ranks: Turbulent Travels in the Promised Land • The Gates of Damascus • Kingdom of the Film Stars: Journey into Jordan

NORTH AMERICA Alaska • Boston • Boston City Map • Boston Condensed • British Columbia • California & Nevada • California Condensed • Canada • Chicago • Chicago City Map • Chicago Condensed • Florida • Georgia & the Carolinas • Great Lakes • Hawaii • Hiking in Alaska • Hiking in the USA • Honolulu & Oahu City Map • Las Vegas • Los Angeles • Los Angeles City Map • Louisiana & the Deep South • Miami • Miami City Map • Montreal • New England • New Orleans • New Orleans City Map • New York City • New York City City Map • New York City Condensed • New York, New Jersey & Pennsylvania • Oahu • Out to Eat – San Francisco • Pacific Northwest • Rocky Mountains • San Diego & Tijuana • San Francisco • San Francisco City Map • Seattle • Seattle City Map • Southwest • Texas • Toronto • USA • USA phrasebook • Vancouver • Vancouver City Map • Virginia & the Capital Region • Washington, DC • Washington, DC City Map • World Food New Orleans **Travel Literature**: Caught Inside: A Surfer's Year on the California Coast • Drive Thru America

NORTH-EAST ASIA Beijing • Beijing City Map • Cantonese phrasebook • China • Hiking in Japan • Hong Kong & Macau • Hong Kong City Map • Hong Kong Condensed • Japan • Japanese phrasebook • Korea • Korean phrasebook • Kyoto • Mandarin phrasebook • Mongolia • Mongolian phrasebook • Seoul • Shanghai • South-West China • Taiwan • Tokyo • Tokyo Condensed • World Food Hong Kong • World Food Japan **Travel Literature**: In Xanadu: A Quest • Lost Japan

SOUTH AMERICA Argentina, Uruguay & Paraguay • Bolivia • Brazil • Brazilian phrasebook • Buenos Aires • Buenos Aires City Map • Chile & Easter Island • Colombia • Ecuador & the Galapagos Islands • Healthy Travel Central & South America • Latin American Spanish phrasebook • Peru • Quechua phrasebook • Read This First: Central & South America • Rio de Janeiro • Rio de Janeiro City Map • Santiago de Chile • South America on a shoestring • Trekking in the Patagonian Andes • Venezuela **Travel Literature**: Full Circle: A South American Journey

SOUTH-EAST ASIA Bali & Lombok • Bangkok • Bangkok City Map • Burmese phrasebook • Cambodia • Cycling Vietnam, Laos & Cambodia • East Timor phrasebook • Hanoi • Healthy Travel Asia & India • Hill Tribes phrasebook • Ho Chi Minh City (Saigon) • Indonesia • Indonesian phrasebook • Indonesia's Eastern Islands • Java • Lao phrasebook • Laos • Malay phrasebook • Malaysia, Singapore & Brunei • Myanmar (Burma) • Philippines • Pilipino (Tagalog) phrasebook • Read This First: Asia & India • Singapore • Singapore City Map • South-East Asia on a shoestring • South-East Asia phrasebook • Thailand • Thailand's Islands & Beaches • Thailand, Vietnam, Laos & Cambodia Road Atlas • Thai phrasebook • Vietnam • Vietnamese phrasebook • World Food Indonesia • World Food Thailand • World Food Vietnam

ALSO AVAILABLE: Antarctica • The Arctic • The Blue Man: Tales of Travel, Love and Coffee • Brief Encounters: Stories of Love, Sex & Travel • Buddhist Stupas in Asia: The Shape of Perfection • Chasing Rickshaws • The Last Grain Race • Lonely Planet ... On the Edge: Adventurous Escapades from Around the World • Lonely Planet Unpacked • Lonely Planet Unpacked Again • Not the Only Planet: Science Fiction Travel Stories • Ports of Call: A Journey by Sea • Sacred India • Travel Photography: A Guide to Taking Better Pictures • Travel with Children • Tuvalu: Portrait of an Island Nation

Index

Abbreviations

BI – The Big Island
K – Kauai

M – Maui
Mol – Molokai

O – Oahu

Text

A

AAA (American Automobile Association) 219
AARP (American Association of Retired Persons) 219
accommodations 35-7, see also individual types
Acute Mountain Sickness (AMS) 52-3, 108, 160
After Dark in the Park 122
Aiea (O) 95
air travel 223-5
 baggage restrictions 225
 cheap tickets 224
 interisland 224, 225
 international 224
 to/from Molokai 174
 to/from US mainland 223-4
akepa 25
Ala Moana (O) 66
Alakai Crossing (K) 216
Alakai Swamp (K) 214-17, **215**
albatross 25
alcoholic drinks 38
altimeter 47
altitude problems 52-3, 108, 160
amakihi 25
amau 20
American Association of Retired Persons (AARP) 219
American Automobile Association (AAA) 219
amphibians 24
animals 22-5, see also individual species
anthurium 20
apapane 25
arboretums 74
 Keahua Forestry Arboretum (K) 199
 Lyon Arboretum (O) 71, 73
area codes 221

astronomy 107
Awa'awapuhi Lookout (K) 212-14, **214**
axis deer 22

B

B&Bs 36
Baldwin, Henry & Samuel 15
baleen whale 23
bamboo 21
banyan 21
beach morning glory 20
beach naupaka 20
Bellows Air Force Base (O) 79
bicycle travel 226
Big Island Visitors Bureau 99
Big Island, The 96-143, **98**
bird-of-paradise 20
birds 24-5, see also individual species
blue gum 21
boat travel
 interisland 227
 international 225
booby 25
books 41-2
bougainvillea 20
bus travel 226
business hours 222

C

cabins 35-6
camera 42
camping 35-6
candlenut tree 21
Canyon Trail (K) 211, **212**
Captain Cook, town of (BI) 112
Captain Cook Monument (BI) 111-24, **113**
car travel 226
 driving license 218
 road rules 226

cattle 22
CCC (Civilian Conservation Corps) 81, 91, 171, 180
cell phones 221
cereus 20
children, hiking with 38-9
Chinatown (O) 66
ciguatera poisoning 55
Cinder Desert (M) 160
Civilian Conservation Corps (CCC) 81, 91, 171, 180
Cliff Viewpoint (K) 211
climate 18, see also weather information
clothing 44-8
clubs, hiking 41
coconut palm 21
compass 46
condos 36-7
conservation 26, 34, 181
 organizations 27, 33, see also individual organizations
consulates 219
Cook pines 22
Cook, Captain James 15, 86, 96, 111, 112, 202
Crater Rim Trail (BI) 131-3
craters, see individual craters
creepy crawlies 25
cultural considerations 29
currency 220
customs regulations 219-20
cybercafés 222
cycling 226

D

Damien, Father 176, 178
dehydration 53
dengue fever 55-6, 165
Department of Land & Natural Resources (DLNR) 40
Department of Parks & Recreation 99

Devastation Trail (BI) 129
Diamond Head (O) 95
diarrhea 54-5
digital resources 41, 222
Dillingham Airfield (O) 91
diseases 54-6, *see also* health, *individual diseases*
Division of Conservation & Resource Enforcement (DOCARE) 22, 60
Division of Forestry & Wildlife (DOFAW) 41, 74, 93, 99, 187
Division of State Parks 99
DLNR (Department of Land & Natural Resources) 40
DOCARE (Division of Conservation & Resource Enforcement) 22, 60
documents 218
    storing 219
DOFAW (Division of Forestry & Wildlife) 41, 74, 93, 99, 187
dolphins 23
drinks 38
driving license 218

E
Earthjustice Legal Defense Fund 26
email services 222
embassies 219
emergency
    rescue 60-1
    telephone numbers 221
environmental issues 26, *see also* conservation
equipment 48-9
    altimeter 47
    backpack 48
    check list 45
    clothing 44
    compass 46
    GPS (Global Positioning System) 47
    hiking poles 49
    sleeping bag 48
    stove 49
    tent 48
evacuation 60-1
exchange rates 220

Bold indicates maps.
For a full list of maps, see the map index (p3).
For a full list of hikes, see the hikes table (pp4-5).

F
false sandalwood 21
false staghorn fern 20
fauna 22-5, *see also individual animals*
ferns 20-1
festivals 222
film (camera) 43
first aid 50, 51
flash floods 149, 168
flora 19-25, *see also individual plants*
flowers 19-20
food 37, 52
footwear 44
Friends of Malaekahana 85
frigate 25
fungal infections 58

G
geography 16-18
giant white golf balls 93, 95
giardiasis 55
ginger 20
GPS (Global Positioning System) 47
Great Mahele land act 15
green sea turtle 24

H
Haena (K) 190-1
Halape (BI) 139, 142
Halawa Valley (Mol) 183
Haleakala crater (M) 155-62, **158**
Haleakala National Park (M) 26-8, 155
Haleakala Visitors Center (M) 155
Haleakala volcano (M) 155
Haleiwa (O) 87
Halema'uma'u (BI) 124-9
Halema'uma'u Crater (BI) 133
Halema'uma'u Overlook (BI) 128
Halemanu (K) 217
Halemau'u (M) 161, 162
Hali'imaile (M) 159
Hamakua Coast (BI) 103
Hana (M) 164-9
Hanakapiai Beach (K) 192
Hanakapiai Falls (K) 193
Hanakapiai Valley (K) 189, 191
Hanakoa Stream (K) 193
Hanakoa Valley (K) 189, 192
Hanalei (K) 189-90
Hapu'u fern 20

hare's foot fern 21
Hau'ula Loop (O) 84-6, **86**
Hawaii Audubon Society 33
Hawaii coot 25
Hawaii Nature Center 74
Hawaii Volcano Observatory (BI) 128, 132
Hawaii Volcanoes National Park (BI) 26-8, 96, 120-42
Hawaiian crow 24
Hawaiian hawk 24
Hawaiian hoary bat 22
Hawaiian monk seal 22
Hawaiian short-eared owl 24
Hawaiian stilt 25
Hawaiian Trail and Mountain Club 81
Hawksbill sea turtle 24
health 50-61, 97
    common hiking ailments 52
    immunization 50
    insurance 50
    women 58-9
heat exhaustion 53
heatstroke 53
heiau 167
heliconia 20
Hi'ilawe Falls (BI) 105
hibiscus 20
hiking
    books 41-2
    children, with 38-9
    equipment 48-9
    history 15-16
    itineraries 32
    permits 33-4
    safety 39, 59-61
    women 38, 58-9, 186
Hilina Pali (BI) 138-42, **139**
Hilo (BI) 97-9
Hipalau Camp (K) 208, **153**
history 15-16
hitching 226
Hoapili (M) 151-3
holidays 222
Holua Cabin (M) 161, 162
Honoka'a (BI) 103
Honolulu (O) 62-8, **64**
Honolulu Watershed Forest Reserve (O) 74
Honolulu Zoo (O) 76
horses 22
Hosmer Grove Campground (M) 159
hostels 36
hotels 35
hypothermia 54, 160

I

i'iwi 25
Iliau Nature Loop (K) 206
ilima 20
immunization 50
insurance
    health 50
    travel 218
Internet
    access 222
    resources 41
ironwood 21
itineraries 32

J

jacaranda 22
Jackass Ginger Pool (O) 71-3
Jaggar Museum (BI) 128, 131, 132
Japanese white-eye (bird) 25
Judd Trail (O) 73

K

Ka'aha shelter (BI) 142
Ka Lae (BI) 143
Ka Lu'u o ka O'o (M) 160
Ka Moa o Pele (M) 160
Kaena Point (O) 89-91, **91**
Kaena Point Satellite Tracking Station (O) 90, 94
Kaena Point State Park (O) 89
Kaena Point State Park Beach (O) 91
Kaho'olawe 27
Kahului (M) 147-8
Kahului Bay (M) 151
Kaiaka Bay Beach Park (O) 87
Kainaliu (BI) 112-13
Kalalau (K) 188-96, **192**
Kalalau Beach (K) 189
Kalalau Lookout (K) 214
Kalalau Valley (K) 191
Kalanai Point (O) 85
Kalapawili Ridge (M) 161
Kalaupapa National Historic Park (Mol) 175-8, **177**
Kalaupapa Peninsula (Mol) 175
Kaluahaulu Camp (K) 208
Kaluahine Falls (BI) 105
Kamakou Preserve (Mol) 179-81, **179**
Kamehameha I, see Kamehameha the Great
Kamehameha III 15
Kamehameha V 170, 171, 176

Kamehameha the Great 15, 62, 69, 96, 102, 144, 184
Kamo'oho'opulu Ridge (K) 199
Kanaio Beach (M) 153
Kanaloa Point (M) 151
Kanoa Ridge (M) 151
Kapa'a (K) 195-6
Kapalaoa Cabin (M) 159, 160
Kauai 184-217, **185**
Kaunakakai (Mol) 172
Kaunala (O) 86-9, **88**
Kaupo Gap (M) 161
Kawaikoi Camp (K) 216
Kawaikoi Stream (K) 216-17
Kawilinau (M) 160, 162
Kea'au Beach Park Campground (O) 94
Keahua Forestry Arboretum (K) 199
Kealakekua (BI) 112-13
Kealia (O) 91-3, **92**
Keanakakoi adze quarry (BI) 110
Keanakakoi Crater (BI) 132
Keck observatories (BI) 110
Ke'e Beach (K) 188
Kekaha (K) 203
Keone'o'io (M) 152
kiawe 22
Kihei (M) 152-4
Kilauea (BI) 116
Kilauea Iki (BI) 129-30
Kilauea Iki Crater (BI) 129, 131
Kilauea Iki Overlook (BI) 130, 133
Kilauea Visitor Center Area (BI) 123
Kilauea Volcano (BI) 96, 116, 120
Kilohana Lookout (K) 216
King's Highway (M) 146
Kipahulu (M) 155
Kipahulu Campground (M) 168
Kipahulu Visitors Center (M) 167
Kipuka Puaulu (Bird Park) (BI) 143
knee strain 52
Koaie Canyon Trail (K) 206-11, **207**
Kohala Coast (BI) 142-3
Koke'e State Park (K) 209-17
kokio keokeo (hibiscus) 20
Kolowalu Trail (O) 77
Ko'olau Gap (M) 161
Ko'olau Range (O) 83, 84
Kuaokala (O) 93-5, **92**
Kuilau Trail (K) 197-9, **198**
Kukui Trail (K) 206-11, **207**
Kukuihaele (BI) 104

Kula (M) 159
Kula Forest Reserve (M) 162
Kula's agriculture 163
Kuli'ou'ou Ridge (O) 77-8, **78**
Kumuwela Lookout (K) 212

L

La Perouse Bay (M) 151
Lahaina Pali (M) 153-5, **154**
Laie (O) 85
Lake Waiau (BI) 110
Lanai 169
language 29-31
lava 91, 114, 120, 129, 115-19
leatherback turtle 24
leprosy colony (former) 170, 176
leptospirosis 55
Lihue (K) 187-9
lilikoi 20
Liliuokalani, Queen 15-16
Limahuli Garden (K) 191
local Hawaiian food 100
Lolo Vista Point (K) 214
Lonomea Camp (K) 209
Lyon Arboretum (O) 71, 73

M

maile 20
maile-scented fern 20-1
Makaha (O) 94
Makahiku Falls (M) 168
Makahoa Point (O) 85
Makamakaole Valley (M) 151
Makaopuhi Crater (BI) 136
Makapu'u Point (O) 79, 95
Makiki Forest Baseyard (O) 73
Makiki Valley (O) 73
Makiki Valley Loop (O) 74
Makiki-Tantalus (O) 73, 74
Malaekahana State Recreation Area (O) 85
Malama Hawaii 26
Malo, David 15
mammals 22-3
Manana Trail (O) 83-4, **82**
Manawainui Gulch (M) 155
mangrove 22
Manoa Cliffs (O) 73-5, **72**
Manoa Falls (O) 71-3, **72**
Manoa Valley (O) 76
maps 39-40
Maui 144-69, **145**
Maui (demigod) 157
Mauka Powerhouse (K) 205
Mauna Iki (BI) 136-8, **137**
Mauna Kea (BI) 18, 97, 106-11, **109**

Mauna Kea Ice Age Natural Area Reserve (BI) 110
Mauna Kea State Recreation Area (BI) 108
Mauna Loa (BI) 97, 140-1, 116
Mauna Ulu (BI) 135
Maunawili Demonstration Trail (O) 78-81, **80**
Maunawili Falls (O) 78-81, **80**
medical assistance 53
medical kit 51
menehune 203
Millimeter Valley (BI) 110
Moalepe Trail (K) 197-9, **198**
mobile phones 221
Mokuleia Beach (O) 93
Mokuleia Beach Park Campground (O) 90
Moleka Trail (O) 75
Molokai 170-83, **172**
Molokai Ranch (Mol) 170
money 220-1
    costs 220
    taxes 221
    tipping 221
mongoose 22
monkeypod 22
Mo'okini Heiau (BI) 142
Mo'omomi Dunes (Mol) 181-3, **182**
Mo'omomi Preserve (Mol) 181
Mormons 85
mosquito bites 56
motorcycle travel 226
Mountain View (BI) 124
mule trail (Mol) 170
Muliwai (BI) 102-6, **104**

Na Ala Hele Trail (O) 76
Nahuina Trail (O) 75
Napau Crater (BI) 134-6, **135**
Napau Crater Campground (BI) 136
national parks 26-8
    Haleakala National Park (M) 26-8, 155
    Hawaii Volcanoes National Park (BI) 26-8, 96, 120-42

Nature Conservancy, The (TNC) 26, 33, 159, 171, 181
navigation equipment 46-7
nene (goose) 24
noddy 25
North Pacific humpback whale 23
North Shore (O) 86, 91
North Shore Surf & Cultural Museum (O) 87
Nounou Mountain East (K) 196-7, **198**
Nounou Mountain West (K) 197, **198**
Nualolo Cliffs (K) 212-14
Nualolo Trail (K) 213-16
Nu'uanu Pali Lookout (O) 69
Nu'uanu Trail (O) 73
Nu'uanu Valley lookout (O) 73, 74, 75, 95

O
Oahu 69-95, **70**
observatories 110
Ohala Heiau (M) 167
Oheo Gulch (M) 155
Okoleho (K) 217
Olowalu (M) 154-6
Onizuka visitor center (BI) 106, 107
orchids 20
organizations
    conservation 27, 33, *see also individual organizations*
    government 40-1
    hiking 81
    search & rescue 61

P
Pacific bottle-nosed dolphins 23
Pacific golden-plover 25
Pala'au State Park (M) 175
Pali Kapu O Keoua (BI) 114
Paliku Cabin (M) 160, 161
paperbark eucalyptus 21
parks, *see* national parks, *individual parks*
passionfruit 20
Pearl Harbor (O) 16
Pele (goddess) 119
Pele's Paint Pot (M) 162
Pelekunu Overlook (Mol) 181
people 28
Pepeopae Bog (Mol) 181
permits 33-4
petroglyphs 143
phonecards 221

photography 43
pidgin 31
Pihea Vista (K) 216
place names 40, 71, 97, 172
plank-and-cable suspension bridge 144, 149, 150
plants 19-25, *see also individual plants*
Polihale State Park Campground (K) 203-4
Polipoli (M) 162
Polipoli Springs State Recreation Area (M) 162
Pololu Valley (BI) 142
population 28
postal sevices 221
Powerline Trail (K) 199-203, **200**
prickly heat 53
protea 20
Protect Kaho'olawe Ohana (PKO) 27
Puako petroglyphs (BI) 143
public holidays 222
Pu'u Huluhulu (BI) 135
Pu'u Koae (BI) 138
Pu'u Loa petroglyphs (BI) 143
Pu'u o Kila Lookout (K) 215
Pu'u Ohia (O) 95
Pu'u O'o Trail (BI) 143
Pu'u O'o vent (BI) 120, 134, 135, 136
Pu'u Pia (O) 77
Pu'u Poliahu (BI) 107

Q
Queen's Bath (BI) 114

R
rainbow eucalyptus 21
religion 28-9
rescue 60-1
responsible hiking 34-5
road rules 226

S
safety 39, 59-61
    basic rules 59
    crossing rivers 59
    on the Big Island 122
    on Kauai 186, 190, 194
    on lava 120
    on Maui 149
sandalwood 21
screw pine 21
sea hibiscus 20

Bold indicates maps.
For a full list of maps, see the map index (p3).
For a full list of hikes, see the hikes table (pp4-5).

search & rescue 60-1
senior travelers
    senior cards 219
shaka 30
shearwater 25
shrubs 21-2
Sierra Club, The 26, 33, 99
silversword 19
Silversword Loop (M) 162
Skyline Trail (M) 169
Sliding Sands Trail (M) 156, 160
South Point (BI) 143
Southwest Rift (BI) 132
Space Rock (K) 193
special events 222
spiders 25
spinner dolphins 23
spirits, ancient 90
spotted dolphins 23
sprains 56
stoves 49
Sulphur Bank (BI) 131
sunburn 53

T
Tantalus (O) 73
taxis 227
telephone services 221
    emergency numbers 221
    weather information 42-3
telescopes 107, 110
tern 25
thrush (infection) 58
Thurston Lava Tube (BI) 129,
    131, 133
time 222
tourist offices 218
transport, see individual
    methods
tree snail 74
trees 21-2

U
University of Hawaii
    Observatory (BI) 110
urinary tract infection 58-9

V
Vancouver, Captain George 15
visas 218
vog 97, 118, 125
volcanic haze (BI) 97
Volcano (BI) 123-4
volcanoes 96, 120, 115-19
    Haleakala volcano (M) 155
    Hualalai (BI) 96
    Kilauea (BI) 96, 116, 120
    Kohala (BI) 96
    Loihi Seamount 116
    Mauna Kea (BI) 96, 97,
        106-11
    Mauna Loa (BI) 96, 97,
        140-1, 116
    Pu'u O'o vent (BI) 120

W
Wa'ahila Ridge (O) 75-7, **76**
Wa'ahila Ridge State
    Recreation Area (O) 75, 77
Waiahuakua Valley (K) 193
Waiakoa (M) 169
Waianapanapa State Park (M)
    165-7, **166**
Waihe'e Ridge (M) 150-1
Waihe'e Valley (M) 149-50, **150**
Waikiki (O) 67
Wailua (K) 194-5
Wailuku (M) 148-9
Waimanalo (O) 79
Waimanalo Bay (O) 79
Waimanalo Bay Beach Park (O)
    79

Waimano Trail (O) 81-3, **82**
Waimano Waterfall (O) 83, 84
Waimanu Valley (BI) 105-6
Waimea (K) 201-2
Waimea (O) 87-8
Waimea Canyon (K) 204-5,
    205
Waimea Canyon Lookout (K)
    201
Waimea Canyon State Park (K)
    201-9
Waimea Valley (O) 86
Waimoku Falls (M) 167-9, **168**
Waipio Beach (BI) 105
Waipio Valley Overlook (BI)
    105-6
Waipio Valley residents (BI) 103
Waipouli (K) 195
Ward Center (O) 66
water 51-2
waterfalls 81, 83, 105, 151, 191
    Blue Pool (M) 164
    Hanakapiai Falls (K) 193
    Hi'ilawe Falls (BI) 105
    Kaluahine Falls (BI) 105
    Makahiku Falls (M) 168
    Manoa Falls (M) 71-3
    Waimano Waterfall (O) 84
    Waimoku Falls (M) 167
weather information 42-3,
    102, 108, see also climate
whale 23
wildlife 19-25, see also
    individual species
Wiliwili Camp (K) 208
women hikers 38, 58-9, 186
women's health 58-9, 125
WWII 16

Z
zoo (O) 76

LONELY PLANET OFFICES

Australia
Locked Bag 1, Footscray, Victoria 3011
☎ 03 8379 8000 fax 03 8379 8111
email: talk2us@lonelyplanet.com.au

USA
150 Linden St, Oakland, CA 94607
☎ 510 893 8555 TOLL FREE: 800 275 8555
fax 510 893 8572
email: info@lonelyplanet.com

UK
72-82 Rosebery Ave, London, EC1R 4RW
☎ 020 7841 9000 fax 020 7841 9001
email: go@lonelyplanet.co.uk

World Wide Web: www.lonelyplanet.com *or* **AOL keyword: lp**
Lonely Planet Images: www.lonelyplanetimages.com